ACROSS THE GREEN SEA

Connected Histories of the Middle East and the Global South
Afshin Marashi and Houri Berberian, Series Editors

ACROSS THE GREEN SEA
Histories from the Western Indian Ocean, 1440–1640

SANJAY
SUBRAHMANYAM

University of Texas Press
AUSTIN

Copyright © 2024 by Sanjay Subrahmanyam
All rights reserved
Printed in the United States of America
First edition, 2024

Requests for permission to reproduce material from this work
should be sent to:
Permissions
University of Texas Press
P.O. Box 7819
Austin, TX 78713-7819
utpress.utexas.edu

∞ The paper used in this book meets the minimum requirements of
ANSI/NISO Z39.48-1992 (R1997) (Permanence of Paper).

LIBRARY OF CONGRESS CATALOGING-IN-PUBLICATION DATA
Names: Subrahmanyam, Sanjay, author.
Title: Across the Green Sea : histories from the western Indian Ocean, 1440-1640 / Sanjay Subrahmanyam.
Description: First edition. | Austin : University of Texas Press, 2024. | Series: Connected histories of the Middle East and the Global South | Includes bibliographical references and index.
Identifiers:
LCCN 2023033196 (print)
LCCN 2023033197 (ebook)
ISBN 978-1-4773-2877-4 (cloth)
ISBN 978-1-4773-2878-1 (pdf)
ISBN 978-14773-2879-8 (ebook)
Subjects: LCSH: Indian Ocean Region—History—15th century. | Indian Ocean Region—History—16th century. | Indian Ocean Region—History—17th century. | Indian Ocean—Navigation—History—15th century. | Indian Ocean—Navigation—History—16th century. | Indian Ocean—Navigation—History—17th century.
Classification: LCC DS336 .S83 2024 (print) | LCC DS336 (ebook) | DDC 909/.0982405—dc23/eng/20230809
LC record available at https://lccn.loc.gov/2023033196
LC ebook record available at https://lccn.loc.gov/2023033197

doi:10.7560/328774

For Saddy
Who left us much too soon

Between my finger and my thumb
The squat pen rests.
I'll dig with it.

S℞AMUS H℞ANEY

Contents

List of Maps *ix*

List of Illustrations *xi*

Preface *xiii*

A Note on Transliteration *xvii*

A Note on Currency and Tonnage *xix*

Introduction: Conceptual Issues in Connected Histories *1*

Chapter 1. An Epoch of Transitions, 1440–1520 *25*

Chapter 2. The View from the Hijaz, 1500–1550 *95*

Chapter 3. The Afro-Indian Axis *133*

Chapter 4. The View from Surat *161*

A Conclusion: Toward Polyphonic Histories *203*

Notes *217*

Index *263*

Maps

Map 1. Hurmuz and the Persian Gulf   6
Map 2. The western Indian Ocean   27
Map 3. Coastal East Africa   70
Map 4. Daman and South Gujarat   150
Map 5. The city of Surat   176

Illustrations

Figure 1.1. Illustration from a Gujarat *Sikandar Nama*, ca. 1500.   58
Figure 1.2. Arabic letter from the Swahili coast.   74
Figure 2.1. Port of Jiddah as drawn by Gaspar Correia, *Lendas da Índia*.   106
Figure 2.2. Port of Suakin drawn by Dom João de Castro.   124
Figure 3.1. Sidi Bashir Mosque at Ahmedabad.   148
Figure 3.2 Inscription of Malik 'Ambar, Antur Fort.   155
Figure 3.3. Portrait of Ikhlas Khan Habshi with a petition.   157
Figure 4.1. C. H. Braad's plan of Surat.   175
Figure 4.2. Surat in an eighteenth-century Indian cloth map.   181
Figure 4.3. Krishna devotion in Boullaye's text.   196

Preface

Maritime history has been a central focus of my work from the very beginning of my publishing career as a historian in the mid-1980s. This was the same period when I had my first proper exposure to the maritime dimension of India, which until that point had largely been restricted to periodic summer visits as a child to Chennai (Madras) and strolls at sunset on Marina Beach by Gandhi's statue, accompanied at times with a strong smell of drying fish. While doing the archival research for my doctoral dissertation I returned several times to Mumbai (Bombay), staying on the splendid campus of the Tata Institute of Fundamental Research thanks to dear friend Kapil Paranjape, and to Goa, staying in Panaji's Altinho district. The significant difference between the life of a maritime urban center and one in the interior, which I had grasped earlier as a mere bookish idea, became far clearer to me as an existential proposition. Since that time, I have come back periodically to the Indian west coast, especially for some memorable visits to Kerala in the company of historians rooted in that region, as well as to diverse sites on the Bay of Bengal, on the east coast, ranging from Puri to Tarangambadi. It has also been my privilege to have seen the western Indian Ocean from a very different viewpoint while visiting the island of Réunion for lectures and seminars in September 2008.

When Houri Berberian and Afshin Marashi invited me to submit a book for their new series "Connected Histories of the Middle East and the Global South," from the University of Texas Press, there was an obvious temptation to turn to the western Indian Ocean as a subject. I had been exploring different aspects of the maritime region in the past two decades in a variety of ways in my research, whether it was Gujarat, Goa, Kerala, East Africa, the Red Sea, or the Persian Gulf. Whenever I turned to these subjects, my thoughts were drawn to a group of French scholars who had played an important role in my early career in the late 1980s and 1990s. The youngest of them, Denys Lombard, had not really worked on the western Indian Ocean but was instead a scholar of maritime Southeast Asia. In that capacity, he helped found an important journal, *Archipel*, and wrote significant monographic works on Aceh and Java, besides editing some crucial texts such as the travel account of Augustin de Beaulieu. A second figure was Geneviève Bouchon, who wrote on both Kerala and coastal Sri Lanka at the beginning of the sixteenth century and went on to publish several significant documents from the early years of the Portuguese presence in the Indian Ocean. But the most formidable personality in the group was Jean Aubin, who began his career as a historian of medieval Central Asia and Iran but was then progressively drawn into studying the Indian Ocean of the fifteenth and sixteenth centuries. Aubin was never attracted to the monograph as a form, and he much preferred the essay; he also edited several intriguing texts in both Persian and Portuguese. I knew him well in the last decade of his life before his untimely death in January 1998 (a mere two weeks after that of Lombard), and I treasure our conversations and the advice and comments he gave me on my drafts, usually written in his minute and meticulous hand. In the last years, aware of his unreliable health, he sometimes spoke of drawing his scattered works together and eventually published the first volume of what became a trilogy, *Le Latin et l'astrolabe*, of which the last two volumes were published posthumously. It was my privilege, albeit an increasingly sad one, to be the discussant for the release of each of these volumes in Paris at the Calouste Gulbenkian Foundation. Over the years, Aubin's influence on Indian Ocean studies has grown in some circles through the Portuguese historian Luís Filipe Thomaz, Aubin's close associate, and Thomaz's students in Lisbon. On the other hand, one has the impression that with the passage of time Aubin's work has been progressively neglected in the world of Anglophone scholarship, something Aubin feared might in fact be the case.

A good part of this book was written in Covid times, during which the companionship of Caroline Ford was indispensable for me. These years have been a rough ride, with both our neighborly and our professional milieu having deteriorated, a tendency notably exacerbated by the growing hold of unfortunate forms of identity politics and social media in our times. It will probably be diplomatic to pass in silence over the attitude of my home department leadership and the university administration in this context. On the other hand, I have had reason to appreciate those colleagues and friends who have held on to their sanity and sense of humor, even when they have been my interlocutors at a distance. In no particular order other than an alphabetical one, my thanks go to Ned Alpers, Francisco Apellániz, Jyoti Gulati Balachandran, Evrim Binbaş, Guy Burak, Subah Dayal, Malika Dekkiche, Indravati Félicité, Jorge Flores, Naveen Kanalu, Arash Khazeni, Mike Laffan, the late Pier Larson, Giuseppe Marcocci, Roxani Margariti, Claude Markovits, Søren Mentz, Hiromu Nagashima, Mike O'Sullivan, Keelan Overton, Kaya Şahin, and Tunç Şen. A special word of recognition for the late Cornell Fleischer and Cemal Kafadar, friends and colleagues of very long standing, who were my coauthors in relation to the #Selimgate affair in Ottoman and global history in 2020, when so many of our fellow historians simply failed to rise to the occasion. To these names I will add three elder statesmen: Saul Friedländer, Carlo Ginzburg, and Velcheru Narayana Rao, whose intellectual company has ever been a delight. As usual, Muzaffar Alam collaborated generously with me on several projects, the results of which have been regularly employed in this work, and I thank him profoundly for his help and intellectual companionship. I am also grateful to Bill Nelson, who prepared the maps with his customary efficiency.

It remains difficult to come to terms with the loss of my close friend and long-term intellectual conversation partner Sunil Kumar, who left us in January 2021. He loved the craft of history as he loved walking through and savoring the sights of his difficult city (and to a lesser extent mine) of Delhi in the company of friends and students. I still feel his warm hand on my shoulder and believe he would have enjoyed this book, which reflects so many discussions, both serious and frivolous, we had over the years.

A Note on Transliteration

The linguistic complexity of the western Indian Ocean as a region poses challenges to the historian in terms of schemes of transliteration to be used. Diacritical marks have generally been dispensed within this book. For Persian and Arabic, a slightly modified form of the Steingass system is used here: Nur-ud-Din rather than Nur al-Din, Abu'l Fazl rather than Abu al-Fadl, and so on. Apostrophes and single opening quotation marks are used for hamzas and ayns, respectively. The normal modern conventions are in use for the occasional citations from Ottoman Turkish. For Indian languages, standard transliteration is followed, without diacritics for consonants, and long (and short) vowels are also not marked.

A Note on Currency and Tonnage

A number of different currencies and measures of weight and shipping tonnage are referred to in this book. The currencies vary somewhat in their values over time. The equivalences presented below are therefore only by way of indication.

1 real de a ocho = 40 Ottoman akçe (ca. 1550)
1 cruzado = 420 reis (1554)
1 pardau = 300 reis (1554)
1 xerafim = 300 reis
1 Muzaffari tanka = 0.6 Mughal rupees
1 Mughal rupee = 2 xerafins (ca. 1650)
1 Mughal rupee = 2.4 mahmudis (1620)
1 real de a ocho = 2 Mughal rupees (ca. 1615)
1 Mughal rupee = 1.2 Dutch florins (24 stuivers) (ca. 1620)
1 quintal = 51.4 kilograms
1 bahar (Kochi) = 166 kilograms (1554)
1 bahar (Kannur) = 206 kilograms (1554)
1 khandi (Goa) = 220 kilograms (1554)
1 khandi (Chaul) = 235 kilograms (1554)
1 tonel (Portuguese) = 877 liters
1 tonneau (French) = 1,440 liters

ACROSS THE GREEN SEA

Introduction
Conceptual Issues in Connected Histories

> In a word, let us cease if you please to speak endlessly between one national history and another, without ever understanding each other.
>
> Marc Bloch, "A Contribution towards a Comparative History of European Societies" (1928)

NO ISLAND IS AN ISLAND

Seas can be unfriendly, even to experienced mariners. Toward the end of the Islamic lunar month of Muharram in the year 962 AH (December 1554), the Ottoman admiral and intellectual Seydi 'Ali Re'is found himself in Ahmedabad in Gujarat, putting the final touches to his work *Kitabü'l-Muhit* (Book of the Ocean).[1] Seydi 'Ali had not intended to be in Gujarat and found himself there only because of the vagaries of navigation, having suffered a shipwreck in a massive storm while trying to take his fleet around the Arabian Peninsula from Gwadar to Yemen. An experienced sailor in the Mediterranean, where he had served with the great Hayreddin Barbarossa, the Ottoman admiral was clearly unfamiliar and rather ill at ease in the more easterly waters where he now found himself. This is what seems to have motivated him to write his text, based on the experience of having "discussed nautical matters day and night with the pilots and mariners who were on board" during a period of roughly eight months spent first in Basra, then in the Persian Gulf, and eventually off the coast of western India.[2] With remarkable ingenuity, he had also managed to lay his hands on several important geographical works in Arabic by earlier writers, whether classic medieval texts or those of more recent vintage written by men such as Ahmad ibn Majid and Sulaiman al-Mahri.[3] As he had learned to his own cost, Seydi 'Ali stated, "it was actually extremely difficult to maneuver in the Indian seas without them [such works], since the captains, commanders, and sailors, who were not experienced in these maneuvers always needed a pilot because they themselves lacked the necessary knowledge."[4] Constituted as a companion volume to his better-known travel text *Miratü'l-Memalik*

(Mirror of Kingdoms), the *Muhit* may be considered a textual tribute of sorts from the Mediterranean to the Indian Ocean, an admission that to know the one was not to know the other.[5]

To draw the obvious lesson, every ocean needs its own histories, just as it needs its own navigational treatises.[6] Neither the Mediterranean nor the Atlantic can provide a simple model to be imitated, however much modern historians have been tempted to do so.[7] The reasons for this may be evident, but they bear reviewing. The Mediterranean, after all, was a relatively small body of water, one-thirtieth the surface of the Indian Ocean, with only two very limited points of exit into the Black Sea and the Atlantic respectively.[8] It could sometimes be dominated by a single political system, as had been the case with the Roman Empire, a model for the ambitions of later empires. Given its oblong shape, it was also relatively quickly traversed from its northern to its southern shores, with navigation on the east-west axis more cumbersome. As a consequence of this geography, the Mediterranean was the theater for a particularly dense set of crisscross interactions, the point of departure for Fernand Braudel's exploration of the sea as an object of historical study in the early modern period.[9] The Atlantic Ocean, for its part, poses problems of quite the opposite order. For centuries, until Iberian empire-building in the late 1400s, its eastern and western shores barely maintained any form of regular contact. Even after 1500 the ocean as a whole showed little or no coherence; and as even enthusiasts for Atlantic history have admitted, there are serious issues posed by "the real disjunctions that characterized the Atlantic's historical and geographic components."[10] Atlantic history has thus usually been sliced into various segments corresponding to the various European empires that attempted to dominate one or the other set of circuits in the ocean. Furthermore, in the three centuries from 1500 on, the relationship between the two seaboards remained deeply asymmetrical, resembling neither the Mediterranean nor the Indian Ocean in this respect.

Let us turn to our real object, the western Indian Ocean or Green Sea (*al-bahr al-akhzar*). Since histories must begin somewhere, this one may as well commence in the kingdom of Hurmuz in the Persian Gulf, a small but complex maritime state centered on the tiny and singularly arid island of Jarun, with its striking multicolored array of soils. Though the island was probably an ancient site of human habitation, its role as the center of a kingdom was consolidated only from around 1300, at a time when the Mongol Il-Khanid dynasty had come to rule over a good part of the mainland to the north after having ended the five-century-long career of the 'Abbasid Caliphate in Baghdad in 1258.[11] Jarun's immediate neighbor farther up the Persian Gulf was the much larger island of Qishm, which was certainly much richer in natural resources but neither as defensible nor as strategically situated to control the waterways. By the middle decades of the fourteenth century Jarun and Hurmuz were well positioned to take over the dominant role as entrepôt that had once been held by the port of Siraf on the Iranian mainland, and then by Qais. The best known of the travelers of that time, the Moroccan Ibn Battuta, testifies to that; he seems to have visited it at least twice on his way to and from India. Ibn Battuta noted that the earlier settlement called Hurmuz had been on the mainland, in the region known as Mughistan, but that a newer town had then been created on "an island whose city is called Jarun," separated from the mainland by a channel that he overstates as three farsakhs, or ten miles, wide. He describes it as "a fine large city, with magnificent bazaars, as it is the port of India and Sind, from which the wares of India are exported to the two 'Iraqs, Fars and Khurasan." This city was the residence of the sultan, who at the time of Ibn Battuta's visits was Qutb-ud-Din Tahamtan bin Turan Shah. He had taken the island in the late 1310s after a protracted contest and then added various other islands and territories to its domains on the two shores of the gulf. The sultan initially made a poor impression on Ibn Battuta, who described him as "an old man, wearing long cloaks, both skimpy and dirty, with a turban on his head, and a kerchief for a waist girdle," but he later came to realize that he was actually "one of the most generous of princes, exceedingly humble, and of excellent character."[12] Ibn Battuta also noted that the royal family was given to periodic bursts of internecine violence, notably between Tahamtan and his brother Kaiqubad and Kaiqubad's descendants. However, it appears that the initiative to build up Jarun and make it a real political center had in fact come from outside this family. The most significant figures in the matter were a couple of enterprising former Turkish slaves, Baha-ud-Din Ayaz and Bibi Maryam, who in the last years of the thirteenth century had managed to stave off pressure from rival groups of Mongols on the mainland in order to carve out a coastal domain including Qalhat (in Oman), but centering on Jarun, where Ayaz himself settled and ruled for a time during the first decade of the fourteenth century.

After the political consolidation that Tahamtan and his allies then brought about, the central place of Jarun and Hurmuz was assured in the next century and a half, despite regular bouts of internal political turbulence. Although there is a paucity of contemporary sources from the second half of the fourteenth century, Chinese sources of the Ming dynasty during the first three decades of the fifteenth century shed a fair amount of light on Hurmuz's role in the Indian Ocean trade.[13] Several of the celebrated expeditions of the admiral Zheng He put in at the port and usually followed a fairly regular pattern of spending two months there from mid-January to mid-March before embarking on their return voyage to China. As an authoritative analysis of these Chinese materials puts it: "All 'first-hand information' on Hormuz, as on many other distant ports and polities, was collected in the days of Zheng He—by Ma Huan, Gong Zhen and Fei Xin, who accompanied Zheng He on his expeditions. Later sources merely repeat what these three authors had to tell, without adding anything new to the stock of data then available."[14] The account by the translator Ma Huan is particularly intriguing, since he was himself a convert to Islam.[15] Rather than an ethnocentric or condescending view, he paints a highly idealized picture of Hurmuz, in which everyone in the kingdom is a devout Muslim who follows every aspect of the shari'a to the letter and beyond. Not only are the people "refined and fair," but they are also "stalwart and fine-looking; their clothing and hats are handsome, distinctive and elegant." Besides, he provides an extensive list of the different commodities traded on the market, though he omits to mention perhaps the most significant of them, the horses that were brought in from the mainland in order to be exported to Indian destinations in Gujarat, the Deccan, and Kanara and Kerala ports such as Bhatkal, Kannur, and Calicut (Kozhikode).

The picture that can be gleaned from the Ming sources becomes still clearer because of a narrative account in Persian from the early 1440s, written by 'Abdur Razzaq Samarqandi. 'Abdur Razzaq was the envoy sent by the Timurid ruler Mirza Shahrukh to Kerala in order to assert his preeminence in the maritime world of the western Indian Ocean at that time, in competition with the Yemeni Rasulids or the Cairo-based Mamluks. Arriving in Hurmuz from Herat in the early part of 1442 in order to take a ship bound for Kerala, he describes the port:

> Hurmuz, which they call Jarun, is a port in the midst of the sea, with no equal on the face of the earth. Merchants from the seven climes, Egypt, Syria, Anatolia, Azerbaijan, Arabian and Persian 'Iraq, Fars, Khorasan, Transoxiana, Turkestan, the Qipchaq steppe, the Qalmaq regions, and all the lands of the east, China, Machin, and Khanbaliq, all come to that port, and seafaring men from Machin, Java, Bengal, Ceylon, the cities of the Land below the Winds [*zirbad*], Tenasserim, Soqotra, Siam [*shahr-i nav*], and the Maldive Islands, to the realm of Malibar, Abyssinia and Zanj, the ports of Vijayanagara, Gulbarga, Gujarat, and Cambay, the

coast of the Arabian peninsula to Aden, Jiddah and Yanbuʻ, bring to that town precious and rare commodities.¹⁶

This is an extensive list, running all the way from East Africa to the ports of China. ʿAbdur Razzaq notes that goods and people from the world over can be found in Hurmuz, and further that the trade is taxed a very reasonable tenth save for gold and silver, on which no duties are paid. In contrast to Ma Huan, he also emphasizes that "adherents of various religions, even infidels, are many in the city, but they deal equitably with all." According to the Timurid envoy, the town was known as the Abode of Peace (*dar al-aman*), while the residents were "as flattering as Persians, and as profound as Indians [*tamalluq-i ʿIraqiyan wa taʿammuq-i Hindiyan*]." His later experience with the Hurmuzis when he was on his mission in southern India would lead him to modify this opinion somewhat.

Thanks to the meticulous research of the French savant Jean Aubin in the 1950s and 1960s, it is possible to reconstruct the principal elements of the morphology of Hurmuz in the later fifteenth century, even in the absence of reliable cartographic evidence.¹⁷ The new settlement of Hurmuz was initially built around 1300 on a spur of land at the extreme north of the island of Jarun, which pointed toward the Iranian mainland. There were two port sites, to the east and west respectively, both considered to be of good quality. The fortified residence of the kings was in this same area, south of Point Murna, with nine bulwarks and several points of entry. This structure was on high ground and supposedly the most imposing royal palace in that part of the Persian Gulf, at least in the view of most sixteenth-century commentators. Between the palace and the seafront to the west were several elite residences. These included the residence of the Fali clan of viziers, while another building was generally used to house princes who had been blinded to keep them out of succession struggles, a common practice of the time. In front of the palace was an important madrasa and infirmary complex with a minaret, which had been constructed by the ruler Turan Shah (r. 1347–1377).¹⁸ Some of these significant buildings were heavily damaged or destroyed, however, in an earthquake in February 1483. In the center of the town itself, some 250 meters south of the royal palace, was the imposing congregational mosque founded at the beginning of the fourteenth century and considerably enlarged at that century's end. The Dutch Jesuit Gaspar Berze described it, undoubtedly with some exaggeration, as "the largest and the most beautiful mosque that there is in all of Moordom."¹⁹

It was in the eastern port and anchorage that one found the customhouse (*gumruk*), located there because the eastern side was the one pre-

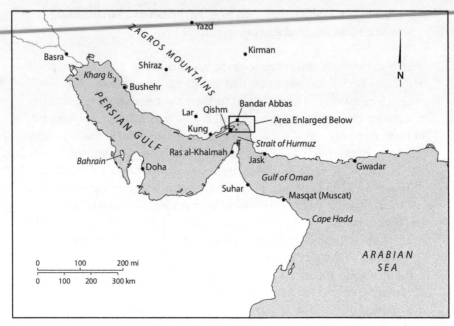
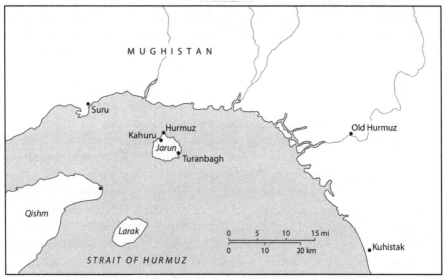

1. Hurmuz and the Persian Gulf

ferred by ships for its facility except on those occasions when they needed to shelter from rough winds blowing in from the Indian Ocean. On the same side, farther to the south along the coast, one encountered the wharfs for ship construction as well as the main warehouses to stock goods. In the town itself were several squares (in Portuguese, *praças*). Contemporary Persian authors refer to the largest, which housed the major market, probably at the eastern end of the urban space, as the Maidan-i Jarun. It is unclear if the town was really organized on a regular chessboard pattern, as some conventional drawings from a later period suggest. There was certainly an important street leading south directly from the palace and intersecting the city's main avenue, which ran from east to west, at right angles not far from the congregational mosque. It appears likely from descriptions that most of the other streets were deliberately narrow and winding, so that houses could provide shade for one another. Most of the houses appear not to have had gardens or courtyards, were between two and four floors high, and had been built of a porous volcanic stone that kept out the heat. As one approached the southern edges of the town, the houses became less frequent, and instead there were reed huts thatched with palm fronds in which the poorer islanders lived.

At a few kilometers' distance from the town, at Kahuru on the west coast, was an area where the townsmen went out on pleasure trips, and where one of the two royal cemeteries was located. The other main royal cemetery could be found on the east coast of the island, near a shrine dedicated to the legendary prophet Khwaja Khizr, a figure of some significance in the gulf.[20] Not far from Kahuru was an area that the rulers and their retinues used as a polo ground, and this was the same zone the kingdom's elites used for occasional retreats and to take shelter away from the urban center after an earthquake like that of 1483. This liminal area, between the town and the southern hills, housed some other interesting sites, such as those where the minority Shi'ite population engaged in its Muharram celebrations, or where a handful of Indian yogis resided in caves, and other "Hindu" groups maintained their own shrines in order to be outside the town proper. Much beyond these, closer to the southeastern extremity of the island, was a site designated as Tolombak (or Turan Bagh), which had its own water source and small garden as well as a royal pavilion where it was claimed one could post a lookout in order to discern the approach of ships arriving from India.

The last decades of the fifteenth century were quite turbulent ones in the Hurmuz kingdom, after the extended reign of Fakhr-ud-Din Turan Shah (r. 1436–1471), the ruler at the time of 'Abdur Razzaq's visit. The long reign of Salghur Shah (1475–1505) was punctuated by numerous struggles both within the gulf itself and with mainland powers such as the Aqquyunlu. The ruler himself had had some difficulty in seizing the throne after protracted civil wars involving his brothers, notably Shah Wais, whom he defeated at Julfar through a combination of military force and subterfuge. Although a variety of Omani clans played some role in his success, his main allies seem to have been a set of powerful families from the Iranian coast, who had fleets of boats equipped with efficient archers. It was therefore no surprise to see the emergence during his reign of one of these families, the powerful Fali clan, which came to occupy the position of vizier held earlier at Hurmuz by first the Baghdadi family and then by the Iji Sayyids. Among them we may note the preeminent figure of Ra'is Nur-ud-Din Fali, who also came to control the lucrative customhouse at Hurmuz and its revenues. At the same time members of the corps of royal slaves (*ghulams*), who had quite diverse origins, carved out a significant role during Salghur Shah's reign. The complex nature of the trading links in Hurmuz had created a highly diversified slave market there, with slaves imported from the Iranian mainland as well as Ethiopia and India. Among these slaves, the most important at the end of the fifteenth and the beginning of the sixteenth century was the powerful eunuch Khwaja 'Ata Sultani (d. 1513), who would play a key role in resisting the first Portuguese attempts to control Hurmuz in 1507–1508.[21]

The case of Hurmuz, however atypical it may appear at first sight, holds important lessons for the historian of the early modern western Indian Ocean.[22] We should obviously avoid the construct of the microcosm here, since a small space such as the kingdom of Hurmuz can hardly stand in for the far larger oceanic space in which it was located, no more than Malta can be made to stand in for the Mediterranean or Madeira for the Atlantic. Rather, let us reflect—even if briefly—on the methodological questions that its study raises and how these questions have been addressed by generations of historiography. The most remarkable aspect of Hurmuz is the complex layering of historical source material that is available for the site. Beginning with the Persian and Arabic narrative sources (including Ibn Battuta) in the fourteenth century, later periods bring other materials to the fore as well, such as collections of diplomatic correspondence, travel texts, and archival documents from the sixteenth century and beyond. For the late fifteenth century, one of Jean Aubin's chief sources was an unpublished chronicle, the *Tabaqat-i Mahmud Shahi* by 'Abdul Karim Nimdihi, which he read together with Nimdihi's *insha'* (belles-lettres) collection in manuscript, and which sheds light on dealings among Hurmuz, the Persian Gulf more generally, and western India.[23] Nimdihi himself, who spent a part of his career in southern Iran and the Persian Gulf and another part in the Deccan and Gujarat, is one of those figures whose trajectory breaks down the conventional geographical boundaries that historians have been wont to employ, and much the same can be said for his chief patron and employer, Khwaja Mahmud Gawan Gilani (d. 1481).[24] Weaving together these intersecting but different sources can thus produce a rich tapestry in which Hurmuz proves to be an indispensable knot.

In turn, the production of context enriches our reading of any text, however trivial it may appear to be at first sight. We can see this logic at work in relation to a small handful of letters written in Persian and Arabic from early sixteenth-century Hurmuz, preserved today in Lisbon's Torre do Tombo. Khwaja 'Ata Sultani, the de facto controller of the island-state, composed these letters in September 1508 and addressed them to the Portuguese commander Afonso de Albuquerque. Albuquerque had attempted in the previous year on his own initiative to seize control of Hurmuz but was obliged to abandon his attempt, since many of the other captains under his command refused to follow his lead. By the time of his return to Hurmuz in late 1508, Khwaja 'Ata had taken the precaution of contacting Albuquerque's superior, the viceroy Dom Francisco de Almeida. In one letter he plays one off against the other:

> He [In His Name]
>
> Great Captain Afonso de Albuquerque, know that the envoy of Dom Francisco the viceroy came to us from Cochin, and he brought a letter on which there is the seal of Portugal. The letter with the seal is addressed to us, and also there is a letter for you and for the captains who are with you. Look at it. The original is for you. We know what it contains. Read the letter of your sultan. Listen and take the proper path. If you come [to us], you will see the seal of your sultan of Portugal. Let the captains come near the shore, so that we can send the envoy from Portugal to you and the seal that is on the letter addressed to us, you will see it. The prisoners who were with you, and whom you sent to the lord of Cochin, [namely] Nakhuda 'Ali Mubariz and his companions, have been sent back to us and he treated them well. Know this. Salutations.[25]

The letter is written in a fair hand, but as Jean Aubin, who carefully analyzed it, notes, it was certainly dictated and not written by Khwaja 'Ata himself. It is characterized moreover by its strange informality and, to quote Aubin, "confused and dialectal style," perhaps because Khwaja 'Ata was himself of Bengali origin and had not received an advanced literary education. Albuquerque is addressed by name and as the *nakhuda kabir* or "great captain"; the term "viceroy" is not translated as, say, *na'ib* or "deputy" but simply rendered as *abu zurray*, a loan word from the Portuguese term *vice-rei* or *visorei*. Interestingly, we have a sixteenth-century translation into Portuguese of this letter, which we may also consider in order to obtain a sense of the distinction between original and contemporary rendering. This translation quite closely approximates many—but not all—elements of our version in more or less the same sequence. The name of the chief prisoner sent back from Cochin is rendered differently as Nakhuda Qaisar. Some small details are left out, such as the fact that the Cochin ruler (*sahib al-Kuji*) had treated the prisoners well. The exchange of a couple of letters immediately following this one is also interesting. Albuquerque attempted in these to question the authenticity of the Portuguese letters he was sent from Hurmuz, claiming, for example, that the wax on one of the seals looked suspicious. Khwaja 'Ata responded indignantly that he would never have forged a letter from the viceroy and that Albuquerque was merely using this as an excuse to be a "traitor to the King of Portugal" (*haram-khwar-i padshah-i Burtukal*, which the contemporary Portuguese translation baldly renders as *tu es tredor a el Rey de Portugal*). Besides, he pointed out that the letters carried the signatures of the Portuguese viceroy and the official secretary (*nawisinda*). He also suggested that the translator or "reader" (*khwananda*) Albuquerque employed to deal with Persian and Arabic correspondence was incompetent and had created pointless confusion.[26]

A careful reading of even this small body of correspondence in its proper context thus allows us to understand that even as Albuquerque was attempting to exploit the political differences in Hurmuz between the rulers, the Fali family and Khwaja 'Ata, the latter was no less well informed and able to exploit the fissures that he knew existed between Albuquerque, the other captains, and the Portuguese viceroy based in Cochin. His complex strategy, which proved largely successful until his death in 1513, cannot be understood with reference to stereotypical ideas of "Muslim statecraft" or the alleged gulf between "merchants and rulers" in the Indian Ocean world.[27] It must instead be understood as the well-considered defense of a freeport (*dar al-aman*), which guaranteed a neutral space for different groups of merchants, rather than the fortified outpost it would become after its eventual capture by the Portuguese.

COMPARATIVE HISTORY AND BEYOND

One way of posing a history like that of Hurmuz would be in comparative terms, whether those comparisons were made within the limits of

Asian history or extended as far afield as Venice, Genoa, and Lübeck. The classic formulation is that of Max Weber, which cast a long shadow extending well into the 1960s and 1970s, a period when the comparative fashion in history was probably at its peak.[28] This was also a time when the dominant framing in social science–inflected history was provided by the master concept of "modernization," particularly in the variant set out by the economic historian Simon Kuznets. Kuznets's work, which involved processing an enormous body of data on a large number of countries, identified what he saw as a standard trajectory of long-term economic and social change, which (it was imagined) would diffuse from the Western world and then set the pattern for "less advanced" countries in Asia, Africa, and Latin America.[29] Though Kuznets was influenced by thinkers of an earlier generation such as Joseph Schumpeter, he lacked their sophisticated historical understanding. Therefore, while he may have not intended it as such, his studies became a somewhat inflexible and doctrinaire framework to understand general processes of economic (and even social) change. This in turn led to critiques and modifications from other intellectuals who had emerged from the milieu of late tsarist Russia, such as Alexander Gerschenkron (1904–1978). Gerschenkron's celebrated collection of essays on the question of "economic backwardness" from 1962, despite its somewhat unsystematic and dispersed character, intended to critique the more mechanistic conceptions present in both the standard Marxist analysis of the time and other simplistic stage theories of change, such as those put forward by W. W. Rostow.[30]

Although most questions addressed by these economists and historians were explicitly framed through comparisons, these could be multiple and complex comparisons or simpler paired comparisons, such as those between India and Japan or between India and Indonesia.[31] The same predilection for comparative analysis remained in place when one moved back from the more recent period to studying the sixteenth and seventeenth centuries. One such exercise could be to compare the workings of the Dutch and English East India Companies, which had been founded in 1602 and 1600 respectively in order to trade in the Indian Ocean, one apparently a sizable, centralized body with access to large amounts of capital through the Amsterdam stock exchange, and the other a rather loose and unstable institution, lacking a centralized chain of command and with a complex and ambivalent relationship with networks of private traders.[32] In the 1970s and 1980s there was a notorious tendency to idealize the Dutch Company (Verenigde Oostindische Compagnie, or VOC) and treat it as the most efficient and most advanced of the chartered trading companies, whether in the Indian Ocean or the Atlantic.

This was again very much the consequence of a Weberian influence on such comparative studies, as can be seen from the important work of the influential Danish historian Niels Steensgaard. In particular, Steensgaard contrasted the Dutch Company not with its English counterpart but with the Portuguese *Estado da Índia* and various Asian state structures, which he saw in quite radical terms, portraying it as an "institutional innovation" when compared to a purely "redistributive enterprise" like that of the Portuguese, Safavids, or Ottomans. As he announced at the outset of his work, his real purpose had been "a study of the victorious companies," but he had concluded that "a satisfactory study would have to be made on a comparative basis, taking into account what evidence might be unearthed concerning the losers."[33] His schematic representation of Portuguese Asian society, based largely on the mocking accounts of foreign travelers who had visited there, was that it was "a social system in which the ambitions are archaic although the situation is dynamic." The entire "normative system" was in his view one oriented toward jockeying for petty advantages of social status rather than profit maximization, and furthermore in the grip of a "constitutionally determined corruption" that was impossible to reform. In contrast, the Dutch Company was characterized as a rational enterprise oriented toward "solving ... problems, [having] turned them, so to speak, to their own advantage."[34] Thus, if the central concept in relation to the Portuguese is "corruption," with the Companies, "the key words are flexibility and planning." Steensgaard sums up the whole matter quite pithily in an early section of the book: "The downfall of the caravan trade, the defeat of the Portuguese and the triumph of the Companies was an episode in the historical process during which the Middle East and the Mediterranean region relinquished the economic leadership in favor of the Atlantic regions. It was part of the clash between the Catholic Iberian powers and the Protestant Channel powers, and it was part of the confrontation between older and newer entrepreneurial forms—a step towards the development of modern economy."[35]

We will have occasion to return briefly to Steensgaard, notably his selective understanding of both the *Estado da Índia* and the Islamic "gunpowder empires," with its emphasis on customs collection and redistribution rather than trade. It is worth noting that two other major historians who had studied the Dutch Company did not quite share his view, even if they never expressed their own opinions outright. The self-taught English historian Charles Boxer had spent several decades from the 1920s onward studying both the Portuguese and the Dutch and had written major works of syntheses in the 1960s on both seaborne empires. However, he had usually shied away from an explicit comparison between the two, even though he had studied the conflicts between them in both the Atlantic and Indian Ocean contexts, and even as far east as Japan.[36] The American historian Holden Furber, for his part, produced a bold and wide-ranging survey of European commercial activity in the Indian Ocean between 1600 and 1800, which appeared at about the same time as Steensgaard's work.[37] In this book he covered many major and minor participants, including the Dutch and English, but also the French and the Danes. Furber's profound immersion in the archives did not allow him many illusions regarding the Dutch and the English. He was perfectly aware of how deep the issue of "corruption" ran in the Companies and how little they corresponded to an ideal of flexibility and profit-oriented dynamism. His earlier studies had amply demonstrated that beneath the surface of the English Company serpentine networks of private interest and familial jockeying for advantage were to be found.[38]

It should be clear therefore that the weighty heritage of comparative history is something that scholars of my generation, largely trained in the 1980s, have had to confront and struggle with since the very outset. But the comparisons that have been summarized in the preceding pages have usually been large in both their temporal and institutional dimensions and structural in their orientation. Frequently they have been influenced by the practice of historical sociologists, whether Marxists or Weberians, rather than the reflections of historians such as Marc Bloch, notably in his celebrated essay on comparative history from 1928.[39] When one rereads Bloch's essay, it is striking to note not only its vagueness about some matters but also its remarkable sophistication about others. Obviously Bloch was not particularly concerned with comparisons that would lead the historian outside Europe, though he does not seem to rule this out as a principle. Equally, he was aware that comparative history had its limits and was not, as he put it, a "new panacea." He also distinguished between two types of comparisons: one set that would lead to a consideration of societies distant in space and time that neither had common origins nor had influenced one another (here he had in mind James Frazer's *The Golden Bough*); and the other where the comparisons were between broadly contemporaneous and neighboring societies, such as France and Germany or France and England. For such comparisons to be useful, he went on to argue, two conditions were necessary: there should be some level of similarity between the cases under study, and there should also be some dissimilarity in the two contexts. Without the first there was no basis for comparison, and without the latter there was no interest left in it.

Writing at a time when comparative history was still somewhat unpopular, Bloch could not have foreseen certain of its less desirable effects as its use became more and more widespread, indeed a veritable industry in certain academic contexts. There are several obvious issues with how comparative history came to be practiced: (1) the idea that the simple juxtaposition of two (or more) cases is in itself somehow significant or reveals some hidden truth; (2) the use of comparison to reinforce a predetermined hierarchy between the cases under examination, a procedure usually reinforced by a sharply asymmetrical knowledge of the two cases; (3) the reification of the objects (or cases) being studied by exaggerating their uniqueness or specificity; (4) the repetitive and somewhat slothful use of the same units of comparison rather than a flexible approach to them; and (5) the use of comparison for simple list-making or the creation of typologies for their own sake, thus, for example, enunciating some more or less random claim such as that there are seven types of empires, or five types of cities, or eleven types of religious systems.[40] Certain comparative historians have even taken to openly fabricating bodies of statistical data in order to lend a spurious air of scientific precision to their exercise, claiming for example to have an "index of social development" for different societies over five or ten or fifteen thousand years.[41]

It was in the context of a profound dissatisfaction with the state of comparative history that in the late 1990s I proposed an alternative in terms of "connected history" in order to rethink the geographical and spatial conceptions that underpinned the units of analysis used by historians.[42] The original essay was presented initially as a critique of a project by Victor Lieberman, an American historian of Southeast Asia, who had sketched out a comparative macrohistory to be written in order to show the "strange parallels" between developments in distant parts of Eurasia, especially with regard to state formation. Embracing a thousand years of history beginning in about 800 CE and drawing for the most part on secondary literature, Lieberman attempted to make a typology of state forms, listing and dividing in the familiar exercise to produce an "intra-Eurasian classification."[43] In its schematic outlines it immediately became evident that the exercise was one in the reification of boundaries and in reproducing certain entrenched stereotypes (such as a blunt-edged contrast between imperial unification in India and China) rather than one that led to any surprising or innovative conclusions. More than one specialist of the regions in question is likely to have winced when reading Lieberman's claims such as this one: "in other critical aspects, both synchronic and diachronic, I have found precious little difference between, say, France, Burma, Japan, and Vietnam."[44] This was of course a very different approach than the one Carlo Ginzburg identifies with Marc Bloch: "Bloch evokes the persistent prejudice which identifies comparative history with the search for analogies, including the most superficial ones. However, the central point of comparative history, Bloch insists on the contrary, is to emphasize the specificity of the *differences* between the phenomena that are being compared."[45] Clearly, then, there are better and worse ways of practicing comparative history.

The central propositions where connected history was concerned laid the emphasis on rather different questions. The first of these was the problematic effect of nationalism and national boundaries on how historical problems themselves were formulated by imposing rigid teleologies. While these boundaries were clearly appropriate in many cases, especially for the nineteenth and twentieth centuries, they had little utility when one moved back in time into the early modern and medieval periods. Not only did they obscure the importance of the study of large spatial units that cut across such boundaries, such as empires, but they also downplayed the significance of smaller regions that were often historically crucial and might be found traversing current national boundaries. But historians were often ill equipped to study such historical phenomena precisely because they refused to combine the diverse archives and texts that were necessary to do so, failed to come to terms with the multiple historiographies that had to be mastered, and instead fell back on the lazy habits of their conventional training.[46] It thus appeared to me that a crucial question for the historian was to find the means and the skills to break down conventional spatial boundaries when those boundaries were no longer useful but instead had become impediments to the study of the real historical problems that one encountered.

A second problem, once the conventional boundaries had been called into question, was the reconstitution of fresh spatial parameters appropriate to the new problems that were to be studied. Here the central idea in connected history was spatial flexibility, because what might be appropriate in order to study a merchant network like that of the New Julfan Armenians of the seventeenth and eighteenth centuries might be quite inappropriate if the object of study was the cultural world of the great fifteenth-century poet and intellectual 'Abdur Rahman Jami (1414–1492).[47] The writings of some members of an older generation of historians were a considerable inspiration in order to think through this issue, whether one looks back to Jean Aubin or the American sinologist Joseph Fletcher. Both had reflected considerably on the complex and overlapping jurisdictions of political and cultural formations of the early modern period.[48] Neither had embraced a version of global history based simply on deploying and synthesizing secondary material, as had become common in the Anglo-American historiography in the wake of William McNeill in a form that still dominates in the production of popular history in the United States and Britain.[49] Rather, both Aubin and Fletcher showed a restless ambition with regard to spatial units, moving from the study of cities to the analysis of empires and to other liminal spaces. In the case of Aubin, he followed some fascinating individual trajectories of the later medieval and early modern periods, namely of minor or neglected intellectuals who moved from service in one political formation to another and then to a third or fourth.[50] This had little or nothing to do with the "liberal cult" of mobility, as some Marxisant sociologists have recently claimed, but rather with a historically rooted understanding of the nature of the activities of chroniclers, poets, and courtiers in the Islamic world.[51]

The initial set of examples used in the 1997 essay on connected history were diverse and included political legends that circulated across wide spaces in Eurasia with divergent valences (such as the legend of Alexander), as well as the use and reuse of millenarian schemes and materials between the late fifteenth and seventeenth centuries in a large swath of territory in which different politico-cultural regimes were in close communication. In the time since its initial publication there have been several reactions to it, some drawing upon it as an intellectual resource, others based on fundamental misunderstandings, and still others hostile for a variety of reasons. The fact that it was meant to be a set of skeptical proposals in relation to a dominant paradigm—namely, a comparative history rooted in nationalism with relatively rigid units of comparison—has often been forgotten in the process. Many scholars who were studying rather banal commercial, political, or other spatial connections began to claim that they were consequently and automatically practicing some form of connected history. Among the misunderstandings, perhaps the most perilous is the view that connected history can be transformed into a sort of third-worldist discourse of symmetrical history (*histoire à parts égales*) in which the West and the Rest would somehow be given equal voice. This was the construction of a French political scientist, Romain Bertrand, who in midcareer turned to writing early modern history.[52] Despite his modest acquaintance with European and Asian primary sources of the early modern period, Bertrand was able to convince a part of the French public that he could become a ventriloquist and speak in the voice of the oppressed Asiatic Other of the European colonizer, when no scholar before or since has been able to do so. In reality, Bertrand's writings thus revisited and misread the work of established historians of early modern Southeast Asia who had never wished to give their work such a "politically correct" turn.[53]

A different and certainly more fecund line of development was to try to combine connected history and early modern imperial history on a broad scale with no claims to symmetry of treatment. The earliest explicit attempt in that direction was by the French scholar of colonial Mexico Serge Gruzinski in an essay published in 2001 in a special number of the well-known journal *Annales HSS*.[54] Gruzinski begins his essay by noting, "The chronological and geographical frameworks of historical research at times become heavy. Their rigidity often masks ethnocentric reflexes concealed behind historiographical traditions." After some skeptical remarks directed at the contributions of scholars in Anglophone world history and postcolonial studies, he goes on to note that it was necessary to confront the issue in early modern history of "mixed landscapes, frequently disconcerting and always unpredictable":

> The exhumation of these historical "connections" has led our path to cross that of Sanjay Subrahmanyam, when he prefers research in and development of "connected histories" to a comparative history that is imprecise, redundant, and full of a priori assumptions. This implies that such histories should be multiple—the fact of being plural and small-scale does not make them unimportant—and that they should be interlinked and can communicate. The presence of a baroque altarpiece in the interior of Hopi Indian chapel raises problems of interpretation which go far beyond the study of a community, a region, or a type of object. When confronted with realities that necessarily have to be approached on multiple scales, the historian should become a sort of electrician capable of reviving continental or intercontinental connections that national historiographies have long worked to disconnect or avoid by rendering their frontiers impermeable. Those that separate Portugal and Spain are an example of such blockages.[55]

Gruzinski's point of departure was therefore the sort of "mestizo objects" that had long fascinated him, and his metaphor (not mine) was that of an electrician reconnecting what had been disconnected. My own conception took as its point of departure social, cultural, or political phenomena that were not necessarily concrete objects such as paintings, ivories, or altarpieces. The conversation with Gruzinski was pursued in a creative way over a seminar (called "Amérique-Asie" in shorthand) that he and I jointly directed over several years in the EHESS in Paris in the late 1990s and early 2000s, in which he initially developed his ideas on the Catholic monarchy in the sixteenth and seventeenth centuries through a connected histories approach. By the time he transformed his essay into a book-length project some years later, though, Gruzinski had embraced the overarching framework of globalization or *mondialisation*, a concept regarding which I was not (and still am not) enthusiastic.[56] I myself have returned to the question of combining imperial and connected histories since that time in a variety of venues and publications.

For the sake of completeness, it may be necessary to mention two other attempts to critique connected history as a proposal, albeit from very different angles. One of these comes from a well-known historian of nineteenth-century Britain and the British Empire. This takes the form of an essay that, as its title clearly suggests, is meant to be a defense of comparative history and whose idea is that the best form of defense is to attack alternative approaches.[57] The author, Philippa Levine, thus begins by making a series of broad claims that simply do not bear serious investigation, such as that comparative history is rarely practiced (and must hence be protected as a sort of infant industry); that it has no real relationship with or investment in national boundaries; and that any problems we might identify in the comparative approach are in fact general problems that can be found in all history writing. Having thus distorted the critiques of comparative history, the essay then proceeds to claim that all alternatives are redundant because comparative history already does what they claim to do. After a highly selective summary of one of my essays on the connected history of millenarian movements in the Eurasian space, the author declares, for instance: "Subrahmanyam fails to demonstrate why a comparative rather than a connected approach would not reveal the synchronicity he finds between these various forms of millenarianism."[58] The point is that the essay is not simply about identifying synchronicity, which is merely a point of departure rather than (as this author mistakenly believes) the point of arrival; the essay is actually about the complex relationship and cross-fertilization between a whole series of political movements and ideologies operating with highly flexible geographies.[59] For such historians, the objects of study have already been fixed and have a rigid predetermined geography to them, given to them (for example) by a type of highly conventional British and British Empire history. In this view, one can apparently either work with the universal or the particular, and the particular leads ineluctably to the national.[60]

Critiques from a different angle have come from a few authors using the vocabulary of postcolonial studies. In the 1990s, the same intellectual conjuncture that produced the exchanges concerning comparative and connected histories referred to earlier also produced a different form of critique of Eurocentrism, at the level of metahistory. The best-known work in that context was the Indian historian Dipesh Chakrabarty's *Provincializing Europe*, which was intended to critique a discursive formation in which it was "impossible to *think* of anywhere in the world without invoking certain categories and concepts, the genealogies of which go deep into the intellectual and even theological traditions of Europe."[61] Chakrabarty explored this critique in relation to various intellectual strands, including Marxism, to which he and others of his school (the so-called subaltern studies collective) were broadly attached. Although he had begun his career as a social and economic historian with a comparative bent (comparing the formation of the Indian and English industrial working class), in this later book Chakrabarty had thus moved to a sort of metahistory or intellectual history with limited implications for general historical practice. Like many other subaltern studies historians, he continued even after this critique to remain wedded to conventional geographies of nation-state (India) and region (in his case, Bengal) and to a chronological focus that was largely on the period after 1800. There was thus little or no intersection at this point between postcolonial studies and connected history.[62]

Other postcolonial scholars working on the early modern Indian Ocean have also periodically attempted to develop a critique of connected history, which they portray as having become dominant and even "ubiquitous" over time. In one of these essays it is claimed that "twenty years of 'connected history' writing have brought little clarity over whether 'connectedness' refers to connections as the object of study, a quality inherent to the objects studied, or the way any object might be studied—or indeed all three, or any given combination."[63] On the other hand, some attention to the relevant literature on the subject should make it amply clear that the purpose has never been the study of connections as such or the "inherent" quality of objects. Confusing the distinct terms "circulation" and "connection" also brings little or no light to the issue. Rather, the crucial question has been one of whether our current geographies are adequate for our research questions or ill fit to deal with them. The problematic character of the ugly neologism of "(dis)connected history" can be seen in some recent studies of the Portuguese in Sri Lanka in the sixteenth and early seventeenth centuries, which seem to scarcely represent an advance on writings from the 1950s and in fact take matters several steps back from Aubin's complex studies of the Portuguese in the Persian Gulf.[64] The historian who wishes to go beyond the conventional geographical conception (not to say cliché) of an island in isolation, into which European invaders erupted and perpetrated gratuitous violence, will remark the need to constantly rethink Sri Lanka's history in relation to other histories, those of Kerala and the Tamil and Telugu countries, for example, or even the Malay and mainland Southeast Asian world.[65] They may wish to address why the great Mappila entrepreneurs from Kerala of the 1530s such as Palassi Marikkar invested so much time, effort, and even lifeblood in trying to maintain their influence in the vestiges of the Kotte kingdom in western Sri Lanka, or analyze why the key intermediaries between Sri Lankan rulers and the Portuguese in the period were often Tamil-speaking Srivaishnavas. In a related vein, the historian would do well to question the facile separation between the two shores of the Gulf of Mannar in this period, in view of the fact that so many historical actors made their living by constantly traversing it.[66]

STRUCTURE OF THE WORK

This work contains, in addition to this introduction, four chapters and a short conclusion. I consider the period from about 1440 to 1520, an epoch that has usually posed serious problems to the historiography, in chapter 1. In a wide-ranging survey of the historiography of the Indian Ocean in the fifteenth century published in 1987, two well-known specialists thus remarked: "Considering the wide area they cover, the sources available on the fifteenth century are few and have been used in very diverse ways. Although the Indian Ocean countries are rich in archeological and epigraphic remains, many aspects of their synthesis have yet to be undertaken. Identified by manuscripts which are too often apocryphal, the chroniclers attached to the royal dynasties showed little interest in maritime activities."[67] While this may be broadly accurate, the intervening decades since the publication of that essay have shown that the sources available are less meager than was once supposed, even if they remain unevenly distributed in space and time. The picture that the Portuguese chronicles and archival materials from the years 1498–1520 present to us can thus be reconsidered in the light of these materials. At any rate, the heavy dependence by historians of the fifteenth-century Indian Ocean on two Portuguese texts from the early sixteenth century, those of Tomé Pires and Duarte Barbosa, can now be shown to be not merely outmoded but unnecessary.[68] I thus am able to recover a history with a far greater variety of actors and interests, which can be written moreover from a diversity of perspectives. The chapter closes by marking an important political transition, namely the defeat of the Mamluk dynasty in Egypt, and the consequent entry of the Ottomans into first the Red Sea and then the wider Indian Ocean.

The next chapter takes us into the sixteenth century but also takes a different point of perspective, that from the Muslim holy city of Mecca. A significant set of sources that has been used by historians from at least the nineteenth century are the texts written by Qutb-ud-Din Nahrawali (1511–1582), a prolific Mecca-based Hanafi *'alim* (or savant) with roots in Gujarat. Nahrawali wrote a chronicle of the Ottoman conquest of Yemen and an account of the notables of Mecca, as well as a travel account detailing his visit to Istanbul in the late 1550s.[69] Some of these works were translated into Ottoman Turkish, while others showed a distinct hostility to the Ottomans and their attempts to dominate the Hijaz. However, in more recent times scholars have also turned to the writings of earlier chroniclers, dating back to the fifteenth century. Using these works, notably those authored by Taqi al-Fasi and the Banu Fahd family, Richard Mortel was able to identify more than two hundred significant merchants based in Mecca in the later Mamluk period, especially after the 1420s. Many of these men used the title *khwaja*, "master," and a significant number of them were involved in the trade with India (Gujarat and Kerala), the Persian Gulf, and Egypt. He concludes: "The mercantile community of Mecca during the late Mamluk period was an upwardly mobile group of individuals, a great many of whom were immigrants, attracted to a life in Mecca because of the sanctity of the town itself, as well as the unique possibilities it offered for participation in the international trade of the age. Not a few merchants were able to amass large fortunes, principally as a result of their activities in commerce, which often included more or less frequent journeys to diverse regions, especially India, the source of much of the merchandise carried by this trade."[70] The Ottoman conquest of the Hijaz in 1517 introduced some changes, but the links to western India in particular remained significant. Drawing on an earlier research project conducted in collaboration with my colleague Muzaffar Alam, this chapter traces the outlines of a narrative extending into the middle decades of the sixteenth century.

Chapter 3 is devoted to a somewhat different set of geographies, those linking eastern Africa to western India. Both sides of this equation involved an intricate patchwork of polities, running on the African side from the kingdom of Mutapa in the south to the Solomonid kingdom of Ethiopia in the north and embracing a variety of states both large and small. Founded in the 1270s, the upland Ethiopian kingdom began an important phase of expansion in the early 1330s during the rule of 'Amdä Seyon (r. 1314–1344), which took its territories to the south and east and also led to the partial subjugation of the Ifat sultanate, which controlled the Red Sea port of Zayla'. These intermittent conflicts with Muslim neighbors then continued into the fifteenth century, with the foundation of the sultanate of Barr Sa'ad-ud-Din (or Adal) that took the place of Ifat. Though the Solomonids appear to have held the upper hand in these struggles for the greater part of a century and half, their dominance began to slip as the fifteenth century neared its close, especially after the reign of the aggressive Zär'a-Ya'iqob (r. 1434–1468), described by the important Ethiopian historian Taddesse Tamrat as "the only monarch who made a serious attempt to grapple with the overriding problem of creating a nation out of the manifold communities which constituted his extensive empire."[71] Farther south from the Horn of Africa, a Muslim coastal presence and Islamic influence can be traced in the fifteenth century all the way to Mozambique, interspersed with significant non-Muslim populations. Textual, linguistic, and inscriptional evidence together with an accumulating archaeological record provide us a longer and more complex chronology of the emergence of Islamic city-states on the Swahili coast than what was available a generation or two ago, with the consolidation of materials from that time on Kilwa and its environs.[72] It has been noted that the period from about 800 to 1100, sometimes termed the Shungwaya period, witnessed the creation of the first urban centers in the area, the gradual consolidation of Swahili in the north, together with trade with the Persian Gulf. In the next phase, between 1100 and 1300, the focus of the northern links was transferred to the Red Sea, and a number of new towns such as Mogadishu were founded. This was also a phase of increasing Islamization on the coast, as well as of the increasing prominence of Sayyids (and pseudo-Sayyids) from Yemen. The pendulum then swung back to an extent between 1300 and 1600, with the "Shirazi" period, in which prominent coastal families who had accumulated wealth and power started to claim prestigious Shirazi origins in order to distinguish themselves from both mainland Africans and immigrants from the Red Sea. These elites built elaborately decorated tombs and stone houses, founded new mosques, and adopted "new paraphernalia and dress."[73]

The whole of this coast was in direct or indirect contact with western India in the early modern centuries, whether with Gujarat or the Konkan, in circuits of exchange that included trade goods such as textiles, ivory, and beads, as well as a human traffic in slaves, who came to occupy a variety of social niches in western Indian societies. Known variously as Habshis and Zanjis in Persian vocabulary, these slaves played roles in state-formation processes in the western Indian sultanates, which had usually emerged in the process of the fragmentation of the Delhi Sultanate in the fourteenth and early fifteenth centuries.[74]

The last chapter takes us then to a prominent western Indian port, Surat, and the view of the western Indian Ocean that is afforded from there. In the seventeenth century, Surat enjoyed extensive connections with the Red Sea, Persian Gulf, the Horn of Africa, the Swahili coast, and the Indian Ocean archipelagos, as well as other ports on the Indian west coast from Goa to the southern end of Kerala. William Finch, an employee of the English East India Company, describes it (with some inaccuracies) in the following terms in 1610, not long after the English had first settled there:

> The citie is of good quantitie, with many faire merchants houses therein, standing twentie miles within the land up a faire river. Some three miles from the mouth of the river (where on the south side lyeth a small low island over-flowed in time of raine) is the barre, where ships trade and unlade, whereon at a spring tide is three fathome water. Over this the channell is faire to the citie side, able to beare vessels of fiftie tunnes laden. This river runneth to Bramport [Burhanpur], and from thence, as some say, to Musselpatan [sic]. As you come up the river, on the right hand stands the castle, well walled, ditched, reasonable great and faire, with a number of faire peeces [pieces of ordnance], whereof some of exceeding greatnesse. It hath one gate to the green-ward, with a drawbridge and a small port [i.e., gate] on the river side. The Captaine hath in command two hundred horse. Before this lyeth the medon [*maidan*], which is a pleasant greene, in the middest whereof is a maypole to hang a light on, and for other pastimes on great festivalls. On this side the citie lyeth open to the greene, but on all other parts is ditched and fenced with thicke hedges, having three gates, of which one leadeth to Variaw, a small village, where is the ford to passe over for Cambaya way. Neare this village on the left hand lieth a small aldea [village] on the rivers banke very pleasant, where stands a great pagod, much resorted to by the Indians. Another gate leadeth to Bramport; the third to Nonsary [Navsari], a towne ten cose [*kos*] off, where is made great store of calico, having a faire river comming to it. Some ten cose further lyeth

Gondoree [Gandevi], and a little further Belsaca [Valsad], the frontire towne upon Daman."[75]

Finch then goes on to describe other features of the city, such as its water tanks and customhouse, its various bazaars, and satellite settlements such as Rander (on the other bank of the river), before concluding with a short reflection on the sailing seasons. Yet the city had a longer and far more complex history than the English were able to discern, going back well into the sixteenth century. The chapter thus seeks to reconsider this history as well as its impact on the character and structure of the city itself.

The purpose of this book, modest in size and compact in its conception, is not to provide a comprehensive history of the western Indian Ocean over two centuries. Neither is it to provide a schematic view, by resorting to a high level of abstraction or generalization. Rather, its strategy may be conceptualized as providing a set of incisions in order to look into various aspects of this maritime world, which was in this period a space of considerable variety and complexity. While questions relating to cultural and intellectual history will be a recurrent refrain, I should stress that the book will rest on a bedrock of political economy, linked to an analysis of social history. Only a close and careful reading of sources can allow us to approach the complexity that the western Indian Ocean offers us, and it is on this exercise that we shall now embark.

Chapter 1

An Epoch of Transitions, 1440–1520

The dark night, the fearsome waves,
and the awesome whirlpool;
How can those who bear no burden,
and live on the shore,
imagine our condition?

Ghazal of Hafiz Shirazi

It is considered conventional, even obligatory, when writing an Indian Ocean history to begin with a consideration of certain geographical factors, notably the system of seasonal winds termed the monsoon (from the Arabic *mausim*). These winds follow a well-defined pattern. The South Asian subcontinental landmass creates a low-pressure area drawing winds across the western Indian Ocean in the first months of the year, principally on a southwest–northeast axis, so that southern islands such as Réunion and Mauritius experience heavy rainfall between December and April. The same winds, gathering moisture as they sweep across the ocean, typically make landfall on the Indian west coast in May and June, producing abundant rain on the subcontinent over the next few months on which systems of traditional agriculture heavily depended. This wind system is reversed in the latter part of the year, and from November to January, high pressure over continental Asia pushes winds back in the opposite direction toward the southwestern segment of the Indian Ocean. This more or less regular cyclical pattern was known to seafaring communities in the first millennium BCE and was recorded by Greeks engaged in the Indian Ocean trade around 100 BCE. Navigators also became aware, as Edward Alpers notes, that "the monsoon system did, however, have its limits [and] its effect in the western Indian Ocean reached only as far south as the northern Mozambique channel," after which other powerful systems of winds and currents prevailed.[1] Coming to terms with these facts meant that one could move away in part from the cumbersome and time-consuming traditions of coastal navigation that had once linked western India and the Persian Gulf, for instance. Coastal navigation still had a major part to play, but it could now be articulated into a more sophisticated pattern of long-distance sailing that connected distant parts of the western Indian Ocean. In the later fifteenth and early sixteenth centuries, to sail from Aden to Calicut took thirty-five days; from Masqat to Goa twenty to thirty days; from Malindi to Calicut twenty-five days. Even a somewhat painful and unseasonal voyage between Goa and Qalhat took about forty-five days in 1520. These were thus quite reasonable voyage times in comparison to some of the great oceanic voyages of the sixteenth century. To be sure, they did not quite compensate for the very real terror that crossing the sea could evoke, as we see in Hafiz's famous poem, or in the travel account from the 1440s of 'Abdur Razzaq Samarqandi: "When the smell of the ship reached my nostrils and I experienced the terror of the sea, I lost consciousness to such an extent that for three days I was dead to the world, save for the rising and falling of my breath."[2]

What, then, was the nature of the maritime space that is the object of our study? The western Indian Ocean can be conceived of as an irregular quadrilateral, with one more or less open side, the southern one. This size and shape immediately distinguish it from some other relatively closed maritime systems that have been better studied, such as the Mediterranean or the Black Sea. The remaining three sides are profoundly unequal. The long eastern coast of Africa, stretching from the mouth of the Red Sea via the Horn of Africa to the Cape of Good Hope, is undoubtedly its longest segment and is itself conventionally divided into several segments, whether seen in ecological or cultural terms. The shorter northern segment runs from Aden and the Hadramaut to the Persian Gulf and beyond as far as the coast of Makran and Gwadar and marks the southern limit of the Perso-Arabic mainland. Finally, the eastern segment, or Indian side, can be thought to extend from the mouth of the Indus River to the southern tip of the subcontinent at Cape Comorin and could in a generous definition also include the western coast of Sri Lanka. Additionally, the quadrilateral had two significant partial outlets in the form of the Persian Gulf, leading as far as the Shatt-al-Arab and the twin basins of the Tigris and Euphrates rivers, and the Red Sea, an ancient and much used but notoriously treacherous passage that connected the western Indian Ocean to the southeastern limits of the Mediterranean world.

The relative weight of the three sides of our quadrilateral is naturally a difficult matter to resolve, in large measure because one needs first to decide what the appropriate metrics are. A simplistic model that gained a great deal of popularity in the 1970s and 1980s was that of core-periphery relations, much indebted in turn to neo-Marxist developmental schema in which different societies were slotted into a form

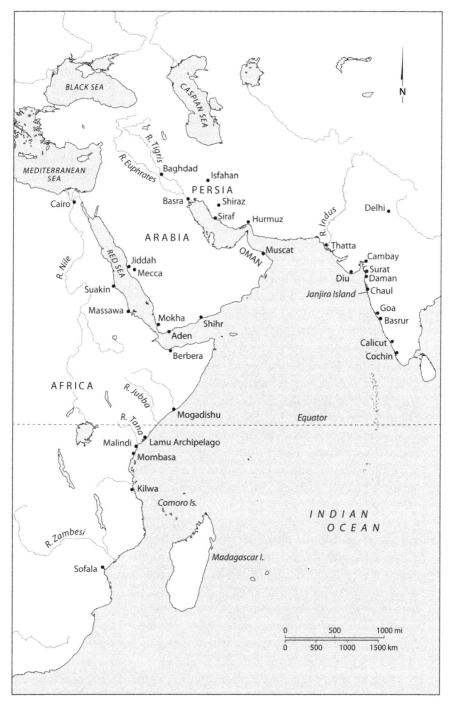

2. The western Indian Ocean

of binary opposition. In this view, one could take any sizable historical space, term it a "world-system," and divide its constituent societies into developed cores on the one hand and less developed peripheries on the other, with a clearly defined hierarchical relationship between the two through which cores would systematically exploit peripheries for their own gain. Though initially developed to describe the emergent colonial Atlantic societies of the sixteenth century in which plantation slavery played a significant role, this model gained some limited popularity among historians of the Indian Ocean through the influence of Immanuel Wallerstein and his direct and indirect disciples.[3] But it also rapidly became clear that this was a case of fitting square pegs into round holes. Attributing the characteristic of cores to societies that had large numbers of artisans or a significant amount of commercial agriculture was not only highly reductive in its materialism but also falsely assumed that such societies were thereby able to project their power over others and engage in forms of unequal exchange such as those that obtained in colonial empires. But power, and more particularly cultural power, has historically stemmed not only from manufactures and surplus rice and wheat; it often had deeper roots and was the result of the interplay of cultural models involving language, religion, courtliness, and a host of other factors. Given the failure of world-system models to prove their utility in the past four decades, I will in general set them aside in this analysis, referring to them only occasionally where they play a significant role in recent historical debates.

Let us begin with a cautious and skeptical survey of certain basic material conditions, such as demography. None of the littoral societies of the western Indian Ocean maintained credible census or cadastral data at any level of detail in the years before 1800 CE, with the partial exception of the Ottoman Empire. Surveys of world population history currently at our disposal are based on little more than educated guesswork or a set of plausible hypotheses. In the case of South Asia, a baseline for 1600 CE is usually established based on partial cadastral data from the Mughal Empire, which is to be found in the *A'in-i Akbari*, which is a part of an official Mughal chronicle of the period.[4] Estimates for earlier years are then constructed on qualitative assumptions regarding the nature of demographic change. The population estimates for Africa tend to fluctuate far more wildly and seem for the most part to be backward extrapolations from periods when reliable data is available, meaning as late as the beginning of the twentieth century. After some speculative estimates several generations ago, based on stereotypes concerning a lack of change, a broad consensus emerged in the 1980s that

TABLE 1.1. Regional population estimates (revised Maddison dataset), in millions

Date/Region	East and Northeast Africa	India	Middle East	World
1000 CE	10	75	20	268
1500 CE	14	110	18	438
1600 CE	16.5	135	22	556

Source: Angus Maddison, *The World Economy: A Millennial Perspective* (Paris: OECD, 2001), 238, 241. This may be compared with the figures in Massimo Livi-Bacci, *A Concise History of World Population*, 5th ed. (Chichester, UK: Wiley-Blackwell, 2012), 25.

placed the total African population in 1600 CE at about 55 million and argued for a fairly steady rate of growth between that date and 1900 CE. A more recent revisionist trend has seen this base estimate revised radically upward to about twice that size, based on the view that the early modern population density in Africa (in, let us say, 1500 or 1600) must have been much closer to that in Eurasia, and also assuming that the slave trade would have only permitted slow and intermittent growth in population after about 1700.[5] In table 1.1, the estimates of the 1980s are presented rather than the later revisionist ones, and it is assumed that East Africa and northeastern Africa represented 30 percent of the total African population. These are juxtaposed with estimates of the population of the Indian subcontinent and the Middle East, running from Iran to the Mediterranean but excluding Egypt.

Even though we would not wish to invest a high degree of faith in this table, which is derived from the very large macro-level data set constructed by Angus Maddison and his colleagues on long-term trends in the world economy, it is nevertheless useful at least in the sense of giving us some orders of magnitude. We can thus say that India (or more generally South Asia) had a dominant demographic weight in the context of the western Indian Ocean when compared to West Asia and the Middle East, as well as eastern Africa. It would nevertheless be erroneous to translate this weight into a qualitative dominance over all matters political, economic, and cultural or somehow to assume that South Asia was the core or center around which the western Indian Ocean was effectively organized.

In order to pursue this question further, it may be useful to return to a schematic analysis by the Dutch historian André Wink contrasting the historical geography of the Indian Ocean with that of the Mediterranean.[6] Wink's intuition is that the Mediterranean analogy is not a particularly helpful one, for reasons I will return to. It should be noted that when the field of Indian Ocean history properly emerged in the second half of the twentieth century, it did so in a self-consciously imitative context. Many scholars who participated in the early formulations of the Indian Ocean as a distinct field of historical study had in mind Fernand Braudel's classic two-volume study of the Mediterranean Sea, first published in 1949 and revised in 1966, despite the many differences between the two spaces in terms of geographical layout, scale, and density of traffic.[7] Even the religious geography of the Indian Ocean appeared far more complex and layered than that of the early modern Mediterranean, which was schematically often divided along a straightforward Christian–Muslim axis of the sort that came to the fore during the celebrated Battle of Lepanto in 1571. But this did not prevent Indian Ocean historians from liberally transferring arguments and models from the Mediterranean, even if some notes of caution were periodically sounded. Wink's principal point, on the other hand, is that the Indian Ocean was constituted quite differently from the Mediterranean in terms of the importance in the former case of some major river systems, which had a significant impact on littoral societies. These included at least three major systems—the Zambezi, the Tigris-Euphrates, and the Indus—but we could also add two other cases that affected the Indian Peninsula, namely the westward-flowing Narmada and Tapti (or Tapi). Each of these created significant basins in which agriculture was concentrated, giving rise to persistent forms of urbanism. A secondary point that Wink makes appears less plausible, namely his bald contrast between the alleged urban instability of the Indian Ocean and the stability of the Mediterranean, which revisits older orientalist cliches that have long been questioned. However, a third aspect of his analysis is of interest, the claim that "the interface of agrarian expansion and pastoral nomadism" provided a crucial historical dynamic on the Indian Ocean littoral, so that "the new capitals of the first half of the second millennium . . . were all located on the fringes of the arid or semi-arid zone and functioned as major centers for the recruitment of man- and animal-power. Situated on the interface of the settled world and the world of the marches, the eccentric new capitals could mediate between sedentary investment and the mobilization of the resources of military entrepreneurs, merchants, and pastoralists."[8] Though initially put forward to characterize trends in the post-Mongol context of the greater Iranian world, it may be argued that the agrarian/urban/pastoral interface can equally be extended to parts of the Indian subcontinent (such as the Deccan), as well as to East Africa.

To conclude this section, some remarks are in order on a different aspect of the western Indian Ocean world, the role of islands. As Roxani Margariti has remarked, "islands and insularity are crucial subjects of study for Indian Ocean history and historiography—as they are for the Mediterranean—and . . . examinations of island lives enrich our understanding of Indian Ocean polities and communities and offer a new view of their participation in an interconnected world."[9] That said, it seems to me necessary to distinguish three types of islands in the western Indian Ocean. The first are the archipelagoes of small islands that dot various zones of the maritime area, such as the Seychelles, the Comoros, the Mascarenes, the Maldives, and the Laccadives (or Lakshadwip). Edward Alpers has examined several of these in their relationship to African history, whether with regard to questions of Islamization, slave trade, or commercial expansion more generally. The Maldives, on the other hand, maintained a relatively close link to Kerala, but they were also a major stop for maritime traffic between the northwestern Indian Ocean and Southeast Asia.[10] A second set of islands, which Margariti herself studies more closely, is located in the two significant interior seas, the Persian Gulf and the Red Sea. The role of the Persian Gulf islands has long attracted historiographical attention, as I have already noted for Jarun (Hurmuz), but also for Qishm, Kish, Kharg, and Bahrain. In the case of the Red Sea, the history of the Dahlak archipelago, located not far from Massawa, is of particular interest. Though we lack a full-fledged study, there is enough evidence to suggest the existence of an autonomous Muslim maritime state there between the eleventh and early thirteenth centuries, which cast a wider shadow over parts of the Red Sea before being subjugated and brought under the direct control of the Rasulid sultans of Yemen. Margariti proposes that it is best to study such islands not separately but as part of a larger set of networks, linking them both to other islands and to mainland polities. Much the same conclusion could be drawn with regard to the Persian Gulf islands.

A third case stands on its own as a category, and that is the very large island of Madagascar in the southwestern Indian Ocean (leaving aside the question of Sri Lanka, which may be seen as a marginal part of the western Indian Ocean). The continuous human habitation of Madagascar appears to have begun only around 500 CE, through what has been described as "a settlement process in which relatively few women, most travelling from Indonesia, founded the Malagasy population— with a much smaller, but just as important, biological contribution from Africa." This population movement of Austronesian speakers has left a significant cultural and linguistic imprint on the island, distinguishing it from the East African mainland. It seems to have occurred either through a formal process of the implantation of small colonies (although this appears improbable), through loosely organized trading voyages from Indonesia, or "via a direct sailing route across the Indian Ocean, perhaps even as the result of an unintended transoceanic voyage."[11] Whatever the case, the Arab geographer al-Idrisi was the first to mention the island and its people in a written source, and then only in the twelfth century. In the same century there appear to have been trading settlements of Arabic speakers on the northeast coast, especially in the area of Vohemar, where considerable archaeological remains and artifacts have been found. Mahilaka on the northwest coast, sometimes termed the first real urban center on the island, preceded this site; emerging in the ninth century, Mahilaka grew to the height of its power in the thirteenth and fourteenth centuries before falling into decline.

By this time small political systems had sprung up in various parts of the island, though few had yet taken on the dimension of kingdoms. These systems often had distinct characters: if some, like those to the west and northwest, reflected the power of pastoralist groups, others to the south appear to have been more closely influenced by the cultural practices of the African mainland. Eventually, the dominant political formation that would emerge would be in the central highlands with the state of Andriana-Merina, but that would only be in the seventeenth century. By around 1500 CE, our most plausible "guesstimates" put the population of the whole island at around 700,000. Summing up these broad trends, Philippe Beaujard has written:

> The arrival of new populations during the thirteenth and fourteenth centuries reflects Madagascar's increasing insertion into Indian Ocean networks. This process would be further enhanced during the fifteenth century, paralleling internal developments based, not only on advances in wet rice cultivation on the eastern and northwestern coasts and in the Highlands, but also on progress made in stockbreeding along the western coast. Rice cultivation fostered demographic growth, which in turn spurred the formation of highly hierarchized kingdoms. Long-distance trade also played an increasing role, with the development of a slave trade from the Highlands toward the trading ports of northwestern Madagascar and other Indian Ocean regions.[12]

In sum, even if the great island's history in this period was not solely the product of external influences—whether from East Africa, the Islamic world, or even the more distant Indian subcontinent—it would be unwise to remove Madagascar from a complex oceanic context.

POLITICAL GEOMETRY OF THE FIFTEENTH CENTURY

In 1433 CE, the series of celebrated maritime expeditions sent by the Chinese Ming dynasty into the Indian Ocean came to an end. This seventh and last expedition, led by the veteran Muslim eunuch-admiral Zheng He after an interval of nearly a decade, had ventured not only as far as the Persian Gulf and the Red Sea but even to the Swahili coast. Over the space of three decades, these repeated expeditions left a lasting mark on maritime Southeast Asia, but they also made interventions (at times violent ones) in the context of Lanka, Kerala, and beyond.[13] Though they created no lasting settlements or colonies on the littoral of the western Indian Ocean, the Ming rulers both gathered valuable and intricate ethnographic information and made themselves and their power known in a wide sphere. While much has been written about these voyages, certain central issues remain unresolved because we cannot locate these activities in relation to a fully articulated political theory. These issues are particularly acute in the context of the western Indian Ocean, where it does not appear that anything like a stable "tribute system" predicated on the sending of envoys and gifts to China was being constructed. This has led to two sets of anachronistic constructions by current-day historians, one of a peaceful sphere of interstate cooperation and the other of a well-designed projection of power in a form of shadow empire.

The first idea is clearly belied by the rhetoric of the Ming court itself, in the preparatory instructions to Zheng He from the emperor Xuande (r. 1425–1435) for the seventh expedition that are found in the *Ming shi-lu* (Ming Annals), and that clearly show a hierarchical conception of the Indian Ocean world.

> The Eunuch Director Zheng He and others were sent with an Imperial proclamation to go and instruct the various *fan* [tribute-paying] countries. The proclamation read: "I have respectfully taken on the mandate of Heaven and reverently inherited the Great Rule from the Taizu Gao Emperor, the Taizong Wen Emperor and the Renzong Zhao Emperor. I rule over the ten thousand states, manifest the supreme benevolence of my ancestors and spread peace to all things. I have already issued a general amnesty to all under Heaven and declared the

commencement of the Xuande reign. All has begun anew. You, the various *fan* countries far across the ocean, will not yet have heard. Now I am especially sending the Eunuch Directors Zheng He and Wang Jinghong carrying this proclamation with which to instruct you. You must all respect and accord with the Way of Heaven, care for your people and keep them in peace. Thus will you all enjoy the prosperity of Great Peace." Variegated silks, as appropriate, were to be conferred upon the rulers or chiefs of all twenty countries through which the eunuchs were to pass, including Hormuz, Lanka, Calicut, Melaka, Cochin, Barawa [Bu-la-wa], Mogadishu, Lamri [Nan-bo-li], Samudera, La-sa, Liu-shan, Aru, Kampar [Gan-ba-li], Aden, Dhofar [Zuo-fa-er], Zhu-bu, Shihr [Jia-yi-le] and so on, as well as the Old Port Pacification Superintendency.[14]

Though several of these sites are currently not identifiable, a clear pattern emerges. It appears that the last Ming expedition, like its predecessors, tended to avoid direct contact with the large polities of the western Indian Ocean and instead preferred dealing with the smaller port cities. In the Islamic world, these included Hurmuz, Aden, and Mogadishu. It appears that two of these Chinese vessels appeared in Aden in June 1432 and were permitted to come as far as Jiddah; this might have been the occasion for some Muslim members of the expedition to perform the hajj, which would have been in August that year. There is no credible evidence, however, that the Ming or their expeditions loomed large on the consciousness of Mamluk sultans such as Barsbay (r. 1422–1438), despite the ruler's considerable interest in the commercial networks of the Red Sea.

The eastern neighbors and rivals of the Mamluks, the Timurid rulers, require a more nuanced analysis in respect of their relations with the Ming. A protracted conflict for succession among various descendants and family members, what has sometimes been termed the First Timurid Civil War, followed the death of Timur in February 1405. The conqueror's youngest son, Mirza Shahrukh, gained the upper hand over other claimants and set about consolidating a Timurid state based in Herat in the 1410s and 1420s. The same period is marked by complex relations with the Mamluks on the one hand and the Ming dynasty on the other. The work of a consolidator is notoriously different from that of a founder, and this was certainly the case of Shahrukh (d. 1447), whose four decades in power have a very different character from the reign of his charismatic and turbulent father. Shahrukh's image, to a considerable extent crafted by members of his own court, is that of a shariʿa-minded, orthodox Sunni ruler who sought to suppress heterodox dissenting groups that at times rose up against him in rebellion, which was the case in 1423, and at others even mounted assassination attempts against him, as happened in 1427. However, it has been argued that this image papers over a far more complex reality of shifting alliances and opportunistic group solidarities. In particular, it has been suggested that the years after Timur's death represent "a period when distinct, and often radical, political ideas found a ready audience in the Timurid Empire." Groups of notables and intellectuals proposed these "different constitutional programs," and Timurid princes who jockeyed for power against one another adhered to them. Scholars have given particular attention to Mirza Shahrukh's nephew, Mirza Iskandar ibn ʿUmar Shaikh (d. 1415), who emerged for a time as the dominant figure in Fars, Persian ʿIraq, and Kerman, with his political center in Isfahan. As Evrim Binbaş has persuasively argued:

> Iskandar failed to carve an independent dispensation for himself out of Timur's empire even though he seems to have identified what politics needed in the long term after the death of Timur. The First Timurid Civil War that raged throughout the Timurid Empire between the sons and grandsons of Timur between 807/1405 and 821/1418–1419 was a battle between political ideas and constitutional programs as well as a brute power struggle. Various contenders to Timur's throne adopted different political concepts formulated around the principles of Chinggisid supremacy, caliphal contractualism, and absolutism. Iskandar was arguably the most innovative of all the Timurids in this period, at least the best recorded one. Although his reign was short, his ultimate solution to the political crisis of his time outlived him.

The reference here is not to the rump ʿAbbasid Caliph at that time resident in Cairo under Mamluk protection, but to a reworked notion of caliphal power that the Timurids would periodically manipulate through the fifteenth century, and which was particularly present in the early part of Shahrukh's reign. At the same time, Iskandar apparently saw that the constant recourse to appanaging would produce an unstable and unsustainable political system, as indeed happened in the second half of the fifteenth century. To return to Binbaş's formulation:

Since his mother and maternal grandfather were Chinggisids, and his tutor Buyan Quli Qanghli was a Moghul officer, Iskandar must have been familiar with Chinggisid political principles, but he chose to formulate his constitutional program in a completely different political discourse. He tried to overcome his difficulties by presenting himself as an absolutist ruler, a ruler who would be the source of law and sovereignty simply because he mastered all the sciences, including the religious and occult sciences. He was certainly supported by a range of intellectual figures in Persian Iraq and Fars, but his idea of absolutism crumbled in front of Shahrukh's idea of redistributive politics, which certainly appealed more to the Turco-Mongol amirs, who were ever eager to share power at the expense of the ruler at the center.[15]

While Shahrukh managed to hold together a fragile system, sharing power with other members of his extended lineage as well as entrenched clans of urban notables, it was nevertheless crucial for him to project his status in the wider world as an upholder of orthodox Sunnism.

We can see this in the tortuous nature of his relations with the Mamluks, sometimes mediated through the sharifs of Mecca. Shahrukh's long period in power corresponded to the reign of several Mamluk sultans who largely emerged from the household world of Barquq (d. 1399), the founder of the so-called Burji dispensation dominated by Circassian Turks. They included the rulers Barsbay and Jaqmaq, who held power for more than three decades in the first half of the fifteenth century. Shahrukh's dealings with these rulers took quite different forms, with notable ups and downs. In the early years of his reign, the Timurid ruler showed a desire to assert symbolic power over the Ka'aba and its elaborate ceremonial routines, and he negotiated with the sharifs to this end. However, by the close of the 1410s and the early 1420s it became clear that the Mamluk sultans were tightening their grip over the Hijaz, and Shahrukh seems to have cautiously beaten a retreat, moderating both his symbolic claims and his diplomatic rhetoric. As Malika Dekkiche has remarked in her analysis of Timurid-Mamluk diplomatic exchanges, there was, however, a period at the very end of Barsbay's reign when relations notably deteriorated; the Mamluks refused to accommodate some of Shahrukh's ceremonial requests, he responded with insulting letters claiming they were mere subordinate rulers who needed to be taught a lesson, and they responded in turn by assaulting the Timurid envoys.[16] The accession of Jaqmaq to the throne apparently calmed matters down, and a higher degree of cordiality obtained in the last decade of Shahrukh's reign. Still, this unresolved struggle for symbolic supremacy with the Mamluks would have consequences in the context of the Indian Ocean.

Shahrukh also maintained diplomatic dealings with the Ming dynasty, notably at the time of the Yongle emperor. This was in part an attempt at restoring some form of normalcy after the low point when Timur had executed a Ming envoy and threatened an invasion because of the Hongwu emperor's clumsy attempt to reduce him to the status of a supplicant. Several authors have analyzed these dealings, most notably Joseph Fletcher, who points out that relations between the Ming and Shahrukh were initially rocky because the Chinese side persisted for a time in its patronizing and haughty rhetorical style, exemplified by a letter from 1412 in which the emperor not only advised Shahrukh on how to deal properly with his family but also referred to the service (khidmat) that the Timurid envoys were to perform, even as he declared himself no less than the "lord of the realms of the face of the earth" who "makes no distinction between far and near and regards all equally and impartially."[17] The Timurid court in return sent back a highly inflammatory response in two versions, Persian and Arabic, advising the Ming emperor to convert forthwith to Islam as many other sensible rulers had done, since his sovereignty and power would be assured only then. Rather than further raise the temperature of the exchange, the Ming court seems to have chosen instead to offer an olive branch, with an embassy in 1416 carrying a letter urging that "from both sides [they] should lift the veil of difference and disunity and order the opening of the door of agreement and unity, so that subjects and merchants may come and go at will and the roads may be secure." Fletcher notes that two years later, in 1418, the Ming court went even further in the correspondence. The Yongle emperor, he observes, "abandons all pretense that he is Shahrukh's suzerain and addresses him as a political equal. In so doing, the Ming ruler violates the neo-Confucian myth that as emperor of China he is suzerain of the world." This was achieved through a form of duplicity or "double standard" in which the Ming regime was willing to compromise its external posture as long as appearances could be kept up in China, including matters involving the public reception of ambassadors.

These relations with the Timurids seem to have fallen off from the mid-1420s with the Yongle emperor's death; as I have mentioned, the maritime expeditions, too, were abandoned in the early 1430s. It is of some interest to note that Zheng He's voyages find no specific mention in these overland diplomatic exchanges, implying that neither side wished to raise the issue concretely. It seems likely that some word of the arrival of the fleets in Hurmuz from 1414 onward would have reached the court at Herat in one fashion or another, especially as Shahrukh's grip over the southern Iranian provinces grew. At the same time, scholars have remarked, the relatively abundant narrative sources in Persian from Timurid court circles make little mention at all of the Chinese fleet. An exception may be found in the little-known chronicle of Ja'far bin Muhammad Husaini, where we find the following brief passage referring to the ruler of Hurmuz in the 1420s: "During this time numerous junks with Chinese products and large quantities of fabrics arrived from China. [The Shah] sold them pearls of all kinds, for which he traded much gold, silver, cloth, and porcelain ware, with which he filled his treasury."[18] This suggests that the Ming maritime intervention principally affected the coast, and the most substantial of the mainland polities, that of the Timurids, did not feel overly concerned by its implications, at least not immediately.

The extensive shadow of Shahrukh's power also reached well into the Indian subcontinent, and especially the Indo-Gangetic plain. Timur's conquest of Delhi and defeat of the Tughluqs in late 1398 had created considerable instability in that region, and it precipitated the formation of a series of compact regional states, none of which could claim realistically to dominate the others. The process had already begun during the reign of Firoz Shah Tughluq (r. 1351–1388) and had accelerated further in the course of two civil wars that pitted rival Tughluq factions against each other in the decade after his death. The governor of the prosperous region of Jaunpur in the central Gangetic valley was one of those who showed his hand in the 1390s, and his descendants created the so-called Sharqi dynasty there.[19] The new and intricate interstate system extended well into central India, where the Malwa Sultanate emerged in the late fourteenth century to be consolidated and placed on firmer ground after 1400. In the area around Delhi itself, the post-Timur vacuum was gradually filled by a variety of fragile claimants. In the 1410s power fell into the hands of a lineage claiming to be Sayyids, one of whose members, Khizr Khan, had been hereditary governor of Multan before Timur's invasion and had opportunistically submitted to him in order to gain political leverage. Khizr Khan and his descendants, who governed Delhi until the early 1450s, maintained relations with Shahrukh's court in Herat in the 1410s and 1420s, and the mid-fifteenth-century chronicle of Muhammad Bihamadkhani tells us that they never declared themselves to be sovereigns and instead sought and received robes of honor and ceremonial paraphernalia (such as banners and parasols) from the Timurids. As Peter Jackson remarks: "Shah Rukh's influence in the subcontinent seems to have been extensive. Bihamadkhani, who includes verses in praise of that monarch's sovereignty (*saltanat*) and refers to him as 'the seal of kings' (*khatam al-muluk*), claims that Sultan Hushang Shah of Malwa appealed to him for assistance against an invasion from Gujarat."[20] But this symbolic power of tutelage did not go entirely unchallenged, since some of these post-1400 rulers also sought out contacts with Cairo and the 'Abbasid caliphs living there under Mamluk tutelage in order to request documents of investiture from them. This can hardly have been pleasing to the court of Herat and may account for some of the actions of the Timurids in the 1440s.

'ABDUR RAZZAQ AND HIS MISSION

In general, the expansive drive of the Delhi Sultanate in the thirteenth and fourteenth centuries did not take it much beyond the Deccan, roughly as far as the basin of the Krishna River. There was one anomaly or exception in the form of a small political system created in the far south of the peninsula, in the area of Madurai, usually designated as the Ma'bar Sultanate. Emerging from a set of episodes of Khalji intervention in the succession politics of the Pandya kingdom in the Madurai region, the polity was initially ruled by governors sent from Delhi, but it then became independent in view of its distance from the Deccan. For about half a century this sultanate also managed to maintain a modest presence in Indian Ocean trade thanks to its trading ports and access to pearl fishing; given its obscure profile in history, we are fortunate to have the narrative account of the Moroccan traveler Ibn Battuta, who not only visited it but was married to the daughter of one of its rulers.[21] The career of the sultanate came to an end when Sultan 'Ala-ud-Din Sikandar Shah was defeated in 1378 by the armies of a powerful new kingdom that had recently emerged in southern India, the kingdom of Vijayanagara, centered on a capital city on the banks of the Tungabhadra River.

These states and regions were far from the mental horizon of the Timurids in the early fifteenth century, unlike the states of northern India with which they maintained relations. It was thus by sheer happenstance that they entered into contact with the small but significant trading state of Calicut (or Kozhikode) in central Kerala in the early 1440s. Now, Calicut was far from unknown in the maritime world of West Asia, since it was a regular trading partner with both the Persian Gulf and the Red Sea as well as Yemen and south Arabia. The port had risen to prominence over the middle decades of the fourteenth century, taking advantage of the decline of the well-known medieval port of Kollam farther south. The French historian Éric Vallet, who has produced a comprehensive study of the commercial policy of the Rasulid Sultanate of Yemen, describes the rise of Calicut from the Yemeni perspective:

> In 770/1369, according to al-Khazraji, "a present arrived from the lord of Calicut, made up of a number of plants and exotic birds. . . . There was white pepper, yellow jasmine, roses and other things." The ties became even closer at the end of the 8th/14th century when the principal Muslim merchants of the city wrote directly to the Sultan of Yemen, al-Ashraf Isma'il, using elevated titles such as "pole of the Sultanic sky; . . . light of the community, of truth, and of religion," and also "Lord of the Sultans of the Arabs and non-Arabs." They attempted thereby to establish a privileged relationship with the Rasulid Sultanate, at a time when the political balance in the subcontinent was being profoundly shaken.[22]

This letter, reproduced *in extenso* in the Yemeni chronicle, marks the high point of these relations, and it carries the name of the *qazi* (judge) of Calicut, Baha-ud-Din, as well as five of the principal merchants, most of whom appear to be Muslims from West Asia. We are led to believe that the Muslim mercantile community of Calicut at this point had relations with many of the important Islamic states of the Indian Ocean littoral, but that it had nevertheless chosen to pay obeisance to the Rasulids in preference to others, such as the rulers of Hurmuz.[23] This is undoubtedly a mark of the success of the Yemeni strategy of blocking direct access to, for example, Egypt, sometimes through the use of outright force and at other times through negotiation and chicanery.

It may be useful at this stage to consider somewhat more closely the nature of the Calicut trading state that had clearly emerged as an important player in the course of the fourteenth century. The early stirrings of this state can be found in the twelfth century, with the end of the Chera superstate of the Perumal rulers centered on Mahodayapuram, on the banks of the Periyar. Different *svarupams* (or households with chiefly pretensions) contested for power, and one of the subordinate chiefs of the region of Eralanadu (or Eranadu) appears to have then consolidated his rule in central Kerala as far as Trissur in the south. These rulers, belonging to the loosely defined Nayar caste, were known in the earliest references under the title of Punturakkon, or "Lord of Puntura," an epithet that appears in the undated thirteenth-century bilingual inscription at the

Mucchunti mosque.[24] Initially, it seems, they were based at Netiyiruppu, an interior area, but in the course of the twelfth century they extended their reach westward toward the sea, claiming that the Chera Perumals had granted these rights to them. They then expanded south to the edges of the region of Valluvanadu, and the mouth of the Perar River, seizing control of the crucial river port of Ponnani. By the fourteenth and fifteenth centuries various literary sources in the genre of "messenger poems" (*sandesha-kavyas*) refer to the trading prosperity of the Calicut (Eranadu) kingdom, with one of them stating that "the ocean knows that his daughter, the Goddess of Prosperity, resides in this town." Unlike some of its neighbors and rivals, the kingdom does not seem to have hosted significant settlements of Syrian Christians or Jewish traders but sought a closer link to Muslim merchants, as that mosque inscription hints and as Arabic sources from the fourteenth century onward confirm.

Despite the significance of trade, and especially maritime trade, this political system was firmly rooted in an agrarian base. Chief among the crops in its importance was rice, though by the fifteenth century rice also seems to have been imported, whether from southeastern India or from Dakshina Kannada ports between Kumbla and Basrur. Besides, we also find coconut and areca groves, as well as the production of fruits and vegetables; prestige export crops such as pepper came from the hilly areas located in the interior rather than the coastal zone. Important sources of pepper included the chiefdom of Vadakkumkur, located in the Idukki region, which had emerged from the fragmentation of the larger Vempolinadu kingdom. Some of the agrarian revenues in Calicut were given as tribute to temples and related institutions and denoted as *devasvam* (intended for the gods), and despite the modest extent of their kingdom, the rulers were significant patrons of such establishments. One of the crucial sites that came under their control in their earlier expansionary phase was the Tali temple, previously held by the ruler of Polanadu.[25] Although this was not a Saiva temple of great antiquity, it was given considerable prominence, and it also occupied a place of proximity to power, to the southeast of the royal palace. The ruler was in the habit of paying it regular visits with ritual processions that are frequently referred to in contemporary documents. This was also the location for a prestigious annual assembly of significant scholars and literati in which debates were held and encomia and titles handed out. A second site of far greater antiquity was the Tirunavaya temple on the northern bank of the Perar River. This Vaishnava temple was closer to the secondary capital of Ponnani, and it was here that two prestigious festivals, Mamakam and Taippuyam, were celebrated every twelve years. The neighboring

Valluvanadu rulers contested control over the temple, however. Besides the lands given over to the temples, there were also a sizable number of distinct agrarian estates (*cherikkal*) controlled both by the extended royal family and by magnates. Fiscal intermediaries managed such estates and levied a variety of taxes, both agricultural and nonagricultural. Based on his analysis of the palm-leaf records of the *Kolikkotan Granthavari*, the historian V. V. Haridas has concluded that although "there is a misconception that prior to the colonial and Mysorean [eighteenth-century] period land tax did not exist in medieval Malabar," various family records attest to "the details of revenue collected from land."[26] The intricacies of this political and fiscal system, largely managed through a matrilineal system of succession at various levels, often proved a puzzle for foreign observers, lending itself to various forms of confused observation.

As I have noted, from the middle decades of the fourteenth century, Calicut had strengthened its trading links with Yemen, sending fleets of ships bearing pepper and other goods to Aden every year. This trading regime, which seems to have remained robust until the 1410s, began to show significant cracks thereafter, during the last years of the reign of the Rasulid Sultan al-Nasir Ahmad (r. 1400–1424). Éric Vallet has reconstructed the sequence of events through a careful reading of a variety of narrative sources. The difficulties, which began with a set of dispersed rebellions, reached the royal family itself when a civil war broke out between the sultan and his brother. In the process of crushing the rebels and attempting to reconsolidate power, Sultan al-Nasir Ahmad was obliged to engage in extensive military expenses and turned to the revenues of the port as a convenient milch cow. He also attempted the forced sale of silk that was in his possession at an elevated price, much to the unhappiness of the mercantile class. This appears to have led to disputes between him and the chief of the sultanic commercial establishment (*matjar*) in Aden, Wajih-ud-Din. The chronicler Ba Makhrama notes that this had important consequences. "When injustices were committed at the time of al-Nasir al-Ghassani, the merchants of Aden fled for Jiddah, as well as to India and Malabar. Salah-ud-Din ibn 'Ali [brother of Wajih-ud-Din] departed for Malabar, and the ruler confiscated his properties."[27] The shipowner merchants of Calicut had thus been alerted by the early 1420s that Aden was a hotbed of potential troubles.

It was one of the most important of the Kerala-based maritime merchants, Nakhuda Ibrahim al-Kalikuti, who took the initiative. Yemeni sources noted that he was among those who had been the subject of "tyranny" at the time of Sultan al-Nasir and that even the death of the ruler in 1424 had not resolved matters. Nakhuda Ibrahim thus came to be the leader of what were termed the "deviants" or "interlopers" (*mujawwirun*), that is, those who decided to abandon the normal trading route to Aden.[28] The core narrative of events is available from the chronicle of al-Maqrizi, to be read in conjunction with other more fragmentary sources. It would appear that Ibrahim's unhappiness with Aden reached a head in 1422, the year when he decided to avoid Aden and take his ships to Jiddah. But on this first occasion, he was mistreated by the Meccan amir, Hasan ibn 'Ajlan, who also controlled the port. Discouraged by this, he then decided to try his luck in the following year in other Red Sea sites such as Suakin and Dahlak, only to find that the political regimes there were even less inclined to be tender to newly arrived merchants. It was only in 1424, therefore, that he and others in his wake were better received in Jiddah, essentially because the Mamluk Sultan Barsbay himself decided to intervene. The elites of Cairo, apparently better informed now of this opportunity to draw revenue (and implicitly political power and influence) away from the Rasulids, began to consider putting in place a new regime for trade in the Hijaz, one in which the amirs would be subordinated to them with regard to the administration of long-distance commerce. In October 1423, Barsbay is reported to have sent a harshly worded letter to amir Hasan, instructing him not to tyrannize the Indian merchants any longer. The next year, Nakhuda Ibrahim found a more diplomatic Mamluk amir, Qurqmas, in charge of affairs in Jiddah. Encouraged by this, he is reported to have brought fourteen vessels in his train in 1425 and as many as forty the next year, including some ships from the Persian Gulf and possibly Southeast Asia. Al-Maqrizi described the new regime: "The administration of Jiddah came under the Sultan's purview [*wazifa sultaniyya*]; and the governor received robes of honor from the prince. Each year, when the ships from India [*marakib al-Hind*] arrived in Jiddah, this official made his way to Mecca, gathered the duties on the goods, and went back to Cairo with the amount. The treasury thus gained 70,000 dinars, not taking into account what was not taken back [to Cairo]."[29]

This new regime offered opportunities to a number of new actors, notably Damascus-based merchants who saw it as an occasion to draw Indian goods in increasing quantities to the Levantine ports rather than Cairo and Alexandria. But it was not destined to be stable for a number of reasons. Though they had misplayed their hand, the Rasulids returned to the charge and attempted in the early 1430s to persuade the Indian captains to return to their port. They also tried to send fleets to patrol the mouth of the Red Sea in order to force vessels from the Indian Ocean into their port. This led to the temporary creation of a dual system by which some ships made directly for Jiddah while others put in at Yemen, with their goods being carried farther on into the Red Sea through smaller coastal vessels. This was also the result of the fact that the Mamluks were unable entirely to inspire confidence in their management at Jiddah. At the same time, the appearance in 1436 of an epidemic plague in Aden was also a source of instability for the latter port. Between that year and 1454, the end of the Rasulid dynasty, the port was unable to recover or reestablish the old prosperity of the late thirteenth and fourteenth centuries. The Tahirids, who took control of Yemen in their wake, were unable to project their power or prestige across the waters of the western Indian Ocean in quite the same way.

It was in the declining years of the Rasulids that an envoy appeared from Calicut in Herat, the capital of the Timurid ruler Mirza Shahrukh. Our main source for this matter is the text of the courtier and intellectual 'Abdur Razzaq Samarqandi, *Matla' us-Sa'dain* (The Rising of the Auspicious Twin Stars), a sprawling history of Timur and the Timurids written in around 1470, in which the author also recounts various aspects of diplomatic history (such as dealings with the Ming and the Mamluks) as well as his own experiences.[30] 'Abdur Razzaq informs his readers that at some point in the late 1430s Shahrukh had sent emissaries to the sultan of Bengal, Nasir-ud-Din Mahmud, to settle quarrels between him and the Sharqi rulers of Jaunpur. While returning by sea to the Persian Gulf accompanied by a counter-embassy, these envoys had "been stranded in Calicut" and had made contact with the ruler, the Samuri (from the term Samudri) and the Muslim community resident in his port. As a result, a Persian-speaking Muslim envoy had been sent to Herat from Calicut, with "all sorts of gifts and tribute." The envoy not only requested that Shahrukh grant permission for the Friday prayer to mention his name in the mosques of Calicut, but he also insinuated that the Calicut ruler could be easily persuaded to convert to Islam. This led Shahrukh's court to dispatch 'Abdur Razzaq, a well-educated but low-ranking courtier, to Kerala via the Persian Gulf in an exploratory mission. He recounts the voyage, which began in January 1442 and lasted three years, in several episodes in his text and sheds interesting light on one set of midcentury interactions in the western Indian Ocean.

The tensions surrounding this voyage already came to be defined in Hurmuz, from where 'Abdur Razzaq wished to set sail. Though the city itself and its cosmopolitan environment impressed him favorably, it soon became clear that the ruler Turan Shah was not eager to help the Timurid envoy in his mission, perhaps out of concern for the spread of Timurid political influence over the waters of the ocean. The delayed departure meant that the party was unable to exit the region promptly and instead had to put in successively at Masqat, Quryat, and Qalhat, with the result that in the suffocating heat of the summer months, 'Abdur Razzaq's brother, who was a member of the party, died. The vessel carrying 'Abdur Razzaq then made a rapid crossing to Calicut, although the accompanying ship was not so fortunate and fell into the hands of corsairs operating out of the Sangameshwar River. The stay in Calicut, which lasted four months from November 1442 to April 1443, was not a happy one. A few days after his arrival, 'Abdur Razzaq was received in the Samudri's palace, accompanied by the head of the Muslim community (*kalantar-i musalmanan*), but this was a disappointing experience. The ruler and most of his courtiers appeared inappropriately dressed from a Timurid viewpoint, and the letters and presents from Shahrukh were treated rather dismissively. Furthermore, it turned out that the idea of converting the Samudri to Islam was far from realistic. Nevertheless, 'Abdur Razzaq was willing to admit that the port city itself had its virtues, not dissimilar in some respects from Hurmuz.

> Calicut is a safe port [*amanabad*], equal to Hurmuz in its mercantile population from every land and region, and the availability of rarities of all sorts from Daryabar, especially the Land below the Winds, Abyssinia, and Zanj. From time to time, ships come from God's House [*Baitallah*], and other towns in the Hijaz, and stop for a while in this port. It is a city of infidels, and therefore is in the Abode of War [*dar-ul-harb*]. However, there is a Muslim population resident, with two congregational mosques, and on Fridays they pray with peace of mind. They have a religiously observant *qazi*, and most of them are Shafi'i by sect.[31]

This last phrase is worth comment, for it indicates that the affinity of Calicut's Muslim population was with the Mamluk Sultanate, whose rulers, unlike the Timurids, were also Shafi'i.

Despite his attempts to gather some ethnographic details, for example on the question of polyandry and matrilineal succession, the tone of 'Abdur Razzaq's account thus becomes increasingly dyspeptic. If the purpose was to extend the symbolic reach of Timurid power to the ends of the Indian subcontinent, this was clearly not the way to achieve it. It was therefore with some relief that the Timurid envoy recounts a windfall in the form of an unexpected contact with the court of Vijayanagara, which asks that he be sent there. This diversion accounts for the bulk of his account and is of considerable interest in its own right.

It is clear that Vijayanagara was not within the geographical horizon of the Timurids, and it also does not feature in contemporary Mamluk accounts of India. The chancery manual of al-Sahmawi from the 1430s, for example, lists six significant Indian kingdoms (*mamlaka*): Delhi, which he compares to Cairo in its importance; Cambay or Gujarat; Bengal; the Bahmani Sultanate (or Gulbarga); Mandu or Malwa; and a last kingdom that appears to be Jaunpur (though written as "Sanbub"), ruled over by Sultan Ibrahim.[32] 'Abdur Razzaq thus takes considerable care to describe the principal features of the Vijayanagara kingdom, stressing its impressive size and control over several hundred ports, the flourishing state of its rural domains, and the sophistication of its craftsmanship. Visiting some temples on his way from Mangalore to the capital city, he even pays compliments to these "idol-houses" (*but-khana*), which are of "extreme delicacy," though it is understood that the worship conducted there is wholly unacceptable from a Muslim viewpoint. Arriving in the city of Vijayanagara itself, he refers to it as being "of enormous magnitude and population, with a king of perfect rule and hegemony whose kingdom stretched from the borders of Sarandib [Lanka] to the province of Gulbarga, and from the borders of Bengal to the region of Malibar."[33] From the perspective of the interior Iranian world, the sight of a walled and gated urban center of such dimensions was naturally all the more impressive because it considerably surpassed the space of Herat. From a consideration of the urban center as a whole, 'Abdur Razzaq moves then to the bazaars, the palace, the scribal class (*nawisindagan*), and revenue administration, followed by a series of exotic features, such as the extensive elephant stables. On being permitted an audience with the ruler Deva Raya, 'Abdur Razzaq was struck by his chiseled features and "tunic of Zaituni [Chinese] satiny silk" as well as the fact that he wore "a necklace of lustrous pearls, the worth of which the jeweler of the mind could scarcely appraise." The court had a proper Persian-speaking interpreter through whom he was able to communicate, and it met the criteria of civilized courtly discourse that the envoy had found so lamentably lacking in Calicut.

'Abdur Razzaq would return carrying a brief letter from Deva Raya for Shahrukh and accompanied by some Khorasani notables whom he found resident in Vijayanagara. However, the latter part of his stay in the city was tarnished by his disputes with some middle-level officials there, and more particularly the rumormongering of an influential group of Hurmuzi merchants in Vijayanagara. These merchants, in all probability linked to the strategic horse trade from the Persian Gulf, made it their task to undermine 'Abdur Razzaq's credentials, even going so far as to claim that he was an impostor with forged documents rather than an authentic envoy. We can thus see that the anti-Timurid hostility that had made itself felt already in Hurmuz continued to trail him across the water. Finally, in December 1443, 'Abdur Razzaq and his accompanying party left for the port of Barkur, and from there for Honavar farther north. The return voyage proved rather difficult, and it was only in January 1445 that the group made its way to Herat to recount their many travails and more limited triumphs. Shahrukh is reported to have summoned the vizier of Hurmuz to his court in order to chastise him for the repeated instances of Hurmuzi misbehavior and to have sent another envoy to Vijayanagara. Unfortunately, we have no further traces of this embassy in the person of Maulana Nasrullah Junabidhi.

Despite its many intriguing qualities, 'Abdur Razzaq's account also has several characteristic lacunae. Little is said about the history of the Vijayanagara kingdom, for example, beyond pointing to its frontier rivalry with the Bahmani sultans to the north. The envoy shows some awareness of tensions within the dynasty itself, which would become more acute in the course of the 1450s and thereafter, until the emergence of the powerful warlord figure of Saluva Narasimha, who dominated the last decades of the fifteenth century.[34] Although he visited at least three west coast ports—Mangalore, Barkur, and Honavar—'Abdur Razzaq also does not closely discuss the nature of Vijayanagara rule in that region. The extensive but dispersed inscriptional record suggests that their penetration of the area around Mangalore had begun as early as 1345 but that it was somewhat slower to come farther up the coast. Groups loyal to the long-ruling Alupa dynasty seem to have resisted incorporation into the broader imperial formation until the very end of the fourteenth century. Thereafter, after crushing a significant rebellion, Vijayanagara rule established itself on a sounder footing after 1400. Nevertheless, at least two sets of groups continued to exercise some degree of autonomy. One of these were strongly entrenched chieftains such as the Chauta and Bangadi rulers to the south or the Jain rulers of Bhatkal and Gersoppa, who entered a tributary relationship with the imperial power. But equally significant were various mercantile groups, often organized into "guilds" or corporations, with titles such as the *hanjamana* or "fifth group." As the epigraphist and historian K. V. Ramesh has written:

> These trade and citizens' guilds and the various officials, mentioned above, were together referred to, in the field of administration, as the *kattaleyavaru* or *samasta-kattaleyavaru*. They helped the imperial governor of the *rajya* [province] to which

they belonged in matters of administration. We have seen that according to the Udipi inscription of A.D. 1437, the *samasta-kattaleyavaru* of the *hattukeri* [community] of Barakuru had acted as the arbitrators in a serious dispute between the imperial governor Annappa-Odeya and the residents of Sivalli. During Vijayanagara administration, these organizations rose to great power, wealth, and influence. An inscription from Yermal, Udipi Taluk, actually refers to the thousand warriors [*saviralu*] of the *samasta-halaru*. From this, it may be concluded that these guilds had their own armed followers whose duty was to protect the interests of their respective guilds. A further attestation to their power is furnished by the Kaikini inscription of A.D. 1427 from which we learn that the *nakhara-hanjamana* was powerful enough to challenge the authority of the governor and thereby invite an attack by the imperial forces.[35]

These semiautonomous mercantile organizations were among those that would face important challenges in the course of the sixteenth century as the level of organized maritime violence was ratcheted up in the western Indian Ocean. As it turns out, they had a sufficient degree of flexibility and imagination to come to terms with the changed circumstances.

THE BAHMANIS AND GUJARAT

During his stay in Vijayanagara, 'Abdur Razzaq was made aware of the importance of the conflict between that kingdom and its northern twin and neighbor, the Bahmani Sultanate. Indeed, at one point in the course of 1443, his chief interlocutor in the state apparatus, whom he terms "the vizier who paid kind attention to me," departed to the warfront for an extended period. There is sufficient evidence to show that like the Mamluks, the Timurids had a fairly clear conception of the Bahmanis in the fifteenth century. To take one example, the great Timurid chronicler and intellectual Sharaf-ud-Din 'Ali Yazdi (d. 1454) worked in the chancery of the prince Ibrahim Sultan at Shiraz in the early part of his career, and we find several letters in his *insha'* (belles-lettres) collection exchanged with the Bahmani domains.[36]

Direct relations between the Konkan coast of India and Iran via the ports of the Persian Gulf long predated the foundation of the Bahmani Sultanate (1347–1538) in the Deccan by 'Ala-ud-Din Hasan Bahman Shah (r. 1347–1358; earlier titled Zafar Khan) in the mid-fourteenth century.

Konkan ports such as Thana and Chaul were quite prominent in the trade across the Indian Ocean in the thirteenth century, even if other regions such as Gujarat to the north and Kerala to the south may have regularly surpassed the extent of their trade. But already in the preceding centuries, Muslim traders from the west had gradually settled along this coast during the rule of first the Rashtrakutas (eighth–tenth centuries) and then the Yadavas of Devagiri (ninth–fourteenth centuries), creating hybrid communities such as the Navayats that were heavily invested in maritime activity in the role of mariners as well as merchants. A steady trickle of evidence from Arab traders and geographers from al-Mas'udi (d. 956) in the tenth century onward makes it clear that the Konkan coast was quite familiar to them and that merchants from Yemen, south Arabia, and the Persian Gulf frequented the area. Merchants from the Iranian port of Siraf and its environs in particular seem to have known and settled in Chaul (or "Saymur," as it is usually referred to in these Arabic texts).[37] The exact size of these Muslim trading colonies appears at times rather exaggerated in the sources, but there is little doubt that these traders considerably preceded the armies of the Delhi Sultanate, when they penetrated the area under the rule of the Tughluq dynasty (1320–1413). They also maintained contact with the sultanates that had emerged in the coastal regions of West Asia in the declining centuries of the 'Abbasid Caliphate (750–1258).

While the Bahmani Sultanate in the second half of the fourteenth century made claims to control the ports of the Konkan, the area in fact remained somewhat autonomous from them for long periods. However, since the sultanate also had no effective dealings with the Coromandel coast, because of difficulties presented by the resistance of the compact yet resilient Reddi kingdom of Kondavidu, its generals and rulers returned periodically to the task of subjugating the west coast, especially in order to gain direct access to the strategic horse trade from West Asia. The early decades of Bahmani rule are somewhat difficult to analyze on account of a paucity of contemporary sources, and historians have usually been obliged to turn to far later narrative histories, from the end of the sixteenth or early seventeenth centuries. These sources—like the chronicles of Muhammad Qasim Hindushah Astarabadi (known as Firishta, d. ca. 1623) or Sayyid 'Ali bin 'Azizullah Tabataba'i (who flourished in the late sixteenth century)—mention that the dynasty's founder assertively claimed descent from the pre-Islamic Sasanian rulers of Iran (224–651 CE) and that his use of the ancient Iranian epithet "Bahman" was a direct reference to this claim. Probably to further buttress this improbable claim, the architectural historian Mehrdad Shokoohy has noted that a good many early Bahmani structures in the capital of Gulbarga carry as a motif a Sasanian emblem in the form of "two open wings surmounted by a crescent and sometimes a disk."[38] Despite this apparent and advertised cultural orientation, there is little concrete evidence that in the first half-century of Bahmani rule substantial migration took place to the Deccan from Iran because of the regnant political strife in the latter area. Recall that the last Ilkhanid ruler, Sultan Abu Saʻid (r. 1316–1335), had died with his offspring in a plague epidemic in 1335, leaving the plateau divided among rival claimants such as the Jalayirids (1336–1432) to the west and the Injuids (1325–1353) and Muzaffarids (1314–1393) to the east. Several decades later, Timur (r. 1370–1405) then invaded the region, setting up the rule of the Timurids over Iran, notably that of his son Shahrukh.[39] It is in fact during the latter part of the Timurid epoch that we see the growth and somewhat stable maintenance of close links between Iran and the Deccan, and this is particularly the case from the 1420s onward, even though the chronicler Firishta later stated that the Sultan Firuz Shah Bahmani (r. 1397–1422) had already inaugurated the custom of annually sending royal ships to the Persian Gulf.

The conventional explanation for this shift, on the other hand, tends to associate it with the contested accession of Ahmad I (r. 1422–1436), who on account of facing entrenched opposition among the elites at Gulbarga moved his capital farther east to the freshly fortified city of Bidar (later named Mahmudabad).[40] The rule of this sultan, and especially that of his successor Ahmad II (r. 1436–1458), saw a considerable influx of Iranians, both men of the pen and robe and those of the sword. These included prestigious descendants of the Sufi saint Shah Niʻmatullah Wali Kirmani (d. 1431), but also a number of other magnates from Kirman and its environs in southeastern Iran, extending east as far as Sistan.[41] A figure who assumed great significance in the Deccan in these years came from slightly farther west: this was the magnate and "portfolio capitalist" Khalaf Hasan Basri, who came to enjoy both the title of vizier and that of *malik-ut-tujjar* (prince of merchants) in the 1420s, and whose career we can follow for nearly a quarter-century. According to Firishta, at the time Ahmad Shah was struggling in 1422 to take over the throne, Khalaf Hasan was already a well-known merchant (*tajir-i mausum wa maʻruf*) as well as a friend of long standing (*ashna-yi qadim*) of the future ruler.[42] His trading investments were clearly considerable, but Khalaf Hasan also soon became known as an active military entrepreneur and general who led several expeditions from the late 1420s onward in order to subjugate areas of the Konkan coast such as Mahim and Salsette Island, both parts of Mumbai today. However, the area was lost to the Gujarat sultans, and this zone came broadly to define the extent of the northward reach of the Bahmanis along the coast. Khalaf Hasan, however, continued to be politically active in the Konkan uplands during the following reign. He was killed in an elaborate ambush in 1446 while leading a campaign against the powerful Sirke family and their allied rajas of Khelna Fort northwest of Kolhapur. Interestingly, Firishta claims that when Khalaf Hasan was killed, he "fell with five hundred noble Sayyids of Medina, Karbala and Najaf" who were apparently the remaining part of an elite corps he had formed some time earlier, "of three thousand, composed of the natives of Iraq, Khorasan, Mawarannahr, Rum and Arabia."[43] Between the 1420s and mid-1440s, Khalaf Hasan thus played the role of a pole of attraction to a number of elite migrants, but he seems to have counted above all on the support of men from the Iranian world in his military endeavors.

In the second half of the fifteenth century, another migrant, this one from southwestern part of the Caspian Sea littoral, inherited the title of *malik-ut-tujjar* that Khalaf Hasan had held. Khwaja Mahmud Gawan Gilani's (d. 1481) glittering career in the Bahmani Sultanate stretches over some three decades from the early 1450s to his death in 1481. By the time of his arrival in the region, already in his forties, the two main ports that were associated with westward trade across the ocean in a stable fashion were Chaul and Dabhol. It was at Dabhol-Mustafabad that Gawan himself disembarked around 1453 and made his way to Bidar, where he quickly made an impression both as an astute trader in warhorses and other precious products and as someone with some political experience in the fragmented courts of northern Iran. Gawan also possessed a superior education, of which clear evidence can be found in the works of *insha'* that he produced in his lifetime, such as the *Riyaz al-Insha'* and the *Manazir al-Insha'*, and letters written on his behalf by his secretary, 'Abdul Karim Nimdihi.[44] By the 1460s, roughly a decade after his arrival in the Deccan, he was thus able to take control of the post of vizier and mount a series of successful expeditions against the rulers of Vijayanagara to the south. The Russian merchant Afanasii Nikitin (d. 1475), who visited the Bahmani Sultanate when Gawan was at the height of his power, has left us a vivid portrait of his spectrum of activities.[45] Besides those that Nikitin mentions, it may also be noted that Gawan was a patron of the arts and builder, as the remains of his impressive madrasa at Bidar testify. Thus, even if our initial impression from the first half of the fifteenth century suggests a dominance of migrants from the southern part of the Iranian world, it would appear that over the course of the century the Caspian Sea littoral regions (Gilan to the west, Mazandaran to the east) also progressively find a prominent place. A full prosopographic analysis of migrants mentioned in the Deccan chronicles, based on place-name suffixes (*nisbas*), has not yet been undertaken, to my knowledge. If this were carried out, it would certainly yield such names over the full extent of the fifteenth century as Gilani, Astarabadi, Qummi, and Simnani as much as Ardistani, Kirmani, or Sistani.

Mahmud Gawan maintained an extensive correspondence with a large number of important personalities of his time, ranging from political actors and rulers to intellectuals and poets and Sufis and men of religion (as table 1.2 shows). It was clearly his ambition to make the Bahmani Sultanate an important magnet for such figures, and in this project he was obviously not entirely successful, as most of his invitations to intellectuals, poets, and Sufis were turned down.[46]

On the other hand, it must be admitted that the Bahmani Sultanate did manage to build a powerful military machine, one that kept the sizable Vijayanagara armies at bay through much of the fifteenth century. In the decades after 1450, this flow of men, passing principally through the Persian Gulf island and entrepôt of Hurmuz, can be divided into various subcategories. Jean Aubin presents the following synthesis of the matter, which is worth quoting at length:

> India did not just drain precious metals [from Iran]. It also drained men. Hurmuz was for the princes of the Deccan a place to recruit mercenaries who were emancipated slaves [*ghulam*], those whom the Portuguese sources term "white people," in contrast to indigenous combatants, or African *ghulams* with a darker skin, who were less valued. "Whoever has more white people [*gente branca*] is the most powerful," observes Tomé Pires who, in the 1510s, estimated that there were ten to twelve thousand Persian warriors in the Deccan. Of these warriors originating from Persia, a good number were Turks. As a result of tribal disorders that were linked to their successive fortunes in the courts of the fifteenth and early sixteenth centuries, Qaraquyunlus, Aqquyunlus, Safavid *qizilbash* [red caps] and Turkmen from Iran, evicted from their usual territories, cut off from their clans, or threatened by vendettas, moved to India, in groups or as individuals, either via the Qandahar route or by sea. Amongst these uprooted men who would seek their fortune in India, a good number were also native Iranians, members of initiatory brotherhoods of wrestlers, who preferred adventure and the *métier* of war to the sad lot of artisans or peasants.[47]

TABLE 1.2. Letters from Mahmud Gawan

Addressee	Category	Source
Notables of Gilan, etc.	political	Riyaz and Kanz
Sultan 'Ala-ud-Din, ruler of Gilan	ruler	Riyaz
Sultan Abu Sa'id Gurgan	ruler	Riyaz
Ottoman Sultan Fatih Mehmed	ruler	Riyaz
Khalil Pasha (Ottoman)	political	Kanz
Ottoman grand *wazir* Mahmud Pasha	political	Riyaz
Qadi-'askar of Rum	political	Kanz
Jahan Shah, ruler of Lar	ruler	Kanz
Uzun Hasan Aqquyunlu	ruler	
Sultan Khushqadam (Mamluk)	ruler	Kanz
Sultan Qait Bay (Mamluk)	ruler	
Yashbak min Mahdi (Mamluk official)	political	Kanz
Sultan Mahmud Begada of Gujarat	ruler	Riyaz
Maulana Shams-ud-Din Lari	*'alim* (religious figure)	Riyaz
'Abdur Rahman Jami	*'alim* and poet	Riyaz
Khwaja 'Ubaidullah Ahrar	*'alim* and Sufi	Riyaz
Shams-ud-Din Lahiji	*'alim*	Kanz
Shaikh Sadr-ud-Din Rawasi	*'alim*	Riyaz
Abu Bakr Tehrani	*'alim*	Riyaz
Shaikh Da'ud Mandu'i, Malwa ambassador	political	Riyaz
Burhan-ud-Din Ibrahim	nephew	Riyaz
'Imad-ul-Mulk	nephew	Riyaz

Some of these had specialized skills, notably as archers (*zihgirpushan*), for which the southern region of Laristan was particularly known. In one of his letters to the prince of Lar, Mahmud Gawan writes of his pressing need in the matter, and it would seem that agents of his such as Amir Faramurz, based in Hurmuz, carried out this recruitment. To cite

Aubin again, "Brigandage or emigration, these were the alternatives that were all too often offered to men from the poor villages of the Garmsirat, whose oases could not feed them."

Powerful though the Bahmani state was in appearance, it was also quite fragile, and it lacked a stable fiscal base or deep cadastral penetration into the countryside and its resources. Aubin has noted, once more, that its resources seemed to be largely based on drawing on booty from ceaseless frontier warfare; in his view, "the military charges, the sumptuary expenses, the prestige-oriented policies that Mahmud Gawan pursued, required considerable sums of money, and the administration that he put in place worked with a heavy hand. His agents had 'tied the turban of excess on the forehead of impudence,' as [the chronicler] Tuni writes in the usual style of Persian *munshis*."[48] The most successful campaigns appear to be those of the late 1460s and early 1470s and involved the capture of several significant fortresses and ports to the southwest, such as Sangameshwar, Kolhapur, Belgaum, Hubli, and Goa. In the aftermath of these, there were also some attempts at administrative reorganization, in terms of drawing more territories into direct royal administration (or *khassa*), and the redefinition of the provinces (*atraf*) and prebend assignments.[49] The inadequacy of these changes was shown in the course of late 1470s and early 1480s, when rebellions broke out in the eastern reaches of the kingdom in areas such as Kondavidu and Kondapalli, precipitating a major political crisis.

Not long after Mahmud Gawan's execution at Nellore on trumped-up charges in 1481, it was therefore no surprise that the Bahmani Sultanate began to fragment, with regional powerbrokers assuming increasing power at the expense of the court in Bidar. Two of these post-Bahmani states were of relatively limited significance, those of Berar and Bidar itself. The remaining three represent interesting studies in contrast. Ahmadnagar (1496–1636), which hived off the northwestern section of the Bahmani Sultanate (including the port of Chaul), was founded by Ahmad Nizam Shah (r. 1496–1510), the son of Nizam-ul-Mulk Bahri, reputedly a Brahmin convert (though this might well be a genealogical topos rather than a fact) who had already been prominent in politics in the 1470s and 1480s. Bijapur (1490–1686), on the other hand, was founded by Yusuf 'Adil Khan (r. 1490–1510), a young man of Turkish origin who had apparently been brought from Hurmuz to the Bahmani domains by a merchant called Khwaja Zain al-'Abidin Simnani. Yusuf was deeply interested in the horse trade, but it is also reported by more than one source that in his youth he was an accomplished wrestler.[50] Again, rising through the Bahmani ranks in the 1480s, he seized the occasion presented by central weakness to set up a state in the southwestern part of the domains, with the main ports at his disposal being Dabhol and Goa, the latter of which he and his son lost to the Portuguese in 1510.

In contrast to these relatively lowly origins is the case of the founder of Golconda, Sultan Quli (r. 1496–1543), a prince from the Qaraquyunlu (1380–1468) lineage who was born in Iran in around 1470. After accompanying his uncle on a first visit to India as a child, he appears to have returned there when it became clear that his political prospects in Iran were limited by the rival Aqquyunlu (1378–1508) clan.[51] Later sources claim that he remained faithful to the Bahmani sultan Mahmud (r. 1482–1518) until about 1507, thereafter assuming full control (*dara'i wa farman-rawa'i*) of Telengana, or the eastern section of the domains, with the title of Sultan Quli Qutb ul-Mulk. Even early Portuguese observers were quite aware of the differing statuses of the three Deccan rulers. Thus, Tomé Pires claims that the rulers of both Ahmadnagar and Bijapur were "slaves" by origin, but that Sultan Quli "was not a slave. He is a man of great worth and highly esteemed in the land [*muito estimado na terra*]."[52] At the same time, neither the sultan nor his successor had direct access to the oceanic trade, and it was only in the latter half of the sixteenth century that the Golconda rulers managed to seize hold of several prominent Bay of Bengal ports.

If the frontier conflict with Vijayanagara was a significant factor through the career of the Bahmani state (albeit with notable ups and downs), a different form of struggle was manifest in relation to its northwestern neighbor, the Gujarat Sultanate. Unlike the Bahmanis, who had already sought to keep the Tughluqs at arm's length in the mid-fourteenth century, the governors of Gujarat only reluctantly declared their independence from Delhi after 1400 and the crisis caused by Timur's invasion. In the following decades, however, they were notably successful in drawing together an ecologically diverse set of areas into a regional kingdom marked by a long and complex coastline, as well as a firm agrarian and artisanal base. Arguably the most prosperous part of this kingdom was made up of the valleys of four rivers, the Sabarmati, Mahi, Narmada, and Tapti, in the southeastern part of the Gujarat sultan's domains. It was here that one found a greater density of population and many of the most significant urban centers and port cities, whether Rander, Bharuch, Baroda, or Khambayat. Moving north of this area brought one to the harsher terrain of the Rajput kingdoms such as the Sisodiya domains of Mewar. A quite distinct zone was located to the west, the sizable Kathiawar Peninsula extending across a gulf into Kacch, known for its extensive set of ports and connections to West Asia. This was also an area where a number of autonomous chieftaincies could be found, dominated by groups such as the Jadeja Rajputs with pastoral origins.

For several decades from the 1970s on, a rather stereotyped vision developed by the historian Michael Pearson dominated the portrayal of the political economy of Gujarat in the fifteenth and sixteenth centuries.[53] Painting in broad brushstrokes and drawing largely on the conceptual apparatus of later colonial ethnography, Pearson argued that Gujarati society in this period was made up of a series of watertight social cellules inhabited by functionally distinct groups such as "rulers" and "merchants," with few means of interaction or communication between them. But most recent scholarship has firmly rejected this viewpoint. Thus, Samira Sheikh in her examination of later medieval Gujarat argues, "There is also evidence to indicate that political authority in central Gujarat was bound up with the trading activities of the region. It is now possible to challenge the traditional thesis that trade had little to do with the politics of the hinterland, and that the rulers, in particular the Sultans of Gujarat, did not derive significant benefit from it. This view emerges from the idea that pre-colonial hinterland empires were primarily based on the exploitation of land resources in relation to which trade was largely autonomous."[54]

More generally, it can be seen that the thesis of social rigidity derives from an underlying idea of spatial immobility. On the other hand, it is evident that once one moved away from the major river valleys and their attendant settlements, the Gujarat Sultanate hosted a considerable mobile population, most notably of pastoralists. To quote Sheikh's study: "Historically, the most important groups in Gujarat were merchants and pastoralists. Rulers were usually former pastoralists, transforming themselves from cattle rustlers, bandits, or pirates into patrons and enforcers of security. 'Merchant' and 'pastoralist' were overarching and sometimes interchangeable identities: merchants could be itinerant, and pastoralists could engage in trade. It was the interaction between the two that fuelled the history of the region."[55] This had already been the case when the Delhi Sultanate controlled the area, and it persisted as a dynamic into the time of the Gujarat Sultanate.

The latter sultanate was founded by a former Tughluq governor, perhaps from a family of Punjabi Khatri converts, who took the title Muzaffar Shah in the early fifteenth century but reigned for only a short time. The political system was effectively consolidated by his grandson Ahmad Shah, who ruled for just over three decades from 1411 to 1442. An important feature of this reign was the decision to move the capital from the older, prestigious center of Anhilwada-Patan to the new site of Ahmedabad, in the vicinity of an older political locus at Ashaval, on the banks of the Sabarmati River. The major congregational mosque was completed there in 1424, and from his new capital the sultan made attempts to act on various fronts. Vigorous campaigns were carried out against the newly emergent Malwa Sultanate to the east, as well as more episodically against the Bahmanis, who contested control of the upper Konkan coast. But the main concern of this reign appears to have been the tussle with a variety of Rajput clans, ranging from the important Rathod chiefs of Idar (north of Ahmedabad) to a congeries of smaller lineages. Eventually, Ahmad Shah seems to have consented to some degree of power- and revenue-sharing with these Rajputs, who thus came willy-nilly to participate in his sultanate, sometimes even intermarrying with Muslim elites. Equally striking is the regular attention paid to the western regions and the repeated campaigns by the sultan and his main generals in Kathiawar, testified to by a number of Arabic and Persian inscriptions.[56]

Recent scholarship on fifteenth-century Gujarat has mainly focused on two related questions: the relationship between the sultans and a set of powerful migrant Sufis who settled in the region such as Shaikh Ahmad Khattu and Qutb-i 'Alam; and the literary patronage of the sultans and their rivals.[57] These help us gain a far better sense of the cultural politics of the sultanate, for on the one hand the sultans wished to assert their preeminence as patrons of Islam in post-Timur South Asia; on the other hand, they were also actors in a world where Sanskrit and the western Indian vernacular languages played a significant role. It is therefore regrettable that we lack a close study of Gujarat elite politics in the fifteenth century through a reading of not only the retrospective accounts produced in Mughal times but also a handful of contemporary texts and chronicles.[58] To the extent that we can produce a schematic view, it would run as follows. The Gujarat Sultanate, like the greater part of the political systems that derived from Delhi, made use of a mix of free nobles (*amirs*) and slaves. Both free nobles and slaves were of a variety of ethnic origins. The free nobles included both those with long family roots in the region and migrants from elsewhere, that is, other parts of the subcontinent as well as West Asia. There were apparently tensions between these two groups of slaves and free amirs, as we see on key occasions such as successions to the throne. An interesting case is that of Malik Sha'ban, titled 'Imad-ul-Mulk, who had the intermediate status of *khanazad* ("born to the house") in the sense that his father Malik Tuhfa Taj-ul-Mulk had begun his career as a slave and already served the sultans from the early years of the dynasty. Malik Sha'ban is described

FIGURE 1.1. Illustration from a Gujarat *Sikandar Nama*, ca. 1500 (Lalbhai Dalpatbhai Museum, Ahmedabad, N. C. Mehta Collection, NCM 355).

as a key player in the troubled years after the death of Ahmad Shah, and he seems in his role as vizier to have mediated the rise to the throne of the most significant of the fifteenth-century rulers, Mahmud Shah (r. 1458–1511), generally remembered by his nickname of "Begada." In the early 1460s, the Malik then prudently withdrew from the political sphere, having constructed a large tomb complex as well as other significant buildings and gardens.[59]

Sultan Mahmud's half-century-long reign still awaits its modern historian. But certain themes from the reign are clear enough. As cultural historian Aparna Kapadia notes:

> By the end of the fifteenth-century, Sultan Mahmud Begada's reputation appears to have been well-established in and around his domains. A variety of sources document stories of his greatness as the most powerful of the rulers of the regional sultanate of Gujarat. His military achievements and administrative measures to bring the local chieftains under control are documented extensively in the Persian writings from the region. These accounts speak of Mahmud Shah's continuous military campaigns to subjugate the ruling chieftains as well as the ever-rebellious nobility, which, in Gujarat, included men of diverse ethnic origins.[60]

Mahmud Shah is also the first of the Muzaffarid sovereigns to have consciously promoted the tradition of history writing in his domains by encouraging the settlement of literati from the nearby Iranian world such as 'Abdul Husain Tuni, 'Abdul Karim Nimdihi, and Shams-ud-Din Zirak Shirazi.[61] There are also a good number of indications that suggest that he pursued a form of charismatic, personalized rule, claiming for example to communicate directly with the Prophet in his dreams. Equally, he sought out trusted agents to implement his rule on various occasions, such as his decision in the 1470s to divide the sultanate into a set of five provincial units. Among his significant agents was Malik Sarang Qiwam-ul-Mulk, reputedly a Rajput convert to Islam. Yet the most striking career, which emerged in the second half of this extended reign, was that of Malik Ayaz (d. 1522).

In 1473, Sultan Mahmud successfully carried out a campaign at the western extremity of his domains against the Chudasama rulers of Kathiawar and seized the important center of Junagadh as well as the port of Jagat (Dwarka). This was also the occasion to attack groups of corsairs operating in islands in the Gulf of Kacch.[62] This action permitted the consolidation of access to the western ports of the sultanate at an opportune moment, for the older medieval port of Khambayat had begun to experience difficulties on account of the progressive silting of the Mahi River. In the 1480s, these western regions were placed under the control of a manumitted slave who had once been a member of the personal guard (*ghulaman-i khass*) of the ruler. The origins of the former slave, Malik Ayaz, are ambiguous. Perhaps our best source, the Portuguese chronicler João de Barros, claims that he was of Slavic origins and purchased—probably in the slave markets of the Black Sea—to be brought to Ottoman Istanbul and trained there.[63] Besides his acknowledged technical skills as an archer, Ayaz obviously acquired a good grounding in Perso-Islamic culture. After time spent in Basra and the Persian Gulf, he was given to Sultan Mahmud by a merchant and soon was able to rise up the ranks. Persian chroniclers depict him as playing an important tactical role in the celebrated attack on the hill fort of Champaner in 1483.[64] By the early sixteenth century he possessed significant prebends both in the eastern and western parts of the sultanate and had built up the port of Diu (until then of secondary importance) as a significant player in regard to commerce to the Persian Gulf, Red Sea, and East Africa. At the same time, he himself acquired a significant fleet of small vessels and galleys, which may have even numbered in the dozens.

But behind the rise of Diu lay a process that still remains obscure, which is the emergence into general prominence of Gujarati merchants across the western Indian Ocean and into areas such as Melaka and Sumatra. The clearest description of their profile is provided in the early sixteenth century by the Portuguese Tomé Pires, who encountered them largely in Southeast Asia. He lists the places to which they traded from Gujarat: from Aden to Hurmuz, the Deccan kingdoms, Goa, Bhatkal, all of Malabar (and especially Calicut), Lanka, the Maldives, Bengal, Pegu, Siam, Pidir, Pasai, and Melaka, with the two main trading links being to Aden and Melaka. Elsewhere he also mentions the extensive Gujarati trade to various ports in East Africa, carried out in collaboration with Yemeni merchants. In Melaka alone, he claims, there were a thousand Gujarati merchants in the early sixteenth century and another five thousand mariners and others who came and went from Gujarat. Pires goes on: "The Gujaratis were the best seamen and those who navigated more than the other nations in these parts, and they did so in ships that were better in terms of size and in their mariners. The Gentiles of Cambay [Gujarat] have great pilots and are much given to navigating."[65] Undergirding this thalassocracy was a powerful mercantile and financial structure in Gujarat itself:

> Since this kingdom [Gujarat] is only ennobled because of its trade, it seems necessary for me to speak of it. Now that we have begun to speak of the trade of Cambay, these are [like] Italians in how they know and deal with merchandise. All the goods of Cambay are in the hands of the Gentiles who are called Gujaratis [Guzarates] as a general name, and thereafter they are divided into lineages [such as] Banias [Baneanes], Brahmins, Bhatts [Patamares]. There is no doubt at all that they control the trade overall; they are men well-versed in merchandise and have a feel and harmony for it as is right. So much so that the Gujarati says that any insults proffered while trading can be pardoned. There are Gujarati establishments everywhere, and some work for others, and still others for these, and they are diligent men who are able in trade, who count with their fingers as we do in writing. They are men who will never give you what is theirs, nor do they want what belongs to anyone else, because of which until now they are esteemed in Cambay [despite] practicing their Gentility because they ennoble that kingdom through their trade.[66]

The Italian comparison is given a more specific dimension in another passage: "they have factors [*feitores*] everywhere who live and are settled, just as the Genoese do in our parts [Europe], both in Bengal and in Pegu, Siam, Pidir, Pasai, [and] Kedah, carrying back to their country the goods that are valued there; so that there is no trading place where Gujarati merchants have not been espied." It may be added, based on other sources, that the family of Sultan Mahmud himself participated in the trade, especially to West Asia, and both he and his son owned sizable vessels. The sultan's own principal ship, titled the *Miri* (or *Amiri*), was estimated by the Portuguese who first came across it in Hurmuz at 600 to 800 *toneis* burthen (a tonel measuring 877 liters in volume).[67] A few years after Pires wrote his text, a Corsican agent of the Portuguese described Gujarati commercial power: "The King of Cambay is the most powerful king [in these parts in terms of goods] and treasure, and also of ships, because between large and small ones he would possess five hundred *naos*, and extensive lands with many supplies, and many goods and all the merchants."[68]

A TWIST IN THE TALE

The first small fleet of Portuguese vessels, captained by Vasco da Gama, made its way into the Indian Ocean via the Cape of Good Hope in the early part of 1498 and arrived after an extended sojourn in East Africa in the vicinity of the Kerala port of Calicut in May that year. The Portuguese were at this time not particularly well informed about the political or economic realities of the western Indian Ocean, and hence they made a number of elementary diplomatic blunders. However, between 1498 and 1505, the year in which the first viceroy was sent out to head the fledgling Estado da Índia (State of the Indies), a far clearer picture had emerged in Portugal of the realities of at least the western part of the Indian Ocean, as seen from the instructions (or *regimento*) given to the new viceroy, Dom Francisco de Almeida. By 1500 or so they had given up their initial hope that there would be a substantial number of Christians in the area and a correspondingly modest number of Muslims. After East Africa and the coastal kingdoms of Kerala, which were their first points of contact, the Portuguese established fragile dealings with south Arabia, the Persian Gulf, the Konkan coast, and Gujarat. In view of their violent actions during the passage of the second fleet, headed by Pedro Álvares Cabral, we are left to imagine that word of these newcomers spread very quickly through the networks I have described in the preceding pages. The second expedition of Vasco da Gama in 1502–1503 would have confirmed this; not only did Gama infamously capture and sink a pilgrim ship returning from the Red Sea to Calicut in September–October 1502, but his relatives the Sodré brothers, who commanded a smaller fleet meant to ensure a stable naval presence, also flouted that directive and instead attacked the Hadramaut ports and their vessels before being lost in a storm.

The initial Portuguese strategy was simple but gradually acquired more complex layers. The main purpose was to acquire an important share in the European pepper and spice market while simultaneously inflicting substantial damage on the Indian Ocean trade of the Mamluk Sultanate. Trading with first Calicut and then Kochi (Cochin) farther south was intended for the first purpose, while attacks on Asian merchants, whether off the coast of Kerala or on open waters, were meant to act as a damper on trade to the Red Sea. No plans of territorial conquest existed in these early years, and the first Portuguese fortress, built in Kochi by the Albuquerque cousins in 1503, was constructed on a parcel of land acquired by consent from the ruler there. The arrival of Almeida in 1505 already suggested a shift, because new fortresses were now projected, one in Kilwa on the Swahili coast, another in Kannur (Cannanore) north of Calicut, and a third in the Anjedive Islands. Meanwhile, attacks on Asian shipping continued, but they do not appear to have made an enormous dent in trade to the Red Sea, though Venetian supplies were certainly affected by turbulent conditions in Yemen and the Hijaz. The captain, Afonso de Albuquerque, then attempted on his own initiative to acquire a fortified outpost in Hurmuz in 1506–1507 but he was outwitted and rebuffed by Khwaja 'Ata Sultani. As for success of the pepper and spice trade, we have a clear view from the return cargoes to Europe in 1505, which are dominated by pepper (1,074 metric tons), followed at some distance by ginger (28 tons), cinnamon (8.7 tons), and cloves (7.1 tons).[69]

The Mamluks, probably urged on by their diplomatic networks in the Indian Ocean and to an extent by the Venetians, did react to this threat and challenge. For their part, the Venetians had been convinced by their Muslim correspondents in cities like Calicut that the situation was potentially disastrous and that the extent of Portuguese naval power was far more significant than was really the case.[70] It is evident that the new sultan, Qansuh al-Ghauri (r. 1501–1516), was not enthusiastic about the idea of a military expedition in the Indian Ocean, and the fragile state of the sultanate's finances and military resources also rendered the task all the more difficult. However, aided by mass confiscations and fines levied on important families, the sultan's agents were able to cobble together the resources to assemble a fleet at Suez and bring together the levies of troops and mariners needed to man it. This fleet of around a dozen vessels, placed under the command of the Kurdish admiral Amir Husain, left Suez in February 1506, and after stopping at Tur, Yanbu', and Jizan they spent a whole year at Jiddah, where the fortifications were improved and taxes and levies raised. By the time Amir Husain left Jiddah for the Indian Ocean in August–September 1507, his reputation as a harsh taskmaster was already widely known among merchants. This did not augur well for the fate of the expedition.

As noted, the later Mamluks such as Qait Bay (r. 1468–1496) maintained dealings with several polities in India, including the Gujarat and Malwa sultanates, the Bahmanis, and also possibly Calicut. In view of this, it is no surprise that the first destination of Amir Husain's fleet was Gujarat, which was apparently intended to be the center of operations. Arriving in Diu, the Mamluk admiral entered into contact with Malik Ayaz and then through him with Sultan Mahmud, by whom he was received, and to whom he gave "a grand present that the [Mamluk] Soldão had sent him, of brocade, silk cloth, swords, and daggers," in the words of a Portuguese chronicler.[71] A decision was made that some of Malik Ayaz's vessels under his direct command would be attached to the Mamluk fleet, and the two sets of ships then made their way down the Indian west coast until, in early March 1508, they encountered a Portuguese fleet commanded by the viceroy's son, Dom Lourenço de Almeida, in the Konkan port of Chaul. In the ensuing naval combat the Portuguese fleet was roundly defeated and its commander killed. It would appear, however, that already in the course of this engagement differences had emerged between Amir Husain and Malik Ayaz, and not long thereafter the Malik began a secret correspondence with the Portuguese viceroy, indicating his unhappiness with the Mamluks and their overbearing comportment. After biding his time for a few months, Almeida set out with a fleet from Cochin in late November 1508. Following an attack on the port of Dabhol, the Portuguese arrived before Diu in early February 1509 to face what appeared to be formidable enemy fleet. The underlying reality was quite different: Malik Ayaz had decided to abandon Amir Husain to his fate and discreetly withdrew his forces from the combat. The Mamluk fleet was thus handily defeated, and a handful of survivors (including the admiral) made their way to the protection of Sultan Mahmud.

The question has sometimes been posed as to whether the Portuguese, by these actions, introduced violence into the affairs of an otherwise peaceful Indian Ocean in which actors coexisted through commerce and other forms of cultural exchange. We need to distinguish several elements clearly in any adequate answer. We may need at any rate to reconsider some aspects of Archibald Lewis's well-known judgment on the matter: "The major maritime skill which the maritime peoples of the Indian Ocean had failed to develop prior to 1500, then, was a skill in naval operations. Their failure in this regard was an historic one, and it proved decisive enough to nullify their advanced maritime technology, their business acumen and experience, their longstanding traditions of large-scale, overseas commerce, and the navigational skills they had developed."[72] First, there is no doubt that in the fourteenth and fifteenth centuries various groups operated at the fringes of large states by attacking and seizing their shipping, as we see from the case of Sangameshwar in the 1440s or the islands of the Gulf of Kacch later in that century. Most such forms of "maritime predation" were localized. The groups that engaged in such activities could be loosely organized through ethnicity or could become incipient state forms, such as those that Roxani Margariti describes for the medieval western Indian Ocean.[73] A second more vexed issue is whether there were states that deployed sizable naval forces to foster their expansion in the centuries before 1500. The examples that are often chosen to illustrate this draw from Southeast Asia and the Bay of Bengal and involve such states as the Cholas and Srivijaya, where the historical record in fact lacks clarity and legibility regarding the actual extent of their maritime power (as opposed to their ritual projection).[74] I have mentioned the case of the Ming fleets of the fifteenth century, and it is true that some recent historians have wished to argue that they bear a far closer resemblance to the Portuguese Estado than conventional analysts have been willing to admit, in terms of both their use of actual and potential violence and how they deployed a tributary dynamic.[75] However, this does ignore several crucial differences, notably the highly intermittent nature of Ming activity (with large gaps of time between some fleets), as well as the absence of fortified settlements manned by imperial agents in distant locations. In turn, this takes us to a third matter, namely the technologies of violence involved and the difference between a maritime strategy powered by guns mounted on ships and earlier, less efficient forms. Taking these aspects together, we may say that the Portuguese Estado did not introduce violence into the Indian Ocean but changed the scale, regularity, and efficiency of its use.

Perhaps the most crucial aspect to be considered is one of the conceptualization of maritime space in the exercise of state power. We do not have a clear explanation of how ideas of maritime sovereignty were theorized by states such as the Ming, and even less the Cholas or Srivijaya. From a legalistic viewpoint it has been plausibly argued that Islamic law generally refused to admit that states had the right to control the open seas and gave them only limited rights over "territorial waters." As Hassan Khalilieh puts the matter, "Islamic law considers the boundless sea to be the common heritage of mankind. No governing authority or nation could either claim proprietorship over it, or exclusive right of navigation." He adds by way of explanation that "the boundless sea neither belongs to any state or nation, nor may it be subject to appropriation because God has subjugated [*sakhkhara*] it just as He has made the sun, the moon, 'and all things in the Heaven and on Earth' serviceable to humans and other creatures."[76] In turn, it should be made clear that the Portuguese themselves were unable to build a consensus on the matter, and both state officials and their ecclesiastical counterparts debated it through the sixteenth century. The chronicler and ideologue João de Barros took the view that the Portuguese monarch could indeed make strong claims on the monopolistic use of the sea based on the support of papal bulls and the pressing need to make war on "infidels." The opinion of the Jesuit Manuel de Carvalho is quite clear and based on his reading of canon law: "Navigation of the sea and commerce thereof is free and unencumbered to all, as is stated by natural as well as common civil law, so that everyone has a right [to protest] against someone who prohibits it to them without reason and justice, and in defense of this right can ask for it to be restituted by whoever denies it to them, and if any damage has been received as a result, can recover it [the amount] from whoever prohibited them and caused the said damage, and if they have the King's authority can even go to war on this matter."[77] This called into question a number of instruments that the Portuguese Estado regularly used, notably the *cartaz* (or navicert) given to the captain or owner of a ship to ply a trading route safely either in exchange for money or as an act of diplomacy. Again, though predecessors of this practice may be found before 1500, there is little doubt that the Portuguese extended the scale and regularity of the *cartaz* as an instrument.

SOME CASE STUDIES

In the decade or so after the engagement at Diu, the contours of the interaction between the various powers and interest groups in the western Indian Ocean acquired sharper definition. The Portuguese Estado itself was redefined through a series of conquests, of which the three most significant were Goa (1510), Melaka (1511), and Hurmuz (1515), all of which became fortified strongholds that would last through the sixteenth century. Of the three, Goa had the greatest territorial dimensions, and beginning with Tisvadi and its adjacent islands, it expanded in the 1530s and 1540s to include the neighboring areas of Bardez and Salcete. The fresh impetus was partly the product of new leadership, notably that of Afonso de Albuquerque, who had now been promoted to governor and who surrounded himself with a group of advisers including his close relatives and some Florentines and converted Jews, as well as men such as the erstwhile "corsair" Timmayya from Honavar. One of Albuquerque's new policies was to create a sort of creole bourgeoisie of settlers, who would act as a support for the Estado, while not being directly employed by the crown. This was in a sense a compromise with the insistent demand of Portuguese elements who argued that official trade and ambitions had attained such dimensions that they were being stifled. This is how Albuquerque described his conception in a letter to Dom Manuel of October 1512.

> The riches of the Indies are very substantial, and if all the expenses that are incurred on the mass of your men and fleet are taken from [the revenues] of your factories, Your Highness will come to realise what is spent here at additional cost [*custa alheya*]; and the 200,000 *cruzados* with which one can pay for four thousand men amount to nothing, because the merchandise that Your Highness carries away is worth 1,300,000 *cruzados*, and if Our Lord gives you Urmuz and Adem, as you now possess Malaca, it will be enough for all the expenses in the world that you want to make; for if Your Highness is contented with the trade between these parts and those Kingdoms [Portugal], and you set aside the trade here, with the tributes, and homages, and perquisites of your fleet you can sustain ten thousand men in India; and if you wish you can raise up four or five powerful men, with great power and great revenues, who will be enough to control everyone, with the help of Our Lord.[78]

At a level below these "powerful men," who would emerge in the 1520s and 1530s, the governor also wished to see the emergence of a larger group who came to be termed *casados*, men who would marry locally and reside in the settlements of the Estado.[79] (See table 1.3.) The peculiar circumstances of the conquest of Goa permitted this. The Portuguese took the territory from its 'Adil Shahi rulers a first time in late February 1510. It was lost to the Bijapur Sultanate over the summer. In November Albuquerque returned to the charge, and the second conquest was a far more brutal affair than the first one. Those male members of the Bijapur elite who did not manage to flee were summarily massacred over a period of four days, and their wives, families and properties were seized; the deaths in the massacre were counted in the thousands.[80] These Muslim women, rapidly converted, were then married by Albuquerque to chosen Portuguese men largely from the group of conquerors of Goa, even if their status was quite varied. A document from 1514 gives us a first list of such couples.[81]

Twenty years later, an extended list of prominent tax-paying *casados* in Goa finds at least some of the same names, suggesting the solidification of the community.[82] However, the Goan "model" proved nearly impossible to replicate in the first half of the sixteenth century. We may consider two such attempts by the Portuguese, first the Swahili coast of East Africa (especially Kilwa), and second Kannur (or Cannanore) in northern Kerala.

When the Portuguese, rounding the Cape of Good Hope, arrived in the Swahili coast from the south at the close of the fifteenth century, they had found the discernible traces of a complex history of Islamization already in place. The anonymous shipboard account (sometimes attributed to Álvaro Velho) of Vasco da Gama's voyage along the Swahili coast in 1498 gives us a first sense of this. On crossing the Cape of Good Hope, Gama's fleet had first anchored at São Brás (Mossel Bay) in late November 1497, where they encountered only a pastoralist population. But some weeks later, when they sailed north to Inharrime River, they found a more complex settlement with thatched houses whose inhabitants proved willing to trade copper for cloth. A little farther up the coast they encountered small boats and the first indications of a more complex trading system where one of their local interlocutors even informed them "that he had seen ships as large as those that we [the Portuguese] had brought."[83] Early in March 1498 Gama's small fleet put in at Mozambique Island, where the Portuguese found (to their apparent dismay) that the inhabitants were not only quite numerous but "of the sect of Muhammad and speak like Moors," besides being dressed in "rich and embroidered" clothes. There were also signs of the presence of "white Moors" from farther north up the coast, bringing cloth and spices in exchange for ivory and gold. Mozambique Island thus marked for them the southern limit of the spread of Islam along the coast at the time.

It was thus no coincidence that it was precisely here that Gama engaged in his first armed conflicts with local populations. He also managed to get hold of two Muslim pilots, who reluctantly took his fleet as far north as Mombasa, where they arrived in early April. Once in Mombasa

TABLE 1.3. First-generation *casados* (settlers) of Goa (1514)

Name	Name of spouse
Bastião Gonçalves	Maria Vaz
Aparício Dias de Macedo, knight	Brites de Morais
Achiles Godinho	Inês Rodrigues
Manuel Taborda	Ginebra de Brito
Manuel de Albuquerque, *tanadar* (revenue official)	Ginebra
Francisco Vieira	Guiomar de Albuquerque
António Brás, knight	Joana Bocarra
Álvaro Godinho, knight	Guiomar Furtada
Vicente da Costa, royal chamberlain	Felipa da May
João Rodrigues, captain of musketeers	Brites Ribeira
Manuel Fernandes, knight	Maria Fernandes
Vasco Fernandes	Catarina Coelha
João Fernandes	Constança de Brito
Cristóvão de Figueiredo, of the royal household	Isabel de Almeida
Álvaro Madureira, keeper of the stores	Brites Fernandes
Mateus Fernandes, judicial scribe	Guiomar Godinho
António Gonçalves, saddler	Guiomar de Orta
António de Azevedo	Leonor da Silva
Fernão de Lisboa, tailor	Francisca Godinha
Cosmo Fernandes	Leonor de Melo
Diogo da Veiga	Maria da Cunha
Álvaro Fernandes, *alcaide* of the city	Brites Baião
Cristóvão Lopes	Maria Lopes
Álvaro do Cocho	Margarida do Cocho†
Fernão Rodrigues, *tanadar* of Panaji	Catarina Álvares
Francisco de Albuquerque	Antónia de Albuquerque

the pilots fled as quickly as they could. In Malindi Gama found another pilot—apparently a Gujarati—who then guided him across the western Indian Ocean to his final destination of Calicut. It was in Malindi, moreover, that the Portuguese for the first time encountered Indian ships and merchants, though it is unclear from which region of the subcontinent they originated. On this first voyage, the Portuguese did not make direct contact either with the Sofala region or with Kilwa farther north, which had already been a prestigious political and commercial center at the time of Ibn Battuta.

The succeeding voyages of the years up to 1505—those led by Pedro Álvares Cabral, João da Nova, Gama (for a second time), the Albuquerque cousins, and Lopo Soares—obviously consolidated the trading knowledge of the Portuguese concerning the Swahili coast. They also led the Portuguese to make an initial bid to attempt to control the gold trade of the region, making use of the textiles purchased in India for this purpose. To do this they decided to build a fortress in Kilwa, a port with which they had established contact in 1500, through the fleet of Cabral. However, this fort, constructed and named Santiago in 1505 by the first viceroy Dom Francisco de Almeida, was abandoned after a short existence in 1512, though we have documents from the archives regarding the day-to-day functioning of its captains such as Pedro Ferreira Fogaça and Francisco Pereira Pestana, as well as the resident commercial agent (*feitor*), Fernão Cotrim. After 1512, the Portuguese then concentrated their activities elsewhere, in sites such as Sofala and Mozambique Island. As Malyn Newitt has noted, the gold trade "had fallen off sharply in the second decade of the century as the gold traders moved their operations to Angoche and as the wars among the Karanga chiefs in the interior interrupted the supply of gold to the fairs."[84] The Portuguese response to this commercial failure was to attack rival trading networks, such as those based in the Querimba Islands (1523) and in Mombasa (1529). But these attacks produced little by way of trading success, so that their focus began to shift to the more dispersed trade in ivory by the 1530s. This enterprise was quickly transformed into the private business of the captains of Mozambique and individual Portuguese entrepreneurs, while, as Newitt notes, "the poverty-stricken royal factory at Sofala carried on virtually no trade at all." The Portuguese official strategy in the region cannot therefore be counted as a great success in the first decades of the century, eventually obliging them—as Edward Alpers has shown—to commence "the gradual occupation of the area which was to become known as the Rivers of Sena" (that is, the Zambezi valley), thereby also forcing a reorientation of other rival networks.[85]

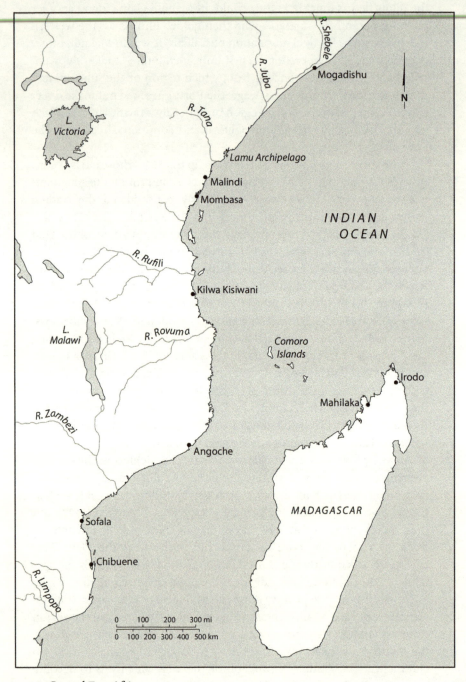

3. Coastal East Africa

Nevertheless, these early years of Portuguese dealings seem to have produced some interesting materials from the viewpoint of the historian of the Swahili coast. I have already noted the documents of the Kilwa fortress and factory, which are rather narrowly focused on internal transactions regarding wages, supplies, and the like. A very different type of document came into the possession of the official Portuguese chronicler João de Barros (1496–1570), who was also the superintendent of the Casa da Índia (India House) in Lisbon, and who therefore oversaw trade on the Cape route. From at least the 1530s, Barros had regularly instructed a number of Portuguese who were on their way to the Indian Ocean to find materials that could help him fill in local historical details in his planned chronicle. One such source is what he referred to in his *Décadas* as "a chronicle of the Kings of Kilwa" (*huma chronica dos Reys de Quiloa*), without clearly stating what language it was in.[86] Most scholars believe that the text would have been in Arabic or that it may already have been put into Portuguese for Barros's benefit, since he was himself not able to read Arabic directly. In his published version there are many signs of the careless rendering of personal names and other details in the relevant parts of the *Décadas* where he uses and cites this "chronicle." Further, following the discovery in the late nineteenth century of the manuscript of an Arabic text, often entitled *Kitab as-Sulwa fi Akhbar Kilwa*, there has been much discussion among specialists of the region's history regarding the relationship between this latter text and what Barros had at hand.[87] The *Kitab* was apparently composed around 1550, if not earlier, though this dating is open to question.[88] Some have argued that Barros's materials must have come from the brief period 1505–1512, when the Portuguese controlled Kilwa, but this is not entirely plausible for it would suppose that they were collected much before Barros was even considered for the position of chronicler. Despite several notable divergences between Barros's account and that of the *Kitab*, they do share some important commonalities. One of these is the insistent reference to the "Shirazi" settlement of the area and its alleged influence on the history of the city-state of Kilwa and its environs. Historians' attitudes toward the idea that traders and other settlers from the interior Iranian city of Shiraz (and the nearby port city of Siraf) arrived in the area several centuries before the Portuguese and played a crucial role there have varied from outright acceptance to cautious skepticism and open rejection (as being purely symbolic).[89] It is nevertheless of some interest that such a construct was current in some elite circles in Kilwa already in the early sixteenth century and was thus communicated to Barros.

Of the remaining centers on the Swahili coast of commercial interest, the Portuguese had dealings in this early period above all with two: Mombasa and Malindi. Alpers has shown that even if Mombasa was a known port in the fourteenth century, its real rise to prominence only occurred late in the fifteenth century, largely on account of what he terms "their early and successful cultivation of the trade with their own hinterland." Besides, Mombasa merchants were active in the Zambezi valley trade via Angoche, and they had some significant relations with western India. It has thus been argued that "by the time the Portuguese came along, it [Mombasa] was the most powerful city-state on the coast," and that it had a particularly resilient trading structure. An anonymous Portuguese description from the late 1510s tells us that it is a "very large city . . . with many fair houses, very tall, of stone and mortar, with well-built streets." Known to be a place of extensive trade (*muy grão trato de mercadorias*), it was famed both for its excellent harbor and its location in a "very fertile land" (*terra muy farta*). However, the sultan of Mombasa was from the very outset, in 1498, reluctant to deal with the Portuguese and their violent ways, and as a result paradoxically had to suffer repeated attacks from them. The same anonymous account recounts how, in 1505, viceroy Almeida's fleet forced the sultan from his city, "and they killed many of his people, and took into captivity many of the men and women, and it [Mombasa] was plundered and destroyed and burned."[90] But this was hardly the end of matters; as Alpers notes, "Mombasa weathered a succession of catastrophic Portuguese attacks in the sixteenth century (1505, 1528–1529, 1589) without ever losing its enormous economic and political vitality."[91] In contrast, the sultans of Malindi chose to play the Portuguese card and openly declared their friendship for the Portuguese from early on; as the same anonymous description of the late 1510s clearly states, "This king and these Moors were always good friends and servants of the King, our lord, and we have always found in the place much welcome and a very tranquil peace."[92] It was a peace that came at a price, as we will see, especially when the Portuguese captains of Sofala sent out fleets to patrol the coast and opportunistically take prizes. In the early 1510s, on abandoning Kilwa, the Portuguese considered opening a regular trading establishment at Malindi, but this does not seem to have lasted long, replaced by the practice of the coastal fleet.[93]

Further intriguing details regarding Portuguese dealings in the region come from a handful of Arabic letters written in the first two decades of the sixteenth century.[94] One of these comes from Sharif Muhammad al-'Alawi, resident at Mozambique ("Musbih" in the text), and is directed (like all the others) to the Portuguese king, Dom Manuel. It is relatively plain and unadorned, with a small ersatz seal drawn in ink on the reverse describing the sender. After formal praise of the Portuguese monarch, it requests from him a document that will perform two functions: guarantee protection to Indian traders in the region of Sofala (presumably from the Portuguese resident on the coast) and allow the sender himself to travel around on a ship without interference from the Portuguese. We encounter a summary of another letter from the same sharif (or, as he is called here, "xeque") elsewhere in the Portuguese archives, albeit without the Arabic original.[95] Here he recounts his own services, also in regard to Portuguese ambitions in Angoche, and requests that he be allowed to bring ten bahars of ivory to Mozambique from Sofala (each bahar being roughly two hundred kilograms). However, the addressee of the letter, the secretary of state António Carneiro, had also received a letter from the Portuguese factor in Mozambique, Diogo Vaz, in which the latter had spoken "very ill of the *xarife* and [said that] he merited severe punishment."[96] In fact, it appears that Mozambique was in a state of turmoil at the time, and the Portuguese had killed the sharif's son-in-law in a fracas. The result was that it was practically impossible for the Portuguese to obtain supplies in both Mozambique and Angoche.

There are also two letters that originate in Kilwa, of which the first is written on behalf of its ruler Sultan Ibrahim. It is again unadorned in its physical appearance but quite well written, possibly by a professional scribe. The writer was the effective ruler of Kilwa at the time of the first contacts with the Portuguese fleets of Cabral and Nova in 1500 and 1501. Portuguese sources relate that he showed little interest in welcoming or dealing with the Portuguese, possibly because he was preoccupied by other threats both within his city-state and from other rivals along the coast.[97] The Portuguese reacted violently in 1502, when Gama during his second voyage to the Indian Ocean threatened to bombard the town, forced a meeting with Ibrahim, and extracted a tribute from him in gold.[98] For a better grasp of the complex political situation in Kilwa in the early sixteenth century, we can draw on the careful modern analysis of Elias Saad, attempting to reconcile Arabic and Portuguese materials. Saad argues that by the middle of the fifteenth century there was "a polarization in the power structure of Kilwa between the throne [*al-mulk*] on the one hand, and another powerful post identified as the emirate [*al-amr* or *al-imara*]."[99] At the same time a larger controlling oligarchy in the city-state emerged in the latter part of the fifteenth century, termed "the people of the major decisions" (*ahl al-hall wa'l-'aqd*) and made up both of those claiming royal descent (from the Mahdali dynasty) and others, such as prominent merchants. In the late fifteenth

FIGURE 1.2. Arabic letter from the Swahili coast (Torre do Tombo, Lisbon, Núcleo Antigo 891, Maço 1, Documentos Orientais, Letter 20).

century, one of the Mahdalis, Kiwab bin Muhammad, had made a determined but unsuccessful attempt to centralize power in his person by seizing the emirate and placing a weak ruler on the throne as sultan. His nephew Ibrahim bin Sulaiman, the central personage of our story, succeeded Kiwab as amir; but it is clear that many resented Ibrahim, both within the broader Mahdali lineage and among the richer merchants. One was Muhammad Rukn al-Daybuli, described by Saad as a "wealthy non-royal notable" (possibly with some oversight of the treasury), who was thus not a part of the extended group of families descended from the Mahdalis. Rukn had made clandestine contact with the Portuguese perhaps as early as Cabral's visit of 1500, and from him the Portuguese had received a slanted understanding of the politics of the Kilwa state.[100] They were thus made aware that besides the kings there were others who held the post of governor (*governador*), and that Amir Ibrahim, "though he was the absolute master of Quiloa, was not called king by the people." Muhammad Rukn was able to maintain his contacts with the Por-

74 / ACROSS THE GREEN SEA

tuguese until 1505, when Dom Francisco de Almeida arrived in Kilwa with his force and summarily captured the town, obliging Amir Ibrahim to flee to the mainland. Barros describes the situation thereafter:

> D. Francisco de Almeida, though he was not that well informed regarding the succession among these kings, as we have now recounted, knew however from Mahamed Anconij [Muhammad Rukn] that the people were not very satisfied with Habraemo [Ibrahim], and how all of them wanted to raise up a king who would be closer to the real lineage [of kings], as well as the reason for which they tolerated him. And therefore, he came to know about the notable persons who were there in the land, and other things about which he wished to inform himself, in order to know about the manner by which to ensure the security and government of the city.[101]

Having had the measure of matters, the Portuguese viceroy and his council then made the extraordinary decision to set aside the Mahdali lineage altogether and decided instead that Muhammad Rukn "should receive the lordship [*senhorio*] of that city, because he had merited it, and gone through our friendship, [and] because besides this he had the stature, was aged about sixty years, and had the prudence to govern even though he was not of the royal lineage, because for the setting in order of that land nothing else would do." This decision seems to have come as rather a shock to Muhammad Rukn himself, who according to Barros was "innocent of the honor to which he had been called." He was then taken on horseback in a ceremonial procession through Kilwa, and the decision was announced before "all the principal Moors of the city."[102]

From the outset Muhammad Rukn appears to have been aware that he might suffer from a serious deficit of legitimacy. We are told that he therefore asked for those whom the Portuguese had taken prisoner in their assault on the city to be set free quickly, and that as a consequence of this gesture "all those who had gone off into the palm-groves of the island as fugitives returned to the city to live in their houses." These conciliatory actions proved insufficient to guarantee a stable basis for his power. Barros gives a detailed narrative of an intricate sequence of events after Muhammad Rukn's rise to power in 1505.[103] Summarized briefly, the new ruler appears to have had tense relations with the Portuguese captain of the fortress, Pedro Ferreira Fogaça, who described him in a letter of August 1506 as "unnecessary" (*pouco necesario*) and an impediment to Portuguese ambitions to expand into the islands of the coast.[104] Ferreira was keen to send ships out to take prizes in the vicinity, claiming an extensive Portuguese monopoly of various trade goods. In one of these expeditions, the Portuguese captured the son of a close relative of Amir Ibrahim, who is described as the ruler of a nearby place called "Tirendincunde." Muhammad Rukn determined to use the occasion to offer an olive branch to the exiled Ibrahim, set the young man and his family free after paying a large gold ransom to the Portuguese, and himself decided (against Ferreira's advice) to accept an invitation to visit the father on a peace mission. Instead, Barros tells us, Rukn was ambushed and assassinated by the other's men as he "lay sleeping in the *zambuco* in which he went." By June 1506, therefore, things were once more in turmoil in Kilwa: the Portuguese factor, some other officials, and several Muslim notables supported the candidacy of Haj Hasan ("Agi Hocem"), the son of Muhammad Rukn, as ruler, while Pedro Ferreira and others around him wished to support the return of the family of Amir Ibrahim in some form. An emissary of the Portuguese viceroy, Nuno Vaz Pereira, was obliged to choose between various options, and he decided in favor of Haj Hasan. The optimistic expectation was that he would stabilize matters and reestablish the commercial strength of Kilwa.

Instead, on taking power, Hasan was determined to make retributive war on those who had killed his father, and with some allies from the hinterland (such as "Munha Monge," perhaps a distortion of the title Mwenyi Mwanya) he launched a series of bloody raids on Ibrahim's clansmen. Various parties sent a series of complaints to India, reaching the ears of viceroy Almeida. It was then hastily decided to reverse the earlier decision; Haj Hasan would be displaced, Ibrahim would be invited back, and in the event that he did not wish to return, power would be handed over to his cousin, Muhammad Mikat, whom some suspected of being the real assassin of Muhammad Rukn. Ferreira was only too happy to implement this decision. In turn, Mikat seems to have ruled for a little more than two years, initially with the help of the Portuguese garrison and officials in Kilwa. But the departure of his chief patron, the captain Pedro Ferreira, and his replacement by the strong-willed Francisco Pereira Pestana boded ill for him. Pestana launched a series of insistent complaints against Mikat, accusing him of creating instability in the town and hinterland and even of making war on his own departed cousin Ibrahim. He managed to persuade the new governor, Afonso de Albuquerque, to remove Mikat from power and to bring the exiled Ibrahim back to Kilwa. Thus, writes Barros, Ibrahim "remained in a peaceful state, reforming the country into a better situation than he had before it was taken from him by us, because the travails he had passed had taught him how to govern." The chronicler seems to relish the irony of all this, calling it "a notable comedy of the cycles of the world."

It appears most likely that the letter from Ibrahim was written after his final return to power and the removal of Mikat, although there is a small possibility that it was written during his first stint in power, just before the Portuguese capture of Kilwa in 1505. In favor of the former hypothesis are both the contents of the letter itself and the title he now used, namely "sultan" (whereas he seems to have titled himself "amir" earlier on). It is written very much in the humble tone of a supplicant, requesting the Portuguese king that "you may order your deputy [na'ib] that he should deal kindly and generously with us." Furthermore, it states that "we are a weak group [qaum], and we are not in a position to quarrel and combat against you." Everything should be done to avoid discord and to ensure that the people in Kilwa do not "scatter in panic." There is also still another letter that is far more complex, richer, but also harder to interpret at times. Written in poor Arabic, with a highly uncertain grasp of the niceties of syntax (moving unsteadily between the first and third person), it was written by Haj Hasan ibn Muhammad Rukn after his displacement from power and at a time when Sultan Mikat still ruled Kilwa. It is a long series of complaints and accusations. To begin with, Hasan notes that his father was killed by Muhammad Mikat because of his loyalty to the Portuguese. Like his father, Hasan has remained loyal but has received no recompense for his loyalty. The chief villain in the matter is apparently the captain of Kilwa, Pedro Ferreira. Ferreira has ensured that Hasan's access to other high-ranking Portuguese, such as fleet commander Tristão da Cunha, has been partially impeded.[105] It is also implied that Ferreira has turned viceroy Almeida against him and that Almeida himself is not honorable. Besides, Ferreira is accused of constantly resorting to extortion. This includes an episode when Haj Hasan was carried off to Malindi on Ferreira's instructions and imprisoned and tortured until he handed over a quantity of gold. Having been further robbed by Mikat's followers (enigmatically termed the "the people of means" or *ahl al-mal*), the writer declares his helplessness and his poor condition: "I now have nothing to eat, nor do I have clothes." Through the letter and a small accompanying present, he hopes to attract the attention and benevolence of Dom Manuel. Several Portuguese officials and others are cited as his character witnesses, including the celebrated go-between and interpreter Gaspar da Gama, who had visited Kilwa more than once in these years.[106] This letter thus forces us to reconsider in part the eminently unsympathetic portrait of Haj Hasan that is left to us by Barros. Barros sums up the end of his career thus: "Hocem, seeing that all the wealth that he had inherited from his father had been spent in the vengeance for his death, and that if he remained in Quiloa, he ran the risk of being killed by his enemies, asked Pero Ferreira to have him carried to Mombaça, as was done, where shortly thereafter he ended his days more miserably than any commoner."[107] In this official version, Hasan and his own lack of judgment are seen as responsible for his fate; yet the reader of his letter is left to wonder whether Hasan, like his rival Ibrahim, was not caught up in a complex web that was not fully of his making, in which actors like viceroy Almeida and captain Ferreira also bore some crucial responsibility.

These Kilwa letters can be read together with some documents from Malindi, farther to the north, and addressed to Dom Manuel by Sultan ʿAli bin ʿAli. The main letter seems largely to concern the activities of the Portuguese captain Manuel Fernandes in the region, particularly in relation to a ship from the port of Diu in Gujarat. Was this ship seized by Fernandes, and was the sultan asking for its release? A few other documents from the period are helpful in providing context on the other hand. We learn that Manuel Fernandes had been the royal agent in Sofala in 1505 and then the captain there in 1506–1507; in February 1507 he had handed over command to Nuno Vaz Pereira, who immediately investigated his predecessor on the charge of stealing gold from the factory.[108] Other documents mention the Portuguese capture of a Gujarati ship near Malindi in March 1510 and the disputes that resulted therefrom, as well as the Portuguese hostility and suspicion toward Sidi Bu Bakr, a great merchant of Malindi, who together with his brother regularly traded with Angoche.[109] In 1513, the Portuguese *feitor* at Sofala wrote to the king of the increasing menace that the Angoche network represented to Portuguese interests, stressing that it was place "where are resident many Moors from Quiloa and Melinde," who were so resourceful that they could "thus fill the land with cloth and cause a great decrease in the trade of this factory." His conclusion was that the Portuguese monarch "should order the said Moors to be thrown out of there or destroyed in such a way that they will not be able to live or trade there."[110] In the face of such an attitude, even the possession of Portuguese documents (*seguros* or *cartazes*) was sometimes not enough to protect such merchants, trading in Indian cloth or trade beads or African ivory from seizure; as the Portuguese historian Manuel Lobato notes, "The alliance between the king of Malindi and the Portuguese did not however prevent the Gujaratis from suffering severe losses in the first decades of the sixteenth century, on account of the vessels that the Portuguese captured from them in that African port."[111] An example of this may be found in 1518, when a Portuguese ship sailing in the vicinity of the island of Soqotra captured "a *nao* of the Guzerates which they said was coming from Melynde to Canbaya, and its cargo was a great quantity of ivory, copper, coir and other goods that might well be worth 12,000 or 15,000 *pardaos*, and 79 *meticaes* of gold and 150 of silver, and also many valuable Moors and captive slaves."[112] Rather than carry the prize to Goa, the Portuguese captain, Fernando Dias, is said to have secretly sold the goods in Chaul and the ship in Diu. Further examples appear in two later letters from the same Sultan 'Ali to Dom Manuel that survive in the archives, one in a Portuguese version and the other in a summary (but without the Arabic originals). Both date from around 1520–1521: the first complains of the behavior of the Portuguese in Malindi, with their "hard words and deeds towards us" which includes robbing some 9,500 xerafins worth of goods; the second points a finger concretely at two Portuguese ships (including the *Taforeia*), whose captains Rui Lourenço and João Fernandes "came to this port of Melindi and corrupted and destroyed it and seized goods in it, saying openly that Your Highness is aware of this and considers it good if the port of Melindi is damaged."[113]

These materials from the first two decades of the sixteenth century suggest that the options open to rulers of the city-states of the Swahili coast in the face of the initial Portuguese challenge were all unpleasant in some degree. A further complication was that individual Portuguese captains and officials often had ideas and projects of their own that were at variance with royal orders as well as the official policies of the Estado da Índia. Open resistance, as the sultans of Mombasa tried, could leave one victim to costly periodic attacks from Portuguese fleets. Cooperation, which the sultans of Malindi attempted to offer, was not a guarantee of safety either, especially if one wanted to balance Portuguese demands even minimally against the interests of other commercial groups and ensure that one's port had a viable fiscal existence rather than a near-asphyxiated trading system.[114] Finally, the case of a Kilwa is a particularly interesting one, where all the strategies—whether of resistance, foot-dragging, or conciliation—were attempted turn by turn between 1500 and 1530. Over the course of the sixteenth century, as Alpers has remarked, Kilwa managed to survive by ceding ground and adjusting "its commercial orientation from one which had previously been exclusively seaward, to one which now looked to its own hinterland."[115] This was undoubtedly a high price to pay.

THE KANNUR CASE

The last case takes us to a port and polity in southwestern India, Kannur in northern Kerala, that also tried in its own way to come to terms with the challenge posed by the arrival of the Portuguese in Indian Ocean waters. Historians of the later medieval period have long expressed an interest in the emerging affairs of the Kola Svarupam that ruled the area, which are set out in texts such as the eleventh-century epic poem or *kavya* of Atula, entitled *Musikavamsha*.[116] By the fourteenth century, it would appear that the chief port in the area was still Madayi, on the Taliparamba River, but it was progressively abandoned over the second half of the fifteenth century, allowing the emergence in its place of the site of Kannur farther to the south. The dominant rulers of the area, the Kolattiris, now came to reside at Valarpattanam, somewhat in the interior, on the banks of the river of the same name. Even so, they retained the historical memory of the prestigious center around Ezhimala and still referred to it in their titles. The area around Ezhimala is associated with the early phase of Muslim settlement in Kerala, at least in the retrospective view of Shaikh Zain-ud-Din Ma'bari's celebrated sixteenth-century text, the *Tuhfat al-mujahidin*.[117] A twelfth-century CE inscription (from 518 AH) also dates the foundation of an early mosque in the area, that at Madayi. When the center of commercial gravity moved to Kannur in the later fifteenth century, this port too became a major center for Muslim trade, both for the Mappilas and various groups of Middle Eastern Muslims, from the Persian Gulf, the Hadramaut, and even as far as Egypt.

The standard work on the Muslim trading community of the Kannur area in the sixteenth century is that of the French scholar Geneviève Bouchon, who published an extensive essay on Kerala Muslims in the sixteenth century in 1973 and followed it up with a monograph, *Mamale de Cananor*, in 1975.[118] Bouchon's main purpose was to set out the complex process by which, by the late 1520s, a group of Mappila Muslims in Kolattunadu had become staunch adversaries of the Portuguese Estado da Índia and its restrictive policies. The head of the group emerged in the course of the sixteenth century with the hereditary title of the Ali Raja and thus founded what Bouchon terms "the only Muslim dynasty to have ruled in Kerala."[119] Rather than generalize over the whole of Kerala or argue that what obtained with the Muslims of, say, Calicut was true everywhere, her purpose is to come back to the specific challenges faced by the Muslim trading community in and around Kannur. This included the fact that their trading and political interests extended quite far into the western Indian Ocean, in the direction of the Lakshadwip and Maldive archipelagos, a fact reflected in the title the Portuguese sometimes accorded to the Ali Rajas of *regedor do mar*, "ruler of the sea."

The complex economic geography of sixteenth-century Kerala also came into play in the matter of the relations between Kannur and the Portuguese. In 1498 the first Portuguese fleet made its way to the Samudri Raja's domains, and this was probably based on the view—which remained largely unchallenged in the first half of the sixteenth century—that the chief sources of pepper lay in central and southern Kerala. The first Portuguese dealings with Calicut in 1498 were already tense, but they exploded into violence two years later in 1500, when the second Portuguese fleet under Pedro Álvares Cabral arrived in Kerala. Cabral then abandoned the establishment in the Samudri ruler's domains and founded a factory in Kochi farther south, which remained a mainstay of Portuguese activities until 1663. In mid-January 1501 he also paid a brief visit to Kannur and took on board a cargo of cinnamon; later the same year, the small fleet of João da Nova also touched on the Kolattiri's domains, returning early in 1502 to set up an irregular Portuguese factory there, the first factor being Paio Rodrigues, actually an employee of Dom Álvaro de Portugal, a powerful trading nobleman. Then in October 1502, Vasco da Gama himself returned with a large fleet to Kannur, where he engaged in extensive and rather frustrating negotiations with the Kolattiri before departing in something of a huff.[120] Not long after his departure, Gama received a letter from the Kolattiri whose contents are reported in some sources but the actual text of which has not survived. In it the ruler made it clear that he was a friend of the king of Portugal (but not necessarily of Gama) and that, if necessary, he would complain to the king about the violent and intemperate behavior of his subject.

By the time of the next Portuguese maritime expedition, that of the Albuquerque cousins in 1503, the difference in the economic roles of Kochi and Kollam on the one hand and Kannur on the other had become clear. As Jean Aubin has written, "Unlike Cannanore, a port for ginger, Kollam and its satellites were pepper ports."[121] A Portuguese factor thus wrote the very next year, in 1504, to Dom Manuel: "If Your Lordship sends a fleet here of foists and brigantines as I have written to you, and if they prevent *sambuquos* from sailing with this pair of caravels that are here, and if besides there is deposited in this fortress 20,000 to 30,000 *cruzados*, you may have it for certain that 30,000 *quintaes* of pepper can be collected every year between here and Coullam, twenty here and further north [*pera cima*], and the rest over there."[122] The northern part of Kerala was thus hardly considered worthy of consideration in this scheme of things. A rather more detailed explanation is presented some sixteen years later, in a letter of 1520. Here the writer, Nuno de Castro, explains matters:

> My Lord, in this land of Malavar—that is—from Belymjaom [Vizhinjam], a port that is beyond Coulão, to [a distance] of 2 leagues beyond Cramganor towards Calequt, I have learnt that there is collected each year 15,000 *bares* of pepper, and as much as 16,000, not counting that which is held over as old [stock] from one year to the other, which is disposed of in this way: that is, in the land itself there is consumed 2000 or 2500 *bares* in their own demand, and on oxen and headloads they carry off as much as 3000 *bares* outside, as there are wide routes open towards Calecare [Kilakkarai] and other parts of the interior [*sertão*], and there is thus a route which is called Putura [Putheri]; and from Belinjam they carry it on headloads towards Comorym, and there are three other routes by which they carry it on oxen and bring back rice on the return; the pepper that is carried in the *paraos* from Panane, Chatua [and] Cranganor each year towards Dio would be 500 to 600 bares, which is carried along the coastline as I have already told Your Highness. From the remaining 9000, they carry over as old [stock] 2000 to 3000 *bares*, and it is in this old stock that they adulterate because it has a greater consistency than the green pepper, in which with a little effort the adulteration can be shown. And though I may have spoken to Your Highness above of 15,000 to 16,000 *bares*, I have learnt this from men of the land who know the matter well and trade in it, who have told me that they collect as much as 20,000 *bares*, and it seems to me that it may well be so, for Your Highness should not believe that the leakages of pepper are small, whether to Ormuz, or to Dio, or to the Moors in the Straits of Meca, or to Choromandell.[123]

Again, while areas such as Chettuva, Ponnani, and Calicut find mention here, Kolattunadu is left out of the discussion on pepper. Geneviève Bouchon has taken matters a step further than Aubin, arguing that overall Kolattunadu's "natural resources were as mediocre in quantity, as they were in quality" and that the real reason for the success of ports like Madayi and Kannur lay in a combination of geographical position and "the dynamism of its merchant population." So, with local production and resources accounting for "only a minute proportion" of trade, it follows that two other factors must have weighed in: the import trade and a role as an entrepôt.[124] With regard to the first, around 1500 Kannur was one of the principal ports through which horses from West Asia arrived in southern India. Ludovico di Varthema, visiting there early in the sixteenth century, noted that it was "a port where they unload the horses that come from Persia. And you should know that for each horse, one pays 25 ducats as duties, and afterwards, they are carried inland to Narsinga, where there are many Moorish merchants." Besides, he noted that the place had "but a little by way of spices, pepper, ginger, and cardamom, myrobalans, and a small amount of cassia."[125] The horse trade to Vijayanagara was one that Kannur shared with Bhatkal, somewhat to the north. As regards its role as an entrepôt, the connection to the Maldives was highly significant for Kannur, as were links up and down the west coast of India and across the western Indian Ocean.

It was because of these functions that the Portuguese were not simply content to have a factory in Kannur. In 1504 a powerful fleet under Lopo Soares de Albergaria had again put in at the port and (somewhat as it had done in 1502) made a great show of ceremony in dealing with the Kolattiri. But the man who had been left in charge of the factory, Gonçalo Gil Barbosa, had over time persuaded himself that his life and the lives of his compatriots were constantly under threat. He thus began secretly to lay the foundations for a fortress while at the same time "letting the king of Cananor believe that it was for a factory-house that would be strengthened, so as to be defensible against the Moors." On the arrival in October 1505 of the viceroy Dom Francisco de Almeida in Kannur, the Portuguese thus presented the ruler with a fait accompli to which he had to acquiesce, no doubt being aware of how his port might well otherwise be bombarded. The Portuguese chronicler Castanheda assures us, though, that "the king conceded it with all good will, showing great pleasure with the trade that the king of Portugal wished to have in his land: because, as he esteemed nothing so much as his profit, he knew how much this amounted to for the increase in his revenues [*suas rendas*]."[126] The fortress, named Santo Ângelo, was very rapidly constructed and its command handed over to Lourenço de Brito.

The very next year, in 1506, the real significance of having such a fortress became clear. Almeida had prepared a coastal patrolling fleet of ten vessels under the command of his son to control shipping from Kerala to West Asia. One of the ships was under the command of Gonçalo Vaz de Góis, who—in the official account of the chronicler Barros—encountered a large ship off Ezhimala that he found suspicious. As it happened, the vessel carried a legitimate navicert from the Portuguese captain of Kannur allowing it to travel. However, Góis decided that the ship really came from the Samudri's territories and that its certificate had been obtained under false pretenses; at any rate, in Barros's words, he "sent the ship to the bottom with all the Moors who sailed in it, all stitched up in a sail so that there would be no memory of them." This murderous act may have been motivated either by Góis's personal greed for a prize or by a cynical disregard for official guarantees and documents. However, the sail burst open, and some of the corpses washed up off Kannur, including that of "a Moor who was the nephew of Mamale, one of the richest and most honored that there was in that Malabar, who was a resident of Cananor." The Muslims of Kannur thus went to Brito, captain of the fortress, and accused him of having "misled them with his certificate [*seguro*]," since it really afforded them no protection.[127] Since Brito was unable to give them satisfaction, the merchants then complained bitterly to the new Kolattiri, who had just acceded to the throne. Incensed by the Portuguese behavior, they even besieged the fort for several months, in the course of which several Portuguese were killed, including Góis himself. What is notable is that the Portuguese effectively refused to accept responsibility for the events, instead blaming it on Muslim treachery and duplicity and the existence of secret contacts between Kannur and Calicut. Certainly they were aware that in the absence of a fortress they would have been sitting ducks, as they had been some years earlier in Calicut. A fortress was what was needed in order for the Portuguese to act with impunity and with little fear of reprisal. The Kolattiri thus rapidly found what the agreement he had made with the Portuguese viceroy was worth and what its effective consequences were.

We thus see his ruminations on the matter in a long, complex letter written to the Portuguese King Dom Manuel in December 1507. Since only the Portuguese version of this letter has come down to us, it has some odd features, including some Christianized vocabulary that clearly came from the scribe rather than the Kolattiri himself:

> I, the King of Eli [*Elrey d'Ely*] make it known to the very high, and very powerful, my Lord the King of Portugal, that in the beginning of the discovery [*achummento*] of Malevaram, your people and ships came to Calecud to trade, where they were robbed and the men killed, and they left from there and went to Cochym; the king, my uncle, who reigned at that time came to know of it, and because he did not want that in foreign kingdoms [*estranhos reynos*] it should be said that the kings of Malabar were bad, and lacking in truth, he at once sent his men to Cochym to invite them to come over here, and Pedralveres

[Cabral], who was then captain, came here, and without asking a price or speaking of payment, he [the king] ordered fifty *bahares* of cinnamon to be placed in the ships, as well as all the other things that they might need, and he the captain ordered them to be paid very well, and he ordered that his great desire to settle trade in this port of Cananor be communicated; and immediately the next year four ships came towards Calecud not knowing what had happened, and they were properly informed by me and laden [with goods], and they were treated with all honor and welcome. And since, besides, the king my uncle knew for certain of their great desires, he made sure that they left behind men, who he ordered to be welcomed and settled in his land, until the Admiral [Vasco da Gama] came and settled the trading terms with us, and left behind a factor and goods, and departed with a cargo. And afterwards the factor [Barbosa] asked for a site for a factory at a distance from the Moors, which was given to him as he wanted, though there had been no contentions with the Moors, and he was given all facilities for this, until the arrival of the Viceroy, at which we greatly rejoiced here on account of some differences that had arisen here [meanwhile] amongst his people, and as soon as he arrived, the king, my uncle went and met him in the same place that had been given, and he agreed on all matters of trade and good friendship forever, in the hope that it would always remain, and the Viceroy asked him to allow a fortress to be made in the said place so that his people might be more secure, and because he wished to leave a very honorable *fidalgo* [Lourenço de Brito] there as captain, in order to look after his affairs, and the king, my uncle, granted it to him with all goodwill, and he ordered that he be given all the facilities that he might need for this, and he [the Viceroy] at once left the said captain there with his people, and departed to Cochy.

What we have thus far is a perfectly anodyne account, corresponding rather well with the official Portuguese version. Indeed, it even appears that the contacts were largely at the initiative of the rulers of Kannur. At this point in the letter, however, the tone begins to change:

And at this time in Coulam, they killed the [Portuguese] factor and the people who were with him, as so his [the Viceroy's] ships went there and they burnt many *zambucos* that were in the port of Coylam, amongst which they burnt six large *zambucos*

> from my kingdom, one with elephants and others laden with many and rich goods, because of which the Moors who are my vassals and merchants raised a great tumult on account of the great loss that they had sustained, and [so] we at once supplied the fortress with the great speed, and placed a great deal of protection over its people, and we ordered some of the Moors who were the most inflamed in this [affair] to be punished according to the custom of our lands, and on this account they were somewhat quelled, though in their hearts they remained bitter on account of their losses. And in the meantime, their ships were [again] seized in this port, [and] when a ship [*naao*] of a Muslim merchant who is my vassal wished to enter it, while returning from Gromuz [Hurmuz] with horses, they carried it off to Cochy saying that it did not carry their safe-conduct [*seguro*], and since the greatest trade there is in this port was always that in horses from Gromuz, the king, my uncle, was much aggrieved, since we well perceived that the said trade was going to be destroyed, as indeed it was undone, and we thus lost great revenues. And after this, the Moors with their ill-will in order to deceive us, killed a boy who was a native of the land, and newly [made] Christian, and the king ordered a Moor killed in exchange, and executed other acts of justice that are usual in our land.

The obvious contrast here is between the justice of the Kannur rulers, who compensate the Portuguese for their episodic losses, and the regular and unjustified violence of the Portuguese, for which no compensation is forthcoming. The letter then continues:

> And at this time, the king, my uncle, died, and I took on the reign with a good and sound will with regard to your people, as he had always held, which was to accord them much honor and welcome in my kingdom. And I called for them and let them know this; and in this situation, even before I was crowned, the first *zambuco* that set sail in my reign, even before it had left my kingdom in the port of Ely, was taken from me [by the Portuguese], whilst its captain was ashore with the safe-conduct [*alvará de seguro*] that the captain Lourenço de Brito had issued for it to sail. And when it was seized in this way, the said captain hastened there with his *seguro*, and he was seized and killed, as were all the other people, and the *zambuco* was carried off to

> Cochy. And with the hatred on account of this and other past affairs, my vassals—before I could control them, for I was not yet crowned, as is the custom of this land—created a tumult and attacked the fortress, and soon as I came to know, I sent my ministers [*alguazizes*] to turn the people away from the fort. And when they reached there, the war was already highly inflamed on account of some deaths, and so we were at war for four months, in which they killed people from my kingdom. And I at once sent word to the Viceroy in Cochy to say that I wanted peace with him, and he told me to make it with the captain Lourenço de Brito and that he would be contented with that, and so I at once made a peace and friendship that was firm forever with the said captain, with all the conditions and agreements that had been in effect before, with all truth [?] from both sides. And in this regard, your captain has my letters, and I have his, and on these matters we are contented, except that both our goods and yours are traded at a fixed price, so that ships cannot be laden here, because in the entire world, goods vary according to the times and novelties, and I would like that Your Highness should organize matters so that we can always trade, because at times your goods are worth more than what is fixed, and at other times less, as is the case with ours.

The account here seems to correspond broadly to that of the *sanbuq* attacked by Góis, albeit with some variants. The Kolattiri presents himself here as an honest broker, rendered impotent by circumstances. But what is also interesting in the last lines is his defense of a form of "free trade," as distinct from the fixing of prices by treaty that the Portuguese demanded. To close the letter, there are also some notable grumblings with regard to the issue of Christianity and conversion.

> And I would also like that some people who in my kingdom I hold as slaves, as do my Nayres, who are of two categories [*leis*] of people, that is Tiues [Tiyyas] and Mucoas [Mukkuvas], should not be converted into Christians, and nor should Nayres or Bramanes. Because if these slaves become Christians, a conflict [*arroydo*] may result between our vassals and your people, because the Nayres of my lands gain their revenues from them and they will not want to lose them. And from now on, with God's help, I hope to deal with you in all truth and good friendship, just as a great lord like you merits, for I am an enemy of

your enemies and a friend of your friends, and because the king of Calecud knows this, he is always hostile to me and I to him. And I also ask you that you always ask that my honor be maintained, and my kingdom be enlarged, and that you should order your people that my vassals should always be protected and honored by them as good friends. Through Tristam da Cunha, who is your Captain-Major of this fleet that is leaving now, I am sending a small gift for the prince, your son, who I hope Our Lord will help to grow and remain alive. Written in Cananor on the sixth of December of 1507.[128]

If things had been difficult under Almeida, matters were to deteriorate still further under his successor, the more active and bellicose Albuquerque. During the six years of his governorship Albuquerque made a series of major interventions and conquests, although his attempt to conquer Aden failed in 1513. In particular Albuquerque's conquest and settlement of Goa had a significant impact on Kannur, since he then decided that Goa would be the great centralizing point for the import trade for horses into the Deccan and southern India. Besides, Albuquerque had in mind a devious plan to make peace with Calicut and resume Portuguese trade with the port; to this end, he tried to persuade other members of the royal family there to poison the Samudri Raja (in which he possibly succeeded).[129] He believed that the investment in a Portuguese factory and fortress in Kannur was misplaced, also because of the poor relations the Portuguese had with the main families of Mappila Muslims there. As he wrote in a letter to the king, Dom Manuel, in April 1512: "Does Your Highness not know of the Moors of Cananor that they call themselves your slaves, and come and kiss the feet of your factor, and come with great humility and submission before your captain, [but] for a very small matter, they have besieged your fortress twice, and have always been displeased at not having been able to carry it off?"[130] Of course, the "very small matter" (*muy piquena cousa*) in question was the sinking of the ship in 1506 and the massacre of those on board, who included several members of notable Mappila families. Or again, at the end of the next year, in a letter written while he was at Kannur: "Cananor is a shyster [*hum regatam*], who sells us supplies for double the price, and from which you have no profit, nor is it worth anything except for the name of having a fortress; everything else that you it possesses, can equally be had at Calecut."[131] Despite this open hostility, Albuquerque continued to deal with Kannur and with the Kolattiri as well as others there. This was for several reasons. First, he feared the influence of the Mappilas resident in the port, and in particularly of the family of Mammali Marakkar, whose reach extended into the Maldives and beyond. Second, there was the question of inertia and the difficulty in dismantling a fort without losing face. Third, as Albuquerque himself recognized, he was unable to control the activities of his own subordinates resident in Kannur, many of whom had their own commercial and political alliances both in the port and at the court in Vallarpattanam. These included Duarte Barbosa, later celebrated, who was crucially placed as interpreter (*língua*) to influence relations between the Portuguese Estado and the Kolattiri.[132]

Once we are into the second half of the 1510s, matters appear to change somewhat during the successive governorships of Lopo Soares and Diogo Lopes de Sequeira, and the level of overt hostilities seems to have even diminished for a time. Lopo Soares in particular showed himself rather accommodating to the Kannur traders and allowed their influence to grow considerably, especially over the Maldives and into the western ports of Lanka. The maintenance of the fortress was apparently rather careless at this time, and the Portuguese possibly began to see Kannur as a relative backwater in their own Estado, as is testified to by a long and resentful letter from the fortress captain, Dom Aires da Gama, younger brother of Vasco da Gama, in 1519.[133] However, this preceded a period of extraordinary violence between the Kannur Mappila community and the Portuguese that began in the early 1520s and continued through most of that decade. The leading role was played initially here by Mammali, and then by Valiya Hasan ("Balia Hacem" in the Portuguese documents), who built up an important fleet of oared vessels (or *paraos*) both for trade and to attack and harass Portuguese shipping. However, the Mappilas were unable to count on the steadfast support of the Kolattiri, who—during the brief visit to Kannur of the new viceroy, Vasco da Gama, in late 1524—even handed over one of the important Mappila leaders to him, who was then summarily hanged in the fortress in early 1525. In the ensuing conflict, many of the major Mappila families ostentatiously burned their residences and abandoned Kannur for a time, moving to Dharmapatam, close to the frontier with the Samudri Raja's territories. However, on the death of the Kolattiri in 1527 (after a reign of some twenty years) they seem to have reestablished themselves in Kannur, gradually coming to exercise a greater and greater influence there in the course of the 1530s and 1540s. The frustration and anger of the Portuguese at this new turn of events then gave rise to sporadic violence, such as the assassination by Belchior de Sousa of Fukar 'Ali (or "Pocaralle"), the Mappila *regedor* at Kannur in 1545.[134] Even such acts could not turn the tide or prevent the emergence of the powerful lineage of Ali Rajas in the decades that followed. As Bouchon writes: "The authority of the Cannanore Mappilas was to go from strength to strength during the sixteenth century, ultimately bringing about the break-up of the Eli kingdom."[135]

Our analysis of Portuguese dealings with Kannur can be given further nuance by having recourse to a small body of Arabic documents from the Portuguese archives in Lisbon (the Torre do Tombo), in the same collection as the Swahili coast documents discussed earlier.[136] Several other documents from the same set in Persian and Arabic have already been published (with text and French translation), written by Khwaja 'Ata of Hurmuz and Baba 'Abdullah, including a document from 1519 that contains several mentions of Mammali Marakkar, referred to as Mam 'Ali al-Malibari.[137] In more recent years, several Persian letters from the same collection have also been published, dealing with affairs of the Persian Gulf and the Gujarat Sultanate. (There is also one from Melaka.)[138] The Kannur letters come to us largely from the Kolattiri or from someone who is styled as his vizier, Chenicheri Kurup.[139] They are addressed to King Dom Manuel, his secretary António Carneiro, and on one occasion to Vasco da Gama, the incoming viceroy of the Estado da Índia in 1524.[140] The bulk of the Arabic letters present serious problems of syntax and word order, which are the characteristic consequence of two features: their orality and the fact that the writers did not necessarily possess a high order of formal education in Arabic. They take us back to one of Aubin's own remarks in editing one of the letters: "The style of Baba 'Abdullah, that of a spoken language, is highly incorrect, grammatically, and the sense is often doubtful or ambiguous."[141] Further, some of them are mere fragments since sections of the letters have been destroyed with the passage of time.

The first document addressed by the Kolattiri to Dom Manuel begins with compliments and protestations of everlasting friendship and love.[142] Its tone then shifts abruptly and becomes one of complaint regarding unjust acts, which seem to include the brutal seizure by the Portuguese of ships returning from Hurmuz to Kannur, which have then been carried off to Kochi. The relationship, which began as a sweet one, has now turned quickly into "poison," writes the Kolattiri, adding that he is so disturbed that he "cannot sleep or eat, until your response arrives." This letter, written in an excellent scribal hand and with superior syntax, appears to be the work of Shams-ud-Din, arguably the Egyptian merchant Shams-ud-Din al-Misri, who was at the time resident in Kannur.[143] The next group of documents all come from the governorship of Afonso de Albuquerque, who is never referred to by name, only as the captain-major (*kabtan-mur*). They are addressed either to Dom Manuel or to António Carneiro, and beneath their exaggeratedly polite surface they show signs of a clear annoyance against Albuquerque and his policies. In particular, it is clear that the interruption to the horse trade from Hurmuz to Kannur is greatly resented. Some flattering remarks are addressed to the captain of the fortress, Jorge de Melo, but it is also pointed out that the Portuguese have a high-handed way about them in the town. Interestingly, the Kolattiri suggests sending two of his own representatives to Lisbon in order both to trade on his behalf and to act as his agents at the court to clear up any misunderstandings. Some gifts were also sent along to smooth matters.

We learn from the following documents that Albuquerque had in fact flatly refused to send the Kolattiri's representatives to Portugal. Further, nothing had been done in the following years to improve the situation concerning the horse trade from Hurmuz or the trade from Gujarat, for that matter. The letters from the Kolattiri adopt a somewhat plaintive turn here, as he realizes that his repeated requests are having no effect. They also mention his having sent an Indian slave to remain in the service of the Portuguese court. Another set of three documents then come not from the ruler but from his vizier, Chenicheri Kurup. The first, fragmented and brief, is addressed to António Carneiro, and it reminds him to keep the interests of Kannur at heart and requests a prompt response. The second, more formal and addressed to Dom Manuel, mentions a continuing series of issues, notably the lack of trade at Kannur because of the interruption in the traffic from Hurmuz and Gujarat. For the first time the relationship between Kannur and the "islands" (Lakshadwip and Maldives) finds some mention here. The last document in the series is addressed to Vasco da Gama in late 1524 (after his arrival in India) and is far more direct. It describes the deteriorating relationship with the *kabtan-mur* (here the governor, Dom Duarte de Meneses) in the preceding years and asks Gama to intervene in order to improve affairs. These documents can finally be read together with a letter in Portuguese, written by the same Chenicheri Kurup in 1549, now claiming to be weary after nearly four decades of mediating between the Kolattiri and the Portuguese.[144] The new ruler in Kannur apparently does not appreciate him very much. Caught between two stools, he pleads for a last grant, of the southern borderlands around Mayyazhi and Chombala, which he can turn to his own advantage and that of the Portuguese king (by this time Dom João III).[145] These were the very lands that a few decades later would become a major base for the great enemies of the Estado, the Kunjali Marakkars operating out of Iringal.

MEASURING CHANGE

The decades between the middle of the fifteenth century and the late 1510s witnessed a number of significant changes in the western Indian Ocean and its littoral societies, thus marking an epoch of transitions. Had 'Abdur Razzaq Samarqandi, who died in the early 1480s, rather improbably managed to live on for another four decades, he would have found a distinctly changed situation from the one that he had seen when he made his voyage to Calicut and Vijayanagara. A number of major polities had been swept away, fragmented, or reduced in size and importance, even though this was the case neither with Vijayanagara nor with Calicut. The Timurid political system, a dominant fact of life in West and Central Asia in the 1430s and 1440s, was a major casualty of these decades, even though many direct descendants of Timur could still be found dispersed across a large space. A low point for this system came with the death in May 1506 of Sultan Husain Baiqara, ruler of Herat. On the other hand, some significant new political forces had entered the scene, notably the Safavid order of heterodox Sufis, whose leaders, Shaikh Junaid and Shaikh Haidar, had been contemporaries of 'Abdur Razzaq. Initially contained (albeit with some difficulty) within the space of the Aqquyunlu polity, the Safavids progressively broke free of it in the course of the 1480s and 1490s, and their charismatic young leader Shah (or Shaikh) Isma'il captured the city of Tabriz in May 1501. Propelled by a messianic aura, which "unified radical Shi'i, Sufi, and Turko-Mongol beliefs and practices that attracted the militarized Turkmen clans of western Iran and Anatolia," Isma'il was able to consolidate his power against difficult odds in the course of the first decade of the sixteenth century.[146] He also actively sought to project his image beyond the Iranian plateau, and we know that in the last weeks of the life of Sultan Mahmud of Gujarat (in 1511), a Safavid envoy named Yadgar Beg Qizilbash arrived in his court for this very purpose.[147]

When Albuquerque first took Goa in the early part of 1510 he was somewhat surprised to find another Safavid envoy there who had been sent to Yusuf 'Adil Khan of Bijapur. He persuaded him to hand over the gifts intended for Bijapur and diverted them instead to Dom Manuel, who noted with pleasure that they included silk textiles, saddles, and saddle cloths, as well as what appears to have been the characteristic Safavid headgear (or *taj-i Haidari*).[148] In his discussions with the Safavid envoy, Albuquerque tried to make common cause and proposed that they build an alliance, since "Xeque Ismael was continually at war with the Turk and the grand Sultan of Cairo."[149] In his own way, and through a particular ideological prism, Albuquerque thus perceived that the emergence of the Safavids could produce a change in the political equilibrium of the zone between the Persian Gulf and the Red Sea, including the Hijaz. What could not be easily foreseen was the direction that this change would take. As has been noted, from the beginning of the reign of Sultan Qansuh, "every diplomatic mission between Constantinople (or Edirne) and Cairo always addressed the unexpected rise of the young Safavid leader Shah Isma'il, even in the face of more pressing concerns." Both Mamluks and Ottomans mobilized the same sort of rhetoric, not only claiming that the Safavids' Shi'ism posed a threat to them ideologically but also asserting that they "did not have any mercy for women, children, or scholars of religion."[150] However, the complicated pas de deux between the two great Sunni polities of the eastern Mediterranean that had seen many twists and turns over a century and a half began to show increasing stress with the accession to the Ottoman throne of Sultan Selim in 1512. In summer 1514, when the Ottoman sultan marched on the Safavids, the Mamluks stood by rather than participate, and thus they did not share in the glory of the victory at Chaldiran through which Shah Isma'il's prestige and charisma suffered lasting damage. The Ottomans may have even suspected that a secret entente had emerged between the other two powers. In the aftermath of this campaign, the Ottomans attacked the small Zu'l-qadri polity (*beylik*), which acted as a form of buffer between them and the Mamluks, and in a calculated insulting gesture sent the severed heads of its chiefs to Sultan Qansuh in 1515. Perhaps this was meant to test the view, increasingly propounded at the time, that the Mamluks no longer had either the military or the fiscal resources of a robust political regime. After a set of elaborate ploys and ruses, in August 1516, almost exactly two years from the battle of Chaldiran, Selim's forces and those of Sultan Qansuh faced each other at Marj Dabiq in Syria. The Mamluk sultan was killed and his army routed; five months later, Ottoman forces entered Egypt and took possession of Cairo and the considerable resources of Egypt, Syria, and beyond.

This somewhat unexpected dénouement and conquest of 1516–1517 found almost immediate echoes in the world of the western Indian Ocean through the Red Sea and the Hijaz. The Ottomans were hardly an unknown quantity in that world, and the Bahmani and Gujarat sultans had maintained relations with them, possibly from the time of the conquest of Constantinople in 1453. Ottoman officials in the Red Sea such as Qasim Sherwani thus made it a point to contact Sultan Muzaffar of Gujarat with a "victory bulletin" in 1517, and it is possible that they sent similar missives to other powers in the western Indian Ocean. The

Gujarat sultan's high-flown and somewhat formulaic answer has been preserved and comes down to us. But far more interesting is a reply to the Sublime Porte written by Malik Ayaz that, while somewhat disingenuous on some matters, nevertheless shows a thorough grasp of geostrategy in the maritime region.[151] As might be expected, he has only harsh words for Amir Husain and the earlier Mamluk expedition, which had behaved disgracefully in his view. Instead he proposes a comprehensive plan for a powerful Ottoman fleet headed by Selman Re'is, beginning with an attack on Hurmuz. Once that place had been captured, the next step would be to create a sizable establishment in Dabhol, in 'Adil Shahi territory. At the same time, some Ottoman forces should be sent as reinforcements to Diu. With Dabhol and Diu as centers, the maritime forces of the Portuguese—which were spread very thin over a number of establishments—could be progressively attacked and destroyed. Malik Ayaz admitted that in the past he had made an accommodation with the Portuguese for pragmatic reasons. With Ottoman support, though, he would once again renew his enmity with them in order to ensure that they were defeated.

This ambitious plan was never put into effect, whether during Malik Ayaz's lifetime or thereafter, though the Ottomans continued through much of the sixteenth century to take interest in the affairs of the Indian Ocean both for commercial and broader political motives.[152] These were the motives that took Hadim Süleyman Pasha into the Indian Ocean in 1538, and then Seydi 'Ali Re'is on his expedition in the 1550s, as noted briefly in the introduction. The shape and nature of Ottoman plans would be altered by the emergence of a new Timurid polity founded by Zahir-ud-Din Muhammad Babur in the 1520s and subsequently consolidated by his son and grandson over the following half-century. The chapters that follow will trace the vicissitudes of this interstate system as it emerged, and in which the Portuguese too played a role, but only as one among many actors.

Chapter 2

THE VIEW FROM THE HIJAZ, 1500–1550

> In this year [1502–1503], the vessels of the Frank appeared at sea *en route* for India, Hurmuz, and those parts. They took about seven vessels, killing those on board and making some prisoner. This was their first action, may God curse them.
>
> TARIKH AL-SHIHR

S patial models employed by historians of oceanic spaces can be as unconvincing as those of continental ones. Just as it is hard to argue that "Asia" as a space had a single dominant logic, the western Indian Ocean cannot easily be slotted into a scheme of centers and peripheries in the period that is our concern in this book.[1] In this chapter I will eschew any rigid schematization and instead observe the ocean from a vantage point without assuming the dominance of our point of departure, which is the Hijaz, the area around the Islamic holy cities of Mecca and Medina in the Arabian Peninsula. The significance of this area is obvious enough for a variety of reasons, though its location is ex-centric, lying as it does in the northwest corner of the western Indian Ocean. The Red Sea, on whose eastern shores the Hijaz lies, had been a channel through which commerce, individuals, and ideas had passed over many centuries.[2] With the rise of Islam in the early seventh century CE, a regular pilgrimage to the holy cities—the hajj (and its pendant, the 'umra)—was organized, drawing Muslims from an ever-widening circle that extended by the sixteenth century from northwestern Africa to the southeastern corner of Asia.

Recent years have seen a marked revival of interest in commercial and political relations between the Red Sea and western India in the period running from the eleventh and the fifteenth centuries—what is usually referred to as the later medieval epoch. This revival corresponds to the consolidation of the use of several sets of historical sources. In the first place, the project begun long decades ago by S. D. Goitein, on the Judeo-Arabic commercial materials of the Cairo Geniza relating to the Indian Ocean, has now matured with the posthumous publication of his "India Book" in 2008.[3] These materials largely relate to the period between the late eleventh and the early thirteenth centuries, and they involve ports and political centers both in northwestern India such as Bharuch, Khambayat, and Nahrwala (Anhilwada-Patan) and in Kerala and Karnataka such as Kollam, Pantalayini, Dharmapattanam, Valapattanam, and Mangalore. They can also be usefully supplemented by a smaller cache of Arabic materials deriving from the port of al-Qusair on the western shores of the Red Sea, largely from the thirteenth century.[4] To these we can add significant bodies of Arabic narrative materials from both the Yemen and Egypt, such as the chronicles of the Mamluks, Rasulids, and other significant dynasties in the area. Such narrative sources continued to be produced in the Yemen even after the Rasulids were replaced by the relatively short-lived Tahirid dynasty, which ruled between the mid-fifteenth and the early sixteenth centuries.[5]

Several analytical works have also contributed significantly to filling out our understanding of the Red Sea and its trade in the fourteenth and fifteenth centuries, thus helping to correct a somewhat distorted picture that had emerged from an excessive dependence on and backward reading of the Portuguese sources of the sixteenth century. A major achievement referred to in the preceding chapter is the work of the French historian Éric Vallet, which deals with the state and commerce under the Rasulid sultans of Yemen between about 1229 and 1454.[6] Vallet painstakingly demonstrates how the Rasulids set about building and then maintaining a commercial system in the course of the later thirteenth and fourteenth centuries that extended its tentacles beyond the Red Sea and well into the Indian Ocean. By combining the control of the coastal plains with that of the interior mountains of Yemen, the Rasulids managed to become central actors "in a world where Islam, trade, and the state had indissolubly linked their destinies."[7] Their system, centered on the port city of Aden but with a complex articulation, was challenged in part by traders from southwest India who decided to bypass the port and proceed instead directly to Jiddah in the 1420s. Aden did not entirely fall into ruin as a consequence, but its prosperity was challenged even as that of Jiddah grew over the course of the middle decades of the fifteenth century.

Another work complements and extends Vallet's analysis: John Meloy's examination of the relations of both the Mamluk sultans and the sharifs of Mecca with trade and traders between the late fourteenth and the early sixteenth centuries. The focus here is far more on the complex of Mecca and Jiddah than the ports and territories farther south in the Arabian Peninsula, and the central sources used are once again narrative materials in Arabic. Like the earlier historian Richard Mortel, Meloy notes that he has drawn extensively on writings "composed in Mecca during the fifteenth century by three generations of the Banu Fahd family," as well as their predecessor Taqi al-Fasi.[8] Using these writings, he is able to track useful data, for example, on arrivals and departures of ships in the Red Sea from India between about 1471 and 1537, notably from Calicut, Cambay, and Dabhol.[9] In particular, he makes extensive use of the text of the Mecca-based chronicler 'Izz-ud-Din 'Abdul 'Aziz ibn al-Najm ibn Fahd al-Makki, *Bulugh al-qira* (The Attainment of the Destination), completed around the time of the Ottoman conquest of the Hijaz in 1516–1517.[10]

The use of such sources as these risks bringing the historian face-to-face once again with an old quarrel between those who use narrative texts and those who use archives. Are these chronicles, which are obviously stylized narratives written within specific literary conventions, as reliable as the fragmented merchant letters of the Cairo Geniza or al-Qusair?[11] How are we to evaluate their truth claims and the conditions of their production? This chapter will not pretend to produce a full resolution to this quarrel. Rather, it will argue that the genre of the chronicle itself is rather capacious and that in some instances such texts actually come rather close to archival documents themselves. This is above all the case when the chronicle (or annalistic text) is not meant

TABLE 2.1. Indian ships arriving at Jiddah, 1483–1496

Year	Number of Ships	Origins
1483	21+	10 Calicut, 4 Cambay, 4 Dabhol
1484	13+	9 Calicut, 2+ Dabhol
1485	-	No available report
1486	11	7 Calicut, 4 Cambay
1487	2	2 Dabhol
1488	4+	2 Cambay, 2 Calicut
1489	21+	12+ Calicut, 4+ Dabhol, 2+ Cambay
1490	19	18 Calicut, 1 Dabhol
1491	12	12 Calicut
1492	17+	14+ Calicut, 2 Cambay
1493	8	4 Calicut, 3 Cambay, 1 Chaul
1494	19	14 Calicut, 4 Cambay
1495	4	2-3 Cambay, 1 Calicut
1496	16	8 Calicut, 4 Cambay, 1 Dabhol

Source: Meloy, *Imperial Power and Maritime Trade*, 249–251. (+) here indicates that the actual arrivals exceeded that number.

for wide circulation and thus has not undergone the process of polishing and rhetorical transformation that one normally expects within the genre. Importantly, the chapter will also try to show what the chronicles in question bring to an old subject that has been dealt with by a number of earlier authors, namely the relations in the fifteenth and sixteenth centuries between the region of Gujarat in western India on the one hand and the Red Sea and the Hijaz on the other.[12] These relations have been hitherto dealt with by using materials from Gujarat in Persian (and to a limited extent Arabic), together with sixteenth-century Portuguese chronicles and archival documents, and even Ottoman chronicles. What has so far been lacking for the sixteenth century is a view from the Hijaz. It is this gap that this chapter makes a claim to fill. At the same time, since the analysis is largely focused on a single text, it is important to begin by addressing the matter of its authorship and the subjective position of its author.

AN AUTHOR AND HIS CONTEXTS

In 2000 an important text appeared in print in Arabic, the existence of which had long been known to savants but had been barely explored by historians. This was the work by Jarullah ibn Fahd al-Makki entitled *Kitab Nail al-muna*.[13] Weighing in at more than a thousand pages in print and in two volumes, the publication hardly created a stir in the field of Indian Ocean history. My own attention had been drawn in the 1990s to the existence of this text, then in manuscript form, by the great French historian and orientalist Jean Aubin, who was attempting at the time to reconstruct the vicissitudes of the pepper and spice trade in the Red Sea in the early sixteenth century using Portuguese, Italian, and Arabic sources.[14] As it happens, only one manuscript of the *Nail al-muna* has been found so far, and that too in a damaged form. However, we do know a fair amount about the author, Jarullah (d. 954 AH/1547 CE), as well as his larger social and intellectual context. He may be inserted into a line of historians going back to the celebrated Taqi al-Fasi (d. 832 AH/1429), followed in turn by Jarullah's own grandfather and father, Najm ibn Fahd (d. 885 AH/1480), and 'Izz-ud-Din ibn Fahd (d. 922 AH/1517), briefly mentioned earlier. Jarullah's own notional successor as a chronicler, though he was not a relative, was the well-known Indo-Meccan intellectual Qutb-ud-Din Muhammad Nahrawali (d. 990 AH/1582), about whom we will say more.[15]

Taqi al-Fasi had already set the intellectual tone in the late fourteenth and early fifteenth centuries. A prolific author, he is known to have written more than thirty works of history, most focused on Mecca and its principal personalities.[16] These works were for the most part organized on three patterns. The first recounts the history of the holy cities of Medina and Mecca, their particularities, and religious, social, intellectual, and cultural features; such texts, numbering about a half-dozen, tend to resemble each other a fair deal and overlap in considerable measure. The second emphasizes the biographies of scholars and other eminent citizens of Mecca, corresponding broadly to the *tazkira* genre; the text entitled *'Iqd al-Samin* is a prominent example of this. The third type of work focuses more on the rulers (*hukkam*) and officials of Mecca in different periods. The most important of these works is *Wulat-u Makka fi al-Jahiliya wa al-Islam*, of which the author himself then prepared a summary version.

Taqi al-Fasi's most significant disciple was Najm-ud-Din 'Umar ibn Muhammad ibn Fahd al-Makki al-Hashimi, who surpassed him at least quantitatively (if not in reputation and influence) by writing more than forty works on history and related subjects. As with his master, the best of these is related to Mecca and the lives of Meccans. The first of his books that is known is a kind of annal entitled *Ithaf al-wara*.[17] This work is based stylistically on such classical authors as Tabari, Ibn al-Asir, Al-Zahbi, and Ibn al-Qasir, and it was Najm-ud-Din's endeavor to join the history of Mecca to that of the Islamic world in general. He begins in the very first year of the Hijri calendar and takes his chronology through to 885 Hijri. Besides this, Najm-ud-Din also wrote a sort of dictionary of the principal people of Mecca. We might see this too as a continuation of his master's work, even though he added a number of subjects and persons that Taqi had either missed or who came after his life. Najm-ud-Din also wrote on the history on the great families (*awa'il*) of Mecca, some five books in all. These great families included his own, the Banu Fahd, the al-Tubur (from which the great chronicler Tabari hailed), the al-Nuwaira, the al-Qustulani, and the Banu Zuhaira. He also commenced a text entitled *Bughyat al-maram*, which was completed with a commentary by his son 'Izz-ud-Din under the title *Ghayat al-maram*. In the next generation, 'Izz-ud-Din ibn Fahd appears to have inherited a love for the history of Mecca from his father. He compiled a continuation (or *zail*) to his father's annals, which began chronologically where Najm-ud-Din had left matters and took them up to the year of his own death. This text, as I have noted, was entitled *Bulugh al-qira*, and ran from the month of Ramazan 885 AH to Rabi' II 922 AH (1517 CE), just before the author's death.[18] In this work, we find numerous details of politics, society, economy, institutional administration, and the like, largely focused on the Haram Sharif and those linked to it, as well as the hajj pilgrimage. Like his father, 'Izz-ud-Din also wrote extensively in a biographical (or semihagiographic) mode on the great shaikhs of the time.

This, then, was the rather unique intellectual heritage of Jarullah ibn Fahd, from the third generation of a substantial and established lineage of chroniclers. He too produced a continuation that he added to his father's work, calling it *Nail al-muna*, with the full title translating broadly as "The Realization of the Desire to Attain the Destination; Notes for the Completion of a Gift to Mankind with the Annals of the Mother of Cities [Mecca]." This text, containing many details of Mecca's day-to-day life, begins in the month of Zi-Hijja 923 AH and ends in Jumada II 949 AH. Jarullah was of course fully aware that he was from a particularly important Meccan family, with a genealogical chain ostensibly extending to Muhammad ibn Hanafiyya. Of high status, albeit not Sayyids, the family had long been settled in Asfun in Upper Egypt, known for its extensive Shi'ite population. They appeared to have moved to Mecca in the eighth century AH or thereabouts, and a few members find mention in at least one of Taqi al-Fasi's books, such as Abu'l Khair ibn Fahd (d. 735 AH) and Jamal-ud-Din ibn Fahd (also d. 735 AH). Besides history, the Banu Fahd family was quite diverse in its intellectual interests, in areas such as hadith and *adab*; four of them (including Jarullah himself) were known as *hafiz* (memorizers) in the matter of hadith, which meant they had memorized thousands of traditions of the Prophet and their chains of transmission (*isnad*). Other prominent Meccan families regularly accepted marriage alliances with them, and several of them also attained significant administrative positions in the Hijaz. Their prominence as a Meccan intellectual dynasty seems to have lasted about three centuries, and one of their last eminent members was 'Abdur Rahman ibn 'Abdul Qadir ibn al-'Izz ibn Fahd (d. 995 AH), in the second half of the sixteenth century, possibly a nephew of Jarullah himself. We are thus dealing with a self-conscious set of intellectuals, aware of their own status and imbued with some sense of importance; we know that two generations before Jarullah, Najm-ud-Din had already written a family history, entitled *Bazl al-jahd* (The Profitable Use of Effort). In his turn, Jarullah, too, wrote a sort of family history as well as another work on their family's residence and stay in Mecca; these works endured, and 'Umar al-Shamma' later composed a commentary on several of the books written by this family.[19]

Turning in more detail to the figure of Jarullah ibn Fahd, a certain number of basic elements of his biography are accessible to us. He was born in Mecca on 20 Rajab 891 AH (July 23, 1486). His mother was also a member of the Banu Fahd, her name being Kamaliyya bint Muhibb Abu Bakr Ahmad ibn Muhammad ibn Fahd. It is reported that his father 'Izz-ud-Din took great care to educate him and began to send him to formal classes at the age of four. Jarullah quickly memorized the Qur'an and was also introduced into the hadith by his father, who obviously was a great influence on him intellectually. But a decision was then taken to widen his horizons somewhat. Jarullah was thus sent off to Cairo in his early twenties, in the year 913 AH, in order to learn hadith; after that he went on to Syria and various Ottoman cities. The very next year, in Rabi' I 914 AH, we find him in Yemen, where he stayed for some four months to study with the historian 'Abdur Rahman Diba' in Zabid, who was sufficiently impressed to mention this disciple in one of his works. Some years later, in 922 AH, he was in Damascus and Aleppo, and it was during this period that his father 'Izz-ud-Din passed away.[20] This was also broadly the moment of the Ottoman conquest of Egypt, Syria, and the Hijaz, and in later years Jarullah undertook several visits to the Ottoman heartland of Anatolia to discuss matters with prominent scholars there, but also to build up his personal library of manuscripts. It was while visiting Bursa and Istanbul in 928 AH that he wrote a work entitled *Jawahir al-Hassan fi manaqib al-Sultan Sulayman ibn 'Usman*, in praise of the Ottoman ruler of the time. From Jarullah's own scattered writings as well as those of others, both contemporary and later, we have a fairly good sense of his chief teachers. These included his own father, Shams-ud-Din Muhammad ibn 'Abdul Rahman al-Sakhawi and Zakariyya ibn Muhammad al-Ansari (from whom he learned *fiqh*), among scholars in several disciplines. Interestingly, they also included two women: Umm Salima bint Muhammad al-Tabari al-Makki and Fatima bint Kamal ibn Sirin (a prominent figure in the matter of the interpretation of dreams).

Like his father and grandfather, Jarullah was a highly prolific scholar. The modern editor of the *Nail al-muna*, Muhammad Habib al-Hila, lists some forty-nine works by him on a variety of subjects, from the history of the Hijaz to hadith, *akhlaq* (political ethics), and related issues.[21] Known titles of texts, many of which do not actually survive, suggest some of the subjects he discussed:

- a text on Ottoman construction activities in Mecca, entitled *Nukhbat bahjat al-zaman bi-'imarat Makka li-muluk Bani 'Usman*;[22]
- On the imams of the four schools of jurisprudence;
- On towns and urbanism;

- a treatise on the entry of plague (*ta'un*) into Mecca and Medina (this text is lost);
- several first-person travel accounts, which are referred to by other contemporaries but again seem not to have survived;
- a text on coffee: *Qama' al-shahwat* ("The uprooting of sexual desire; a refutation of the untruths of the coffee administrators");[23]
- *Mu'jam al-Shu'ara'*, an account of poets of his time from whom he had heard verses;
- *Manhal al-zarafa*, a humorous account that exists in a partial manuscript regarding those who were involved with rulership (*saltanat* and *khilafat*); and finally,
- a somewhat controversial text entitled *Nukat al-Ziraf*, or "Laughter-inducing points," which we know led Jarullah to be involved in some fierce debates and controversies regarding his tendency to mock others for their "disabilities."[24]

Jarullah ibn Fahd died in the early morning of Tuesday, 15 Jumada I 954 AH (July 3, 1547). Several contemporary writers fondly remembered him, among whom we can mention 'Abdur Rahman al-Sakhawi and the chronicler Ibn Tulun, who refers to him on more than one occasion in his *Mufakahat*. Besides being remembered by his disciples for the quality of his teaching, he cast a significant shadow on later generations, as we see from even a later text such as Aydarusi's *Nur al-Safir*.[25]

THE TEXT AND ITS PROBLEMS

As I already mentioned, a sole manuscript of the *Nail al-muna* has come down to us, thus rendering it more like an archival document than most other texts of these dimensions. This manuscript carries the title of the text on its first page in the hand of none other than Qutb-ud-Din Muhammad Nahrawali, and it is conserved today in the Süleymaniye Kütüphanesi, Istanbul (with the reference Collection Şehid Ali Paşa Ms. No. 1961).[26] It is made up of 198 folios of middle size, with thirty-one lines per page not written in a particularly distinguished script, and there are two sets of notations on it. The manuscript seems to have been produced fairly close to the author's lifetime, though it is certainly not in his handwriting. (It is also evidently posthumous, since it refers to Jarullah himself as having passed on.) Because many of the additional notations are from the hand of Nahrawali, we can date it to within his lifetime (Nahrawali died in 990 AH, or 1582). The manuscript then seems to have passed after Nahrawali through various other hands, with one of the owners being 'Abdul 'Aziz, and then his children. From this family, it passed on to Hajji Mustafa, a former *qazi* (judge) of the port of Tripoli in Syria in 1094 AH, and then to Wajih-ud-Din ibn Ibrahim. The anonymous scribe claims, incidentally, that he copied the text from an autograph manuscript, but that the latter was itself difficult and defective, with things that had been frequently crossed out and changed. It would appear that Nahrawali then corrected this scribal copy and made changes that are often rather useful and important, since the scribe had frequently introduced grammatical and lexicographical errors.

The *Nail al-muna* was begun in Zi al-Hijja 923 AH (the end of 1517), very soon after its predecessor, *Bulugh al-qira* ended, although there is a gap between the two, probably owing to Jarullah's absence from Mecca at the time of his father's death. It clearly has a secretive quality, for reasons that will become evident. For it seems clear that Jarullah himself was not interested in widely divulging this work, unlike many of his others, probably because it expressed critiques of various aspects of his time.[27] To begin with, there are a number of quite forceful critiques here of the new Ottoman dispensation. This was natural enough, since the Mamluk-Ottoman transition was obviously not a smooth one, even on sectarian grounds, between a Shafi'i administration (the Mamluks) and a Hanafi one (the Ottomans). As for Jarullah himself, it is clear that he was Shafi'i, as were most of his family members. He also appears to have seen the transition as exacerbating tensions between Turks and Arabs, with the Turks even preferring the so-called 'Ajamis to the Arabs. An example of this was in the administration of the port of Jiddah, which came under a *na'ib* (deputy), Qasim Sherwani.[28] Jarullah also made it a point to describe how at the moment of the conquest of Mecca the occupying Ottoman army misbehaved; more generally, he takes every opportunity to denounce Ottoman corruption, notably in the matter of the management of inheritance.

Jarullah also frequently underlined the ignorance of the *faqihs* (jurists) and *qazis* under the new dispensation. He went so far as to claim that people who did not even know how to read the Qur'an correctly began to lead the prayers, while the k̲h̲utba prayer in the Haram Sharif was regularly read by incompetents. Again, the alms (*sadaqat*) were misused and misappropriated, while newly appointed officials poked their noses into where these alms came from. These were not generalized accusations; for Jarullah even gives individual names in this context, calling them liars, takers of false oaths, quarrelsome, and so on. But this is not some simple nostalgia for the pre-1517 dispensation either. While apparently praising the sharifs of Mecca, Jarullah does not always like their policies, either—their habit of taking one-third of some of the alms donated from afar, for example. Still, all in all, he thought the Ottomans were unjust in their treatment of the sharifs. These forceful and even violent criticisms and claims that the Ottomans were violating the shari'a itself (along with local traditions and social mores) made the *Nail al-muna* a highly problematic text. We can thus understand why Jarullah did not publicize this work, never referred to it in his other works, or even bothered to revise it and produce a clean manuscript copy. He did show it to some friends and intimates, however. These included 'Abdul Qadir al-Jaziri, who in his works refers several times to Jarullah's text without giving its title.[29] Again, Qutb-ud-Din Muhammad Nahrawali in the well-known chronicle *al-Barq al-Yamani* summarizes some passages from the *Nail*, also without citing its title.[30] The text apparently even finds echoes in some later historians such as 'Ali al-Sanjari's *Mana'ih al-Karam* and Muhammad al-Tabari's *Ithaf-i fuzala' al-zaman*.

With regard to Jarullah's methods and coverage as an annalist, it would seem that he followed closely in the footsteps of his grandfather and father. Chronologically, Jarullah's own coverage runs from the month of Zi al-Hijja 923 AH (end of 1517) to Rajab 946 AH (roughly November 1539), more or less twenty-three years, with some gaps when he was absent from Mecca. The chronological order is fairly well maintained through the text, and each year has a proper heading, as does each month. In the month of Zi al-Hijja, he always gives a fair number of details regarding the hajj of that particular year. In a similar fashion, he also gives some details of the *'umra* (or secondary pilgrimage) in Ramazan, including the end of the month and its celebrations. A third month he regularly emphasizes is Rabi' I, the birth month of the Prophet. However, in three years (939, 940, and 941 AH) there seems to be some disorder in the text, possibly because Jarullah was somewhat away from Mecca in these years but perhaps for other personal reasons. Further, there is an enigmatic gap between the end of the work and his death of almost eight years. Either some pages have been lost, or Jarullah stopped writing the annals in his last years.

The text of the *Nail al-muna* is marked by its author's talent for pithy description and evocation. Despite his sympathies, which have been noted, he is very clear in his analysis of the strengths and weaknesses of both the sharifs and their subordinates. Besides the transition to Ottoman rule, which is carefully described, notable attention is devoted to the officials in charge of the hajj, and their relationship both with the sharifs and the Meccans themselves. As regards the outside world, Mecca's relationship with Egypt is well set out, as are the dealings with both Yemen and—more to the point of our discussion—India. Jarullah takes a particular interest in the goings and comings of *'ulama'* and traders, as well as envoys (*qasidun*) of various sorts. Insofar as economic questions go, the functioning of the *suqs* and trade regularly hold his attention. Jarullah also quite meticulously notes the arrival of ships in Jiddah.[31] From a more ethical perspective, the hoarding of goods by traders, and the dispensation's concern with checking this, is also one of his preoccupations. Jarullah tracks the prices of foodstuffs, such as wheat, millet, oil, honey, meats, fruits, and vegetables, noting in particular when prices go up or down dramatically. Social stratification in Meccan society, and a sense of the changing situation of the rich and poor is a subsidiary theme in the *Nail al-muna*. At the level of sociocultural observation, the text notes collective occasions, religious festivals, and the hajj as significant objects of interest, as well as the sighting of the moon in relation to 'Ids. On the matter of urban space, he notes the changes to the rest houses and religious buildings in Mecca, as well as the significant alms and charitable donations by the Ottoman state. The deaths of principal persons are carefully chronicled, with the name of the deceased, date and time of death, type of prayers, and place of burial. Similarly, Jarullah makes it a point to note the births of members of important families. In the case of some marriages he goes into great detail, including who was present on the two sides. From the viewpoint of the historian of food, the text also gives us plenty of information on the kinds of foodstuffs and drinks on special occasions, the stews, rice preparations, meats, sweets, and other things. It turns out that even coffee (*qahwa*) was sometimes offered on these occasions, despite its dubious moral status.[32]

THE HIJAZ AND GUJARAT

As can be seen, the *Nail al-muna* is a text of considerable potential in regard to quite a variety of subjects. This chapter focuses on a particular issue: the references therein to relations between Mecca and the Red Sea on the one hand and Gujarat on the other. Scholars of sixteenth-century commercial and imperial history in the region have dealt with this subject already, in a variety of ways and using a diversity of source materials. Among Ottomanist historians, the chief works of the past decades include those of Salih Özbaran with regard to the Ottomans in the Indian Ocean, Suraiya Faroqhi on the Ottoman administration of the Holy Cities, Jean-Louis Bacqué-Grammont on military and dip-

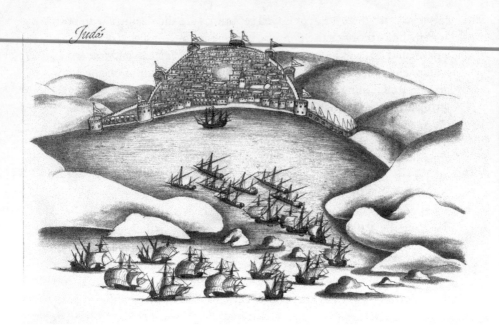

FIGURE 2.1. Port of Jiddah as drawn by Gaspar Correia, *Lendas da Índia*.

lomatic questions, and most recently the ambitious synthesis proposed by Giancarlo Casale, using both Ottoman and Portuguese records.[33] From an Indian perspective, the work of Naimur Rahman Farooqi on Mughal-Ottoman diplomatic relations attempted to cross materials from the two great Sunni-oriented empires of the period.[34] A number of authors since E. Denison Ross in the 1920s have equally approached the question of the Portuguese intervention in the area, among whom the work of Vitorino Magalhães Godinho is notable.[35] In the early 1960s, Robert Serjeant published an important selection of translated Hadrami sources in Arabic regarding the Portuguese, including materials from the *Tarikh al-Shihr* (or *al-Shahar*) of Ba Faqih.[36] In earlier collaborative work with Muzaffar Alam, I have written several essays and chapters with regard both to the western Indian Ocean in the first half of the sixteenth century and Ottoman-Gujarati relations at the time, and to the Mughals and the hajj after the conquest of Gujarat in 1572–1573.[37] In doing so I drew considerable inspiration from the work of the late Jean Aubin on this subject, much of which appeared posthumously, and which drew on a whole panoply of materials in Portuguese, Italian, Ottoman, Arabic, and Persian.[38] Like Aubin, I have proceeded on the understanding that Portuguese sources can give us only a partial picture and that they need constant and careful contextualization.

At the time the *Nail al-muna* begins, the sultan of Gujarat was Muzaffar Shah (r. 1511–1525), while another powerful figure was the governor of the port of Diu, Malik Ayaz, discussed in the previous chapter. In one of the first mentions of Gujarat in his text, Jarullah thus reports the arrival of large sums of money at Mecca from Muzaffar Shah, a feature which he notes had been usual from about 922 AH. These sums, he further remarks, were received by Khwaja Taj-ud-Din Jokdar Lari, an Iranian who held the position of the *amin* of the Gujarat charities in the holy city. He also reports the decision taken on 12 Safar 924 AH (February 1518) that the amount was to be divided half and half between Mecca and Medina.[39] A few months later, in May of the same year, it is reported that Yusuf Zanji, a prominent figure, had arrived from Diu to Jiddah, carrying supplies and other things. At much the same time, another ship, this one a royal vessel, arrived from Cambay belonging to Muzaffar Shah himself.[40] Such royal vessels were apparently quite a regular presence in the Red Sea from Gujarat, for again in March 1519 (Rabi' I 925 AH) a messenger came to Mecca with news that a royal Indian ship from Cambay had arrived off Jiddah in the company of three others, all under the direction of Khwaja Muhammad ibn Shaikh 'Ali Gilani. This small fleet apparently carried a number of Meccan residents who had gone to India on visits and had now returned. There were further arrivals in May, and among the things that were brought for Mecca was a very large Qur'an written in the hand of Muzaffar Shah, which he offered as a gift. The money accompanying this gift was a further sixteen thousand dinars, but there were also rich cloths, lac, indigo, and other goods.[41] Jarullah notes that a great ceremony was held in public for the reception of the Gujarat sultan's Qur'an and its proper installation. It also turned out that Muzaffar Shah had expressed his interest in buying some land for the construction of a madrasa. The land that was acquired belonged to a Syrian trader, who had been in India and even met the sultan personally. But there was some untoward delay in the transaction; the sultan became annoyed and pressed his agents to complete the purchase quickly. He was told that permission had to be obtained from the *na'ib* of Egypt and from the Ottoman Sultan Selim himself, but this delicate task was accomplished through the intercession of the sharifs. Not long after, by the month of Ramazan 925 AH, it was reported that the Muzaffari *madrasa* was now up and running; ten men had been appointed to it at varying salaries and additional stipends, most of them significant Hanafite *'ulama'* but also the odd Shafi'is (two out of the ten).[42]

The image that directly emerges even from these first mentions is of Gujarat as a highly prosperous region, with a devout ruler and a vibrant network of mercantile and religious activity involving a number of ethnicities: East Africans, Iranians, Syrians, and so on. This is further confirmed in a notice from the month of Sha'ban 925 AH (August 1519), which reports the arrival of a number of ships from India, including three of royal origin (*shahi al-muzaffari*), with a great many merchants on board who were natives of Rum, Syria, 'Ajam, and Aleppo, as well as India. Among the prominent shipowners was a native of Aleppo named Barakat Halabi. Jarullah suggests that there had been an earlier depression in trade, but that there was now a visible improvement. This meant in turn that the Meccan intellectuals could think of the Gujarat court as a regular source of support and patronage. When these ships return to India, Jarullah declares, he intends to send two books which he had written of late: one for Sultan Muzaffar entitled *Husn al-suluk fi fazl al-muluk* (containing hadith and other religious traditions), the other for the Gujarat vizier Khudawand Khan, with the title *Tuhfat al-masnad al-'ali bi nukhbat al-asanid al-'awali*. He further notes that many other Meccan scholars had begun to send their *qasidas* and other works for the favor of the Gujarat sultan, while still others were now intending to go to India from Mecca in search of livelihood (*al-rizq*). The latter group included such men as Shaikh Muhammad ibn Abi al-Khair al-Hariri, Shaikh Nur-ud-Din 'Ali ibn 'Abdur Ra'uf ibn Zahira (a relative of the *qazi* of Jiddah), 'Abdul Wahhab al-Ahmadi (a noted singer), and his friend Muhammad al-Badri, as well as Shaikh Nasir al-Muhaddis. Indeed, there were so many of these potential savant migrants that the traders on the ships felt they were becoming something of a nuisance. So it was only with some difficulty that Shaikh Nasir, for example, finally found a passage on Barakat Halabi's ship.[43]

The text now begins to mention the Portuguese (whom it calls Franks) and their threatening activities with increasing frequency, in relation also to Gujarat and India more generally. In the month of Jumada II 926 AH (May 1520), rumors spread that some Franks who were headed from Dahlak to Hind had tried unsuccessfully to attack a Gujarati royal ship bringing gifts and alms for Mecca while it was off Aden.[44] Not long after, in January 1521 (Safar 927 AH), some traders arrived in Mecca from Aden with papers and disturbing news. It was reported that a ship belonging to the Syrian trader Sajur al-Shami had been captured by the Franks near Hind. All those on board had been imprisoned after a fight with many casualties, and the ship itself had been burned. Another ship on its way to India from Aden was also sunk, while two other ships that had left Jiddah, one carrying Malik Muhammad Gilani (the *wakil* of the Muzaffari charities), were also attacked. It was rumored more broadly that in their headquarters at Goa, the infidel Franks were getting ready to mount a major attack on Sultan Muzaffar Shah.[45] By March that year further news came to Mecca from Jiddah, sent by the Indians who had just arrived there, that the Franks who lived in Hurmuz had attacked Muzaffar Shah in Cambay but that he had defeated them despite the fact that they were twenty thousand strong (and some even claimed they were as many as 100,000). The Franks had attempted to land in some towns in Gujarat, and even though they had been defeated they continued to fight, so that Muzaffar Shah then asked the Lodi Sultan of Delhi for aid (it is noted that he was given promises, but no concrete help).[46] The same season brought news of the arrival of two ships in Jiddah from India, of which one was from Bharuch ("Barvaj" in the text), carrying alms and donations from a prominent amir of that port called Khair-ud-Din, as well as from Malik Iyas (or Ayaz), described as the *na'ib* of Sultan Muzaffar. As for the other ship, it came from Diu and belonged to the same Barakat Halabi, whom we have already encountered. The *nakhuda* (captain) of this ship sent some papers to Mecca from Jiddah with distressing news to the effect that when the royal ships for that year had come out from the port of Cambay, they had been attacked by Frankish ships; some had managed to get away, but others had not.[47] Jarullah sounds a skeptical note here, noting that some people believed that this was a false rumor being spread in order to raise the price of the Indian goods on those ships that had in fact arrived.[48] Even so, it is clear from these mentions that the Portuguese were a growing concern for the traders of the Red Sea and Mecca.

The Portuguese interest in Jiddah and its trade dated back to at least the 1510s, during the governorships of Afonso de Albuquerque and Lopo Soares de Albergaria. On the occasion of an unsuccessful attack on the port mounted by the latter in 1517, the chronicler Castanheda provides us the following description of Jiddah and its surroundings:

> After these fifteen days of a westerly wind had passed, there arose a strong breeze from the east so that the fleet arrived in Judá [Jiddah], which is a city on the coast of Arabia 180 leagues from the entrance to the Straits and 165 from Suez which is at its end, at 21 and a half degrees on the side of the North [21° 32']. Two leagues from the port there are many shallows, in which there are many rocks, and from there one has two channels through which one can enter the port, and they are winding, one from east to west and one from northeast to southwest, and whoever follows them must carry a sounding line at hand,

for they are so narrow that one *nao* can barely fit in each one: and on that account this road [*esta barra*] is very dangerous. The location of this city is on such dry ground that there are no groves of trees or greenery, and very little sweet water, for it only rains very rarely: at this time, it would have had a thousand households [*mil vezinhos*]. Its houses are of stone and lime, with multiple levels, with many windows and chimneys. It has a good supply of foodstuff [*mantimentos*], that comes from the outside, and many goods, because it here that are brought together all those that go from India to Cairo and Alexandria, and from these two cities to India. Seven leagues from this city to the interior is the accursed house of Mecca, to which the Moors make their pilgrimages (as the Christians do to the holy sepulcher at Jerusalem), because here is the mummy [*ho çancarrão*], which they say is of the abominable Mafamede.[49]

The suggestion is thus of a compact settlement, with a population numbering around five or six thousand, far smaller than a sizable maritime center such as Hurmuz or Surat later in the century.

There is now an interval of some years in Jarullah's account in terms of mentions of Gujarat. We know from Ottoman sources that these were the very years when they were beginning to make concrete plans to attack the Portuguese positions in India. In 1525 the captain Salman Re'is prepared a report for the Sublime Porte describing the military resources and supplies that the Ottomans had at Jiddah and elsewhere, laying out the possessions of the Portuguese in India, and the situation in Yemen. He wrote: "It is said that the accursed Portuguese hold the above-mentioned ports with [only] two thousand men. Therefore, when our ships are ready, and, God willing, move against them, their total destruction will be inevitable, for one fortress is unable to support another and they are not able to put up united opposition."[50] As we know, however, Salman was not the most discreet of tacticians, boasting of his plans to the Venetian *bailo* (bailiff) in Istanbul, who duly reported his claims to his superiors in December 1525.

> Suliman Rays has spoken to him of the matters of India, on coming [there] from Cairo, and he said he had been named captain of the fleet of the Soldan Gauri [Qansuh al-Ghauri] against the Portuguese, so as to chase the said Portuguese from India, saying that the Signor [Süleyman] wishes to prepare a fleet for India, and send him for that enterprise; and he has ordered the

making in Alexandria of two great galleys and one supply ship with munitions for this end, in which there will be some 2,000 men for this purpose; and he said that in Alziden [Jiddah] there would be 30 galleys in order, and some galliots.[51]

Jarullah, ever with his ear to the ground, also caught wind of some of these rumors. In the month of Zi al-Qa'da 932 AH (August 1526) he noted that a large sum of money had been accumulated in Jiddah for the Ottoman Sultan by the *na'ib* there, 'Ali Rumi, amounting to about 280,000 dinars. But the sultan had now sent orders that this money should be set aside for the force that was being prepared by the captain Salman against the Franks in India (*li-yusraf 'ala al-'askar al-mujahhazin lil-Faranj fi jihat al-Hind al-qabtan Salman*). The sultan had also written a letter to the sharif of Mecca explaining his intentions in the matter and ordered the *na'ib* of Jiddah to implement his command. But some misunderstandings had then arisen between the sharif (at this time Muhammad Abu Numayy) and Salman, since the former felt his revenues were increasingly being encroached upon. The people of Mecca also felt that the preparation of this force in Jiddah was causing them a certain nuisance. Eventually, the *na'ib* of Jiddah had to come to Mecca to placate the sharif, whom he reassured by saying that the Ottomans were not like the Egyptian Mamluks, who often made promises they did not keep. All this was a temporary measure to raise revenues and increase the strength of the Ottomans, he declared. Rumors also spread now that when the captain Salman reached Jiddah he fortified it because he feared that the sharif would attack him, and that the Arabs and Ottomans were headed for an imminent conflict. Fortunately, Jarullah reports, matters calmed down in the end.[52]

One can see clear traces here of Jarullah's skepticism regarding the Ottomans and their policies. Yet, at the same time, he is also clearly admiring of their military prowess in these very years. In the month of Rabi' I 933 AH, when news arrived rather belatedly in Mecca via Egypt of the sultan's victory over the Europeans near Belgrade in the course of his jihad there, Jarullah rejoiced in the superiority of the sultan's tactics in the siege, and the extent of his victory, which apparently involved the taking of fifteen other forts.[53] Jarullah's elation is such at this great victory that he claims the Ottomans have managed to extend Muslim power where it has never been before.[54] On the eastern front, too, it would seem that they stand as a bulwark against the ambitions of the Franks, not only on the sea but on land. Thus, he notes the arrival at Mecca in the month of Muharram 933 AH of a large overland caravan via Yemen bringing Shaikh Rashid ibn Mughamis ibn Saqar ibn Muhammad ibn Fazl, who had been the ruler of Basra and Qatif and came accompanied by an entourage of five thousand persons. That whole area had sunk into chaos because the Franks had killed the chief there, Shaikh Muqrin ibn Zamil al-Jabri, not long before, and a succession struggle had followed. It is implied that a strong external hand had been needed to set this house in order.[55]

The narrative of the eventual failure of Salman Re'is's expeditionary force and his own assassination is known to us from other sources, both Ottoman and Portuguese. As for Jarullah, he notes in Jumada I 936 AH that disturbances had been reported in Yemen against the Ottomans. One of Salman's former lieutenants, his nephew Amir Mustafa Bairam Rumi, who was now governor of Zabid, had been attacked and one of his forts taken by people from Aden. What made the matter particularly complicated was that Bairam had heard that while the Arabs were planning a rebellion against him, a Portuguese fleet was also approaching Aden. So he had at one and the same time to act against the Arabs and send ships out against the Portuguese. This proved too much for him to manage, and the Ottomans in Mecca were greatly disturbed at this news.[56] So great were the tensions at this time that wild rumors began to gain currency. Thus, in the month of Sha'ban 936 AH, news arrived in Mecca that the Indian ships that had been coming that year to Jiddah had been attacked by the Franks near the Bab-al-Mandeb. It was claimed that the prow of Yusuf Turki's ship was damaged, and the ship itself was looted. A small panic set in, and prices of Indian goods rose in Mecca. The ship eventually appeared in Jiddah, as did two others, and the rumor of the attack turned out to be false.[57] But on other occasions rumors of attacks by the Portuguese did have a real basis. This was the case in Zi al-Qa'da 938 AH (July 1532), when some people came in from the south Arabian port of Shihr with news that some of the Franks had invaded their town, captured their ships, and seized their goods.[58]

Later that year word began to spread that the Ottoman court had stirred into action in the face of all this turbulence and that the sultan had appointed a group in Suez to prepare for the fight against the Franks in India.[59] At the same time, the Portuguese too began to make increasingly aggressive moves. In early 939 AH (September 1532), it was reported in Mecca that a *ghurab* (small vessel) carrying Franks had come to Kamaran Island in the Yemen to gather information on the Muslim forces there. This growing menace apparently caused consternation in Mecca. The Portuguese seemed to be spreading their tentacles everywhere, for a few months later Jarullah received word from a friend in Shihr, Ahmad ibn

Muhammad al-Harawi al-Makki, with more detailed news of them. In this message it was noted that on 3 Jumada I 939 AH, a Frankish *ghurab* had menacingly approached al-Shihr, forcing another vessel to come toward the town. An unscrupulous man named Khwaja 'Abdullah al-'Ajami al-Aqta had seized the affairs of this ship from it, dragged it on shore, and broken it up, sharing the proceeds with some other people from among the 'Umayra, who came and took what was left. Jarullah's friend was particularly dismayed that these people (some of whom he seems to suggest are Bedouins) were hand in glove with the Franks and shared the proceeds of looting with them. It was also rumored that year that the many ships heading toward Jiddah from India were now under severe threat. One particularly active Portuguese captain had been making a menace of himself near Shihr and had already plundered several ships, including a Turkish vessel heading to India from Jiddah.[60]

Jarullah's correspondent further informed him of news regarding Gujarat that had been received in Shihr through a small ship that had arrived there, carrying the son of Yusuf Khatuni. He reported that when they were in the vicinity of Diu they had been surrounded by some thirty-eight Frankish ships, which were followed by an even larger fleet of 150 vessels that intended to capture Diu fort.[61] The Franks had run rampant that year, capturing as many as twenty Muslim passenger ships belonging to Yemen, Aden, and al-Mahra. They had also had some vigorous fights with ships from Jiddah, one owned by Muhammad 'Ali. A ship's captain (here, *nakhuza*), Muhammad Malu, had fought bravely against them but was eventually overpowered, even though he managed to drive a Portuguese *ghurab* onto land. Many passengers had jumped from their ships from fear and been carried off by the waves. In all of this, it was said that some two hundred people died like sacrificial goats before the Portuguese butchers. They included some prominent persons: the son of Khwaja Qadir-ud-Din, who was the son-in-law of Khwaja Barakat Halabi; the son of Khwaja Zain-ud-Din al-'Ajami, formerly *nazir* in Jiddah; and many others, especially among the so-called 'Ajamis.[62]

It was reported that when news of these depredations reached the Gujarat court, the ruler, Bahadur Shah, was furious. Among the ships that survived the first wave of attacks was one belonging to the so-called Rumi *sanjakdar* (perhaps the Ottoman governor at Jiddah), which had made its way first to a port generically termed "Fattan" (possibly Somnath), and then to Diu. Here its luck ran out, for it was again attacked by the Franks, driven aground, and set on fire. A few other ships did manage to flee to Somnath in safety, but once again the Franks caught up with them, burned them mercilessly, and captured the people on board. In

India and many other coastal towns there was great consternation as a result. Rice had become scarce, and prices had risen fourfold in many places, with only hay and feed still easily available. In Indian markets, Syrian goods had become very expensive, while Indian goods were at seven times their normal price to the west. Meanwhile, Bahadur Shah—of whom much was expected in the fight against the Portuguese—had gone off instead to fight the infidels (*kuffar*) in Chitor. He had told the inhabitants of the Gujarat ports not to set out overseas, especially from Diu, since he wanted those places to be well defended. So the poor inhabitants of the Gujarat coast had no hope left but had to wait for the arrival of the fleet of the Ottoman ruler (*Khunkar*). There was naturally great disappointment when it had not turned up that year.[63] But Jarullah equally notes that in that year Jiddah was starved of Indian goods, and the traders were all plunged into a state of despondency.

THE AFFAIRS OF BAHADUR

Unfortunately, things did not take a turn for the better. Rather, Jarullah reports the arrival on a certain Friday of the month of Jumada I 942 AH of six ships at Jiddah from India (*bilad al-Hind*).[64] This was unusual in view of the season, it being October 1535.[65] The local merchants were rather surprised, and it was soon learned that the sultan of Cambay (Sultan Kanbayat), referred to here as Bahadur Shah ibn Muzaffar Shah ibn Mahmud Shah, had recently lost a big part of his territory to the Mughal Sultan Muhammad Humayun, the son of Babur and the lord of Delhi. It was even said, noted Jarullah in passing, that this Humayun was the descendant of that "great tyrant" Timur (the epithet probably being a reflection of Ottoman influence on the author).[66] After a number of reverses one after the other, Bahadur retreated to his capital (*takht-i mamlikat*) called Champaner.[67] He then fled in the direction of Diu. He had gathered together extensive gifts of jewels and cash, got hold of some ships in the area, and sent off his brother, his wife, and a group made up of his family as well as some special associates—some two thousand persons in all, including some excellent scholars (*al-fuzala' al-mu'tabarin*)—led by one 'Abdul 'Aziz ibn Hamid al-Mulk, titled Asaf Khan, in the direction of the Red Sea.[68] These were the ships that had arrived in the royal docks (*al-farza al-sultaniya*) in Jiddah. Among their number were two special ships with gifts for the great *Khunkar*, the sultan of 'Arab and 'Ajam, Süleyman ibn 'Osman. One contained the goods of Mustafa Rumi, who was in Hind and an intimate of Bahadur Shah.

This Mustafa had betrayed Bahadur and gone over to the Mughal sultan along with his supporters, and so his goods had been seized.[69] The remaining ships carried Bahadur Shah's family and the goods of his family and army. It was said that there were some 350 boxes of goods and diverse presents, including gold coins (*salasa mi'at wa khamsin sanduqan min al-tuhaf wa al-naqd al-zahb al-mazrub waghayrahu*). Some of the boxes contained seven thousand to ten thousand dinars meant for charity for the men of three of the important mosques, as well as some others.[70]

This unexpected arrival apparently caused much consternation. Jarullah reports that the governor or "deputy" (*na'ib*) of Jiddah, who was a Rumi, kept these affairs in his custody for a while in order to assess them. He also gave out that he was waiting for a response from the Ottoman Sultan in Istanbul or the governor of Egypt. He did this because the sum of money was very significant, and this sort of unsavory behavior was anyway his habit. The boxes contained studded dishes destined for the sultan, as well as a precious sword for the governor of Egypt. Other gifts were meant for notables in Mecca and elsewhere. But the Jiddah governor seized everything except for some household effects. Jarullah clearly and strongly disapproves of these actions, though he notes that his report is based largely on hearsay. He also comments that the helpless Indian party did not resist the governor too much and requested only a few things back.

Apparently, Jarullah was not far off the mark here. This we can conclude from a confidential report sent by the incoming Ottoman governor of Egypt, Hadim Süleyman Pasha, to the sultan not long after the events. The report recounts:

> What follows is that which is represented to the Exalted Court, Refuge of Felicity [*asitan-i sa'adet*], would that God—may He be exalted—preserve it and aid it till the End of Time.
>
> Earlier, when the treasure and the effects of Bahadur Khan arrived in prosperous Jiddah, and when Hüsrev Pasha came to know of it, he wrote a letter to the *emin* of Jiddah and had all the goods and effects [of Bahadur] seized. Now [the *emin*'s men] have sent a letter to Hüsrev Pasha saying: "Act quickly and present a request to the Sublime Porte, because some of these goods are meant as votive gifts [*nezir*], and some are for our expenses, and there is nothing else besides these." [Hüsrev Pasha] as for him, had represented to the Sublime Porte that these were votive gifts, and having issued an exception to the sacred order, sent it with [the caravan of] the pilgrims through the mediation of

its superintendent [*ketkhüda*] called Ferhad. When this person arrived there, at Mecca the venerated, he took away on behalf of Hüsrev Pasha—besides muslin, aloes-wood ['*ud*], raw amber and other gifts—some thirty thousand *mithqals* of gold. As for the superintendent, the above-mentioned Ferhad, he took [for himself] six thousand *mithqals* of gold, which makes a total of thirty-six thousand *mithqals* of gold. Each *mithqal* consists of 80 *akçe*, so that this makes 2,880,000 *akçe*, which in terms of *kise* units represents 57 *kise* and 30,000 *akçe*.

But in reality, not everything was by way of votive gifts as had been reported by him to the Exalted Court. One part would have been gifts, and the rest would have been his [Bahadur's] treasure [*khazine*].[71]

Here is a forthright admission then of the unscrupulous and grasping practices of local Ottoman officials at Jiddah, in the face of what was a rather vast sum of liquid wealth. The report then concludes:

As for the above-mentioned Bahadur Khan, until now there is no news of him. It is not known if he is dead or alive. If God wills, when the season [*mevsim*] comes and news of him arrives, they will be presented in detail and in a truthful manner to the foot of the Exalted Throne. But, since there is no news of him until the present, it is not certain that he is still alive. So that, when the season comes, if news of his death arrives, all of his treasure will become *beyt-ul-mal* and will be seized on account of the Royal Treasury [*miri*], for he has neither children nor relatives. He only has one wife. As for the treasure that they have brought, it is beyond measure. According to their own declarations, besides other effects, they have brought in cash 350 *bedre* of gold coins, each *bedre* consisting of 7,000 gold coins, which in all makes up 2,450,000 gold coins.[72]

What has happened is thus presented through this humble [written] page to the foot of the Exalted Throne. As for the rest, it is for the Exalted Court to issue an order [*ferman*].

[From] this poor servant [*bende-yi faqir*], the humble Süleyman.[73]

Having been plucked of a good part of their valuable resources, some members of the Indian party then made their way to Mecca; they included the important noble 'Imad-al-Mulk, and the nurse of Sultan

Bahadur's family, as well as a larger group of women accompanied by soldiers.[74] Their obvious refuge was the madrasa constructed by Sultan Muzaffar Shah, and it was here that they took up residence at the Bab al-Safa, near the Haram Sharif itself. The presence of this royal party, with rumors of its enormous wealth, caused a major disturbance in the town, if Jarullah may be believed. They were regularly approached by various supplicants and pensioners, and their arrival immediately caused prices to rise dramatically as the value of coined metal fell sharply. Among the goods on which there was a run were butter, meat, and other basic items of household consumption, for it seems that the fragile Meccan market of the off-season could not resist these big spenders.[75] Soon after, the Gujarat vizier Asaf Khan also arrived with some slaves and the remaining soldiers of his party, and they camped at another spot and not in the madrasa itself. But since their numbers were large, they had to take on other houses on rent. Jarullah gives us a certain number of minute details of the negotiations on these matters, which led to a house being found belonging to a Shafi'i *qazi*, who was also a charitable trustee (*mutawalli*). But what Jarullah and other Meccan residents found particularly dismaying was that the Indian party was always throwing its money around, offering huge rents, so that the families who rented out to them made very sizable windfalls. The Indian party also received some gifts from the local officials and beneficiaries (*arbab al-waza'if*) and gave generously in exchange. Jarullah makes it evident that all this caused quite a buzz, and there was much activity around them in the town. But he also makes it clear it was not all for the best and sets out several hostile comments regarding this Gujarati-inspired inflation.

On the other hand, the Gujarati party also had its virtues. It is noted that 'Imad-al-Mulk—portrayed in Jarullah's text as a pleasant and virtuous man—regularly gave out presents to local teachers and dervishes. As for Asaf Khan, he also continued to give gifts to the muezzins and others in need of financial aid. But once again quarrels arose around this charitable activity. The Hanafite imam Muhammad ibn Ahmad Bukhari was accused of controlling the distribution of funds to the detriment of others. The newly appointed Shafi'i *qazi* became increasingly annoyed with Asaf Khan as a result, feeling that he was wholly under the thumb of the Hanafites. Eventually, 'Imad-al-Mulk left Mecca for a time on a visit to Medina, along with Shaikh Mahmud Rumi (who held the title of Shaikh al-Haram al-Nabawi) and several other notables and leading *qazis*. Despite the flaring up of petty conflicts and jealousies between the sharif and Mahmud Rumi, matters were eventually resolved.

As time went by it became clear that the affairs of the Gujaratis were not about to be resolved rapidly. For one thing the Ottoman court was too preoccupied elsewhere; it was around this time that a messenger arrived in Mecca from Cairo with news of Sultan Süleyman's recent and comprehensive victory over the Safavids.[76] It developed that the monarch had left a deputy in charge of the new conquests and returned to Istanbul; in several of the empire's cities such as Cairo and Jiddah, there were major celebrations on the occasion. Early in the month of Rajab 942 AH, Asaf Khan decided to organize a discussion in his house on Muhammad al-Bukhari's hadith collection. He expressed a wish to invite all the communities in Mecca there, and he asked Jarullah to supply some commentaries on the text, especially the Shafi'i theologian Ibn al-Hajar 'Asqalani's *Fath al-bari*. At the same time Asaf Khan continued to receive worrying news from India, so that he asked that every morning in the Hanafi part (*maqam al-hanafiyya*) of the Masjid al-Haram, the *Sura al-An'am* chapter of the Qur'an should be read for the spiritual benefit of Sultan Bahadur, who he knew was in difficult straits. Some fifty *'ulama'*, from both 'Arab and 'Ajam, were asked to participate in this, including Jarullah himself. But the same Hanafite *'alim* Sayyid Muhammad ibn Ahmad Bukhari was placed in charge of this, so that the Shafi'i *qazi*, 'Abdul Latif al-Zaini, felt quite aggrieved. Since he was the chief *nazir* of the Masjid al-Haram, and a powerful man, he wrote to the Ottoman *na'ib* at Jiddah complaining and asking for the cancellation of the reading. To render matters more piquant still, Jarullah also claims that the Mughals from India had sent their agents to influence people with secret payments, in order to prevent this from happening. The claim was further made that the very same Sura had been read over the past two months, but in order to ensure the victory of Sultan Süleyman over the Iranians, and that the new practice would interrupt that reading. The *na'ib* then intervened, saying that the prayers for Süleyman should be resumed, since they were the real priority. It was also decreed that public celebrations be produced in honor of his victory, and that the houses of even the traders from 'Ajam should be decorated. Naturally, this caused resentment among those who had Safavid sympathies, and this led to quite a stir and dispute, with each side claiming it had been insulted.

In Jarullah's view, the root cause of all this commotion was the huge influx of money from India, and also 'Abdul Latif al-Zaini's desire to control it. Later in the month of Rajab, Asaf Khan personally went to the Ka'aba and, accompanied by the Maliki *qazi* and some other senior people, distributed more alms all around. He thus tried to mollify people by showing that he was not favoring the Hanafites alone. Over the next few months, he continued to show great generosity, distributing presents and money to various people, including Jarullah himself, sometimes amounting to as much as a hundred gold coins (ashrafis) a head.[77] In late March 1536, at the end of the holy month of Ramazan, Asaf Khan again distributed substantial gifts and money publicly after nightly prayers. In the following month of Shawwal, there was quite a stir with the arrival in Jiddah of some twenty ships from "Hind" (here meaning both India proper and Southeast Asia). Jarullah clarifies that five were from the lands "below the winds" (taht al-rih), five from Calicut, and the rest from Cambay and Diu. The maternal uncle of Sultan Bahadur was on one of these, as was Asaf Khan's brother Hamid al-Mulk; there was also Shams Khan and Khwaja Khalil Gilani, who was a close confidant in charge of Sultan Bahadur's affairs.[78] Once again the party brought a substantial quantity of gifts and money, though this time the merchants—wise after the previous year— advised them to hide the extent of their resources from the Rumis (or Ottoman officials). Even so, with their arrival, prices began to rise sharply in Jiddah and Mecca, a matter Jarullah found rather regrettable and unfortunate. As for political news from India, the party that had arrived put out that the Mughal Sultan Muhammad Humayun had won some victories and given over many powers to one of his brothers (meaning Mirza 'Askari). Thereafter, his armies had begun to rebel, so that Sultan Bahadur had begun to hope he could return to his own lands.

But the new party brought fresh practical issues that had to be resolved. Some of the Gujarati nobles in it decided to leave Jiddah for Mecca, where Asaf Khan had to make additional arrangements for them. He himself took on a larger house, so that he and his brother could reside together. Khwaja Khalil Gilani also came to Mecca with his ailing father, who died soon after, in the course of the month of Shawwal. Asaf Khan now asked the Maliki qazi, Taji 'Abdul Wahhab ibn Ya'qub, who had emerged as the chief intermediary of the Gujaratis, to arrange a formal meeting and meal with the sharif to discuss some outstanding matters. On this occasion the Gujaratis gave some objects to the sharif, including various presents placed in large Chinese jars (presumably made of porcelain). As a consequence, Jarullah reports, the sharif came to be better and better disposed to Asaf Khan, toward whom he had been somewhat hostile at the outset. Early in the month of Zi al-Qa'da 942 AH he even paid the Gujarat vizier a formal visit at home and was offered sherbets, betel-leaf (tambul), camphor, and other things according to the Indian custom. A very substantial cash gift was offered to him at this time through one of his intimates, Sayyid Nur-ud-Din Ahmad Iji, but the sharif took only half of what was offered, saying that he had come to honor the vizier and not to take his money. In this atmosphere of growing bonhomie, Asaf Khan and the sharif began to frequent each other regularly, and the vizier was even permitted to use a *falki*, a carriage drawn by two horses.[79]

It turned out that Asaf Khan was a rather more able diplomat than had been suspected. On Friday, 18 Zi al-Qaʻda, an official with the rather odd name of al-Kikhia al-Rumi arrived in Mecca from Istanbul along with Asaf Khan's own envoy Yafiʻi and came to the Gujarat vizier's house. He had brought a message from Süleyman's court, saying that the goods of the Gujaratis that had been sequestered so far in Jiddah should be released. Further, a gift of ten thousand ashrafis had been sent from the court for Asaf Khan, as well as three hundred loads of rice, wheat, sugar, and other goods, so that the vizier was naturally overjoyed. The Ottoman envoy did the rounds of Mecca and paid a set of ceremonial visits, possibly to ensure that the royal orders were followed properly.[80] A newly confident Asaf Khan thus profited from the next month of Zi al-Hijja, when the hajj took place. He sought out the members of the Istanbul hajj party and gave them a substantial gift from Bahadur Shah for Sultan Süleyman: this included a waistband (*nitaq*) studded with jewels and stones, but there were also other precious objects and gold coins in the offering. Asaf Khan also resolved to send some of the members of his own party along with the returning Ottomans to Istanbul; these included the young Qutb-ud-Din Muhammad Nahrawali, whose father Jarullah notes was also a well-known Hanafite scholar. Qutb-ud-Din and Abu Saʻud ibn Shaikh ʻAbdul Baqi were officially deputed to accompany ʻImad al-Mulk al-Banani (also called ʻUmdat ul-Mulk) on his journey, carrying a letter from Asaf Khan to the Ottoman ruler.[81]

In view of their growing friendship, Asaf Khan decided at this point to give over the responsibility of handling all the money and alms coming from India to the Sharif Abu Numayy. But this was soon shown to be a major error of judgment. The sharif began to claim a third of these sums for himself as a levy; in absolute terms, this was reckoned to be a very large amount of money, since it included quantities of unminted gold.[82] The sharif placed the rest of the money in charge of a number of other people, including Khwaja Khalil Gilani who had arrived from Gujarat, and it was then distributed to a large number of beneficiaries, including the eternal grumbler al-Zaini. Jarullah implies that too much of this money went to go-betweens rather than to the people of Mecca, who remained somewhat deprived (*mahrum*). He implies too that in these Ottoman times, it would ever be the fate of the Arabs to be shortchanged in this way. Interestingly, Jarullah chooses to reproduce in his text the paper certificate (*wasl* or *wasliyya*) that he himself received along with some money as his part of the alms that were distributed by the Gujaratis. The certificate was from Khwaja Khalil through his financial superintendent, Miyan 'Umar, and is dated 16 Muharram 943 AH. (Nahrawali, in his marginal comments on the manuscript, comments sarcastically that the gold thus disappeared in general into the belly of beasts, though he managed to get a little bit himself.)[83]

The party from Gujarat was at this time in rather good humor, especially in view of news of Bahadur Shah's continued victories over Humayun and the latter's retreat from Gujarat. Some of this news was brought by an envoy called Khojki Muhammad Sherwani, who arrived unexpectedly from India in a *ghurab*, having been sent by Rumi Khan.[84] Asaf Khan was so overjoyed at his arrival that he organized a special celebration. Meanwhile, Jarullah himself received a letter from his friend Ahmad ibn Muhammad in Diu, which had been written in the middle of Rajab 943 AH (late December 1536). He reported that prices had been high in India, especially of rice and other foodstuff, but that they had come down slightly of late. Sultan Bahadur was so busy fighting the infidel Rajputs that he had not had time to stay long in his capital city. It turned out that even the infidels in his own kingdom had betrayed him in his earlier battles and engagements. The sultan had no good advisers left on hand or any virtuous and reputed vizier, so that tyranny was generally on the rise. On the other hand, the Franks had seized the occasion, and some of them had made such a large fort on the Ras al-Khor (in Diu) that none of the sultan's people actually had the courage to enter it. The Franks had also made it clear that they would allow no one in their fortress, and that if anyone entered it, they would not let him out again.[85] A couple of months later, in Ramazan 943 AH, Jarullah reported the fresh arrival of five ships from India at Jiddah. On them was a Turkish vizier from the Deccan called Harsah Khan, who was closely linked to Mustafa Khan. Rumi Khan's ship had also arrived from Gujarat, and with it came news of a major victory of Sultan Bahadur over Humayun some months earlier, in Muharram 943 AH.[86] Asaf Khan, ever the big spender, was so overjoyed at this that he poured hundreds of ashrafis into public celebrations.[87] It also began to appear that the Ottomans were prepared at last to take action on the affairs of India. From some envoys who arrived in Mecca via Jiddah from Egypt on 17 Ramazan, it was now bruited about that 'Umdat ul-Mulk (who had been sent months earlier by Asaf Khan to Istanbul) had finally succeeded in obtaining an imperial *hukm-nama* (order) for the governor (*na'ib-i Misr*) Süleyman Pasha, in Egypt, instructing him to have Amir Janim al-Hamzawi prepare a force to move against India. Apparently Janim had sent his son Mahmud to the Red Sea with these envoys, and plans were being made for over two months in Egypt—since the month of Rajab—to go to the aid of Sultan Bahadur Shah.[88]

But the shocking news from India changed all this. First it appeared as a rumor, and then increasingly as confirmed fact by the month of Zi al-Qaʿda 943 AH: Bahadur Shah had died at the hands of the Franks in an ambush. Here is how Jarullah puts matters in his text:

> Some Indians arrived, met the vizier, and confirmed the news of the killing of the Sultan on 3 Ramazan at the hands of the accursed Franks in Diu. The Sultan had gone in a boat to meet them in the company of about ten of his close companions, and he approached the ship of the [Frankish] captain. He saluted him and disembarked nearby to go to his quarters. The captain asked him [Bahadur] to approach so that he could give him details about the fort. But he refused to advance. Thereupon, members of the [Frankish] group said in a foreign language to seize him [Bahadur]. He divined their intention and drew his sword. He killed the chief of those who advanced. The others then overpowered him. They were numerous and he [Bahadur] had few helpers. So they killed him in cold blood [*baridan*], as well as the other Muslims who were with him. Thus, it was a great blow to the Faith.[89]

The Franks were clearly blamed here for the sultan's death, though whether it was a premeditated act or a plan to seize him that had gone awry remained unclear. Jarullah reports that Asaf Khan was now in a state of consternation but had initially decided to keep the news secret. But on the very next day after the arrival of the Indian traders, on 13 Zi al-Qaʿda, the *naʾib* of Jiddah, Süleyman Rumi, himself arrived in Mecca, ostensibly to condole with Asaf Khan. At this point the rumors could no longer be contained. The *naʾib* then stated that he wished to seal and sequester the goods of Bahadur Shah; the vizier tried to resist this act, and insults and harsh words were exchanged. Eventually, some of the goods were taken away on camelback to the *naʾib*'s residence, amounting to some 250 boxes or even more. The vizier continued to ask for a proper legal document (*mahzar*) confirming that these boxes had been seized, and Jarullah reports that the *naʾib* eventually and somewhat reluctantly gave it to him. It was said that this seizure was enormous in dimensions, amounting to some 700,000 ashrafis, including both very old coins and gold ingots. The Gujarati party decided that the matter should be referred to the Sultan in Istanbul, and the dispute continued for several months (until at least Safar 944 AH), even leading to a delay in the return of the Indian ships in that season. When they did manage to leave, it was at an inappropriate moment, and it is reported that one of them sank near Jiddah with considerable loss.[90]

THE AFTERMATH

The death of Bahadur Shah in the waters off Diu in February 1537 clearly transformed the role, whether real or imagined, of the Gujarati party that had disembarked on the shores of the Red Sea two years earlier. Faced with this new and unexpected situation, and the seizure of the sultan's effects, Asaf Khan initially decided to send 'Umdat ul-Mulk once more to Istanbul. 'Umdat ul-Mulk showed his lack of enthusiasm by stating that he would make this an elaborate pilgrimage and return only via the Bait al-Quds (or Jerusalem) to Mecca. By May 1537 Asaf Khan expressed his intention to go himself to Istanbul with the returning hajj caravan from Egypt.[91] Hostilities between the Gujaratis and the Ottomans were now barely concealed for a time.[92] Toward the end of the month of Safar 944 AH (early August 1537), some of the ships at last set out for Gujarat from Jiddah; earlier, the *na'ib* of Jiddah had stopped the vessels from Cambay and Diu from leaving at the normal time (corresponding to Nauroz, or late March), stating that since Diu had been taken by the Franks, who had also killed the sultan, they had better remain in Jiddah.[93] In contrast, the Calicut ships were allowed to leave at their appointed time. But by the time (i.e., late July or August), the Gujarati ships were given leave, the proper sailing season was over. So the ships tried to make a fast and desperate run across. The consequences were not happy: as noted, one ship sank near Jiddah at Sha'b al-Mahram, and many traders and goods were lost, perhaps as much as three-fourths of the cargo. Among the fortunate survivors was 'Arif 'Ajami, as well as the well-known Shaikh 'Abdul Haqq, who was linked to the Mughals in India.

Asaf Khan's visit to Istanbul did indeed take place, as we learn from Jarullah. Already in the middle of the month of Rabi' I 944 AH (or late August 1537), word had arrived at Mecca from Cairo that Asaf Khan had been given a warm welcome in Egypt and had then set out from Iskandariyya for Istanbul. Not long afterward, most of the confiscated effects of Sultan Bahadur were returned to the Gujarati party in Mecca.[94] It appeared that the Ottoman court was in a triumphant mood and that Sultan Süleyman, after winning what was described as a major "victory over the Franks" on the western front, had recently returned to his cap-

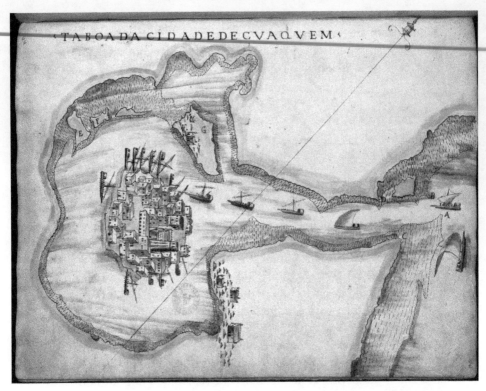

FIGURE 2.2. Port of Suakin drawn by Dom João de Castro (Biblioteca Geral da Universidade de Coimbra, Tábuas dos roteiros da Índia de D. João de Castro, fol. 81).

ital (in fact, he returned on November 22).[95] By May 1538, as the time of the next hajj came around, Syrians from the newly arrived Damascus caravan informed Jarullah that Asaf Khan was on his way back from Istanbul via Jerusalem and the tomb of Abraham at al-Khalil (Hebron). Muhammad ibn Ahmad Bukhari and other important Hanafi divines apparently accompanied him, some of whom were in fact relatives of Jarullah.[96] But Asaf Khan's extended absence from Mecca meant that the Indians there had become quarrelsome and obstreperous; on one occasion, two Indians fought so violently that one died later of his wounds. This became the center of a big debate in Mecca regarding the problematic status of these visitors who had somewhat overstayed their welcome. So it is with some relief that Jarullah reports in Safar 945 AH (July 1538) that Asaf Khan had returned at last to Mecca and was again organizing important and elaborate celebrations.[97]

Whether or not on account of Asaf Khan's visit to Istanbul and his intervention at the court, we learn later in the same month that the long-delayed project of the sending of an Ottoman fleet to India had become a concrete plan. The Meccans received several pieces of news regarding this fleet, which was ostensibly being sent in order to fight a holy war (*ghazw*) against the Franks, who were qualified as the enemies of Allah and the Muslims (*a'da' al-Allah wa al-Muslimin*). This news was followed by the arrival of an envoy to the sharif from the *na'ib* of Egypt, Süleyman Pasha al-Khassi (the eunuch), who stated that in keeping with an imperial order that the latter had received dated 10 Muharram (early June 1538), ships and men for the Indian expedition had been sent from Egypt to Jiddah. This fleet would go to the island of Kamaran and await orders. The Pasha himself was first coming to Mecca for *ziyarat* and would pray there for victory over the enemies.[98]

Portuguese espionage networks had got wind of a version of this plan already almost a year earlier, as we see from the following letter written by Pedro de Sousa de Távora in Rome to the king D. João III, dated July 19, 1537. Here is how Távora saw matters:

> After I wrote to Your Highness with the general news from these parts, a most particular case arose of which I should inform you, and it is that a certain Álvaro Madeira, a native of Sousel, arrived here and told me that he came from India, and he recounts that his coming was in this manner. That he was made prisoner along with one Manuel de Meneses in Xael [Shihr]; and the king of Xael sent him with thirty-four other Portuguese to the Grand Turk as a present, and they were taken by a Turk who came from Diu with permission from Nuno da Cunha in a ship, who handed them over to the captain of Cayro. And this captain informed himself of which of these Portuguese were the most experienced in India, and amongst them he chose this Álvaro Madeira and one Diego Martins, a New Christian, and he sent them to the Grand Turk by the [rapid] postal route [*pellas postas*] to Constantinople, where the Grand Turk informed himself extensively on the matters of India through this Diego Martins, since he was told he was a pilot. And thereafter they were handed over to one Joham Francisco Justiniano, a Venetian, who had already been in Portugal, and on whom the Grand Turk relies a great deal for India affairs.[99]

The events that are referred to in this letter date to 1536, around the time when first Asad Khan's envoy Yafi'i, and then the larger delegation headed by 'Imad-ul-Mulk, had appeared at the Porte. Távora continues:

And then very quickly, around the 25th of last October [1536], the Turk sent Solymam Bassa to make ready the fleet that they have in Suez, in order to go against Your Majesty. Which fleet is made up of seventy galleys, and seven or eight galleons which had been sent to him by the king of Cambay after Diu had been taken: along with these galleons, an ambassador came from the same King of Cambay, and he brought a great tribute [*serviço*] of money for the Grand Turk, which it has been heard would have amounted to four millions in gold, and this in order that the Grand Turk should help him against Your Highness with that fleet and with people, along with which he asked for 30,000 men, saying that the agreement that he had made with Your Majesty's people regarding Diu was to make them more unguarded on believing that since they held Diu, they had secured India, and by this means the Grand Turk could make his fleet ready along with those people whom he was asking for; and that he would give him the port of Çurrate [Surat] or Cambaiete [Khambayat], where they could shelter without Your Majesty's people knowing of it; and that after the Turks had gone there, he would give them Diu as well as the Portuguese who were there; and he also sent him Moorish pilots. The Turk rejoiced greatly on account of that embassy, believing that in that way he would be able to conquer India; and so he at once ordered the fleet and people to be made ready, and he also ordered that all the ships that might come from India to Jiddah and Mecca should be detained, so that they could carry people and supplies for this fleet.

However, it turned out that as late as March 1537 the Ottomans were proving indecisive. The sultan apparently made an initial decision to send "as the Captain-General of this enterprise one of his brothers-in-law, the brother of one of his wives," accompanied by a specialist mariner who was captain of the Alexandria galleys, and the renegade Gian Francesco Giustiniano "as superintendent and adviser, and as pilot-major." But the first part of this decision was clearly rescinded thereafter. Távora, whose information came from Álvaro Madeira (who had somehow managed to escape the Ottomans and flee to Rome), was only able to glean that "the purpose of the Turk's people is to attack Ormuz first, and from there to pass on to Cambay," but also that "according to the monsoons and the time they need to get ready, they cannot leave the straits of Mecca before the coming February [1538]."[100]

This was actually an optimistic timetable. According to Jarullah, Süleyman Pasha arrived in Jiddah only in mid-July 1538 (14 Safar 945 AH). The nervous sharif quickly sent someone out to greet him with gifts and supplies. This envoy met Jamal Muhammad ibn Ahmad al-Marisi in Jiddah and was informed that the pasha had come there with a substantial fleet of about sixty vessels, but an altercation had broken out and the pasha had had Amir Janim al-Hamzawi killed.[101] Since Janim Bey was a person of some prominence, the matter was now the subject of an investigation. The sharif was highly distressed on hearing this news. He decided to make his own inquiries and sent his own oldest son Sayyid Ahmad and a group of Meccans to Jiddah to meet the Pasha. The Pasha welcomed them, but also let them know that Hamzawi had been killed not on his own initiative but on imperial orders (*annahu lamyaqtul al-Hamzawi illa bi-'amr-i Khunkar*). He then handed out robes of honor to various people and sent them back to Mecca. During all this, the ever-arrogant pasha did not even descend from his vessel but simply asked for wood and water for his fleet. Meanwhile, the sharif had begun to prepare a proper reception in Mecca itself, bringing back thirty camel-loads that he had sent to the Dakna Wadi in anticipation of the pasha's arrival.

There now follows a somewhat opaque passage in Jarullah's text concerning Süleyman Pasha's meeting with Khwaja al-Haijari, who is described as the "son-in-law of the Frankish captain" (*sihr-i kaptan al-Faranj*). He was apparently interrogated concerning this Portuguese official and the territories under his control, and he gave a full account of their power. Wild rumors spread that al-Haijari had been killed following his interrogation, but it turned out that he was released.[102] The pasha then decided at last to depart from Jiddah. By now his accumulated fleet was about ninety ships, though some people claimed they numbered more than a hundred. On the morning of 18 Safar, after a short five-day stay, he set sail from Jiddah and went southward at a rapid pace. The sharif's elaborate preparations to receive him were all in vain, though it was said that the Pasha took away 600,000 ashrafis from him. However, as Jarullah notes, these were all contradictory rumors seemingly based on little more than the pasha's rather unsavory reputation. Further, we learn from him that the Turks in Mecca had held a recitation of the *Sura al-An'am* in the Hatim Sharif of the Ka'aba, praying for the eunuch Süleyman Pasha's victory against the Franks in India. Jarullah gives some details of all those who participated in the event but also notes that the Arabs resented being excluded from the affair.[103]

Some seven months after his departure, in the middle of the month of Ramazan 945 AH (early February 1539), an envoy of the pasha arrived in Mecca from the direction of Yemen. He brought news that the fleet had returned from India to Kamaran Island and was planning to come to Yemen. To facilitate his further movements, the pasha asked the sharif for two hundred horses. The sharif then headed out from the city and went to Jiddah along with the envoy. Jarullah reports that the current news regarding the pasha's expedition remained rather confused, since it was not clear what exactly had happened in Diu with the Franks. Had he fought them and won in Diu, or had the Franks simply fled? Did the pasha enter Diu itself, or did he make it only to the ports around there? It was then recounted that when the Ottoman fleet had arrived in India, the chief (*muqaddam*) of Diu, Amir Safar al-Rumi, had met the pasha and exchanged robes of honor, and that the pasha had given him orders to ensure the security of the country. He had then stated he would return to Yemen to pacify and settle it, make the hajj pilgrimage that year (in April–May 1539), and only then come back to India to fight the Franks.[104] He also had made it his priority to ensure the protection of the Bab-al-Mandeb. The pasha had also sent words to the sultan in Istanbul asking for more forces and more supplies. In the Red Sea area itself, he had then sent *nakhuda* Ahmad to the town of Zabid to ask its lord to meet him.[105]

Further details of the anticlimactic expedition emerged in the months that followed. As had been announced, in the month of Zi al-Hijja, Süleyman Pasha duly appeared in Mecca to perform the hajj and formally participated in the ceremony of clothing the Kaʿaba. The sharif for his part treated him with extraordinary respect and caution.[106] But it was also said that the sultan had sent him an angry written message (*marasim*) regarding his poor behavior in India and Yemen and the fact that instead of fighting the Franks he had simply quarreled with other Muslims.[107] The sultan had apparently told him in no uncertain terms that he had not done what he was meant to do and instead had done what was not required. The pasha in due course left Mecca to perform the other parts of the hajj pilgrimage.[108] The next month of Muharram 946 AH (May–June 1539) brought the usual contingent of ships from Calicut, Southeast Asia ("the land below the winds"), and Diu. Two were apparently a special gift for Süleyman Pasha from Safar al-Rumi, the *naʾib* of Diu. It was said that Safar had annoyed the Pasha by broadly hinting he was hastily leaving India for the Arab lands for fear of the Franks, and so this was his belated effort at an olive branch. The pasha took his agent's goods and sent him back summarily. It turned out that the Gujaratis intended nevertheless to continue their struggle against the Portuguese. Jarullah reports that word had arrived in Mecca that Mahmud Shah, nephew of Bahadur Shah, had acceded to the throne and had ordered the destruction of Diu in order to counter the dominance of the Franks.

But this had so far proved of little avail. The young Gujarat sultan had also requested the return of Sultan Bahadur's family members in Mecca. It was therefore left to Asaf Khan to arrange for their departure from Jiddah, carrying at least a good part of their remaining wealth (especially in the form of jewels).[109]

As for Asaf Khan, Jarullah reports that he continued to try and ingratiate himself with the sharif of Mecca.[110] In the month of Safar 946 AH (late June 1539) he lost one of his companions, Shams Khan, who died as he was headed back to India. A proper burial was performed for him in Mecca, with the man in charge of the ceremony being Shaykh 'Ala-ud-Din Nahrawali, one of the regular residents at the time in the Muzaffari madrasa. The last mention of Asaf Khan in Jarullah's text is in the month of Jumada I 946 AH (September 1539), which mentions a ceremony for Asaf Khan's son Qutb Khan in the former's house in Mecca. Jarullah still seems to have retained a fondness for him and continued to praise his good qualities. But by this time Sultan Bahadur's family had left for home, and the great and wealthy Gujarati amir was hardly the man of considerable substance he had once been.[111] He returned to India only in 1548 after an extended absence of twelve years, and once again he played a key role in the sultanate's politics for a time before being assassinated along with his later master, Sultan Mahmud, in 1554.[112]

CODA

The purposes of this chapter have been several, with the central one being to draw scholarly attention to a neglected and important source from the sixteenth century written in the crucial center of Mecca, the spiritual—but also, in some crucial respects, the informational—heart of the Islamic world.[113] In our exploration of this source, Jarullah's annalistic work *Nail al-muna*, I have chosen furthermore to focus on a particular set of aspects, namely those having to do with the Red Sea and the Hijaz in relation to Gujarat. I have attempted to demonstrate that a strong and quite regular political, commercial, and intellectual link existed between the Gujarat Sultanate and Mecca and that mercantile traffic between the Red Sea and the Gujarat ports (Cambay and Diu) was kept alive between the 1510s and 1530s by a number of participants both from South and West Asia, ranging from smaller individual entrepreneurs to the Gujarat sultans themselves. Future historians of trade may wish to look further into the careers of men such as Khwaja Muhammad Gilani, Yusuf Turki, and especially the interesting figure of Barakat Halabi besides the various 'Ajami traders mentioned periodically in Jarullah's text. A systematic reading of the text may also yield further data not only on trade with Gujarat but also between Jiddah and the ports of Kerala, as well as Southeast Asia (which has been mentioned periodically here as "the land below the winds").

In the early 1990s Jean Aubin revealed in the course of conversations his intuition that it was necessary to go beyond the usual Portuguese and Italian sources in order to understand how the spice trade through the Red Sea actually functioned in the first decades of the sixteenth century. As he was later to note, there were "statistics regarding the quantities [of spices] taken by the *muda* galleys at Alexandra and Beirut. Magalhães Godinho has set them out. [But] these numbers have no explanatory value."[114] This led him to a close examination of the narrative sources in Arabic, notably the works of Ibn Tulun and 'Izz-ud-Din ibn Fahd. From these, as well as a reading of other Mamluk and Italian sources, Aubin then came to the following startling conclusion for the period 1501–1504: "It was not in the Indian Ocean, but from Djedda [Jiddah] that everything was blocked. The accumulated delays show, in the sequence of their chronological detail, that the paralysis that struck the Islamic spice route was due to the internal troubles of the Mamluk regime."[115] As a view, this was in keeping with a far more complex (and less Eurocentric) conception of Indian Ocean and Red Sea trade in which not everything was played out in the game between Venice, Lisbon, and Antwerp. Fresh or neglected sources thus allow us regularly to transform our old schematizations and models in political economy. In sum, social-scientific model makers still have much to gain from the work of humanistic historians.

But what may also be at stake is an issue in intellectual history, namely the question of how to gain a better and more balanced understanding of sixteenth-century historiographical production as a whole, in the context of imperial and intellectual competition in areas such as the Indian Ocean.[116] The past few decades have seen important works on the most significant Ottoman chroniclers of the sixteenth century, such as Celalzade Mustafa and Mustafa 'Ali, which can be set alongside the shelves of books that have long existed on Paolo Giovio and Francesco Guicciardini, or the smaller bodies of works on João de Barros, Gonzalo Fernández de Oviedo, or Antonio de Herrera y Tordesillas. Paradoxically, the Arabic historiography of the period has received short shrift in comparison to these other works and to the attention devoted to earlier moments in the Arabic historiographical tradition, whether of the Abbasids or of the chroniclers of Andalusia.[117] An example of this neglect is the figure of Qutb-ud-Din Muhammad Nahrawali, who still awaits a proper monographic study. As Richard Blackburn has written, "Indian by birth, Meccan by adoption, Arab in culture, and Ottoman in political adherence, Shaykh or, as the Ottomans referred to him, Mevla Qutb al-Din al-Makki was recognised among later writers for his depth and breadth of learning and for his skills in Arabic, particularly in poetry and epistolary composition."[118] This allowed him to write works such as *al-Barq al-Yamani*, an important chronicle of the Ottoman conquest of Yemen produced at the command of the vizier Koca Sinan Pasha. Of this text, Jane Hathaway avers, "The Meccan judge Qutb al-Din Muhammad Nahrawali's (1511–1582) sprawling chronicle of Yemen, the Holy Cities and the Red Sea region is virtually unique in its trans-provincial purview; in an example of bilingual cross-fertilization similar to that provided by the circulation of Ibn Zunbul's chronicle, it was translated into Ottoman Turkish and continued by an Anatolian military commander posted to Yemen."[119] Nahrawali also produced a work on the holy city of Mecca, *I'lam bi a'lam*, with biographical notices and other materials, which has long been recognized as a valuable source.[120] To be sure, while frequently being abrasive and boastful, it has also been noted of Nahrawali that "his advocacy of the [Ottoman] sultans did not cause him to withhold criticism of Ottoman officials or policy when he judged these to be deserving of it."[121]

Though Jarullah ibn Fahd stands in a genealogical relationship of some sort with Nahrawali, on account of being a direct source for the latter (as well as a personal acquaintance), it would be hard to place him in the same category as an intellectual. Indeed, recent scholars have mostly portrayed him as a somewhat marginal and cantankerous figure, known more for his backbiting and fondness for slander (*ghiba*) than for any other quality. We thus learn in one recent work that he was "a Meccan historian who wrote a book that controversially exposed some of his contemporaries as being bald under their turbans.... His work so angered these men that they seized the book from his home and washed the pages at the local mosque, dissolving the ink. He attempted to undo their shame (and his own) through public debates with the Meccan theologian Ibn Hajar al-Haytami (d. 974/1567), who had been named in the book as bald, about the lawlessness of revealing others' physical blights and by ultimately rewriting the work, omitting the names of these bald men."[122] Jarullah's defense, when he was morally admonished and physically attacked (his house being stormed in November 1541), was primarily to claim that he was writing for entertainment and admonition rather than in a purely satirical vein; but he also remarked, perhaps tongue in cheek, that he himself had openly admitted to having a "receding hairline."

In any event, whatever moral difficulties he may have had with his censorious Meccan contemporaries, it should be evident to us that Jarullah ibn Fahd remained a very close observer of his times and circumstances. While he was no grand sixteenth-century theorist of history in the sense of an Ibn Khaldun, a Mustafa 'Ali, or an Abu'l Fazl, his work was the humbler one of an annalist, but one with an ever critical and even caustic eye that he deployed to observe the doings of the powers of the day. Such texts as his remain crucial for the writing of a *histoire événementielle* of the Hijaz in the period, as well as for the diplomatic and commercial history of the Indian Ocean in the time. At the same time, we cannot neglect the copious light that a work such as his sheds on the tensions within the Sunni Muslim community of the Hijaz (and eastern Ottoman domains) in the aftermath of the Ottoman conquest, which may in turn help us to understand why it proved so difficult to offer a more sustained and directed resistance to Portuguese ambitions.[123] The view from Mecca that he provides is one that remains rather ambivalent as to the rising Sunni power of the period, the Ottoman Empire. There was no simple religious glue that held the Sunni Muslim merchant communities of the Indian Ocean together, even in the face of an important threat from the Portuguese.

In a wide-ranging consideration of trade in the Red Sea and Gulf of Aden in the sixteenth century, French historian Michel Tuchscherer has suggested that on the one hand the Red Sea was a sort of Ottoman lake from the late 1510s to 1635, while on the other hand Ottomans and Portuguese managed a "real, if precarious, balance of forces in the Indian Ocean" in the same period.[124] Challenging this perspective, Giancarlo Casale has claimed that "by the 1570s, [Ottoman] collective efforts had proven so successful that the Portuguese embargo had been brought to its knees," but that this was followed by "the disappearance of the Ottoman Empire as a visible political presence . . . during the decades after 1589."[125] A close reading of sources suggests on the other hand that there was far more to the trade into the Red Sea than can be explained by the vagaries of Ottoman and Portuguese commercial and imperial policy viewed as a simple zero-sum game and that the complexity of the web of actors and interests requires further consideration.

Chapter 3

THE AFRO-INDIAN AXIS

The noble slave Sidi Sa'id Sultani al-Habashi died in Ahmedabad on Monday, 3 Shawwal 984 H. He belonged to the Hanafi school. He was an orthodox follower of Imam Abu Hanifa to the extent that often he used to criticize Imam Shafi'i. He was well-versed in jurisprudence in addition to possessing great knowledge of other sciences.

'ABDUL QADIR AL-'AYDARUSI, TARIKH AL-NUR AL-SAFIR

In the western Indian city of Ahmedabad, one of the most iconic monuments is a mosque locally termed Sidi-Said-ni-Jali, celebrated for its latticework screens. It was built in the 1570s, in the very last years of the Muzaffarid dynasty in Gujarat. The obituary refers to its builder, Sidi Sa'id Sultani al-Habashi, a noted bibliophile and savant who had studied with the celebrated theologian Ibn Hajar al-Haytami. His origins lay across the western Indian Ocean, as denoted by the appellation "Habashi," meaning that he was from the Horn of Africa. I evoke him because in this chapter I will return to the place of East Africa in the trading and political configurations of the western Indian Ocean by considering the axis that connects the region to western India. I have already noted in earlier chapters that the important role played by the ports and city-states of the Swahili coast of East Africa in the commerce of the western Indian Ocean in the medieval and early modern periods is now generally recognized in the literature. This history has been reconstructed using a variety of sources, ranging from archaeology and the study of material culture to the documents and narratives of European visitors to the region.[1] As noted in chapter 1, we also have at our disposal a small number of letters in Arabic written from Swahili urban centers in the early decades of the sixteenth century.[2]

The Swahili coast letters testify to the wide spread of Arabic across the Indian Ocean by the beginning of the sixteenth century. It has been argued that, like Sanskrit before it, Persian alongside it, and eventually Portuguese after it, Arabic was a cosmopolitan language that sustained not only a religious culture—it was, of course, the language in which the Qur'an, hadith, and much religious commentary were communicated—but also a broader cultural complex that also had "secular" dimensions, in sum, what Ronit Ricci has in a significant work termed the "Arabic cosmopolis."³ Ricci's work, which is fundamentally centered on South and Southeast Asia, makes it clear that some of its arguments could equally be extended to East Africa, where Arabic found a place alongside other vernacular languages that were frequently in the process of taking literary form, often using the Arabic script as a vehicle for the purpose.⁴ A simple measure of the spread and use of medieval Arabic is to look at the celebrated *Rihla*, or travel account, of the Moroccan voyager Ibn Battuta (1304–1377). Departing from Aden in Yemen in the early 1330s, Ibn Battuta made his way first to Zaylaʿ, then to Muqdisho (Mogadishu), and from there to Mombasa and to Kilwa, the southernmost point of his East Africa journey. The entire voyage seems to have taken two or three months, and in its course he encountered a good number of savants (*ʿulama*ʾ) as well as other figures, some of whom came from the Hijaz and the Red Sea as well as other parts of the central Arab lands. The ruler in Kilwa at the time of his visit was Abu'l Muzaffar Hasan al-Mahdali, claiming descent from a family of Yemeni Sayyids and renowned for his generosity.⁵

Drawing on scattered and diverse linguistic, textual, and inscriptional evidence, and above all on the growing archaeological record, it is now possible to offer a longer and more complex chronology of the emergence of Islamic city-states on the coast than what was current a generation ago, at the time of the pioneering work of Neville Chittick on Kilwa and its environs.⁶ Thomas Spear summarizes:

> The "Shungwaya" period, extending from 800 to 1100, saw the cultural genesis of Swahili in the north, the beginnings of trade with the Persian Gulf, and the emergence of the first pre-Muslim towns along the coast. As trade and wealth grew between 1100 and 1300 and trading contacts shifted to the Red Sea a number of new towns were founded, foremost among them Mogadishu; coastal dwellers began to convert to Islam in increasing numbers; and Yemeni *sharifs* became prominent in Mogadishu and Kilwa in a period characterized by increasing "Islamization" of Swahili societies. Trade and wealth reached a climax between 1300 and 1600, the "Shirazi" period, causing prominent families along the coast to claim prestigious Shirazi origins to distinguish themselves from both immigrant Arabs and mainland Africans, adopt exclusive paraphernalia and dress, build elaborately decorated stone houses and pillar tombs, and endow new mosques.⁷

Early scholarly contributions to the study of Swahili urbanism in the pre-1500 period were mainly based on excavations of architectural features and surface collections, especially of imported ceramics. In a second phase extensive area excavations were given more prominence, helping to give a more precise definition of the southern and eastern boundaries of the Swahili world. At the same time, as Stephanie Wynne-Jones has remarked, "the archaeological record upon which we rely for the centuries before 1500 CE does not easily yield evidence for definable social groups."[8] Nevertheless, some useful attempts have been made to combine archaeology and ethnography creatively in order to provide plausible reconstructions of the evolving social structure of the urban centers of the coast. In particular, the work of Mark Horton on Shanga and other areas suggests the emergence from about the eighth century of Muslim settlements organized in a clear town plan around a central open space, with public buildings and a mosque. Such towns (Swahili: *mji*) would have held a mix of pastoralists, fisherfolk, merchants, and craftspeople, some drawn from the interior and others from the wider world of the Indian Ocean.[9] In these emergent urban centers one sees both religious buildings and burial sites, though elaborate individual tombs remained a rarity on the coast before 1800 CE. Further, it is generally acknowledged that Swahili Islamic architecture as it emerged had an indigenous character both in terms of its style and the materials used rather than simply being a copy of received models from the central Islamic lands. By the eleventh century an early mosque structure can be found in Kilwa, and these and other buildings were then extended and enlarged in the course of the thirteenth century in the context of an expanding commercial horizon. In the fourteenth century, as noted earlier, Kilwa had emerged as the largest urban settlement of the coast, though it would eventually face competition from other centers both to the south (notably Sofala) and especially to the north (such as Malindi and Mombasa).[10] Drawing on a broad body of evidence, Abdul Sheriff has suggested that by 1500 all these centers

> were occupied by a stratified society, including the ruling and commercial elites who lived in multistory stone houses, with carved doors and external stone benches to facilitate social interaction in a mercantile society, and a larger class of commoners who serviced the mercantile economy and lived in huts made of sticks, stones and clay. People from the immediate hinterland also settled in the Swahili towns to become new townsmen, but there has also been a continuous seepage of immigrants from

across the ocean who came primarily as traders or sailors; they perennially interacted and intermarried with the local population and eventually became Swahili.[11]

Regarding the Gujarat/East Africa link in the fifteenth and sixteenth centuries, a well-known essay by Edward Alpers from the 1970s still remains a good point of departure. In it Alpers comments:

> Before the arrival of the Portuguese in Indian Ocean waters, trade between India and East Africa was based primarily on the exchange of gold from southern Zambesia and ivory from the coastal hinterland of East Africa for cotton cloths from India and glass beads from both India and Venice. The importance of exotic trade goods for East Africa was vividly recounted in an early sixteenth-century Portuguese report, which suggested that "cloth and beads are to the Kaffirs what pepper is to Flanders and corn to us, because they cannot live without this merchandise or lay up their treasures of it." Among the [other] items involved in the trade were rhinoceros' horn, tortoise shell, and some slaves from East Africa, grain from India, and Chinese porcelain, which was transshipped in western India.[12]

Alpers went on to suggest that the "fifteenth century may have witnessed important changes in both the personnel and organization of trade with the rise to prominence of the Muslim sultanate of Gujarat from 1392 and the domination of Indian Ocean trade by Gujarati merchants," but he was unable to provide many details beyond citing the usual early sixteenth-century Portuguese sources (Tomé Pires and Duarte Barbosa) on the role played by the ports of Khambayat (Cambay) and Diu.[13] On the East African end, he noted the significance by the fourteenth century of Kilwa, Mombasa, and Mogadishu on the Banadir coast and then, farther north, of Berbera and Zayla' around the Horn of Africa.

The relative paucity of textual sources has meant that historians of the Swahili coast in the pre-1500 period have largely drawn their arguments in recent decades from archaeology, numismatics, and the occasional inscription. These arguments were initially set out in broad brush strokes, but we can discern far more precision in recent studies tracing a long history of trade and settlement on this coast prior to 1500.[14] Moreover, the archaeologist Mark Horton has set out interesting hypotheses regarding what he terms a "hidden trade [between India and Africa] in a variety of commodities, such as cloth and beads, that were vital to the prosperity of the whole system, but which are seldom recorded in the texts." Making comparisons based on a close study of material culture and artifacts, he has even suggested that "Indian artisans may have moved to East Africa, [and] Africans may have moved, as well, around the Indian Ocean, not as slaves but as genuine artisanal communities." Despite the "currently insufficient evidence to reconstruct in detail the relationship between northwestern India and East Africa from the eleventh until the fourteenth centuries," Horton goes on to argue, "it is clear that a complex interaction existed between the two regions involving the movement of commodities and artisans in both directions."[15] The regions of India for which he makes this argument seem largely to be Gujarat and Sind. The Deccan features in relation to only one instance, that of an eleventh-century East African bronze lion figurine, "based upon contemporary Indian figurines, possibly from the Deccan region."

EARLY PORTUGUESE CONTACTS AND CONFLICTS

The nature of the textual record obviously changes significantly after about 1500, with the Portuguese arrival in the western Indian Ocean, in ways that are both expected and unexpected. In chapter 1 I summarized some of the main aspects of the anonymous shipboard account of Vasco da Gama's voyage along the Swahili coast in the first half of 1498. But we can also examine, if only briefly, the more elaborate materials made available to us in the narratives of chroniclers such as João de Barros. Rounding the Cape of Good Hope, and after their first encounters with pastoralists, Gama had avoided hugging the coast for fear of currents and thus missed landing at Sofala. Subsequently, Barros writes, he encountered a settlement with people "who seemed to be a mixture of blacks and Moors, who understood some words of Arabic."[16] Thereafter, the fleet was able to put in at Mozambique Island, ruled over by a shaikh, where they found some "white people with caps [*toucas*] on their heads and dressed in cotton like African Moors," and even a merchant with origins ostensibly in Fez. From this point on, encounters with Muslims became regular and the degree of hostility that the Portuguese manifested seems to have risen. The Muslim pilots whom the Portuguese engaged at Mozambique fled in Mombasa, and though that latter city—with its "buildings that were made of stone and lime, with windows, and airy, like those in Spain"—made a positive impression on the surface, it was clear that no pilots were to be had there to cross the western Indian Ocean. Gama's small fleet thus found itself still farther north in the port of Malindi. Here they were visited by "some Moors who were there from the kingdom of Cambay in their ships" as well as by "some men who are called Baneanes, of the same Gentiles of the kingdom of Cambay." It was by frequenting them, Barros claims, that Gama was able to find a pilot to take him to Calicut, a "Gujarati Moor by nation, called Malemo Cana." This name has sometimes been translated in recent times as of Kacchi origin, Kanji Malam.

In the course of the voyages of the early sixteenth century that followed Gama but preceded the official creation of the Estado in 1505, the Portuguese did gradually accumulate knowledge on the trading conditions in southeast Africa. The presence of gold in the region led them to consider a form of triangular trade, bringing in textiles from the Indian west coast. Earlier I considered their attempts to settle in Kilwa and create a fortress there. Abandoning it in 1512, the Portuguese then turned to other sites such as Mozambique and Sofala. As Malyn Newitt has pointed out, however, the Sofala factory "proved a great disappointment to the Portuguese Crown." Though the gold trade was initially promising, the promise did not last, because of the rival networks of Angoche and other centers.[17] Paradoxically, the Crown then tried to tighten up, producing a *regimento* that "sought to prescribe every aspect of the life of the [Sofala] fortress." Naturally, this did not work any better, and soon enough "individual Portuguese jumped ship or deserted the fortress garrisons to settle on the islands and estuaries."

As I have also noted, these early years also produced some interesting materials that historians have found of lasting interest concerning the history of the coast. The official chronicler João de Barros, by virtue of his position in the Casa da Índia in Lisbon, had begun in the 1530s to accumulate texts that would serve as "feeders" for the great chronicle he had in mind, often using slaves or servants as translators and interpreters. Among these texts was what he called "a chronicle of the Kings of Kilwa" (*huma chronica dos Reys de Quiloa*), discussed earlier.[18] This work speaks of links between the Swahili coast and the Persian Gulf, and how traders and settlers from Shiraz and/or the port city of Siraf had arrived in the area in the later medieval period. An alternative narrative that has Muslim settlers arriving in the region from Daybul, at the mouth of the Indus River, has also enjoyed some popularity in recent times.[19]

In the course of the sixteenth century, trade between India and the Swahili coast evolved to a fair extent as a consequence of both Portuguese policies and other factors. The classic analysis by Edward Alpers of aspects of this commerce suggests that "it represented only a small part of India's total overseas trade," not exceeding "four per cent of the total trade of Western India" even as late as 1600. He stresses the role of three commodities: cotton textiles imported from India into Africa and ivory and gold exported from Africa to India. Alpers proposes nevertheless that in the sixteenth and seventeenth centuries, "the East African market for Indian cotton textiles was very small indeed when compared to the domestic market and to those of Arabia, Burma and Malacca." On the other hand, he argues that "before about 1800 . . . the main market for the ivory of East Africa remained the traditional market from India."[20] However, given the nature of the Portuguese records from the period, Alpers cannot quantify either the imports or the exports of these commodities, let alone propose a reconstruction of trends over time. Some two decades after his important work the Portuguese historian Manuel Lobato returned to the question with a closer look at the institutional context of trade, on which I shall draw extensively here.[21] Lobato stresses the importance of the connection between Malindi and Gujarat and notes that the Portuguese tried both carrot and stick to control this trade. However, their use of violence failed to deter those who plied this route, bringing textiles from India and carrying back, gold, ivory, and copper as well as African slaves.[22] At the same time, this led to a deterioration in diplomatic relations with the sultan of Malindi, who complained that "when they [Portuguese fleets] encountered other ships who told them they were going to Melindi, they seized them and entered them by force, and did great harm to them."[23]

Eventually a system emerged thanks in part to the Portuguese acquisition of a fort and trading post in Chaul, in the Ahmadnagar Sultanate. Around 1530 Chaul was declared to be the sole official port where the textile procurement for Sofala and Mozambique was to be carried out. In the middle decades of the sixteenth century, we thus see the emergence of the so-called *navio do trato de Chaul*, which could either be a single large vessel or several smaller ones, with a monopoly over the trade to Sofala. Together with Bassein, the hinterland of Chaul also became the most important area for the procurement of trade beads (*contas*) by the Portuguese for the African market. In turn, a large quantity of ivory was imported every year into Chaul and sold in the markets of the Deccan. What this implied was a division of the Swahili coast trade, roughly north and south of Cabo Delgado. To the north the Portuguese played what was at bottom a predatory role, with the real trade being carried out by Indian and local merchants and the long-distance commerce remaining mostly in the hands of the Gujaratis. If in the initial years Malindi (and to a lesser extent Mombasa) dominated, as the century wore on the port of Pate in the Lamu Archipelago north of Mombasa emerged as the great center for textile imports from India. The Portuguese acquisition and fortification of Mombasa in the 1590s rendered these processes of hide-and-seek even more complicated. On the other hand, the restrictive and monopolistic policies of the Portuguese Estado ensured that in the southern areas over which they had greater control the direct links with the Deccan were greatly reinforced. In addition to the trade with Chaul, the consolidation of Mozambique Island as a way station on the Carreira da Índia ensured that its links with Goa grew ever more pronounced, also through the so-called concessionary *viagens de Moçambique* made, as an account from around 1580 put it, "in a ship fitted out at the cost of the royal treasury, in which they send supplies, and munitions, and Cambay cloth, and beads and other merchandise, which are sent on the King's account."[24] This was important because once Goa became the capital of the Estado in 1530, its population of settlers (*casados*) grew apace, and each settler household became a source of demand for slaves, many of whom were imported from Mozambique, Sofala, and adjacent regions. Most studies remain vague on the numbers involved in Goa until the latter half of the eighteenth century, far beyond the period under consideration here,[25] but by the end of the sixteenth century there were probably several thousand slaves in Goa, of whom a large proportion came from eastern Africa. In turn, at least some of these either fled or may even have been sold into the neighboring Deccan sultanates of Bijapur and Ahmadnagar.[26]

Pedro Machado's long-term view of the trade between East Africa and India draws in turn on Lobato's analysis, adding to it materials from the latter half of the eighteenth century. He points to the fact that "East Africa and Mozambique were not the largest export markets for Gujarati textiles in this period, the greatest number going to the Middle East," and he also stresses the importance of "the widespread African textile production that existed on the coast, islands and interior of East Africa." Further, he argues that it was only in the course of the eighteenth century—and thus beyond the chronological scope of the present chapter—that a new "free trade regime" enabled Gujarati merchants to expand their exports to East Africa, so that "annual imports of Indian textiles stood at 300,000–500,000 pieces from the middle of the [eighteenth] century."[27] It is clear from his discussion that it is imprudent to take such figures (which are already rough estimates for the eighteenth century) backward into the sixteenth and seventeenth centuries. Machado has suggested in another essay that already in the early sixteenth century Gujarati textiles were to be found on the East African coast "in a vast array of styles, colors, and shapes," and that the "bulk were transported into the interior where they were in great demand." His broad conclusion, though relegated to a footnote, is nevertheless significant for us: "due to the limits of the evidence, it is difficult to determine precisely whether Gujarati textiles became more important in these centuries than they had been in earlier ones, or whether they are more noticeable because the documentation improves."[28] At the same time, it is clear that there was a shift in terms of regional emphasis in textile procurement in India. From an initial focus on northern and northwestern Gujarat, the sixteenth century saw the growth in importance of the so-called *panos de Balagate*, produced in the Deccan hinterland of Chaul. In turn, the later seventeenth and eighteenth centuries saw a return to northwestern Gujarat, as Diu emerged to the fore though the activities of its indigenous merchants (*baneanes*) in the East African trade.[29]

FROM THE SWAHILI COAST TO ETHIOPIA

While commercial relations between the Deccan ports and the Swahili coast thus attained a certain importance over the course of the sixteenth century, relations with northeast Africa were in fact of far greater political significance. Again the Portuguese had some role to play in the matter, but in a rather complicated way. By the last decades of the fifteenth century, as they prepared to enter the trade of the Indian Ocean, the Portuguese were anxious to find Christian allies in the region to aid them against the Mamluk Sultanate of Egypt. This led them to send envoys to the ruler Eskender (r. 1478–1494) of the Solomonid dynasty in Ethiopia and to continue efforts to contact "Prester John" (as they termed these kings) in the early decades of the sixteenth century. Intermittent diplomatic relations followed during the regency of Queen Eleni (1507–1516), at a time when the Portuguese under Afonso de Albuquerque first penetrated the interior of the Red Sea and installed themselves in the island of Soqotra.[30] They persisted during the time of Lebnä Dengel (or Dawid II, r. 1507–1540), a period when the Ethiopian rulers gradually found themselves under menace from the coastal sultanate of Barr Saʻd-ud-Din (sometimes loosely termed Adal), under its powerful and charismatic leader, Imam Ahmad ibn Ibrahim.[31] Imam Ahmad, popularly known as "Grañ," the left-handed in Amharic, made an alliance with the Ottomans in the neighboring areas of the Red Sea and was able after initial campaigns in the late 1520s to deal the Ethiopians a severe defeat in 1531. The Portuguese by this time were increasingly suspicious of the Christianity practiced in Ethiopia, which they suspected of being tainted with Judaism. Nevertheless, they felt constrained to intervene, partly to impede Ottoman advances into the area, and they did so through an expeditionary force led by Cristóvão da Gama.[32] Even though Gama was killed (or "martyred") in the southern Tigray region in August 1542, the Ethiopians were thereafter able to gain the upper hand, as Imam Ahmad himself was defeated and killed by the forces of King Galawdewos (r. 1540–1559) at the Battle of Wayna Daga in February 1543.

These campaigns between the 1520s and 1540s had a major impact on the market for military slaves in the Horn of Africa and by a spillover effect into the markets of the Hijaz, Yemen, and Hadramaut. It was precisely in these markets that African slaves were generally procured for Indo-Muslim states. The presence of such slaves—known as *zanji* or *zangi* for those from the Swahili coast and *habashi* (for those from the Horn of Africa)—is known from the time of the Delhi Sultanate and its offshoots, even if their precise numbers are impossible to estimate.[33] Drawing on the earlier, very rough estimates of Ralph Austen, Paul Lovejoy proposed in a classic work on slave trade that the Red Sea and Swahili coast each exported roughly a thousand slaves a year in the sixteenth and seventeenth centuries, with the numbers increasing considerably only after 1700.[34] In turn, these estimates have been subjected to critical scrutiny by the French historian Thomas Vernet, who argues that they are simply "not supported by the assessments given in contemporary documents." Instead, Vernet suggests that the "slave trade run by Swahili, Comorian, and Arab merchants, who provided themselves in Madagascar and the Cape Delgado and Juba areas, might have fluctuated between 3,000 to 6,000 slaves a year in the seventeenth century . . . [with] a low estimate of around 3,000 to 4,000." As regards the destinations, he states that the "Arabian Peninsula and the Persian Gulf probably absorbed the majority of the captives, followed by the Swahili towns, and finally, the Portuguese settlements."[35] Revised estimates for the trade across the Red Sea have not been made to date. Recent works of a qualitative nature have nevertheless pointed to the steady participation of both Christian and Muslim actors in this slave trade, arguing that "one should cease to think of slave trade in the Horn of Africa as a phenomenon uniquely linked to Muslim merchants, but rather envisage it as a system in which Christians and Muslims participated with shared interests as well as real competition."[36] It can be argued that the trade also followed rhythms and that there were certainly peaks and troughs exacerbated by conflict, with the decades from the 1520s to the 1540s representing a significant peak. It should also be stressed that unlike the case of the Atlantic, historians of the western Indian Ocean are currently not in a position to speak with any clarity of the gender composition of the slave trade, though it seems that the proportion of women was far lower than in the Atlantic.

While it is impossible to produce numerical estimates, African elite slaves were probably outnumbered in India for long periods by Turkic slaves originating from Central Asia, who dominated the *mamluk* (or *ghulam*) institution in Delhi in the thirteenth and fourteenth centuries.[37] Periodically, however, groups of habashis did emerge into prominence, as they did by briefly seizing direct power in the Bengal Sultanate in the late fifteenth century. It is no coincidence that this was in a period when the Bengal sultans had opened direct relations with Mecca and were periodically sending envoys and funds there. A new dynasty was founded by a Meccan Sayyid, who took the title of 'Ala-ud-Din Husain Shah (r. 1494–1519). But even during his reign, if Tomé Pires may be believed, the habashis continued to have a major role: "The people who govern the kingdom [Bengal] are Abyssinians (*Abixins*). These are looked upon as knights (*avidos por cavaleiros*); they are greatly esteemed; they wait on the kings in their apartments. The chief among them are eunuchs and these come to be kings and great lords in the kingdom. Those who are not eunuchs are fighting men. After the king, it is to this people that the kingdom is obedient from fear."[38]

Elite slavery was also known in the fifteenth-century Bahmani Sultanate, as we see from reading the chronicles of the region, and habashis were particularly present in the palace interior. But the historiography abounds in vague generalizations and is able to give us only a limited number of concrete examples of their power. Relating events from the late 1480s, for example, the chronicler Sayyid 'Ali Tabataba'i claims that "a clique of Habshis in the service of the Sultan [Mahmud Shah II] had the utmost confidence placed in them; and owing to the power they possessed in the affairs of government, used to behave in a very imperious manner."[39] Names of some these notables have come down to us, in particular that of Dilawar Khan Habashi, an opponent of the Turkish group at the court led by Qasim Barid (who was later to found the Bidar Sultanate). Tabataba'i makes this rivalry one of his great themes to explain the collapse of the Bahmani state and the emergence of its successors. In another passage we learn:

> At this time the power and authority of the people of Habshah and Zangbar in the service of the Sultan had increased a thousand-fold, and the other State officials had no longer any power except in name. The whole country and the offices and

political affairs of the kingdom and the government treasuries they divided among themselves, and arrogantly ignoring the sovereign, themselves governed the kingdom. But since the star of their good fortune had now reached its zenith, after continuing for a long time undiminished: as is invariably the rule with fortune as well as the revolving heavens—the star of that clique began to decline.

The key figure here is not Dilawar Khan (killed in a military accident involving an elephant), but another person. Pires, writing in the 1510s (but referring to a past time), mentions a handful of great "lords" in the declining Bahmani polity and states: "Milic Dastur [Malik Dastur] is an Abyssinian slave of the king [*abixi escpravo del Rey*], and is almost as important as each of these. His land borders on the Narsinga [Vijayanagara] frontier, and he lives in Gulbarga where he has a garrison."[40] Other Portuguese chroniclers refer to him as a eunuch (*capado*), and the Deccan chronicles identify him as Malik Dinar Dastur-i Mamalik, who was killed around 1509–1510 at the order of Yusuf 'Adil Khan.

Malik Dinar thus failed to do what several other notables of varying origins did, that is to lay the foundations of a regional state from the vestiges of the moribund Bahmani Sultanate. But he still features prominently in at least one literary text of the late fifteenth century, the *Fath-Nama-yi Mahmud Shahi*, which is concerned with the politics of the early 1490s. Its author, the poet 'Iyani, had apparently migrated to the Deccan from Iran in the mid-fifteenth century, and he claims to have been resident there for between four and five decades by the time the *Fath-Nama* was written, sometime in the 1490s.[41] The text begins with lavish praise of the Bahmani ruler Mahmud Shah (r. 1482–1518), who is extravagantly compared to ancient heroes such as Faridun and Sikandar. Highly conscious of his own identity as a migrant from West Asia (one of the so-called *ghariban*), 'Iyani makes it a point to stress that one of the ruler's greatest virtues is the fact that he is "the bestower of patronage on these nightingales ['*andaliban*]," as opposed to other groups. Still, the situation in his kingdom turns out to have been full of turbulence, as "a hundred rebellions appeared everywhere." The chief troubles were located in the area of Gulbarga and the fortress of Sagar, and this is how they are described:

O King, may you rule as long as the world exists!
[But] beware of circumstances in your kingdom.
It so happened that the Habashis joined together,

And turned bright day into dark night for themselves.
One of this lot, Dastur Dinar by name,
With much gold and riches, and a whole army,
Joined a scattered group of the same type [*ham-jins*],
And deviated from his faith and belief.
They abandoned their regular service,
And turned against the king of exalted rank.
Rebellion alone was on their minds;
only by gathering an army could it be cured.⁴²

The sultan was thus obliged to march personally against Malik Dastur, enlisting the aid of two other warlords, who brought in large forces of troops and elephants. In the ensuing fierce combat an arrow pierced Malik's horse, and Malik was captured and brought before Mahmud Shah. However, some important courtiers such as Qasim Barid and Fakhr-ul-Mulk apparently interceded for him and urged that he be treated with mercy. The kind-hearted ruler therefore pardoned him and even returned most of his wealth to his possession. As I noted, Malik Dastur's career continued for almost two decades after this, and he was further involved in a number of intrigues as the Bahmani Sultanate entered its twilight.

The first third of the sixteenth century represents a low point for the fortunes of Ethiopians in the Deccan, partly because this was a high point for Shi'ism in the region, and the Ethiopians were usually devout Sunni converts. In order to comprehend their later upswing we need to return to the conflicts in the Horn of Africa, as well as political processes in neighboring Gujarat. One of the earliest scholars to pay attention to this question was the British orientalist E. Denison Ross while editing an Arabic chronicle written in Gujarat by 'Abdullah Hajji-ud-Dabir Ulughkhani.⁴³ Ross proposed that in spite of the presence of some prominent figures in the fifteenth century (such as one Sidi Bashir, who constructed a major mosque in Ahmedabad), the really major influx of habashis into Gujarat was in the 1530s, and that this process accompanied the move of a certain number of Ottoman subjects—and in particular a group around the figure of Mustafa Bairam, titled Rumi Khan—from the Red Sea to Gujarat.⁴⁴ These Ottomans (or *rumis*) played an important role in Gujarat politics from the time of Sultan Bahadur Shah (d. 1537) and extending into the following decades. Some of them, like Khwaja Safar Khudawand Khan, were instrumental in shoring up the significance of port cities such as Surat, which they fortified and rendered defensible against Portuguese attacks. The reader of the text of Ulughkhani, *Zafar al-Walih*, can also discern that the number of important habashis in the upper strata of the Gujarat Sultanate's administration grew apace at this time. Ross listed a number of these, such as (1) several notables with the title of Jhujhar Khan, including Bilal Habashi and his son Marjan Sultani;[45] (2) at least two persons, Sandal and 'Abdul Karim, father and son, with the title of Fulad Khan; (3) and Yaqut Habashi, Ulugh Khan (d. 965 AH/1557 CE), followed by his son Muhammad Ulugh Khan, who was the chief patron of the chronicler.[46] He further argued that many of these Ethiopians were purchased in the slave markets of the Red Sea or acquired as tribute by the Ottomans from Imam Ahmad in the course of his campaigns in the late 1520s and early 1530s. As a consequence, they often continued to show a considerable (though not complete) loyalty to the Rumis and their families in Gujarat politics, especially in the difficult decades of the 1550s and 1560s. This was particularly so in the reign of Sultan Ahmad in the late 1550s, when two significant factions, led respectively by 'Abdul Karim I'timad Khan and 'Imad-ul-Mulk Aslan Rumi, faced off. Among other significant habashi figures mentioned in the chronicles of the period are Yusuf Khan, Dilawar Khan, Bahram Khan, and Bijli Khan, all of whom seem to have participated in court politics and held significant appanages.

HABASHIS AND PORTUGUESE

Historians of the period have probably not paid adequate attention to an additional set of sources that shed considerable light on the role of the Ethiopians in India at this time, namely those in Portuguese.[47] The chronicler Diogo do Couto (1542–1616), in his *Décadas da Ásia*, for example, returns time and again to the place of some figures who for whatever reason are too insignificant to appear in the Perso-Arabic materials, even if he too remains focused on male figures with a military-commercial profile.[48] Couto is an intriguing figure who cannot easily be pigeonholed into the stereotype of the Catholic crusader-historian, and who took a certain pride in incorporating elements gathered from renegades and indigenous informants in his narratives.[49] Some of these were persons with whom the Portuguese Estado had extended dealings, because they were in close proximity to places like Diu, where they had a fortress. Consider one case from the 1550s, that of Habash Khan (or "Abiscan"), who appears several times in Couto's text. In his version, after the assassination of Sultan Mahmud in 1554 various Gujarat notables moved to seize autonomous control of several territories. Habash Khan thus took "the lands of Dio from the hills of Una to those of Junager and made his residence in the city of Novanager."[50] He also appointed an agent, Sidi Hilal, to ensure that he received half the proceeds of the customhouse of Diu. This led to a series of skirmishes between the Sidi and the Portuguese, and if the Portuguese were initially successful in brutally raiding the Ethiopian settlement close to their fort, they began to suffer significant losses. Alarmed by this, they sent a diplomatic message asking the power broker 'Imad-ul-Mulk at court to intervene in their favor. As a consequence, Sidi Marjan replaced Sidi Hilal, but Habash Khan retained broad control of the area. After a brief pause, he continued to raid the Portuguese at Diu, leading them to try another tactic. They thus corresponded with Tatar Khan, a rival notable who had seized hold of Junagadh, and complained to him that Habash Khan was "a weak and false Abyssinian, possessing no merits" (*Abexim fraco, e falso, e sem merecimento algum*).[51] They prevailed upon Tatar Khan to march on the coastal lands and seize Porbandar, Mangrol, and other sites. Caught between these attacks and the Portuguese, Habash Khan reportedly was obliged to abandon the area and retire to the east. Refusing the demands of Tatar Khan and his agents to develop Ghogha as a center of maritime trade to the Red Sea, the Portuguese were able for a time to centralize shipping at Diu, which remained their customhouse and chief port in the area.

The Ethiopian elite in Gujarat is thus presented in the Portuguese view as a formidable and intractable group, determined to resist them where possible. After these events in Kathiawar, their next set of confrontations occurred a few years later, in the context of the frontier region of south Gujarat. Here the Portuguese Estado was troubled by the rise and consolidation of the port of Surat, which had emerged as an important commercial center in the 1540s. Consequently, the Portuguese attempted to obtain a foothold nearby, and they managed to persuade first 'Imad-ul-Mulk and then I'timad Khan to cede the area of Daman, south of Surat, to them. A group of Portuguese began to settle the area from late 1556, but the matter proved complicated, mainly because of the presence of a powerful set of Ethiopians in the area who were quite deeply entrenched.[52] Our main information again comes from Couto, who notes that the chief figures who resisted were Sidi Bu Fath ("Cide Bofatá"), assisted by Sidi Ra'na ("Cide Rana"), as well as a Turk by the name of Qarna Bey ("Carnabec"). This resistance was finally broken when the viceroy Dom Constantino de Bragança arrived in February 1559 with a large fleet and substantial reinforcements, so that Sidi Bu Fath was obliged to abandon his small fort at Daman and withdraw to the north beyond the Kolak River and as far as Parnera and Valsad.[53]

FIGURE 3.1. Sidi Bashir Mosque at Ahmedabad (Image: Cemal Kafadar).

However, on the viceroy's return to Goa, the Sidis returned to the attack, and a see-saw struggle followed over several months. First, the Portuguese mounted an attack on Valsad, and then the habashi cavalry swept down as far as Sanjan, Dahanu, and Tarapur, causing considerable destruction to these southern territories. Despite their best efforts, they were unable to take Daman itself, where the captain Dom Diogo de Noronha managed to hold out. In a last throw of the dice, a new actor entered the scene: this was, in Couto's words, "an Abyssinian called Cide Meriam [Sidi Marjan], a man considered to be a great knight, and who had five hundred horses in his stables." Gathering together a total force of some eight hundred cavalry and a thousand foot soldiers, four hundred of whom were gunners, he descended on Daman from the north in October 1559. On this occasion the Portuguese decided not to wait in their fort but instead sent out a force to meet him, hoping for combat in the "fields of Parnel [Parnera]." Couto's account of the fight is initially somewhat romantic.[54] Two cavaliers, Marjan and the Portuguese Garcia Rodrigues de Távora, after an exaggeratedly courteous exchange of letters, apparently met on horseback in single combat and charged at each other, lance in hand. They then fell to the ground in a mêlée, surrounded by others. An anonymous Portuguese soldier then killed Marjan with a lance.[55] What Couto does not mention, though Jesuit sources from the 1580s do, is that his men carried Marjan's body back to Surat, where it was buried with honor in the mausoleum of Khwaja Safar Khudawand Khan. By the mid-1570s the Sidi had acquired the posthumous reputation of a protector of mariners and a performer of miracles, and Hajji-ud-Dabir reports that when he visited his tomb in 1575, crowds gathered there on Fridays. In his brief account, he notes that Marjan had come from Bharuch to Daman to conduct a holy war (*fi al-jihad*) against the Portuguese and that on his death he was therefore remembered as "the holy warrior and martyr" (*al-mujahid al-shahid*) Marjan.[56]

The end of Sidi Bu Fath's regime at Daman arguably had more significant consequences for the habashis of western India than has generally been realized. If Couto is to be believed, there were "three thousand Abyssinians" in the settlement in 1559, and Bu Fath may have taken some two thousand with him when he fled. It is of some interest that the Portuguese chronicler does admit that the Estado came to terms with some of those who remained. He writes: "Because there were few Portuguese here who wished to accept villages [in grants], the viceroy granted them to Abyssinians [who had become] Christians, so that they might remain here, with the obligation of maintaining firearms [*espingardas*]."[57] This was a process known as *aforamento*, which the Portuguese had already followed in the 1530s in other nearby territories such as Bassein; the grantees (*foreiros*) received villages and collected revenue in exchange for rendering some basic military services. A later fiscal document from 1592, the *Tombo de Damão*, gives us an indication of some of the most significant grantees and their locations.[58] A few may be found in the central *parganas* of Moti Daman and Nani Daman, but most are located in the outlying areas of Lavachha, Sanjan, and Tarapur, bordering on the lands of the "rei de Sarzetas," the Koli Raja of Jawhar. But it is obvious that a much larger exodus took place southward into the Deccan. This was also

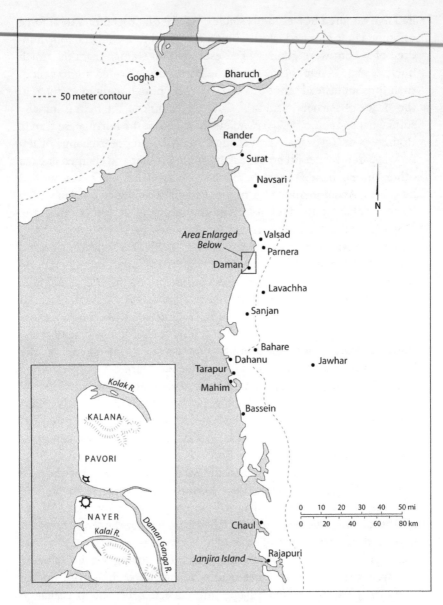

4. Daman and South Gujarat

because the 1560s and 1570s would prove relatively unwelcoming for the habashis in Gujarat. The Mughal conquest of the region in 1572–1573 left little room for them in the political system by contrast to the preceding fifty years. As we know, the Mughal *mansabdari* system—though it might have been accommodating to a variety of groups—never could

TABLE 3.1. Ethiopian-origin *foreiros* (grantees) in the Daman region, 1560–1590

Name	Village	Value (in réis)	Pargana
Paulo Pires	Adacari	3,200	Nayer (Moti Daman)
Barreto da Barca	Palarim	21,163	Pavori (Nani Daman)
Pedro Lopes	Varai	7,380	Pavori
Afonso Gonçalves	Siri	15,920	Kalana (Nani Daman)
Cristóvão Gonçalves	Batacara Vara	5,433	Kalana
Jerónimo de Sousa	Chalda	1,200	Kalana
Francisco Lopes	Panchalai	2,258	Lavachha
Luís de Moura	Borigão	10,675	Lavachha
Paulo de Moura	Loaça	20,545	Lavachha
António Barreto	Calambacala	923	Lavachha
Pedro de Almeida	Umbargão	11,623	Sanjan
António Lopes	Tumba	18,005	Sanjan
Gaspar Nunes	Vadagão	12,285	Sanjan
Jorge Mendes	Sarai	1,640	Sanjan
Paulo Afonso	Timbi	15,110	Sanjan
Lucas de Morim	Sarai	2nd purchaser	
Jerónimo Afonso	Deva Compa	7,520	Tarapur
Domingos Gonçalves	Vardum	17,320	Tarapur
Heitor de Sá	Vardum	New aforamento	Tarapur

Source: Artur Teodoro de Matos et al., eds., *Tombo de Damão, 1592* (Lisbon: CNCDP, 2001).

find a real place for the habashis with rare exceptions such as Sidi Miftah Habash Khan, commander of Udgir.[59]

But this was certainly not true for the sultanates of the Deccan, in particular Ahmadnagar and Bijapur, to a lesser extent Golconda. During the second half of the sixteenth century there was a great deal of mixing between these courts, owing not only to frequent intermarriages among the royal houses but also because notables (amirs) regularly switched loyalties between them. In the last third of the century, in the late 1560s and 1570s, the growing shadow of the habashis is first discernible in Ahmadnagar, during the reign of Murtaza Nizam Shah, as they intervened in a number of key struggles. In the first of these they helped Murtaza against his mother and the former regent, Khunza Humayun, who was determined to keep control of power; she was arrested and sequestered in Shivneri fort near Junnar.[60] Not long thereafter, in 1570, the sultan launched an attack on the Portuguese at Chaul, resulting in an extended siege that failed to attain its purpose. Contemporary Portuguese sources report the arrival on December 15, 1570, of the Ahmadnagar general Farhad Khan with "eight thousand horse, and many foot soldiers, and twenty elephants." They add: "Faratecão [Farhad Khan] was an Abyssinian captain, of great reputation, who greatly liked the Portuguese from the time of that great second siege that the Moors laid on Diu when Dom João Mascarenhas was captain, when this Abyssinian was in the service of the king of Cambay." In other words, he had already been in Gujarat in the mid-1540s and possessed long experience of dealings with the Estado da Índia.[61] Others involved in the siege operations included another habashi commander, Ikhlas Khan ("Agalascão"), described as "a very important person in the kingdom and captain-general of the field."[62] While this siege failed, when the Ahmadnagar armies came back to attack Portuguese Chaul again in the mid-1590s, they were led on this occasion by Fahim Khan, apparently a eunuch of Bengali origin, and the Ethiopian Farhad Khan, probably the same person chronicled in the 1570s. According to the Portuguese histories, Farhad Khan fought desperately on this occasion but was wounded and captured along with his wife and daughter. Couto recounts that before dying of his wounds Farhad Khan converted to Christianity and was hence buried with ceremony in Chaul; his wife produced a sizable ransom and left for Ahmadnagar, while the daughter also converted and was taken off to Lisbon.[63]

While the Ethiopian group had emerged by 1570 in a position of prominence in Ahmadnagar, in turn, the murder of 'Ali 'Adil Shah in 1579 opened up the possibility for them of profound changes in Bijapur. In the 1580s, the éminence grise who emerged was Dilawar Khan Habashi, together with two other Ethiopians, Ikhlas Khan and Hamid Khan. The early years of the reign of Ibrahim 'Adil Shah in Bijapur thus witnessed a turn toward a moderate form of Sunni Islam (unlike the Twelver Shi'ism favored by his uncle) and a gradual reconfiguration of courtly style toward the end of the century. But despite his early tutelage by Dilawar Khan, Ibrahim proved too wily to be dominated by any single group, even promoting Maharashtrian Brahmin ministers when it suited him better. On the other hand, by the end of the 1580s, the habashis were prepared to consolidate power in Ahmadnagar, apparently through a tactical alliance with the Dakanis against the long-dominant Iranian migrants. A period of considerable turmoil ensued as various rulers were displaced and assassinated from the late 1580s onward and scores were settled between political factions through bloodletting on the streets of the sultanate's capital. A number of habashis stand out in this context: Yaqut Khan, 'Ambar Khan, Shamshir Khan, Ankas Khan, Bulbul Khan, Habash Khan, and Abhang Khan (as well as the near-ubiquitous Farhad Khan), along with the main figure, the millenarian sectarian leader Jamal Khan (d. 1591), whom the Persian chroniclers regarded as bearing a great deal of responsibility for the turmoil. Adding to the problems, and perhaps even the root cause of them in some versions, was the growing pressure of Mughal expansion from the north. It would appear that by the end of the 1590s the Mughals were expecting their superior armies to advance easily beyond the Narmada River and handily defeat the weakened Ahmadnagar state, as they had done in the Rajasthan, Bengal, Sind, and elsewhere.

THE RISE OF THE MALIKS

Matters proved far more complicated in reality. The submission of Ahmadnagar took more than three decades and that of the other two major Deccan sultanates until the late 1680s. There were several causes for this delay, including the diplomatic acumen of some of the Deccan sultans. But one of them was the emergence of a powerful habashi elite in the Deccan, which built up clever regional alliances and offered substantial military resistance. As late as 1609, Philip III was writing to his viceroy in Goa with the view that opposing the Mughal armies was a hopeless task. He recalled that the earlier governor

> had written to me of [the state] in which the conquest of the Deccan was, with gave great reason for trepidation, because though the Mogor [Mughal] claimed to be our friend and had again sent an ambassador who was in waiting, he had heard that he [Jahangir] did not have good intentions with regard to his affairs; and because of the state in which even the walls of my fortresses in the North [Province] were, there was nothing to stop him except some resistance from the Idalcão ['Adil Khan], who had sent ambassadors to the Malik, and to the Cotta Maluco [Qutb-ul-Mulk], king of Masulupatão, and Avancatapanaique [Venkatappa Nayaka of Ikkeri], to all get together.[64]

In reality, even if Ibrahim 'Adil Shah did apply himself to diplomacy, mixed with a generous dose of bribery to Mughal frontier commanders, the real obstacle was in Ahmadnagar. In 1600 the Mughals had taken the capital city of the sultanate after some years of resistance mounted by Chand Sultana, regent and sister of a former ruler. But her own power had rested, as an earlier Portuguese viceroy had remarked, in an alliance with a protégé of the deceased Jamal Khan, namely Abhang Khan. This powerful figure—referred to both as Habashi and Zangi in the records—based himself in the fortified center of Junnar, west of Ahmadnagar, and this in turn became the initial base of one of those in his entourage who emerged in a position of prominence, 'Ambar Jiu or Malik 'Ambar.

Much has been written about 'Ambar, and a great deal of it is either open speculation or generous exaggeration.[65] Richard Eaton's short study of 'Ambar remains one of the most useful in recent times and carefully sifts plausible versions of his history from less plausible ones.[66] It would seem that 'Ambar was born with the name of Chapu in the Horn of Africa around 1548, then sold in the slave market of Mokha before being shipped off to Baghdad. From Iraq he was then sold to an important Ahmadnagar amir, Khwaja Mirak Dabir, titled Chingiz Khan, who was *wakil* and *peshwa* of the kingdom in the early 1570s.[67] After his master's death he was apparently manumitted and spent some time without fixed employment. At any rate, a decade and a half later, in the early 1590s, he appears to have spent time at the frontier fortress of Kandhar forty kilometers southwest of Nanded in order to secure it for Ibrahim 'Adil Shah (perhaps during the rebellion of his brother Isma'il), and he even constructed a bastion (the *burj-i 'Ambar*) and left two inscriptions there.[68] This seems to have been a custom of his, for other inscriptions bearing his name can be found at Antur fort and in the Shivneri Hills, the latter still referring to him, interestingly enough, as "Chingizkhani."[69] After his time in Kandhar, Malik 'Ambar returned to Ahmadnagar service and joined Abhang Khan Habashi, rising quickly to command 150 horsemen. After the fall of Ahmadnagar in 1600, he then seems to have hesitated in terms of his loyalties and considered offering his services to the Mughals. The account of the Mughal envoy Asad Beg Qazwini, present several times in the region in the early seventeenth century, gives us a good number of details, suggesting that on at least two occasions the subject of winning 'Ambar over had been discussed in high Mughal circles, such as with 'Abdur Rahim Khan-i Khanan. Of particular interest is Asad Beg's highly positive portrayal of the Ethiopian: not only was he "the bravest of the men of the time," but he was also apparently exemplary both in his courtesy and piety, giving large sums

FIGURE 3.2. Inscription of Malik 'Ambar, Antur Fort (author photo).

in alms and ensuring that in his camp, on every Friday evening, twelve thousand recitations of the Qur'an were carried out by *'ulama'* of caliber.[70] The chronicler Firishta, also a contemporary, describes his rise:

> After the return of Akbar Padshah from Burhanpur to Agra [April 1601], two persons of the late Nizam Shahi government distinguished themselves by their enterprise and conduct and, in spite of the Mughal forces, down to the present period, have retained almost the whole of the Nizam Shahi dominions. The one, Malik 'Ambar Habashi, possesses the country from the borders of Tilang to within one *farsakh* of the fortress of Bir, and four *karohs* of Ahmadnagar, and from twenty *karohs* west of Daulatabad to within the same distance of the port of Chaul. The latter, known as Raju, possesses lands from Daulatabad as far north as the Gujarat frontier and south to within six *kos* of Ahmadnagar: both officers from necessity profess the semblance of allegiance to Murtaza Nizam Shah the second.[71]

In the following years, 'Ambar first defeated Miyan Raju and then expelled the Mughals from Ahmadnagar. In 1610 he moved his capital from Junnar to the prestigious center of Daulatabad and began the process or reorganizing the land cadasters of the region in an effort to rationalize the revenue administration. Further, he showed a quite distinct interest in maritime affairs, as we see from his repeated dealings with the Portuguese in Chaul, as well as with regard to Danda Rajapuri, slightly to the south. Later in the 1610s and 1620s, we find references to ships owned by him and his associates, plying the routes to the Red

Sea and the Hadramaut. English Company records inform us that the master of their ship, the *Andrew*, reported in September 1621 the seizure of "a juncke of the Mellick Ambers, which he had taken coming from the Red Sea, upon consideration of wrongs which hee had donne unto our marchants in Mogulls country by robing their caffely in coming downe from Agra."[72] This retaliation for an attack on a caravan in central India carrying English goods (for which they incorrectly accused 'Ambar) became the occasion for a long drawn out dispute. The English even sent a representative, Robert Jeffries, to Daulatabad, but he was unable to make much headway.[73] Nevertheless, these dealings in the first half of the 1620s showed that Malik 'Ambar was active as a maritime trader from Chaul and nearby ports, using other Ethiopians—such as Sidi Sarur, *nakhuda* of his captured ship—as his agents. He also appears to have used these ships to the Red Sea to carry "rice for the poore [pilgrims], which hee yearly sendes" a confirmation of his reputation for alms-giving (*sadaqa*).[74]

Unlike the case of late fifteenth-century Bengal, Malik 'Ambar did not choose to directly seize sovereign power, instead reserving for himself the more modest title of *peshwa* (first minister). After his death in May 1626, his son Fath Khan as well as a number of other Ethiopians continued to play a significant political role in Ahmadnagar and thereafter in Bijapur. An analysis of the Bijapur *umara'* in the middle decades of the seventeenth century continues to show a sizable place for these men, some of whom even emerged as important literary and cultural figures in the Dakani language, such as Malik Khushnud (fl. 1630–1645), author of the important versified work *Jannat Singar*.[75] They also play an important role in the southward campaigns that took the Bijapur Sultanate in the direction of the conquest of a good part of the Kannada and Tamil country in the 1640s and 1650s. Those involved in the southward push included Sidi Raihan, first titled Ikhlas Khan, and then Khan-i-Khanan (d. 1657), who was a prominent commander; Randaula Khan, titled Rustam-i-Zaman, who controlled parts of the Konkan and the port of Rajapuri; and other prominent figures including Sidi Jauhar of Karnul and his son-in-law Sidi Mas'ud.[76] In the course of the seventeenth century a group of Ethiopians also gradually took control of Janjira, a fortified island off Rajapuri south of Chaul, and made it the center of their activities as purveyors of maritime protection and violence. After the fall of Ahmadnagar in 1636, their level of autonomy grew, and in the 1660s they entered into open conflict with the expanding Maratha state of Shivaji for control of the Konkan and its trade. The Marathas mounted repeated attacks on Janjira in 1669–1670, 1675–1676, and so on;

FIGURE 3.3. Portrait of Ikhlas Khan Habshi with a petition (San Diego Museum of Art, Edwin Binney III Collection, 1990.442).

the Sidis, for their part, were driven to seek an alliance with the Mughals and managed to survive the Maratha onslaught.[77] We cannot be certain of the migratory paths that most of these individuals and families (for the most part less well documented than Malik 'Ambar) actually took. Unlike him, some of them may in fact have belonged to a second or third generation, with roots going back perhaps to an earlier moment in Kathiawar or Daman.

A COMPLEX AXIS

This chapter has focused on certain aspects of human and commercial mobility across the western Indian Ocean, notably between the African East Coast and western India in the early modern period. As noted at the outset, this is a less-studied theme than the relatively robust and historically continuous maritime commercial link between the Persian Gulf and India, a link made even stronger with the establishment in the Deccan of the Bahmanis and their successors.[78] On the other hand, relations between the Deccan and eastern Africa were probably indirect in the medieval centuries and were rendered more stable and direct only in the sixteenth century, with the emergence of direct contacts between Chaul and Goa on the one hand and ports such as Sofala, Mozambique, and Mombasa on the other. The migratory movements involved are also contrasting. Though some military slaves certainly made their way from Iran via the Persian Gulf ports to the Deccan, the bulk of the movement was of free individuals. These were mostly male, but there also some women, even if their individual movements and careers prove far harder to follow and track down. Further, there was also a real process of circulation, for these Persians often retained contact with their *watan* (homeland) and even returned there on occasion.[79] In contrast, the Africans, usually habashis, who found their way to the Deccan and western India more generally did so in their vast majority in the context of slave trade. The names that they had in India often reflect this fact and include precious or semiprecious stones and objects—Marjan (coral), Yaqut (ruby), 'Ambar (ambergris), and Sandal (sandalwood)—or titles using terms of loyalty or ethnicity; they are for the most part not the names they would have had in their eastern African places of origin. We also have little or no evidence of continued contacts or correspondence with their places of origin, unlike the cases of some of the prominent Ottoman *kul*, for instance.[80]

Nevertheless, some memories remained or were maintained in place. The most intriguing instance of this comes from 'Abdullah Hajji-ud-Dabir Ulughkhani, who served not one but two habashi masters, as we have seen. Among the textual sources he uses and cites are some from India and Gujarat, but one stands out, namely the Arabic chronicle of Shihab-ud-Din Ahmad 'Arab Faqih, *Futuh al-Habasha* (or *Tuhfat al-Zaman*). Written in the Red Sea region early in the second half of the sixteenth century—its author originally came from the port of Jizan—this text was meant to exhort the Muslims of the region to return to their combat against the Ethiopian Christians, and as such it was intended at the same time to recall the life and circumstances of the now-deceased hero Imam Ahmad. It is clear that Hajji-ud-Dabir possessed a manuscript of this text, for he paraphrases long passages from it in order to provide some context to the many habashi notables who people his own history.[81] He obviously had spoken with at least some of them, for he adds details that do not appear to come from the text of 'Arab Faqih. In sum, the bulk of the habashis of Gujarat and the Deccan in the early modern period looked back not to a Christian past in the Horn of Africa but to a history that located them squarely in the struggle to establish a place for Islam in the western Indian Ocean.

Can we advance our understanding of this particular set of histories by placing it in a larger comparative context, either that of the Atlantic or of the Mediterranean? One comparison that is frequently made is in quantitative terms to measure the African slave trade eastward in the Indian Ocean in relation to that westward into the Atlantic. The fact is, however, that not only are the statistics for the Indian Ocean far less reliable than those for the Atlantic, but any comparison in such terms is also largely debatable. Slaves were transported across the early modern Atlantic essentially in a context of plantation slavery or on some occasions as household slaves in an urban context. With relatively few exceptions, such as the Mascarene Islands (Mauritius and Réunion) after the 1670s, plantation slavery was not the norm in the Indian Ocean.[82] On the other hand, the possibility of crossing the waters to be integrated as an elite slave into a distant political system was a real possibility in the western Indian Ocean until 1750, whereas no African headed westward could consider this a realistic outcome in Portuguese Brazil, in Spanish America, or Anglo-America (even if former slaves could sometimes enjoy considerable economic success).[83] The habashis of Gujarat and the Deccan could thus become powerful agents and political actors, at least in some conspicuous instances, rather than subaltern performers in a history dominated by other groups. Of course, this does not mean that it is not useful or interesting to compare individual trajectories or microhistories across the two oceanic spaces. This is precisely what historians of Islam in Brazil or colonial America have helped us to do in recent times.[84] At the same time, extending the comparison to the relatively minor—but nevertheless significant—phenomenon of African slavery in a space such as the early modern Ottoman Empire helps us give nuance to the contrast between the Indian Ocean and Atlantic spaces. The crucial post of the habashi "chief eunuch" in the Ottoman court gives us access to a series of fascinating figures, ranging from Mehmed Agha (d. 1590) in the high Ottoman period to Beshir Agha (d. 1746) a century and a half later.[85] While becoming powerful political intermediaries on the one hand, and thus at some remove from the African Americans of the colonial era, these figures were nevertheless usually unable to be more than power brokers, more limited and circumscribed in their scope and ambitions than their South Asian counterparts. Comparison could thus lead us to better comprehend the specificity of these politico-social regimes, as well as their trajectories over time.

Chapter 4
The View from Surat

> The traffic of Sourat is great, and the revenue of the customshouse prodigious, because of the quantity of vessels that one loads up there for diverse parts of the world, in keeping with the tides, the seasons, and the winds, which regulate [affairs] in the Tropics.
>
> François le Gouz de la Boullaye, *Les voyages* (1653)

In her evocative study of the Yemeni port of Mokha (Mocha), the art historian Nancy Um has noted a preference in recent Indian Ocean studies for painting with a broad brush, producing works "which oblige readers to traverse vast tracts of maritime space in the course of a single page," and contrasts this with her own proclivity for "a more focused case of a port city within the worlds in which it functioned."[1] Nevertheless, Um argues for the need to broaden the implications of the case study itself through the judicious use of comparative material from elsewhere while at the same time eschewing the temptation to "draw all-encompassing conclusions about the greater Indian Ocean region." In her closing pages she returns to similar issues of method, stressing "Mocha's particular site, as a port city in communication with the Yemeni interior and the Indian Ocean" and arguing that while "wider regional patterns may be drawn from its example . . . its geographic and temporal specificity are of key significance here."[2] As microhistorians have warned, the devil does really lie in the details.

This chapter is also focused on a port city, but it is equally a reflection on a vexed concept. Much has been written in the past few decades on the idea of "cosmopolitanism," and it is certain that in an era like ours, when violent expressions of patriotism, exclusionary identity politics, and local assertion are growing, the concept will regularly find itself under challenge. So who is a cosmopolitan, and where and when can one find a phenomenon, attitude, or ideological posture that may be called "cosmopolitanism"? Writings on cosmopolitanism as a historical phenomenon (as distinct from simply a vague transcendent ideal) often seem to draw it directly into a history of ideas, and more particularly Western ideas. A common point of departure is to turn to the brief but quite dense article in the first edition of the *Encyclopédie*, with the title "cosmopolitain, ou cosmopolite."[3] Here it is noted that the word derives from two Greek elements, *kosmos* (*monde*) and *polis* (*ville*), and that it means "a man who has no fixed abode" (*un homme qui n'a point de demeure fixe*) or "a man who is a stranger nowhere" (*un homme qui n'est étranger nulle part*). Less remarked is the fact that the article begins by commenting that "one uses this name at times as a joke" (*on se sert quelquefois de ce nom en plaisantant*), suggesting that such an attitude was seen already in the mid-eighteenth century as ridiculous and perhaps pretentious. We are further given to understand that it is an ancient word and attitude, but one that is being revived in recent times, especially in the context of the Enlightenment.

The revival of the word in French has been traced to the sixteenth century, notably to the sulfurous figure of Guillaume Postel (1510–1581). His 1560 work *De la république des Turcs* states on its title page that its author is "Guillaume Postel cosmopolite," and Postel goes on then to claim in his usual tortuous style in the dedication that he calls himself a "cosmopolite" because of his desire to see the emergence of "universal peace" (*la paix universelle*), but further that he would like above all to see it brought about "under the French Crown" (*sous la Couronne de France*). In other words, he perceived no contradiction between his quite overt French patriotism and his claims to be a cosmopolitan.[4] In the late sixteenth and early seventeenth centuries, the term "cosmopolitan" or "cosmopolite" was then picked up and used as a self-definition by a series of somewhat obscure alchemists, such as the Scotsman Alexander Seton (d. 1604), active in Prague, and author of *Cosmopolite, ou Nouvelle lumière de la physique naturelle*. In the course of the seventeenth century, as Paul Hazard has remarked, the term became more and more frequently used, and also used interchangeably with the phrase *citoyen du monde* (citizen of the world).[5] An example of the latter may be found in a letter written in October 1655 by Abraham du Prat in Paris to Thomas Hobbes, at that time in London, introducing him to "Monsieur De la Boulaye, a gentleman . . . who is esteemed in Paris by all honest people. He has travelled up to the borders of China, and very judiciously observed everything of significance in all the lands through which he passed. . . . He is one of those who call themselves citizens of the world [*il est du nombre de ceux qui se disent citoyens du monde*]."[6]

We happen to know a fair amount regarding this person, François le Gouz de la Boullaye (1623–1667). Born near Baugé in the Anjou region, he studied at the Jesuit Collège de la Flèche, as the celebrated René Descartes had done just before him.[7] He began his early travels in the early

1640s and returned to France, after visiting a vast number of countries, in the early 1650s. He published the first edition of his *Voyages et observations* in 1653. In this text, he presented himself as a protean character who sometimes took on the character of "Ibrahim Beg" when in the Ottoman Empire, Safavid Iran, and Mughal India, but who was also known as *le voyageur catholique*. By the mid-1650s, when du Prat wrote his letter, La Boullaye was well regarded as a man of the world and had apparently been introduced into the court of the young Louis XIV by an Angevin nobleman, Guillaume Bautru, comte de Serrant. His self-presentation was one of a gentleman of sophistication and knowledge, who liked dressing up in exotic clothes and often signed his letters in Persian characters as "La Bulay." But some of his contemporaries, such as the Huguenot jeweler and traveler Jean-Baptiste Tavernier, found him unbearably pretentious and precious, scarcely capable of living up to his own self-image as a bridge between cultures.[8] La Boullaye ended his life under shadowy circumstances in eastern India in 1667, and if Tavernier is to be believed, his death may be partly attributed to his incompetence in the matter of communication across cultures.

We can nevertheless see through such a career how one became a cosmopolitan in western Europe in the early modern period. It was often a matter of travel and the knowledge of other cultures, as well as the claim that one had a certain openness or tolerance toward such experiences. The knowledge of foreign languages was undoubtedly of help, especially if added to a classical education, and the status of a gentleman (if not a proper noble title). This is the point of view that Margaret Jacob encapsulates as a particular sort of "benign posture": "They [cosmopolitans] accept the foreign hospitably, without necessarily agreeing with, or practicing, every cultural value associated with it. They enjoy people different from themselves, live next to them comfortably, or socialize and trade with them respectfully."[9] A spate of recent publications has tried to address the question of whether there are one or many cosmopolitanisms. At first sight, this appears to be a variant of a familiar strategy from the "multiple modernities" literature. But "cosmopolitanism" is a different animal, analytically speaking, from "modernity." It is not tied to temporal sequence in quite the same way, and few would deny that it is also a perfectly reversible phenomenon or attitude (if one takes it in that more subjective sense).

Jacob also offers us an opening into a rather different way of approaching cosmopolitanism, namely one that is more sensitive to questions of variations in place. As she states it, cosmopolitanism "happens when circumstances or situations, times, and places exist that are propitious."

There were then certain times and places that made it possible to "experience people of different nations, creeds and colors with pleasure, curiosity and interest, and not with suspicion, disdain, or simply a disinterest that could occasionally turn into loathing." Perhaps certain political structures were more propitious than others. Again, perhaps certain cultural formations were better able to sustain the complex of attitudes implied in cosmopolitanism than others. One place that historians have frequently looked at in their search for cosmopolitan attitudes are thus the great imperial capitals, which were nearly by definition places of great mixing, where many languages, peoples, and cultures came together. London in the seventeenth and eighteenth centuries may be evoked, as can the Istanbul of Sultan Süleyman, the Paris of Louis XIV, or the Prague of Rudolf II; far earlier, for the thirteenth century, Thomas Allsen called the capital of the Mongols in Qara Qorum a major center with a "cosmopolitan flavor." "When the Franciscan friar William of Rubruck arrived there in early 1254," Allsen writes, "he met in quick succession a Hungarian servant, a French maid, a Greek soldier, a Nestorian interpreter, a Russian carpenter, and a Parisian goldsmith. By the time of his departure in late spring he had encountered Chinese physicians, Uighur scribes, Korean princes, and Armenian priests, as well."[10] Indeed, Allsen goes so far as to write of "the cosmopolitanism inherent in the Mongol system of governance," which extended well beyond the elites.

In this chapter I approach the question of cosmopolitanism using a different yet familiar site: the port city. I have chosen to do so for at least two reasons. First, if one were to choose a great imperial city such as the Mughal capital of Shahjahanabad-Delhi, there might be some suspicion (as with Qara Qorum) that we are in the presence of a form of forced mixing, brokered by the naked use of political power.[11] Rather than evoking "pleasure, curiosity and interest," might these not be places where different peoples lived uneasily cheek by jowl, simply because they were obliged to do so as a consequence of serving a great imperial household and its offshoots? A second reason is on account of a desire to explore the intriguing relationship between commerce and cosmopolitanism in the western Indian Ocean, developing themes already present in an implicit fashion in earlier chapters. Theorized in part by later Enlightenment philosophers such as Adam Smith, there is once again a danger that this relationship slips imperceptibly into a history of European exceptionalism.[12] This is why it is important to consider a port far away from Europe, even if it did house a certain number of Europeans: I refer here to the Auspicious Port (*bandar-i mubarak*) of the Mughals, the western Indian port of Surat.[13] Surat's reputation as the quintessence of

Indian Ocean cosmopolitanism would be confirmed even in Europe at the end of the eighteenth century, when Bernardin de Saint-Pierre chose it as the setting for his allegorical Enlightenment tale about religious difference and convergence, entitled "Le café de Surate."[14] By that time the port was arguably in decline.

HOW SURAT EMERGED

It is often forgotten that in the beginning for Surat there was the sticky matter of an artillery fortress. In the early sixteenth century, when the first Portuguese descriptions of the Indian Ocean littoral come to us, Surat appears as a somewhat minor site, one of many ports that dotted the Gujarat and Konkan coastline. The two dominant ports for long-distance trade were rather Diu to the west and Khambayat (or Cambay) to the east, the latter closely linked to the great centers of inland power and consumption. In the celebrated account of Tomé Pires (ca. 1515) for example, Surat appears alongside Daman and Rander as ports controlled by a Gujarat notable called Dastur Khan.[15] But it is evident that rather than Surat, it was Rander (which the Portuguese sources term "Reinel"), located slightly farther up the Tapti River and on its opposite bank, that was the more important center for overseas commerce. This was partly because Rander had been settled earlier and boasted an important community of Nawayat Muslims, many of whom were thought to be expert navigators in the context of the western Indian Ocean. Nevertheless, some of the great Gujarati merchants of the early sixteenth century such as the Brahmin entrepreneur Malik Gopi (or Gopinath) did take a certain interest in Surat; in his case, he is responsible for the construction of the large water tank there known as Gopi Talav.[16]

But conflicts between the Gujarat sultans and the Portuguese in the 1520s and 1530s then had a significant influence on matters. The Portuguese were keen to acquire Diu, which they saw as an important port both in and of itself, and on account of its close connections to the Ottomans (or *rumis*). When the Gujarat sultans resisted their pressure, Portuguese fleets frequently raided the coastal settlements not only in Kathiawar but also on the banks of the Tapti River, with one particularly important attack being carried out in 1530 by the captain António da Silveira on both Surat and Rander. As the Portuguese chronicler Castanheda would have it, Rander was at this time an important settlement "with good houses of stone and chalk, many with an upper storey, and very well-made."[17] On this occasion, Silveira landed first in Surat and "for a whole day and a night, burnt it entirely so that no house remained standing, and the gardens and palm-groves around were all cut down and destroyed, and many small vessels [*cotias*] laden with supplies that were bound for Diu were also burnt." The Portuguese force then moved on to Rander, where the inhabitants did put up a fair amount of resistance, with improvised fortifications and even the use of some artillery. The Portuguese were able to penetrate into the main street (*rua principal*) of the town and proceeded to sack the houses ruthlessly, with the chronicler nevertheless noting with admiration that many of the buildings had gilded facades with semiprecious stones embedded in them. In Castanheda's view, Rander was among "the principal places that traded with China," and as a result it had residences and stores filled with merchandise, "principally copper, and ivory, and porcelain, and other things of much value." However, since Silveira soon realized that it would be impossible to load his vessels with all the goods that were to be found there without risking the lives of those on board, he decided instead to set fire to the houses in Rander as well as to some twenty large ships that he found at anchor in the river, along with a number of smaller vessels.

Five years later, in 1535, the weakened Gujarat Sultan reluctantly ceded Diu to the Portuguese in the hope of buying peace. But the former Ottoman subjects who were by that time active in his domains had other plans. They managed to persuade Istanbul to send out a fleet to besiege Diu in 1538 (as noted in chapter 2), and after this expedition failed to produce significant results, they appear to have moved their activities to centers in south Gujarat such as Bharuch, Surat, and Daman. Chief among these men was an enigmatic character, Khwaja Safar al-Salmani, who had once been in the entourage of the Ottoman corsair Salman Re'is. Originating from the region of Otranto and of either Italian or mixed Albanian and Italian origin, Safar was a convert to Islam who could still speak Italian and retained strong cultural connections to the Mediterranean world.[18] He first appeared in Gujarat in the late 1520s, accompanying Mustafa Bairam, a nephew of Salman Re'is, and even after Bairam's defection to the Mughals in 1534 he at least remained loyal to the Gujarat sultans. This loyalty, which included accompanying Sultan Bahadur of Gujarat on his fateful visit to see the Portuguese governor Nuno da Cunha in February 1537 (in the course of which the sultan was killed), meant that he was rewarded with the title of Khudawand Khan and allowed to use Surat as his headquarters. It was he who then chose the unusual option of building a square artillery fortress on the banks of the Tapti River in order to ensure that there would be no further Portuguese raids there.

Writing several decades later, the Mughal chronicler Khwaja Nizam-ud-Din Ahmad was one of those who paid attention to this event. The occasion for him to return to it was in his account of the campaign of 1572–1573, when the Mughal emperor Akbar personally had to besiege this fort and force it to surrender. Nizam-ud-Din begins by noting that the fort had been built by "a slave of Sultan Mahmud Gujrati, named Safar Aqa, who had the title of Khudawand Khan," in order to deal with "the disturbances caused by the *firangis*."[19] After Khudawand Khan's death in 1546 it had been for a time in the hands of another Gujarat Sultanate notable by the name of Chingiz Khan, and after his death it had in turn fallen into the hands of Akbar's rebellious cousins, the Timurid Mirzas. In both Nizam-ud-Din's text and the subsequent one of Badayuni, the principal purpose is to describe the actual Mughal siege and capture of the fortress, which was apparently under the temporary control of Hamzaban, a former employee of Akbar's father Humayun who had deserted his service. We learn from Badayuni that in the month of Ramazan 980 AH (January 1573), Akbar began a quite elaborate siege; "he threw up immense mounds and high batteries, and the gunners and artillerymen kept up such a fire from under the cover of them, that not an individual of the garrison of the fort dared to show his head."[20] After nearly two months of this, the garrison sued for peace and the fort was taken; the chronogram for the victory was declared as *'ajab qil'a girāft* (he has taken a marvelous fort). Akbar then ordered repairs to be made and recovered some large Ottoman cannons, which it is claimed were leftovers from the time of the expedition against Diu in 1538. (In reality, they seem to have come from Seydi 'Ali Re'is's fleet of 1554.)

Now, the Mughals had successfully besieged and taken a number of fortresses in the preceding decades. But this particular artillery fortress seems to have attracted Nizam-ud-Din's and Badayuni's attention precisely because it was a maritime fort defending a port town. Nizam-ud-Din thus notes that "before it was built, the *firangis* had caused damage and injury of various kinds to the Musalmans," while Badayuni stressed that "the Franks [Portuguese] used to exercise all kinds of animosity and hostility against the people of Islam [*ba ahl-i Islam*], and used to occupy themselves in devastating the country, and tormenting the pious." While the fort was being constructed, the Portuguese allegedly tried to bombard the site on several occasions. But this was all to no avail:

> Khudawand Khan collected expert masons at the time and arranged for the strengthening of the fort. The skilled engineers planned the building in such a way that on both the landward sides of the fort moats were dug twenty yards in width which

reached to the water, and the walls were built of stone and lime and burnt bricks from the water. The breadth of the double walls was five yards; and their height twenty yards. One of the curiosities of the construction was this, that the stones were fastened together with iron clamps, and molten lead was poured into the joints and interstices. The turrets and embrasures were built in such a way that the eyes of the spectators were astonished on seeing them. On each bastion, a *chaukandi* [turret] was built, which in the opinion of the *firangis*, belonged especially to Portugal.[21]

Unable to stop the construction, the Portuguese are then reported to have tried to suborn Khudawand Khan so that he would desist; however, "Khudawand Khan, having made up his mind to set the opinion of the *firangis* at defiance, rejected all their prayers and completed the construction of the *chaukandis*." A few years later, in 1546, the Portuguese had come to learn that this fort now had a garrison of about two hundred, including some forty Rumis (or former Ottomans) and thirty Malays commanded by a Rumi, with the aid of an Abyssinian commander in the city; it also had some small vessels (or *fustas*) at its disposal for defensive ends. They also learned through their intelligence network that Khudawand Khan and another rich merchant called Malik "Mamenade" had several vessels coming and going from Surat (as well as Rander) to such partner ports as Aceh, Jiddah, and Tenasserim (in the Bay of Bengal), and that these included rather large ships (or *naos*) of some 1,200 khandis burthen (a khandi being roughly 330 kilograms).[22] In the previous year there had already been complaints by Portuguese officials that "the ships that set out from Cambaia [i.e., Gujarat], principally from Çurrate and Reinel, set out with [Portuguese] *cartazes* and go with their goods and claiming to make for Malaca, and take the route in that direction; and if they do not encounter any Portuguese ship that might impede it, as soon as they are in the [Andaman] islands or in Nicubar, they turn their prow towards Achem [Aceh], and sell their goods to great advantage there, and load up with pepper."[23]

Khudawand Khan was killed in June 1546 while supervising an attack on the Portuguese in Diu. Soon after his death, the chronicler Diogo do Couto reports that the Portuguese governor Dom João de Castro received a message to the effect that Qara Hasan (or "Caracen"), Khudawand Khan's son-in-law, was now the captain of Surat, but that he had at his disposal "very few people, and it was so unprotected [*tão descuidado*] that the fortress could very easily be captured."[24] The governor therefore sent off his son Dom Álvaro with eighty vessels, instructing him to enter the Surat River at night and effect the capture.[25] The latter arrived near the port, and sent an advance party of seven light vessels upriver to scout out the situation. But they were detected soon enough, and the guns in the fortress fired at them so that the Portuguese were obliged to withdraw. While doing so, it is reported that they attacked an Abyssinian settlement (*a villa dos Abexins*) near Athwa, "which is a watering spot [*poço*], where the ships from Mecca anchor." Another nearby target was a small Hindu temple (*hum pagodinho*) in the vicinity. After a set of further skirmishes had taken place, Dom Álvaro eventually decided to pull out to the mouth of the Tapti River, much to the discontent of some of the other captains, who wished to fight on. A few days later, his father Dom João de Castro joined him there with reinforcements. By this time, news had come to the Portuguese from a spy that many more men had joined the defense of the Surat garrison. The governor therefore decided to abandon the attack, and after a short time in and around Bharuch he went on to Diu.

The Portuguese then returned to the attack a decade and a half later, in around 1560. Meanwhile, emboldened by the construction of the fortress, the merchants and governors of Surat took an increasingly defiant stance with regard to the Portuguese, as we see when the Ottoman admiral Seydi 'Ali Re'is was shipwrecked in the vicinity in 1554 and was granted asylum for a time in Surat.[26] It seems that not a year went by in the later 1540s and 1550s when ships from Surat did not set out on the one hand for Southeast Asian destinations and on the other for the chief Red Sea port of Jiddah. It was therefore a matter of some surprise when secret letters arrived in Goa in 1560 for the viceroy, Dom Constantino de Bragança, from a number of sources, including the man who now bore the title of Khudawand Khan ("Cedemecan, Senhor de Surrate") and who was reported to be the younger son of none other than Khwaja Safar. In these letters he reported that he was being besieged by Chingiz Khan, one of his close relatives, and "that he was in such risk of losing his fortress that he would rather hand it over to the King of Portugal, and the Portuguese, in whom he had always found much love and friendship."[27] The viceroy consulted with the captain of Daman, Dom Diogo da Silva, who told him that "that fortress [Surat] was the most important thing that could be offered to him. Because besides the fact that one could expect great revenues from its customs-house, on account of the commodity of its port, it protected the lands of Daman and Bassein." The viceroy was much taken with the idea of this unexpected windfall and promptly dispatched a fleet of fourteen oared ships under Dom António de Noronha, which left Goa in the middle of the month of April 1560. Couto claims for his part that the reasons for these tensions were that Chingiz Khan was much aggrieved on account of the death of his father, 'Imad-al-mulk, for which he blamed Khudawand Khan. He had thus decided to besiege Surat with a large force, and in his party there was even a group of Timurid Mirzas, footloose cousins of the Mughal dynasty.

The go-between who was designated by the Portuguese to deal with Khudawand Khan was apparently a rather enigmatic Jew called Khoja Abraham. He maintained the channels of communication open, assuring him that the Portuguese would support and defend him. A few days later, the Portuguese fleet made its way up the Tapti River to the vicinity of the fortress. There were various skirmishes between them and Chingiz Khan, at the end of which the latter rather surprisingly withdrew from the region without having sustained major losses. Couto claims that he was persuaded to withdraw by his mother, who it turned out was the daughter of Khwaja Safar, and who feared that he too would be killed by the Portuguese like his grandfather. After this initial success, it is reported that Dom António de Noronha began negotiations with Khudawand Khan for the quick handover of the fortress. But Khudawand Khan claimed that Chingiz Khan was still in the vicinity and that he wanted the Portuguese to expel him entirely before acting further. A formal meeting was finally arranged between Noronha and Khudawand Khan, with Khoja Abraham present. But the Khan kept putting matters off, week after week, until it was mid-May. Fearing that he would be trapped in the Tapti on account of the imminent monsoon, Noronha was then obliged hastily to come out of the river into the open sea with his fleet and departed for Daman without having accomplished his mission. Once again the fortress proved to be out of the reach of the Portuguese. However, Couto reports, Khudawand Khan had in the meantime become very insecure himself. The powerful Nawayats of Rander had apparently witnessed his dealings with the Portuguese and begun to suspect that he would hand them over "with their wives and sons" to the Portuguese.[28] They began to make plans to depose and assassinate him, and the Khan—who had caught wind of this—is reported to have become increasingly erratic in his behavior. A Jesuit letter from Daman written in February 1561 reported that "a month ago, he killed 24 people, who included three or four who advised him, such as a very knowledgeable Brahmin who was his financial advisor [*seu veador da fazenda*]. He is so distrustful of the others that he personally kills the sheep with his hands, and himself stews what he intends to eat." Another letter of the same period claimed that "having killed ten or twelve of his principal men, he rushed out of the fortress like a madman, saying that he did not know whom to trust, for they were planning a treasonous plot to kill him. He remained six days out of the fortress and shaved himself down to his eyebrows, saying that he wanted to become a *jogue* [mendicant]."[29]

Such a situation of extreme neurosis could clearly not last long. Soon after, Couto tells us that he was obliged to take a small escort of fifteen men and escape the fort at night, leaving his wives and treasure behind. He then made his way to the Gujarat Sultanate's court in Ahmedabad, where the vizier, I'timad Khan, welcomed him. Chingiz Khan reportedly came to know of his movements and cleverly bribed two men—a Circassian Turk and an Abyssinian eunuch—to kill him.[30] Using the opportunity of a hunt they managed to do so, and the news of his death quickly arrived in Surat. Those who had taken control of the fort in his absence therefore called upon his brother-in-law, Jahangir Khan (apparently the title of the same Qara Hasan whom we encountered in late 1546), and requested him to become the fortress commander. More prudent than his predecessor, he made peace with Chingiz Khan. So, Couto concludes: "When a son was born to Chinguiscan, Caracem went to celebrate the occasion in Baroche, where I visited him, as I found myself at that time in that city, and because I was a great friend of his, since we both read Italian, and I showed him [works by] Dante, Petrarch, [Pietro] Bembo and other poets, that he enjoyed seeing."[31] Italian Renaissance authors thus proved a cultural bridge between a Portuguese chronicler and a renegade Ottoman at the very moment of Surat's emergence.

Meanwhile, commercial traffic between Surat and the ports of West Asia remained impressive throughout the period. In 1560, for example, Couto notes that while the Portuguese fleet was in the Tapti in front of Surat fort, "nearby [was] a most lovely *nao* called *Rupaia*, which means the silver ship, because every year it arrived from Mecca with a great sum thereof, as well as other riches, since it was a vessel in which the richest merchants from all the kingdom of Cambaia travelled; and the people on the [Portuguese] fleet considered it to be larger than any ship on the *Carreira da Índia*, to the point that almost all the soldiers in their fleet could fit into it." Couto also states that in 1568, for example, the Portuguese viceroy sent a fleet of six vessels "to go in August to Surrate, to prevent the ships that leave there for Achem without *cartazes*, and those which were to come back from Mecca to that river, which always return laden with silver and rich goods." The Portuguese apparently sighted one large ship (*huma fermosa nao*), which managed to evade them, but captured two others from Jiddah, whose booty is said very easily to have exceeded 100,000 cruzados.³² This was in spite of an arrangement that had been arrived at in late 1561 between Qara Hasan and the Estado, reported in a letter by the Portuguese viceroy that year. He wrote: "From Çurrate, Caracem asked me for a truce and some sign of favor. . . . I granted him the peace on the condition that he should give me and the Estado 12,000 cruzados a year, besides a small quantity of cottons, which he should either pay me, or all the naos of Çurrate should go and pay in the customs-house in Damão."³³

Thus, while historians of the Mughal Empire have sometimes claimed that the prosperity of Surat can entirely be attributed to the Mughal conquest of 1572–1573, it is worth stressing that the Mughals only helped along a process that was already well under way.³⁴ In particular, it is likely that they strengthened the ties between Surat and the Mughal heartland in northern India, whereas earlier the port had a hinterland that would probably have been largely limited to Gujarat and central India (through the important inland entrepôt of Burhanpur). A brief but intriguing description of Surat comes to us from the late 1570s and the pen of the Jesuit Antoni Montserrat, who visited there en route to the Mughal court.

> Surat stands on the river Taphaeus [Tapi], which enters the sea six miles from the town. The citadel is in a naturally strong position, is well fortified, and is guarded by a garrison of two hundred mounted archers. The town is adorned by a lake [the Gopi Talav], which is much the largest and the most beautiful (by reason of the pains which have been taken to embellish it artificially) of all the lakes that are to be seen in India. . . . The place is also dignified by the tomb of Qhoja Sopharis [Khwaja Safar, Khudawand Khan], who is frequently mentioned by our writers for his treachery and abandoned character. This tomb is rather an extraordinary structure but is elaborately and expensively decorated. Close by is the grave of another worthless fellow, an Ethiopian renegade from, and enemy of Christianity, who was the leader of Qhoja Sofaris's troops. The common people revere him as a saint, solely because he was executed by Garcia [Rodrigues de] Távora, governor of Daman. The women bring wreaths and garlands of flowers to his tomb. Surat is thronged with merchants, and the nearby port is full of ships; for it is a safe anchorage, since the river extends deep and broad from the sea right up to the city.³⁵

Here then is an early reference to the so-called Marjan Shami, the mausoleum of Khwaja Safar Khudawand Khan, and one of the most striking monuments of pre-Mughal Surat; equally intriguing is the reference to the popular cult of the Abyssinian warrior-martyr Sidi Marjan, associated with the same tomb complex, and clearly at the origin of its name.[36]

CONSOLIDATION AND COMPLEXITY

In the century and a quarter following Mughal conquest, Surat grew to be the most important port city in the Indian subcontinent and one of the great centers of Indian Ocean trade, with its population apparently exceeding 200,000.[37] Of its competitors on the west coast, it outstripped Diu, Dabhol, Chaul, Goa, Basrur, and Bhatkal, as well as Calicut and Kochi (Cochin) further south. Reading the correspondence of the Portuguese administration, one notes a persistent preoccupation with the links of Surat's merchants with two destinations: on the one hand, the sultanate of Aceh, and on the other hand Jiddah and the Red Sea.[38] Repeated instructions were given to the captains of the coastal fleets to patrol the bar of Surat, but usually to no lasting avail. On the other hand, this continued hostility was undoubtedly an irritant, as we note from a few episodes of the late 1570s and early 1580s. In 1578, the minor Mughal servant Bayazid Bayat decided to go on the hajj to the Red Sea. After a long delay and elaborate negotiations with the court, he was eventually allowed to embark at Surat in March 1580 in the ship *Muhammadi*, which had been recently constructed by two important Mughal officials, Qutb-ud-Din Khan and Qilij Khan Andijani.[39] From the very outset, however, the Portuguese began to meddle with the ship and insisted it come to Daman for inspection, so that it could pay the "Diu toll" (*'ushur-i Div*). This was levied to the extent of ten thousand mahmudis (each worth slightly less than half a rupee), which were eventually handed over by Bayazid from his personal fortune to the chief *nakhuda* of Surat, Hasan Chunu (who was acting as go-between), and only then could the ship depart for the Red Sea. In the following years difficulties seem to have continued, as Qilij Khan made various attempts to defy the Portuguese and send ships to Jiddah. The chronicler Couto claims that at least on one instance, in 1585, his ship was attacked and sunk not far from Surat by the Portuguese coastal fleet.[40] However, the Portuguese Estado was also obliged to concede *cartazes* regularly for ships under Akbar's direct protection to make the Jiddah run, both for the purpose of conveying pilgrims and to keep commercial links with the Red Sea (from which increasingly large quantities of bullion were imported) alive. Major Mughal officials such as 'Abdur Rahim Khan-i Khanan and Sadiq Muhammad Khan also built their own ships for trade to Jiddah, of which we have several traces in the 1580s and 1590s.[41]

When the newly formed English Company's ships arrived in the Indian Ocean in the early seventeenth century, Surat was logically one of their principal destinations, a situation consolidated after their victory over a Portuguese fleet in the Battle of Swally in late November 1612.[42] The Dutch East India Company (Vereenigde Oost-Indische Compagnie, or VOC) also maintained an important trading factory there from about 1620 onward.[43] On the east coast, its main competitor—or perhaps mirror image—was the port of Masulipatnam, which was closely associated with the Golkonda Sultanate until the Mughal conquest of the region in the 1680s.[44] Then, as the seventeenth century drew to a close, English East India Company settlements—first Madras, then Calcutta and Bombay—gradually began to emerge as significant nodes of commerce and power. The history of these colonial port cities has often been recounted, either by depicting them as "bridgeheads" of westernization or more recently through some other prism such as "colonial hybridity." But in order to understand Surat in its Mughal heyday, we must look back to another tradition, that of complex multiethnic ports such as medieval Aden and Quanzhou or fifteenth-century Melaka.[45] Even if many significant European visitors came through here in the seventeenth century, it is important to recall that this was not in the final analysis a city that was dominated—whether economically, politically, or culturally—by Europeans and their political institutions until the 1750s.

The difficulty in achieving a balanced depiction of the city during its seventeenth-century heyday lies in the considerable body of European texts and archives we have for the period. Besides Portuguese materials dealing both with Surat as a hostile target and then as a port to which they came to be reluctantly reconciled, the English, Dutch, and French all produced imposing documentation on their respective involvement with this commercial center. A small but growing body of material in Persian has emerged to balance this European perspective to some extent.[46] These include administrative documents regarding the farming out of local offices (such as that of the *mutasaddi* or city governor), *parwanas* and other documents issued by these officials (as well as the occasional imperial *farman*), a small body of documents regarding marriage contracts and property disputes, including the opinions of jurisconsults (*muftis*), as well as a number of complaints and petitions, including in

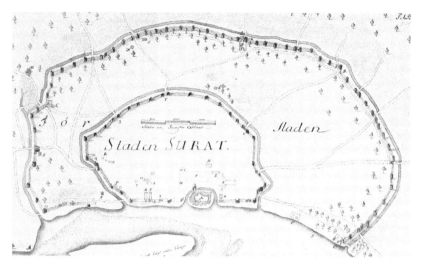

FIGURE 4.1. C. H. Braad's plan of Surat (Göteborgs universitetsbibliotek, Sweden, "Beskrifning på skeppet Götha Leyons resa till Surat och åtskillige andre indianske orter").

the form of the *suwalnama*, "distress note."[47] In one of these documents of the 1630s, the Iranian-born *mutasaddi* Sadra Shirazi (titled Hakim Masih al-Zaman) made it a point to stress to merchants coming to Surat from Persian Gulf ports such as Bandar 'Abbas that his intention was to "properly rectify the injustices and oppression committed on anyone, no matter how small." As a consequence, he had instituted a system of proper escorts for caravans (*qafilas*) coming from inland and had also put an end to a series of abuses in the maritime customhouse "whereby the goods and merchandise of the merchants were first over-valued, and then customs ['*ushur*] assessed and realized." He assured them that despite the blandishments being offered to merchants, including the Dutch and English, by the governors of rival ports such as Khambayat (Cambay), it was Surat which was destined to attract "all kinds of people to come to this port and settle here."[48] Coming as it did in the aftermath of the rather severe Gujarat famine of 1630–1632, one can see that such a document reflects a pressing need to shore up Surat's reputation as the principal port of the west coast, and the evidence from the decades that followed do suggest that such a strategy worked quite well with respect to both the Europeans and others.

But what impression did Surat make on the Europeans who arrived there after 1600, in its heyday? We may commence with the succinct but rich *Remonstrantie* written in October 1615 by Dutch Company employee Pieter Gillis van Ravesteyn, laying out the pros and cons of setting up a

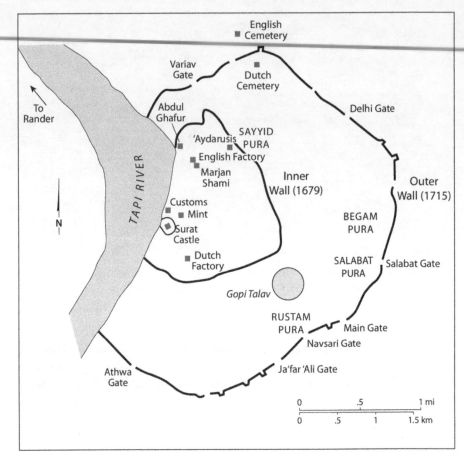

5. The city of Surat

factory in the port city.[49] He begins by noting the maritime traffic of large ships (*groote schepen*) that make their way to Aceh, Pariaman (on the west coast of Sumatra), and Kedah on the one hand and the Red Sea on the other; but there are also smaller vessels that ply the coastal routes up and down the west coast of India, despite the fact that they have to negotiate with the nuisance of Portuguese patrols. The port city itself is "reasonably great and well-built," at a distance from the mouth of the river and surrounded by an earthen wall. He mentions the existence of the artillery fortress, though it does not seem to impress him too much. But there is no escaping the sheer wealth of the city, which is demonstrated by its considerable revenues that he counts as two million mahmudis annually at the time when ʿAbdur Rahim Khan-i Khanan governed the region, but which has more recently fallen to 900,000 mahmudis. The city is linked in turn to a whole set of subordinate centers in Gujarat: Daman, Gandevi, Bharuch, Jambusar, Baroda, Khambayat, Ahmedabad, and so on. The principal interest of many of these centers is their manufacture of textiles (*doecken*), such as *baftas* and *patolas*, but it is also clear that the city represents a substantial market where many imported goods, ranging from pepper and the fine spices, to copper, lead, tin, camphor, and ivory, can find a ready market. Ravesteyn also briefly lists some of the principal merchants (*princijpaelste coopluiden*) of the city, who include Khwaja Nizam, Khwaja Hasan 'Ali, Mir Ishaq Beg, Mir Ja'far, and Khwaja 'Arab among the Muslims and Tapi Das and a certain "Happa Wara" among the *baniyas*.

Later in the century the French Huguenot jeweler Jean-Baptiste Tavernier claimed that Surat was "the sole port in the whole empire of the Great Mogul" (*le seul port de tout l'Empire du Grand Mogol*) and noted the considerable precautions taken to protect the town from European attacks. Dutch and the English vessels were apparently not allowed beyond the site of Suwali on the coast, "neither being permitted to enter into the Surat river." Further, the English and Dutch, both of whom had been permitted to trade in the port in the course of the first quarter of the seventeenth century, were allowed only "hired houses" (*maisons de loüage*); Tavernier adds that "the King does not permit any Frank to possess a house of his own, fearing that one might convert it into a fortress [*par la crainte qu'il a qu'on n'en pût faire une forteresse*]." His overall view of the port is as follows:

> Surat is a city of moderate size, with a poor fortress [*une méchante forteresse*], close to which you must pass, whether you approach it by water or by land. It has towers at each of its four angles; and as the walls are not terraced, the guns are placed upon scaffoldings. The Governor of the fortress commands merely the soldiers of the garrison, and possesses no authority in the city, which has its own separate Governor to receive the customs and the other revenues of the King throughout the extent of the Province. The walls of the city are built of earth, and the houses of private persons are like barns, being constructed of nothing but reeds, covered with cow-dung mixed with clay, to fill the interstices, and to prevent those outside from seeing between the reeds what goes on inside. In the whole of Surat there are only nine or ten well-built houses, and the Shahbandar or chief of the merchants, owns two or three of them. The others belong to the Muhammadan merchants, and those of the English are

Dutch and not the least fine, every President and Commander taking care to keep them in repair.[50]

We thus see that the city now—and we are in the 1670s—still has earthen walls to protect it, in addition to the fortress or "Surat Castle." Tavernier's compatriot, the French East India Company employee François Martin, offers us a somewhat more nuanced view of Surat. In a letter written in February 1700, possibly to the minister, Pontchartrain, he laid out an ample vision of both the problems and prospects of Surat. The city, he declared, had many advantages over all its competitors in India, since all the goods that were brought from Europe normally found buyers there quite quickly, with no leftover stock. Of course, there were ups and downs depending on whether the ships arrived all at once in a season, or with gaps. He then went on:

> This is a city that is greatly populated through its connections in all the States of the Mogol, which this city furnishes with all that they need. It is a concourse of all sorts of nations, from the month of October when the trading season [*la moisson*] begins until the end of May. The city is not agreeable within its walls [*dans son enceinte*]; however, this confusion, this tumult of so many people who are so different in clothes and customs, this infinite number of so many diverse sorts of merchandise, which one brings here from other parts of the world, with which its shops, its warehouses, and its public squares are filled, give it an air of grandeur such that it is easily recognized as the premier city in the world for trade [*la première ville du monde pour le commerce*]. There are Muhammadan and Gentile merchants who are extremely rich. But it is not by the means possessed by its inhabitants alone that the city sustains this great trade. Many of the seigneurs from the Mogol court, many officers, and the principal traders of other significant cities from the states of this Prince, all have their representatives in Surat, where they send large sums that these people [the agents] invest in trade, or lend out at interest, depending on the orders they have received.[51]

Martin went on to note that the greatest trade from Surat was carried out to ports in the Persian Gulf such as Bandar 'Abbas, Kung, and Basra, but also to Mokha and Jiddah in the Red Sea. He claimed that he had kept track for a whole year of how much gold and silver had been brought back from these two areas and had found that it amounted to some twenty million livres, besides that which the traders managed to bring through while avoiding the customhouse. Besides, the Surat traders also had important investments in the gold-export trade of Aceh, in the commerce of the Malabar coast, in Bengal, and in the whole area stretching from Siam to Manila. He pointed out that in 1668, when the French had effectively begun to trade in Surat, the merchants there had only possessed some fifteen or sixteen three-masted vessels for oceanic trade, whereas by 1686 (when he had left there for Pondicherry), there were seventy-two, including some which were of as much as seven hundred to eight hundred *tonneaux* (each roughly 1,440 liters).[52] On the other hand, Martin was well aware that the period when he wrote was a difficult one, when the trade of Surat was in something of a trough, largely owing to the attacks in the 1690s by English corsairs on Surat shipping in the western Indian Ocean. But this was a crisis that would eventually be surmounted once the Surat administration had strong-armed the European Companies to providing adequate protection. Despite some hiccups, the port would continue to flourish well into the eighteenth century.

The Indian historian Ashin Das Gupta's studies of Surat are particularly valuable in giving us a clear sense of the port's situation as it had crystallized in the course of the seventeenth century. We may approach the question from the viewpoint of a trader from West Asia arriving in Surat in the period. Entering the Tapti River from the west, ships normally went upstream past a series of fishing hamlets until they arrived at Swally (Suwali) Hole, the preferred anchorage for larger vessels. Then, pursuing one's route in smaller ships and barges, one went past first the imperial Mughal wharf and then the village of Athwa on the right bank, where the family of Surat's most important merchant of the late seventeenth century, Mulla 'Abdul Ghafur, had its own wharf. After a few other gardens and wharfs, still on the same bank, the visitor would presently reach the recently constructed outer wall (*'alampanah*) and the inner wall (*shahrpanah*), while the older settlement of Rander sat further up on the opposite, or left, bank. Within the walls, still on the right bank was the Surat Castle and its moat, followed by the customhouse and the mint. Nearby was the castle green or *maidan*, an important public space for petty mercantile transactions and beyond it the *darbar*, or the residence of the governor (*mutasaddi*). Das Gupta further adds:

> Men lived mostly in the inner town which had its attractive corner in the complex of the castle with its green and the *darbar*. Beyond the *darbar* and further away from the castle, lived the local Mughal officials in a locality called Sultanpura. As you

faced the *darbar* and Sultanpura from the castle, the mercantile city was on your left, the locality by and large being given the name Saudagarpura. Within Saudagarpura the rich ship-owners and some aristocrats had built houses in a stretch along the river which came to be called the Mulla chakla, named almost certainly after Mulla Abdul Ghafur who lived there. The English Company had its factory here by the river and they were next door neighbours to Ghafur. The grandson of Ghafur built a mosque in 1723 which is still in use by the members of Surat's Patni *jama'at*. The Turkish family of the Chellabies lived in the neighbourhood and had their own mosque, which still stands. The French and the Portuguese lived in the locality, when they lived at Surat. But the Dutch were tucked away at a point where Saudagarpura merged, round the *maidan*, with Sultanpura.[53]

In other words, there was a great deal of mixing in the port, far more than in those urban centers which followed a strict model of ethnic quarters. A European Company employee who lived in Surat in the seventeenth century was hardly insulated from the mercantile and political world of the city at large and did not have the prospect of the same distance from "natives" as his counterpart in Madras or Bombay, both towns with a far stricter spatial division between communities and races. Besides, if one were interested in private trade, as was the rule rather than the exception among Europeans, this necessarily meant some proximity with the Asian traders of the port. Some Company employees may have seen this as an unpleasant necessity, but others did not. Das Gupta reminds us, for example, that the Dutch Company factor Jan Schreuder in the 1740s spent many afternoons in the *gaddis*, or commercial establishments of the Hindu and Jain *baniyas* in Nanavat (an area of Surat where they dominated), "collecting information on who had how much money at Surat."[54] A whole century earlier, another Dutchman Wollebrant Geleynssen de Jongh had been employed Bharuch and Surat, and his *Remonstrantie* gives ample evidence that he frequented Asian merchants—both Hindu and Muslim—socially and had some understanding of both Persian and a vernacular Hindustani.[55]

Unfortunately, Das Gupta did not have access to two valuable visual documents that help us gather a far better sense of the port and its morphology in the first half of the eighteenth century. The first of these is a bilingual Persian-Hindawi map, preserved today in Jaipur, and dating from the early eighteenth century.[56] It gives us a detailed listing of a whole host of important sites, mansions, and public buildings in Surat,

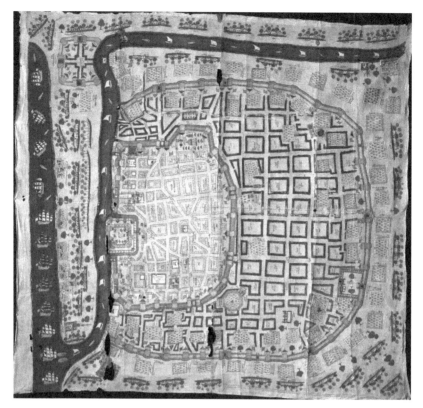

FIGURE 4.2. Surat in an eighteenth-century Indian cloth map, Maharaja Sawai Man Singh II, City Palace Museum, Jaipur, No. 118 (Image courtesy of the Trustees of the Museum).

accentuating the impression of great ethnic mixing that we have already seen. Also visible in the map are some remarkable (and largely ignored) spaces, such as the enormous site occupied within the first city wall of the great establishment of the 'Aydarusi Sufi *silsila* from Hadramaut. Recent analyses by the Japanese historian Hiromu Nagashima have given us a detailed breakdown of these different sites.[57] A second map, this one from the middle of the eighteenth century, comes from the drawings of the Swedish trader Christopher Henrik Braad, who found himself in Surat in these years. Drawn as a far more conventional map than its Jaipur counterpart, the Braad map can be complemented by a series of other drawings that Braad himself made, including of the Gopi Talav and the Marjan Shami.[58] Table 4.1 reproduces the names of a series of sites marked on the first map, in the part of city within the inner walls, but to the north of the fortress. I follow the Persian names rather than those in the more approximate Hindawi version.[59]

TABLE 4.1. Locations in Surat, inner city north of the fort

Northwest locations	Northeast locations
Hammam-i Badshahi	Haweli Basant Ray
Darwaza-i Khwurd	Marjan Shami
Darwaza-i Furza-i Sultani	Shahpur
Tanksal (Mint)	Muhalla Kot Nawal Sah
Darwaza-i Bandar	Muhalla Shahpur
Haweli Shahbandar	Chakla Shagupur
Darwaza Sayyid Sa'dullah	Haweli Muhammad Sa'id Nakhuda
Haweli Yaqut Khan	Muhalla Bali Bev
Haweli Frankis	Pol Bhai Das
Haweli Sayyid Sa'dullah	Haweli Sayyid Zain
Darwaza Mulla 'Abdul Ghafur	Bari Sayyid Zain Basti
Haweli Angrez	Kubhar Wara
Haweli Mulla Muhammad 'Ali son of 'Abdul Ghafur	Haweli Sayyid 'Ali
Mahsul-i Khushki (inland toll station)	Rubel Wara
Pol Basant Ray	Macchi Wara
Saray Begam	Minara Sayyid 'Aydarus
Saray Mughali	Kabza Sayyid 'Aydarus
Haweli Angrez	Kabza Bala Pir
Kaghazi Pura	Saudagar Wara
Haweli 'Umar Sindhi	Pura Bari Bibi
Bukhar Lal Bhai Shahukar	Pathan Wara
Haweli Mirza Zahid	Muhalla Fatehpur

Several distinct types of names are used here, such as *darwaza* (door), *haweli* (mansion), *muhalla* (quarter), *chakla* (quarter), *pura* (quarter), *basti* (settlement), and *wara* (quarter). The mansions usually bear the name or title of a prominent person, or of a group such as the English or French. The *waras* are usually quarters that indicate the concentrations of professions such as potters, fishmongers, moneychangers, papermakers, merchants, and so on. In addition, there are what we may term the "public" buildings such as the baths (*hammam*), the mint (*tanksal*), and the residences of officials such as the *shahbandar*. Moving away from the inner city, we would find other locations, including some of the magnates' gardens and settlements where artisan groups such as weavers resided.

Some of these again bore the names of individuals who had apparently been associated with their founding or consolidation, such as Rustam Pura, Salabat Pura, Haidar Pura, and Begam Pura—the last named for the princess Jahanara Begam, who had connections with Surat in the middle decades of the seventeenth century. As it happens, this particular map gives us locations not only within the two walls but even beyond the perimeter of the outer wall, where we find both private gardens and a series of villages. Also to be found beyond the outside perimeter wall was a series of tombs and cemeteries.

SITES AND MOTORS OF COSMOPOLITAN ENCOUNTER

One of the most penetrating accounts of Surat by a European visitor in the seventeenth century is that of the East India Company chaplain, John Ovington, whose work *A Voyage to Suratt in the Year, 1689, giving a large account of that City, and its Inhabitants, and of the English Factory there* appeared in print in London in 1696.[60] Born in Yorkshire in 1653, Ovington was educated first in Trinity College (Dublin) and then briefly in Cambridge. In April 1689, he sailed for India on the Company ship *Benjamin* as chaplain. His first point of arrival in India was Bombay, a place that he found degrading and full of vice and immorality, the abode of "debauched broken tradesmen and renegade seamen," which he qualified as "little better than a charnel house." It was with some relief, then, that Ovington was able to depart from there in September 1690 for Surat, where he gratefully accepted the post of chaplain of the factory that he would hold for some two and a half years. In February 1693, he embarked again for England, returning to Gravesend in early December of that year. His conduct as chaplain while at Surat was apparently regarded with approval by the Company authorities, and this may have encouraged him to publish his *Voyage to Suratt*. Subsequently, he also published an *Essay upon the Nature and Qualities of Tea* (1699), which brought the wrath of several contemporaries on his head, including the notoriously irascible Alexander Hamilton (not to be confused with the Nevis-born American revolutionary). Hamilton, in his own work *A New Account of the East Indies* (1727), declared that much of Ovington's knowledge came to him "by Second or Third Hands," since he had barely traveled beyond Bombay or Surat.[61] On the other hand, a comparison of their two accounts of Surat shows Ovington to have been far the better informed, both in a historical and ethnographic sense.[62]

Ovington's description of the city of Surat notes that it has "the Form of a Semicircle or Half Moon, because of the winding of the River, to which half of it adjoyns." He, far more than Tavernier, appears impressed by the fort or "Castle," and also notes the existence by the late 1680s of the city wall with six or seven gates manned by guards. Again his description of the urban settlement is again far less contemptuous than the view of the French jeweler. "The Houses," he writes, "are many of them fair and stately, tho' unproportionable to the Wealth of the Inhabitants, who are always concern'd to conceal their Riches, and therefore never exceed in any Luxurious Furniture, lest it should prove too powerful a Temptation to the Avarice of the Mogul." This familiar trope of a form of oriental despotism aside, Ovington does concede that a number of residences are "cover'd with Tiles, and the Walls made of Brick or Stone." To be sure, there are also far more flimsy and poor houses to be found huddled together, made of fragile materials, which he terms "Cajan-Houses." Again he contrasts many streets that are very narrow with others that are "of a convenient breadth" and concludes that some of the public market streets are "more populous than any part of London; and so much throng'd that 'tis not very easie to pass through the multitude of Bannians and other Merchants that expose their Goods."

At the heart of the matter is not state power, whether in the form of the "Governour of the Castle" (or *qil'adar*) or that of the town. Rather, it is commercial effervescence, since "Suratt is reckon'd the most fam'd Emporium of the Indian Empire, where all Commodities are vendible, though they never were there seen before." These include goods not only from Europe but also from China, Persia, Arabia, and a variety of Indian regions, ranging from silks to precious stones, gold, and silver and to a variety of more basic goods of day-to-day use, including those brought overland from the interior. Above all of this, the state seemingly rules with a light hand. The *mutasaddi*, "to whose management and Care is committed the Trust of all Civil Affairs," nevertheless functions through "the Consultation and Concurrence of other Officers of the City," notably the *qazi* (judge), the *waqi'a-nawis* (newsletter writer), and the *kotwal* (warden). The first of these is "skilled in the Municipal Laws," the second is the "publick Intelligencer" who reports to the Mughal court, and the third is described as "somewhat resembling a Justice of the Peace."[63] Thus, from his initial nod in the direction of despotism, Ovington gradually moves toward a view of more or less orderly and rational government. In an interesting passage, he then adds:

> Tho' this City is frequented by a conflux of several Nations, and Peopled by abundance of Foreigners as well as Natives, whose

mixt Concourse and mutual Conversations might be apt to raise Tumults and Disputes, yet they very rarely happen, so much as to cause even a slight Punishment. And for Capital Inflictions, there are seldom Criminals so daring as to merit or incur the Guilt of them. The In-offensive Conversation of the Gentile Indians, who are very apt to receive, but seldom to give an abuse; keeps them Innocent, and at a distance from all hainous Crimes, and timorous in approaching the commission of any such gross Offence, as Murther, Robbery, and such like; and for petty Failures, a drubbing is a sufficient Atonement to publick Justice.[64]

While Ovington's observations are quite extensive and range from funerary rites of different groups to hunting and chess, it is clear that he was unable to enter into any form of close intellectual intercourse with the varied elites of Surat. He was aware that a diversity of literary and scholarly practices obtained there, in languages ranging from Persian and Sanskrit, to what he refers to as the language of the "Gentiles" or "Heathens," who "maintain . . . their own Tongue," meaning presumably vernaculars such as Hindawi or Gujarati, which he knew were sometimes written in a different script from Persian, about which he wrote, "The Court Language is Persian, which obtains with all the Honourable Omrahs, and with all Persons of Ingenuity and polite Conversation through that Empire." In contrast was Sanskrit, a language that was "very difficult to be attain'd, which several of themselves therefore understand not." Ovington was aware that this was a language in which "the Records of their Nation," as well as such subjects as Indian theology, religion, and philosophy, were recorded, but he complains that he was unable to gain access to it because "few of the learned Bramins live near Suratt." Indeed, Ovington leaves the reader with the impression that Surat was a city of great commercial vivacity but intellectual dullness, and he even complains broadly of the inhabitants that "they have not many Learned among them."

This view, while perhaps widely shared among Europeans living there in the seventeenth century, is not quite in consonance with what we know from other sources. A careful examination of the *mutasaddis* of Surat would show that several of them were men of culture and considerable discernment, such as Muqarrab Khan, Mir Musa Mu'izz al-mulk, Hakim Sadra Masih al-Zaman, or later Mustafa Khan.[65] There were also other Muslims of considerable intellectual attainments in the town, such as those associated with the 'Aydarusi establishment that I have mentioned briefly. This *silsila*, or religious lineage, originating from the Hadramaut (or South Arabia) had apparently settled in Surat by the mid-sixteenth century and built its chief mosque not far from the Marjan Shami as early as 1563–1564, about a decade before the Mughal conquest of the city. From Surat, they went on to extend their influence to areas such as Bharuch, but their principal center remained the great port, where—as a recent historian has put it—they deployed "the twin support of the [Mughal] state and the local merchant community" to great effect.[66] Their supporters included Haji Zahid Beg, an important merchant and shipowner, but they also received special grants and stipends from both local and provincial officials. Among the prominent texts written by members of this *silsila* was the celebrated *Tarikh al-Nur al-Safir*, composed by Sayyid 'Abdul Qadir bin Shaikh al-'Aydarus in Surat in 1603.[67] As late as 1735, it is noted in the context of a crisis when the port of Surat was being blockaded that it was the 'Aydarusis who came forward to "lead the whole city in prayer."[68] Equally prominent was a lineage of Surat-based Naqshbandi Sufis, whose key figure was Sayyid Jamal-ud-Din Khwarezmi, popularly known as Dana Sahib Surati (d. 1606–1607). Already well known in Gujarat before the Mughal conquest, he had been allied to the Timurid Mirzas by marriage in the 1560s. But this did not serve to discredit him; on the contrary, on arriving in Surat to settle there he was well received by the Mughal governor, Qilij Khan Andijani, while later his annual *'urs* ceremony was funded through the revenues of a nearby village.[69] Further, his *dargah* in Gopipura became a significant intellectual center in the city, and he had several disciples and descendants who were prolific writers. A third Sufi center in Surat was that of the Qadiri-Rifa'i order, whose *khanqah* (or lodge) was founded by 'Abdul Rahim Mehbub-Allah in around 1626 after he migrated to the port from Medina.[70] Taken together, these three sets of centers consisted of considerable intellectual resources, and to them we must add those of other Sufi *tariqas* (or orders) like the Chishtis, also active in Surat at this time.

Thus, despite the almost exclusive emphasis in a good part of the historical literature on Surat as a commercial center, it would be an error to neglect other aspects of the town. It is clear, for example, that several important private libraries and book collections existed in Surat, as we learn when Europeans attempted to purchase works there. In late February 1634, the Stuart ruler Charles I—possibly influenced by William Laud, the archbishop of Canterbury—wrote to the Court of Directors of the East India Company asking for a supply of Arabic and Persian manuscripts; the Company's factors in Iran responded in late November of the same year: "Our Soveraignes requiries of your worships to furnish him with some varyties of Persian and Arabian manuscripts we shall have regard to."[71] But it was the head of the Company's Surat establishment, William Methwold, who responded at some length regarding the problems in such an enterprise.

> We are exceedingly greived that we cannot in all points accomplish His Majesties royall pleasure. Heere is no want of Persian bookes of all sorts, most men of quality in this citty and kingdome being either Persians borne, discended from them, or educated in the knowledge of that language; so that Persian bookes are plentifully to be had, and we have sent 10 such, of severall subjects, although we doe beleive that there are few in England that will understand them; for howsoever the character resembles the Arabique (every letter carryeing the same denomination and pronunciation) yet for want of those pricks, both above and below, which point out the vowells, and are alwaies used in the Arabian character, the Persian is very difficultly read and understood but by them which are conversant therein. But we will hope that some industrious young man will make use of the opportunity he may injoy, and attayne to so much perfection as to give some light at least to direct more able linguists.[72]

It is possible to trace some of the manuscripts that were actually sent by the Company's servants to England in this period. The most celebrated of these, now in the Bodleian Library, is an illustrated one, the so-called Laud *Ragamala*, containing some eighteen *raga* paintings, a dozen other miniatures, and many specimens of calligraphy. This album was certainly in Laud's possession by the 1630s, and it is now clear that its paintings were produced in the Deccan atelier of the great Mughal aristocrat, general, and patron 'Abdur Rahim Khan-i Khanan (1556–1627), who resided for an extended period of time in the town of Burhanpur, some four hundred kilometers due east of Surat on the Tapti River.[73] We cannot be certain that the English acquired it in Surat, though it is certainly a possibility. Another significant manuscript from Laud's collection is the *Diwan-i Anwari* of the great twelfth-century poet, which had once been in the library of the sixteenth-century ruler of Ahmadnagar, Burhan Nizam Shah I. A striking feature of Laud's relatively small collection of Persian manuscripts, which he gifted to the Bodleian Library in Oxford, was its haphazard nature; not only are they an odd miscellany, but there are as many as three copies of a single text, 'Abdullah Hatifi's sixteenth-century verse account, the *Timurnama*. Other Persian materials that came into Laud's possession—almost certainly acquired in Surat in the same period—included the *Diwan-i Mukhtari* of a fairly prominent Ghaznavid poet, a paraphrase of Qazwini's *'Aja'ib al-makhluqat*, and—more predictably perhaps—the *Dastan-i Ahwal-i Hawariyan*, a Christian-themed text of the lives of saints produced by the Jesuit Jerónimo Xavier and 'Abdus Sattar ibn Qasim Lahauri at Jahangir's court. What this meant in effect was that the archbishop came to possess a mix of poetry and diverse prose, his agents in Surat did not at the time lay their hands on any of the great Indo-Persian chronicles of the close of the sixteenth and the dawn of the seventeenth centuries, the works of Shaikh Abu'l Fazl, Khwaja Nizam-ud-Din Ahmad Bakhshi, or Muhammad Qasim "Firishta," for example, nor great classics of Timurid historiography from the fifteenth century such as Mir Khwand's *Rauzat al-Safa'*. This suggests not so much that such works were not available or read in Surat at the time as that the English Company's factors were not sufficiently connected to the intellectual life of the town. A precocious work like that of Henry Lord, English Company chaplain at Surat, who wrote an account of the *baniyas* and Parsis (or Zoroastrians) in that city in the 1630s, though claiming to be based on "a booke of theirs called the Shaster, which is to them as their Bible," seems in fact to be based purely on oral accounts.[74]

If the Europeans sometimes faced such difficulties of cultural access, their interlocutors in the city seemed often to traverse boundaries of language and community far more easily. An excellent example of this is provided to us by the Julfan Armenians. While historians have doubted the most ambitious claims of an Armenian presence in the city already in the 1570s, it is clear that they were present there in some numbers by the second half of the seventeenth century. Ovington terms them "universal Merchants," who are not only "subtle and diligent in their Traffick" but also traded inland through an extensive network.[75] At much the same time, the French Company factor Georges Roques noted that they were to be found "in a great quantity in Surate, which has given us occasion to have a deep knowledge of them [*de les connaître à fond*]."[76] Like François Martin, Roques claimed to heartily detest the Armenians and their business practices, but he was also aware that the French could not easily do without them, especially because of their multilingual capacities in respect to Persian and the European languages. The Armenians thus clearly participated in the Persophone world of Surat, as did a number of other communities, including the *baniyas*.[77]

Among the *baniyas*, certain families are known to have been expert brokers both for Muslim administrators and merchants and eventually for the East India Companies. In the latter context, two well-known families stand out. One was that of Kishandas, who acted as a Dutch broker (*makelaar*) in the second half of the seventeenth century and was then succeeded by his descendants Rasikdas and Bhagwandas. The other was that of the brothers Tapidas and Tulsidas, who worked for the English Company and were succeeded generation after generation first by Bhimji Parekh, then by Laldas Vithaldas, and then, in the eighteenth century, by the controversial Jagannath Laldas. Tulsidas is described by the Company factors in 1662 as "having lived many yeares in great repute, abounding with riches, much respected for his faithfull dealing," but lately reduced to poverty on account of massive debts owing to him.[78] Such men, though they undoubtedly dealt on a day-to-day basis in a vernacular such as Gujarati and probably kept their commercial accounts in that language, nevertheless were regularly required to deal in Persian at the *darbar* of the *mutasaddi*, as also in other public transactions. It would be naïve to assume that they simply acted at the behest of the Companies or were subordinate to them. The career of the Sthanakvasi Jain merchant Virji Vora provides a telling instance.[79] Virji, who played a major role in Surat through the middle decades of the seventeenth century, first appears in the English Company's records in the late 1610s, acting as a broker or purchaser for imported goods such as spices, coral, and quicksilver and as a lender to the Company (which often needed to be tided over financially from year to year).[80] In a 1624 document intended to resolve conflicts between the English and Surat authorities, he is one of two *baniya* merchants who appears as a signatory, together with the well-known Hari Vaishya.[81] His star appears to be very much on the rise in the 1630s, especially after the economic shock of the great famine of 1630–1632. In March 1634, the English Surat Council complained of him:

> The potency of Virgee Vorah (who hath bene the usuall merchant, and is now become the sole monopolist of all European commodities) is observed to beare such sway amongst the inferiour merchants of this towne that when they would oftentymes buy (and give greater prices) they are still restrayned, not dareing to betray their intents to his knowledge and their own sufferance, insomuch that the tyme and price is still in his will and at his owne disposure. This makes the Councell weary of his unprofitable correspondence, which they intend to shake of by degrees and incline to others that promise more fairely.[82]

The English thus attempted to build up Tapi Das as a rival entrepreneur but found that this was something of an uphill task. Two years later, in 1636, they thus wrote:

Here in Surratt all merchants, as well towne dwellers as those that come from abroad, are so overawed by the overgrown greatnesse of Verge Vora that, if it be a commoditie which he is accustomed or doth intend to buy, no man dares looke upon it, nor the broker (even our owne, which have sole dependance upon your businesse) dare not accompanie such a merchant into our house; for when it comes to passe that although we sould the fine corrall unto Tapidas almost two years since, which he not dareing to avowch, for feare of Verge Vora, continues still in our possession under our names, there hath not bin in all this time one man that hath desires to see it or buy it, butt here it lies still unrequested and unregarded.[83]

Such was his prestige, as Farhat Hasan reminds us, that in 1636 the Mughals "had to remove Hakim Masihuz Zaman from the governorship of Surat and Cambay on the representation of the *bania* merchants, after he had committed the blunder of imprisoning Virji Vora, an extremely rich and influential merchant of Surat."[84] Yet, as far as we can tell, Virji Vora never chose to become a significant ship-owning merchant, instead preferring to freight space on board the vessels of others, whether Asians or Europeans. Nevertheless, he did come to have a formidable network of *gumashtas* (factors), ranging from Aceh and other Southeast Asian centers to the ports of Kerala to Sind, the Persian Gulf, and beyond. Well into the 1650s, he assertively promoted his own claims and interests with the English Company, while assuring their principals in London that "I have ever been a true ffriend to you and your servants here, and soe resolve to continue, and I hope you will soe bee to mee."[85] Even as late as 1660, the English were contemplating borrowing around 150,000 rupees from him on the grounds that "none but Virgee Vorah hath monye to lend or will lend; all but he havinge beene so abused by perticular persons borrowing and not paying."[86] While his "estate" was estimated by some in these years (perhaps with an element of exaggeration) at 8 million rupees, his star would eventually wane during the urban violence of the 1660s, and the last years of his career to his death remain somewhat obscure.

Still another remarkable and well-documented case from the late seventeenth and early eighteenth centuries is that of the Parsi (or Zoroastrian) merchant and broker Rustamji Manakji (ca. 1635–1721). Rustamji acted as *dallal* (broker) for the English as well as the Portuguese and was sufficiently important in the life of Surat to eventually have a quarter, Rustam Pura, named for him. The family originated from Navsari and migrated to Surat at some time in the latter half of the sixteenth century. Rustamji was not only a shrewd businessman but also initiated into the Zoroastrian priesthood, and he prided himself on his charitable works. Interestingly, he commissioned an encomium for himself in Persian and had it written by a certain Mubad Jamshid Kaiqubad. This verse text, the *Qissa-yi Set Rustam Manak*, while undoubtedly formulaic in some respects, nevertheless brings out several salient aspects of the self-image of the Parsi merchant.[87] He is portrayed as a leader of his community who managed to get the poll tax (or *jizya*) commuted by the Mughals, and who also was tireless in his charitable acts. Among these was the extensive help he apparently gave to his community when Surat was attacked in January 1664 by the Maratha "marauder" (*ghanim*) Sivaji, who is portrayed as an inveterate enemy of the community.[88] Further, we also learn of his capable diplomacy, whether in dealing with the Abyssinian warlord at Danda Rajapur, Sidi Yaqut, or in the thorny affair of a ship of the Surat-based shipowner 'Osman Çelebi that had been seized by the Portuguese in the western Indian Ocean in 1708. Portuguese documents from between 1691 and 1709 demonstrate that Rustamji was their broker (*corretor*) at Surat and that he delivered *cartazes* (safe-conducts) on their behalf to Mughal officials, and even intervened in diplomatic matters with the Mughals for them in the region of Daman over several decades.[89] It is clearly possible that Rustamji had some knowledge of Portuguese, and he may even have used this language to deal with other Europeans such as the English and French. What is certain is that in his dealings with his own community, and other Surat merchants, he used both Gujarati and Persian. Many of his charitable works thus carry a bilingual Gujarati-Persian inscription.[90]

BOULLAYE IN SURAT AND WESTERN INDIA

Intriguing light is also shed on seventeenth-century Surat and its networks of sociability by the travel account of a French *gentilhomme*, François le Gouz de la Boullaye. Boullaye spent slightly less than a year in western India, eventually departing Surat for Bandar Kung (in the Persian Gulf) and thence to Basra in early March 1649. In this time, he mostly stayed on the coast and did not spend any appreciable time in the interior of India. His initial base was Surat, which he came to know somewhat well, mainly through frequenting the English factory and its chief Francis Breton there.[91] Breton's second in command at the Surat factory was Thomas Merry, who also came to be a friend of Boullaye. But his closer connection was with Breton for reasons that become clear on some investigation. The records of the East India Company show that Breton had arrived in India in the mid-1630s and remained attached to the Gujarat establishment throughout his stay, ending in his death in July 1649. Initially placed in charge of the finances and accounts, he gradually rose through the hierarchy under the command of the formidable William Methwold.[92] There are suspicions that Breton and Methwold were complicit in running a sizable private trade operation out of the factory (especially in silk), but Methwold was far too well connected socially and politically to face the consequences of this. Breton, on the other hand, is a more obscure character. He came from a large family. One of his brothers, Daniel, was a linen draper in Newgate Market, and another, William, was a minister in Clapton. A third brother, Thomas, joined him in India and served as head of the Company establishment in Ahmedabad until his return to England in 1653. It is also likely that he was related to (possibly the brother of) John Breton, briefly vice chancellor of Cambridge University in the early 1670s. Francis Breton himself had been extensively involved in trade in France, particularly at Bordeaux, and spoke French fluently; his entry into the Company was at the recommendation of several London-based French merchants.[93] One can quite easily see how a bond could form between him and Boullaye. It is very likely that he was one of the principal informants from whom the Frenchman derived his account of the Mughals and their government in Surat.

On the other hand, despite some claims by him to the contrary, there are few indications that Boullaye frequented the employees of the Dutch Company, whether in Iran or in India. In the case of Surat, this is somewhat comprehensible, as the situation of the Dutch in the city was at a low ebb in the late 1640s. Provoked by the Dutch Company's high-handed policies with regard to trade between Gujarat and Southeast Asia (as an outcome of their capture of Melaka, earlier in the 1640s), an attack had been mounted on the Dutch factory in April 1648, leading to the death of one Dutchman and the looting of some goods. The Mughal authorities denied their responsibility, but it is quite evident that they were at least complicit in the matter. The Dutch therefore sent a fleet under Arend Barentsen, the former head of the factory, to threaten and harass Surat shipping while at the same time appealing to the Mughal court to intervene in their favor. This tactic initially failed to yield results, but the following year the Dutch had greater success by holding one of Shahjahan's own vessels hostage and seizing goods from it. It was only in 1650 that they would return to some form of normalcy by sending Joan Tack on an embassy to Delhi.[94] At any rate, only one Dutchman is mentioned among Boullaye's Indian informants, a certain Jong, a "gentleman from

Haarlem." This may also be the consequence of the fact that Boullaye distinctly preferred the company of the English to that of the Dutch.

It is not entirely clear how strong the presence of the French in coastal western India was at this time, and they would have largely been there as individuals rather than a collective body. Boullaye's main French interlocutor was the Capuchin missionary, Père Zénon, who had already been in Surat since the early 1640s. Zénon, who was some two decades older than Boullaye, hailed from the same small town of Baugé and apparently belonged to a family that was friendly with Boullaye's. After having served as a missionary in Palestine, he had been persuaded to move to India and had installed himself in a rather improvised manner in Surat, while his companion, Père Ephrem de Nevers, had gone on to Madras. Here Père Ephrem had run afoul of the Portuguese clergy who were not well disposed to the Capuchins, and since Père Zénon decided to intervene in his favor, he persuaded Boullaye to accompany him to meet the authorities at Goa. So far as we know, since the time of his arrival in Surat in April 1648 Boullaye had remained there, no doubt waiting for first the summer and then the heaviest part of the monsoon to pass. In mid-September he set out with Père Zénon, traveling at times by boat and at times over land, passing first through Daman and then Bassein, Chaul, and Vengurla, eventually arriving in Goa in late October.

The main concern here is the Frenchman's view of Surat and how he came to acquire it. Boullaye's account of his stay in India occupies some 144 pages, roughly a third of his entire text. It is divided into several distinct sequences, some having to do with his stay in different places such as Surat, and Goa, others more thematic. Here, leaving aside his somewhat eccentric chapters on the flora and fauna, we should pay some attention to two central themes: the first on the Mughals, which begins with chapters on "the kingdom of Guzerat," "the great Mogol and the extent of his empire," and "on the policy and government of the great Mogol"; and the second on "the Indous and their habits" (which begins the second part of the text). He notes that the emperor speaks Persian and that the Iranians (or what he calls "Keselbaches," viz. *qizilbash*) hold the highest positions [*premieres charges*] in the empire, even when they have come from humble origins. Contrary to the view held by the Jesuits in their letters and other writings, by the Englishman Sir Thomas Roe, and by later travelers in the seventeenth century, Boullaye is careful not to suggest that the political system is a despotic or arbitrary one. He writes: "His [the Mughal's] policy is extremely soft [*douce*], and he does have his brothers strangled or blinded, nor does he imprison his children, or kill his Omaras or Nababs for some trivial fault. He permits all sorts of religions, so long as they aid the expansion of his empire and makes use of pagans in his military."[95] And again, returning to the same theme a few pages later: "the great Mogol is a Muslim of the Sonni sect [but] his vassals are of different religions: Christians, Jews, Muslims, Parsis, and Indous. They cannot change their religion or beliefs, unless they become of his [the Mughal's] law, but they are allowed to live and die with perfect liberty in the religion in which they were born and can nevertheless attain the highest offices of the State." He also presents the emperor Shahjahan as extremely accessible: "It is very easy to talk to him and ask for justice, even though he is the greatest, richest and most superb monarch in Asia." From this, Boullaye goes on to draw a somewhat unexpected conclusion: "If the Europeans utilized the policies [la politique] of the Indians as well as they do their drugs for the health of their bodies, everything would be better; the authority of the kings would be more stable, and their subjects would be more content."[96]

The chapters devoted to the question of religion are also particularly interesting in their own right, all the more so since everything points to the fact that they largely came from Boullaye's time in Surat. These chapters begin with an introductory statement: "In the East Indies, there is an infinity of Gentiles, amongst whom are the Indous, divided into 125 tribes, who receive no Jew, Pagan, Christian or Muslim into their religion, considering them to be unworthy, which they give as the reason for valuing their [own] sect. They write from the left to the right and have a particular script; they never enclose their women and are never jealous." Possibly aware that the term "Indou" would be unfamiliar to his European readers of the time, Boullaye (or perhaps his publisher) provides an odd paratext: "India in Indian is called Indoustan, the residence of the Indou, who are the ancient inhabitants of the Indies." Here, he seems to distinguish between the three categories of "Gentile," "Pagan," and "Indou," with the last being a smaller group included among the larger ensemble of Gentiles. If on the one hand they can be distinguished from the others by their appearance and their habits, their main particularity lies in what he terms their "general belief" (creánce génerálle) and their "faith" (foy). Thus we have the first elements of a definition: "The first article of their faith is that Ram is God, and the First of the Beings, who at another time was living here below, and gave them the sacred law which they obey from father to son, over 120,000 years." In this first definition, then, what we have is a monotheism, where this single God is accompanied by other lesser saints such as Sita ("Schita"), Lakshman ("Locman"), Kanha ("Kan"), Bhagavati ("Bagoti"), Lakshmi ("Glacmi"), and Hanuman ("Hermand"). Boullaye then adds some remarks regarding ablutions, pilgrimages, and visits to temples (*pagodes*), as well as the abstinence from eating beef. Thereafter he turns to a description of the principal social categories to be found among the "Indous," prefacing his discussion with the following statement: "The differences that one observes among the 125 tribes of Indous are so marked, that it seems that they have never been united; each tribe has its own particular language which is not otherwise understood by the others on account of the long time that their law has been in vigour; their *pagodes* are separate according to the tribe, and served by one, two or three Bramens, according to the people of the tribe." Among these tribes, he counts (besides the Brahmins), *baniyas*, *khatris*, *rajputs*, and *sarrafs*, but also *darzis* (tailors). Lacking exposure to them, Boullaye has little or nothing to say about peasants or persons living outside the city.

These chapters also carry short narrative sections that derive from the traditions of the *Ramayana* (for Rama) or the *Bhagavata Purana* (for Krishna). Here is how Boullaye presents the first of these: "At a distance of three leagues from Sourat in the kingdom of Guserat, there is a stone figure of Herman [Hanuman], to which one attributes several miracles; many pilgrims go there because of the great pardons that one obtains from making such a visit, and from giving him some anointments [*oignemens*] and gifts. Regarding this monkey, I had a history translated for me by the Bramens, which I wish to insert in my book, in order to provide more knowledge of the religion of the Indous."[97] The story that follows concerns Sita's abduction to Ceylon and Hanuman's mission to her, but it ends with him burning down the island with his flaming tail "and generously carrying off his mistress Schita, whom he placed in the hands of Ram." Boullaye then delivers a short reflection on how such a "fable" could be credible to people in India, suggesting that it is "because they imagine that animals are reasonable." On the other hand, turning to his own tradition, he notes that in the Christian scriptures too various creatures seem to talk, from the serpent who tempted Eve to Balaam's ass; further, Solomon had sustained (in Ecclesiastes 4:19) that "man was no better than the beast, and the condition of the one and the other is equal."[98] If Boullaye's knowledge of Vaishnava traditions can be somewhat inexact, he seems to have absorbed very little from the Shaivas of Surat at all: for him Mahadev (or "Maedov") is merely a saintly and ascetic figure "who lived a solitary life in the woods, given to the contemplation of God, and self and nature," while Bhagavati ("Bagoti") is described by him as "a saint who had the force to combat and defeat giants . . . in my opinion, she was another Joan of Arc [*pucelle d'Orléans*] who would have fought with success for the zeal of her religion, and the liberty of

FIGURE 4.3. Krishna devotion in Boullaye's text (Biblioteca dell'Accademia Nazionale dei Lincei e Corsiniana, Rome, Fondo Corsini, Ms. 34.K.17).

her patria, or even a heroine of antiquity." Again, it is worth noting that while Krishna ("Kochetna"), also known as Kanha ("Kan"), finds a place in his account, he is given a secondary place in relation to the central figure of Rama. Of him Boullaye writes: "This saint is reputed to be a heavenly angel, of whom several miracles are recounted to us." It is thus

196 / ACROSS THE GREEN SEA

possible that his principal informants, those who structured his account overall, belonged to the Ramanandi community of Surat or one of the other groups from northern India that were raising Rama worship to the fore from the late sixteenth century onward.[99] However, his only specific remark on the question is coy: "it is very difficult to be informed on everything one wishes, and if I had not found some astrologers and doctors who, against their law, were addicted to wine, I would never have extracted anything from them; but in getting them half-drunk, and exciting their imagination, they told me more than I even wanted, and even interpreted their books."[100] Some of the possible suspects can thus be found in table 4.2.

Boullaye concludes his discussion of the "Indous" of Surat on a moderate tone, certainly by the standards of the Europeans of the time:

> There you have what I have remarked of the Indou religion, from the dealings I have had with their Bramens and doctors; I request the apostolic missionaries into whose hands this account may fall not to act with too much zeal against the law of these Pagans, which is founded in nature; but instead that little by little they make them see that their mysteries are an effect of the policies of their sages, and [instead] they reveal to them that the source is God, infinite and eternal ... in order to gradually bring them towards the evangelical truths and render them faithful, and make them participants in the glory [and] knowledge of Jesus-Christ, the true Messiah, in whom the happiness of all creatures lies.[101]

A few remarks are also worth making in relation to Boullaye's use of images in his *Voyages*. These images fall into several distinct categories: (1) some seem to be based on the traveler's own rather crude sketches, especially of flora and fauna; (2) several are either "portraits" or ethnographic depictions of figures such as an "Indou cavalier," an "Indou woman," or "a Parsi"; (3) several—in fact the largest number—represent gods and divinities and their iconography. The discovery of a partial manuscript version of the travels has considerably advanced our understanding of these. Now, the importance of these images is justified by Boullaye himself in the following terms: "The painting being to discourse what the original is to the painting, I believe I would satisfy the reader more with some figures of Mogol costume than by the descriptions I could make of them."[102] Nevertheless, some of the claims he makes regarding these figures are manifestly absurd, such as his attempt to pass off a generic

TABLE 4.2. Boullaye's informants in Surat and elsewhere

Name	Description
Indian	
Sanga	vania (or baniya, merchant) from Gujarat
Mahadev	Brahmin physician from Gujarat
Ganesh	Brahmin astrologer from Gujarat
Lachman	vania from Bengal
Mir Musa (Mu'izz-ul-Mulk)	governor of Surat (Qizilbash)
Musa	Indian merchant from Agra
Da'ud	Kotwal of Surat (Qizilbash)
Muhammad	merchant from Tibet
Mahadev	interpreter of the Bijapur governor of Jaitapur
British	
Francis Breton	president of the English at Surat
Thomas Merry	second-in-command
John Adler	English factor
George Oxenden	English captain from Mokha
Theophilus May	English physician
Jeremy Blackman	English ship's captain
John Millet	English ship's captain
William Bewes (Bevis)	English ship's captain
Andrew Baines	English minister
Other European	
Lescot	jeweler from Orleans
Du Boults	watchmaker from Geneva
Isaac del l'Estoile	jeweler and watchmaker from St-Jean-d'Angely
Jongh	Dutch gentleman from Haarlem
Dom Francisco da Costa	mestizo gentleman from Daman

portrayal of a woman with a lamp in one hand and a fly-whisk in the other as a portrait of Shahjahan's "beautiful daughter, who has full [rein] over the will of her father," which is to say Jahanara Begam. He presents another generic and well-known image of a woman standing atop a stool and performing her toilette "covered with a *cambrésine*" with heavy innuendoes concerning his own sexual experiences in Surat, especially with regard to the "perfumed oils" that these women use.[103] These images seem to derive from modified copies or versions of Mughal paintings, very likely produced in or around the port city; on the other hand, the illustrations on religious themes appear somewhat less influenced by Mughal courtly styles. Nevertheless, while assuming they emanated from the same hand, art historian Marta Becherini has proposed that these original illustrations from which the printed images in Boullaye's *Voyages* came were all made by "a painter [in Gujarat] accustomed to work for local patrons, based on his acquaintance with Hindu iconography and ... his reuse of compositions typical of Mughal court miniatures."[104] In turn, the images—possibly in the form of loose sheets—would have been quite faithfully reworked into the manuscript today in Europe by a professional European illustrator who also added some of his own drawings (including of Boullaye himself), while the original illustrations or some version thereof eventually made their way to the publisher in Paris, who then produced a far poorer and more schematic version that nevertheless retained some distinct traces of the originals.

Read together with other seventeenth-century materials—whether the factory records or more elaborate narratives such as those of Peter Mundy or John Ovington—Boullaye's account thus provides an evocative account of a certain slice of life in Surat, one in which Europeans lived not apart from but instead in a lively (if at times inebriated) conversation with their Asian counterparts from the middle classes. This is not to deny the existence of ever-present tensions, with the Dutch Company regularly flexing its maritime muscle in the middle decades of the seventeenth century and English privateers doing the same as the century drew to a close.

SOME TENTATIVE CONCLUSIONS

In recent years, several historians (as well as scholars from other disciplines) have explored the question of a cosmopolitanism that might have existed beyond the geographical confines of Europe, as well as the temporal limits of the Enlightenment and post-Enlightenment worlds.[105] If some have searched for it in the history of philosophical traditions, others have sought it out in the political attitudes of courts or the quotidian practices of travelers and merchants. In this chapter I have sought to return to a close consideration of place and focused attention on a single urban center—the great port of Surat in western India—to examine the nature of exchanges (both commercial and intellectual) and interactions in such a setting. The exploration has been intended to open up the questions of whether and to what extent a place such as Surat was conducive to the production of a cosmopolitan milieu, even if it may never have been articulated as such in any explicit theory of "cosmopolitanism."[106] As an exercise, this is thus somewhat distinct from the attempt to follow the career of a complex concept such as *sulh-i kull* ("peace toward all" or "universal civility") set out at length by Mughal ideologues in the sixteenth century and both developed and contested thereafter.[107] Two main considerations dictated the choice of Surat as a site. The first is the relative abundance of diverse materials on this port, in contrast to other fine potential candidates in South Asia such as Dabhol, Masulipatnam, or Hughli. The second is the fact that Surat emerged in the sixteenth century as an explicit challenge to European power and remained a port that was autonomous of European political domination until the "Castle Revolution" of 1759.[108] To study Surat, it seems to me, is an entirely different affair from studying a port such as Kochi (or Cochin) in southwestern India, about which several writers have theorized regarding such matters as "alternative cosmopolitanism and cultural pluralism."[109] From the Portuguese arrival there in 1500 to the Dutch conquest in 1663, Kochi was in fact radically segregated into two parts: the lower city, *Cochim de baixo*, or "Santa Cruz," where the Portuguese and other Europeans lived under a captain of their own; and the upper city, *Cochim de cima*, where the local raja's sovereignty still held to a fair extent.[110] It was only in the latter area that the Kochi Jews—today the object of much nostalgic celebration—could openly practice their faith (and that too within certain limits). Muslims too were almost entirely excluded from *Cochim de baixo*. To be sure, the Dutch conquest changed these rules, but the degree of fluidity and integration in the port remained far more limited even in those later times than at Surat. Indeed, there could be no greater irony than the fact that the author of the iconic early modern text on the Kochi Jews, *Notisias dos Judeos de Cochim* (1687), spent a much greater part of his time in Surat than Kochi and may even have completed his work there.[111]

In sharp contrast, the picture that has been presented here of Surat is of a relatively fluid and open space over two centuries, where communities did not live in quarters wholly segregated by race or faith, where an Italian convert to Islam could ally with neighboring Rajputs to defend an artillery fortress, where a Parsi trader acted as a commercial and diplomatic agent for the Portuguese, and where an inquisitive European could apprentice himself to a Chishti Sufi or become an admirer of the Mughal intellectual Shaikh Abu'l Fazl. To be sure, some concentration by occupations existed, and we may presume that the great merchant/ magnate households tended to gather their clientele around them. But social and commercial dealings regularly cut across sectarian lines. Critiquing K. N. Chaudhuri's claim that in early modern India "it was unusual for a Hindu merchant to conduct business with a Muslim," Irfan Habib emphatically pointed to considerable evidence to the contrary from Surat, including the fact that the family of Mulla 'Abdul Ghafur regularly used *baniya* brokers with names such as Gangadas and Rajaram. Habib also returned to examine events such as the celebrated 1669 conflict between the family of Bhimji Parekh and the *qazi* of Surat, when a large number of *baniyas* first threatened to leave for Bombay and then decamped to Bharuch until they were placated and persuaded to return. Here, too, where Chaudhuri had claimed that "the Surat disturbance of 1669 was far from being an isolated incident," Habib suggests that "the sympathies of the local Mughal officials during the incident were clearly with the Banyas and not with the *qazi*."[112] Such a view certainly goes against a construct that attributes the eighteenth-century British conquest of the port and its hinterland to a set of deep and immutable cleavages and hostilities between the communities resident in the port.[113]

For a last small glimpse into the cosmopolitan aspects of Surat in the period under our consideration, let us take a moment to stop by the graveyards of the city. The English and Dutch graveyards lie to the north of the old city, the latter within and the former beyond the outside wall. The first Dutch tomb dates to 1642, and the first English one—that of Francis Breton—to 1649. Of the two graveyards, the English one is the more interesting and hence the better studied. It houses, among others, the tombs of the brothers Christopher and George Oxenden from Kent, the latter being a friend not only of Le Gouz de la Boullaye but also of the celebrated poet Samuel Butler.[114] The Dutch graveyard does have some notable and monumental graves, such as that of Hendrik Adriaan van Rheede (reputedly built to eclipse that of the Oxendens), but they seem stylistically to correspond fairly closely to other Dutch colonial graveyards, such as those in Pulicat (north of Madras/Chennai). However, with regard to the English graves, and particularly those of the seventeenth century, here is the judgment of two architectural historians:

There is little evidence in the form or details of the buildings themselves for the presence of European craftsmen, and local builders would no doubt have been primarily responsible for their construction. The latter must have drawn up the designs in accordance with the instructions of those who commissioned them, but both the general conception of the tombs—free-standing monuments with domes and pinnacles—and the details of the designs and decoration—place them firmly within the Indo-Islamic architectural tradition. This conclusion is reinforced by the indigenous nature of the construction technique (painted and moulded stucco over a brick core); the use of stucco, in particular, has a long history in India.[115]

The same authors add that "in a broad sense the earliest tombs in the cemetery may be held to derive from the adoption in India of Timurid tomb forms in the early sixteenth century. Octagonal free-standing mausolea such as the Sabz Burj and Nila Gumbad at Delhi, dating to the 1530s or 1540s, provide obvious parallels in both their general conception and decorative details." The sixteenth and seventeenth centuries saw a veritable explosion in the construction of public buildings in Surat and its neighboring areas such as Phulpara—such as tombs, mosques, temples, and the like. Perhaps they too could provide us with material evidence of complex borrowings and conversations across groups and communities.

Given the richness of materials available on early modern Surat, it may be said that this chapter has still left plenty of stones—both literally and figuratively—unturned. In particular, it may be worth returning with a fresh eye to the archives of the Dutch, English, and French resident in Surat, reading them not as a part of the history of "European expansion" but somewhat differently. This would be a just tribute to Ashin Das Gupta, the first historian who really sought to do so and thus provided an inspiration to scholars working elsewhere in the broad region, such as Nancy Um. But there are also fresh frontiers to be charted, by looking to underutilized materials in Armenian, Sanskrit, or Gujarati. All of these would suggest that the study of the complex and cosmopolitan life of western Indian Ocean ports remains as much a challenge as the study of ports in the Atlantic, the Mediterranean (including the Black Sea), or the China Seas.

A Conclusion
Toward Polyphonic Histories

God, he said quietly, isn't the sea what Algy calls it: a great sweet mother? The snotgreen sea.

James Joyce, *Ulysses*

The past two generations have seen an efflorescence in historical studies of the western Indian Ocean in the early modern period, including studies of areas that had once been relatively neglected. In the 1990s, when I was still a relative novice in matters of history and teaching in the University of Delhi, a visiting European student, now a senior museum curator, returned from a visit to Sind with a set of photographs he had taken of the celebrated necropolis in Makli. Among images of the splendid mosques and other structures was one of the broken gravestone of a regional notable. The upper part, which must have included the name and the obligatory Qur'anic verses, had been destroyed, but the Persian verse ended with a chronogram that provided the date of his death (1048 AH or 1638–1639 CE). It read: "[He] from whom the *wizarat* received a hundred embellishments, / when he intended to leave this house full of sufferings, / from the unknown came a beautiful, resonant, voice, / the date of his death comes from: *ja-yi sharr fani ast* [this evil world is but transient]." Intrigued, I began to read further into the history of Mughal Sind and found several interesting works on political and administrative questions based in part on the Persian chronicles and other works of the sixteenth and seventeenth centuries.[1] But I could find very little that would link the region and its great riverine port city, Thatta, to the commerce of the early modern Indian Ocean, the subject of my interest.

Delving then into the published records of the English Company that were somewhat ready at hand, I found several references from the very early decades of the seventeenth century. Thus, the English factors at Surat wrote in 1614:

In November 1613 the *Expedition* arrived at Laurebander [Lahori Bandar], the port of Sinda, and there disembarked Sir Robert Sherley and his company, at which place there are continually resident many Portingals, by whose plots and persuasions the port governor denied our people trade, by which means they departed towards Pryaman etc. without knowledge of our factory at Suratt; after whose departure Sir Robert sought his way into Perseia, but was by the governor detained for the king's answer, wherein being delayed he attempted his departure without license, but was fetched back again, one of his people slain, and the rest beaten and robbed.[2]

At the same time, they noted the excellent prospect of riverine trade on the Indus, a "fair river, whereby we may transport our goods to and from that goodly city and country near Lahor." Intriguingly, the editor of these volumes also listed a document from November 1614 that had been catalogued but lost: "the report of Brinzee, Nahuda of a junk from Larree describing the Province of 'Zinde,' subject to the Mogul; the value of English commodities at that market; and of exports thence fit for England; with the coins in circulation at Negrotat [Nagar Thatta], the capital, and Bunder Larree [Lahori Bandar] the Port."[3] Within a few years of this lost report, however, Sir Thomas Roe was discouraging the Company from pursuing this avenue: "Syndu you may freely goe too, lade and relade; but it is inhabited by the Portugall; lies noe way well for your stock (except you scatter it); it vents only your teeth [ivory] and affoords good cloth and many toyes."[4] Once again, we find the same insistence on the substantial (and nefarious) Portuguese influence in the area.

The standard works on the Portuguese presence in the waters of the Indian Ocean said little about their connection with Sind. In the early decades of the sixteenth century, Tomé Pires had written somewhat disparagingly that even though Sind boasted "a large town . . . with many ships and merchants both heathen and Mohammedan," it was past its glory days and only "used to be very famous" (*foy amtigamemte mujto nomeado*).[5] On the other hand, describing the trade of Hurmuz in the 1540s, Bastião Lopes Lobato had certainly noted that the trade from Sind accounted for roughly 7 to 10 percent of the port's revenues, "when Diul [Dewal], which is otherwise called Sinde, is at peace and there is navigation to Urumuz."[6] A brief mention in various texts referred to an episode of hostilities from the 1530s, when a Portuguese fleet had attacked a small redoubt of the Arghun dynasty in Wari Creek at the mouth of the Indus River.[7] It thus seemed reasonable to turn to the obvious resource, namely Diogo do Couto's *Da Ásia*, a work that the present book has drawn on repeatedly. Sprawling, unwieldy, and complex in its construction, this multivolume text has never been given its due place among sixteenth-century European works. Yet it is a gift that keeps on giving, since Couto drew upon a very large network of informants and periodically lifted passages somewhat unscrupulously from other authors.[8] In his *Década sétima*, covering the governorship of Francisco Barreto in the 1550s, he thus enters into a discussion of the Sind region, notably "the City of Tanta [Thatta], the principal one of the Kingdom and amongst the largest and richest in the Orient, both on account of the dimensions [*grossidão*] of its merchants and because of the fineness [*louçainha*] and subtlety of its artisan-work, in which it precedes and has an advantage over all, save the Chinese."[9] Couto informs his readers that late in the year 1556 the ruler of lower Sind Mirza 'Isa Tarkhan had sent an ambassador to the governor in Bassein to ask for Portuguese help against a rival, Sultan Mahmud, described as "a rebellious tyrant" (*hum tyranno alevantado*). Barreto, who was known for his adventurism and aggressive policies, promptly agreed and sent out a fleet of twenty-eight ships and seven hundred men under the command of one of his relatives, Pêro Barreto Rolim.[10] It was stressed that the ruler of Sind "was a friend of the Estado, and from trade with him everyone enjoyed great profits." On an earlier occasion, in 1549, he had asked a passing Portuguese fleet to intervene on the coast against some of his enemies in Balochistan, and he clearly had a positive impression of the Portuguese.[11] Rolim and his fleet arrived off Sind early in 1557 and entered the mouth of the Indus, making their way gradually up the twists and turns of the river to Thatta, where they found not Mirza 'Isa, who had gone off to besiege a distant fortress, but his minor son. Couto has it that despite several emissaries sent on land by Rolim he could get no response other than that he had to wait until Mirza 'Isa's return and that his expenses for supplies would be met in the meantime. The captain-major grew restive as February began, the more so as he received word from Thatta that "if he wished to leave, he could do so." Couto is quite explicit on the nature of the pressure that he faced, which was from the undisciplined Portuguese soldiery. He writes:

> Pêro Barreto was disgruntled with this disappointment, and in the entire fleet there was a common sentiment, because the soldiers wanted at once to avenge themselves; but Pêro Barreto put the matter off because he did not want to have a rupture until he saw what the King [Mirza 'Isa] ordered. And since sol-

diers in in India are very loose and free, at night they created a great rumpus around the captain-major, called him weak, pusillanimous, and that out of fear he did not avenge such a great offense; and they said these and other things to him so many times, that he lost his confidence to the extent that without taking counsel with anyone, he ordered the foists to get ready their ammunition. At this news, the soldiers rose up [in jubilation], and began to get ready their harquebuses, and clean their arms, and meanwhile, the captain-major with great dissimulation sent men off to buy supplies in the city, with which he furnished the fleet plentifully.[12]

Couto's description is thus hardly one of a glorious feat of arms under proper leadership. Rather, the expedition that was ostensibly intended to help Mirza 'Isa ("a friend of the Estado") turned into one of pillaging, because the Portuguese were tempted by the prosperity of Thatta, "full of great and rich goods, spices . . . and other materials." Using the flimsy excuse that Mirza 'Isa's absence was an insult (*affronta*), the Portuguese thus disembarked from their fleet and "entered the city, and put to the sword every living thing they could find, even dumb animals; and since they had no more targets for their fury, the captain-major ordered that they should sack the city, which they did at once, with all of them seizing quantities of goods that were [then] laden on the ships." The chronicler further reports that large sections of the city were set on fire, killing an estimated eight thousand residents, including many helpless people (*gente inutil*), and with the overall damage at "two million [xerafins?] in gold." One of their chief targets was at the edge of the town, in the form of a "very large mosque, similar to our temples, with three doors" (probably the Jami' Masjid, built on the orders of Shah Hasan Arghun in 1531–1532).[13] The Portuguese not only set fire to and damaged the structure using barrels of gunpowder but also brought about a partial collapse, killing numerous people inside in the "most cruel and miserable sort of death that could be imagined."

This episode was sufficiently traumatic to leave clear traces in the Persian chronicling tradition of Sind. The *Tarkhan Nama*, for example, notes that Mirza 'Isa Tarkhan was engaged in a dispute with Sultan Mahmud Arghun and had absented himself from Thatta. "Meanwhile, news was received that the Frankish people [*mardum-i firang*] who were coming from Bandar Lahori to help Mirza 'Isa Tarkhan, on finding the city of Thatta unprotected, had plundered it, set it on fire and taken its inhabitants hostage [*asir karda*]."[14] Faced with this treacherous behavior,

Mirza 'Isa was obliged to rush back and abandon his struggle with Sultan Mahmud. The Ottoman admiral Seydi 'Ali Re'is, who had been in the region not long before this episode and had dealings with both the Tarkhans and the Arghuns, provides the larger context for this dispute.[15] He makes it clear that Thatta was the meeting point of several routes, some terrestrial and some fluvial. To the east, for example, lay Gujarat, with which Sind had long-standing political and economic ties. It was from Gujarat that the Ottoman admiral himself made his way to Thatta, following a route that took him from Ahmedabad via Patan, Wanga (the frontier with Sind in the 1550s), and Junagadh to Thatta. Again, later on in his peregrinations, Seydi 'Ali sought to make his way from Thatta to the Mughal domains in order to make contact with Humayun's court. On this occasion he went up the Indus via Nasarpur, Sehwan, Darbela, and Bhakkar (mentioned earlier) to Mau, Sultanpur, and Ucch until he crossed the Sutlej River to make his way to the great distribution centers and inland entrepôts of Multan and Lahore. These two trading towns commanded the trade from northern India to Central Asia in large measure and were also crucial for the trade to Kabul and Qandahar, and thence to the cities of Iran.

But it was equally possible to bypass these towns and make directly for Qandahar from Bhakkar. These overland routes from Sind into Safavid Iran thus waxed and waned with the ebb and flow of the maritime trade from Lahori Bandar to Hurmuz and other Persian Gulf ports, and the twinned relationship was a structural constant that held as much for the early seventeenth century as it had done for the 1550s.[16] By about 1590, it is reported that there was a Portuguese factor sent from Hurmuz who normally resided at Thatta. This remained the case after the Mughal conquest of Sind in 1591–1592, when the Portuguese attempted to build a proper commercial foothold in the region to consolidate their trade to the Persian Gulf and Masqat. It was thus reported in 1597 that "the Mogores are peacefully in possession of the kingdom of Cinde, and the Portuguese who go there for their commerce are well treated." Initially the Portuguese concern had been that the Mughals would build a fleet in the upper reaches of the Indus and mount an attack on Hurmuz and other centers under Portuguese control.[17] But these fears waned with time, and as we have seen from the English Company records, the English saw the Portuguese trading presence in Sind as a formidable obstacle by the 1610s. In 1620, of fifty-four ships recorded arriving at Hurmuz, as many as eight were from Sind, exceeded only by those from Goa.[18] Such a view of an established Portuguese presence finds confirmation in António Bocarro's account of the *Estado da Índia* in the mid-1630s, where he devotes several pages to Sind, in particular Thatta and Lahori Bandar (*o Bamdel*). Bocarro has a somewhat exaggerated idea of the size of Thatta, and a poor opinion of the character of the local population ("they are a very weak people, pleasure-loving, superstitious, and lying, Gentiles and Moors all mixed together"). According to him, the region, conversely, was "very productive in foodstuff, wheat, rice, sesame, maize, lentils, barley, all sorts of meats with few exceptions, and most excellent sheep." A particular specialty was the production of cotton textiles, which was so extensive that the local raw cotton production was insufficient for the purpose, so that cotton had to be imported from Kacch and Jamnagar. Bocarro goes so far as to claim that "in the city [Thatta] alone, there are thirty thousand or more weavers."

As a result of the plentiful availability of these trade goods, private Portuguese traders came there in sizable numbers; "in 1633, there came together twenty-one [Portuguese] ships, between galliots, pinnaces, and foists, with some two hundred Portuguese." Some of these vessels were richly supplied in terms of silver, gold, and pearls, with capital that could amount to as much as 200,000 patacas (the equivalent of a Spanish *real de a ocho*). The customs duties levied at Lahori Bandar were officially quite modest at 3.5 percent, but Bocarro suggests that there was a constant tussle between the Mughal officials who tried to overvalue the goods and the Portuguese who bribed them not to do so. Besides this trading presence, which varied depending on the seasons and monsoon, there was a more permanent Portuguese presence in the area by the 1630s with two dimensions: secular and religious. In Thatta itself, the Carmelites had a church with two priests, to take care of some fifteen or sixteen Portuguese *casados* there; charity rather than money sent from Goa maintained the priests. In Lahori Bandar, where there were roughly equal numbers of permanently resident Portuguese, there were two Augustinians who, unlike the Carmelites, did receive a handout from the Portuguese Crown. And finally, there was a Portuguese trading factor resident in Thatta, who received no salary from the Estado but whom the Mughal administration permitted to pay 40 percent less on his goods at the customhouse than did normal merchants. He apparently abused this privilege in order to carry the goods of other Portuguese merchants through the customhouse as well. It seems that this factor was a rather obstreperous person who was given to throwing tantrums in the Mughal governor's presence and trying to threaten him with Portuguese naval power, which was by then much diminished. Bocarro also adds a curious note about another source of income for this factor: "He has the liberty to produce wine which, as it is against their law of the Moors, produces much profit and they come to buy it from him at night. The wine is made from jaggery, and the bark of a tree called *joto* [*Acacia nilotica*]. But the factor makes his principal living from his merchandise and ship."

These years in the early 1630s clearly represented the high point of private Portuguese trade in Thatta and Lahori Bandar, when Bocarro boasts that they were able to prevent the Dutch Company from gaining ground there. But this situation was not to last, perhaps because—even by Bocarro's own admission—there were frequent violent incidents in Lahori Bandar where "the Portuguese are treated very badly, with great abuses [*perrarias*], of which they themselves are the cause because they carry out a hundred thousand unreasonable and spiteful acts on the natives, frequently beating them up and even killing them, which they try to cover up with money, and even those who are badly treated are silenced with whatever they give them." In the early 1640s, the English succeeded in making considerable trading inroads into the area, even though they were subsequently unable to keep up the pace of their expansion. In the latter half of the seventeenth century, their Thatta factory failed to meet English expectations save in brief phases. More and more, especially in the 1640s and 1650s, as the Mughals took an active interest in the trade of the western Indian Ocean, it would appear likely that the trade of Sind fell into the hands of Mughal princes such as Aurangzeb and Dara, as well as Sind-based *baniya* (merchant) traders. In time they were joined by the Dutch Company, which continued to trade intermittently from the Indus delta and its ports over the next century or so.[20]

Not every maritime region of the western Indian Ocean is as well served as Sind in terms of the diversity of its overlapping historical materials. This becomes clear when one looks even at a region just to the west of the Indus delta, the area of Gwadar and Makran.[21] The Balochi populations of the area included some who were quite invested in maritime matters, termed "Naitaques" or "Noutaques" by the Portuguese from the time of their first forays into the Persian Gulf. Based in centers such as Gwadar and Tis, these mariners were not constituted into a form of political system that the Portuguese were able to recognize easily, and they thus tended to treat them with deprecatory terms such as "pirates" or "thieves" (*ladrões*). As a result of Portuguese raids on the Balochi sailors in the 1510s, writers such as Tomé Pires did come to have some conception of the unique features of their social organization.[22] He points to a division between an interior population that practiced agriculture, nomadism, and raising horses in the Dasht River (*rio dos Noutaques*) system, whom he broadly compares to the neighboring Rajputs, and a population that he terms "corsairs" (*cosairos*), who formed war bands that could number as many as two hundred and went out in light boats, armed principally with bows, arrows, swords, and lances. Their geographical sphere of activity, in Pires's view, extended as far as Hurmuz and the Gulf in the west and Gujarat in the east. He is struck by the fact that despite their being surrounded by Muslims, they "are Gentiles; there are no Moors among them." Pires also underlines the fact that "they have no king and live in bands [*cabilas*]," with their own distinct language that is neither Arabic nor Persian.

Periodic conflicts between these seaborne Baloch subalterns and the Portuguese characterized much of the sixteenth century. The chronicler João de Barros reports a minor incident from the late 1510s but uses it to add a few reflections on

> the Nautaques, peoples who live on the seafront of the regions of Quermam [Kerman] and Macram [Makran], that lies between the river Indus and the mouth of the Straits of Ormuz. These people, though their real name is Baloches, are called Nautaques on account of their profession of thieves, for in their language it means sea-robbers or corsairs. The life of these Nautaques consists of sallying out of their ports in small and light vessels, and if a *náo* went by their station, unless it was well-armed and defensible, they would attack it and rob it.[23]

He notes that as a consequence the rulers of Hurmuz before the Portuguese conquest were in the custom of maintaining a patrolling fleet during the sailing seasons. Some decades later, the Portuguese realized how serious a threat these Baloch "corsairs" could really be. Diogo do Couto's chronicle reports, under the year 1549, the case of a Portuguese fleet under the command of Luís Figueira, which was requested by the rulers of lower Sind (possible the Tarkhans) to raid some Baloch settlements on the coast. He writes:

> They sailed along the coasts of the Nautaques, attacking some of their ports and settlements, in which process they did some damage. And while on that [coast], one of our ships ran aground, in an area where the people of the land came upon them, and they cut off the heads of all the Portuguese, and took the ship with all its artillery, without our people being able to resist; and things went from bad to worse, because another ship was caught on a sandbank, where it was lost, but the people on board escaped in the other ships.[24]

This was a form of warfare, then, with no quarter either given or taken. This explains the best-known of such conflicts, which took place in 1581, when Dom Luís de Almeida decided largely on his own initiative and against the wishes of the captain of Hurmuz to mount a coastal raid on the region. He put together a fleet of galleys, oared ships, and smaller vessels called *taranquins*, considered ideal for such purposes. According to Couto, again our main source, the attack began with the "city of Penani [Panwan], which was very lovely, and located on the open seacoast."[25] The inhabitants had been forewarned of the approach of the Portuguese, and most of them had fled into the interior. Nevertheless, writes Couto, "the city and all its contents were in the power of our people, who sacked it as they pleased; and then, when there was nothing left to rob, they set it on fire, which consumed it totally; and they did the same thing to the forty-seven longboats [*terradas*] that they found in the dock and at sea, leaving nothing intact." From there, the fleet then moved on to their main target, which was Gwadar, where the inhabitants had also anticipated the raid. "This city," writes Couto, "was large and rich, as it was a very commodious port, and generally frequented by rich merchants from Cambay and other parts, who had already fled into the forests; our people disembarked in the city and did what they had done in the other [city], for there was no resistance, collecting many prizes and supplies, and then went on further to the city of Teim." This final raid would appear to have been carried out still farther east in Kalmat (the "rio de Calamate," according to Couto), an area inhabited by a people distinct from the Baloch, whom the chronicler terms the "Abindos, barbarous and ferocious people." This seems in all likelihood to be a reference to the Brahui population in the area.

While there is no Baloch chronicling tradition that allows us a different perspective on these matters, a distinct possibility does exist in the form of oral epics. Some of these are concerned with Mir Hammal Jiand (or Jihand) of the Hot lineage, resident in Kalmat. One deals with a combat with a lion that Mir Hammal overcomes and kills, while another concerns his conflicts with a significant local figure and rival, Mir Chakar. Of greater significance for our purpose is a sequence that concerns Mir Hammal's struggle, ultimately unsuccessful, with the "Franks" (*Parangan*).[26] This begins with the hero's sailing his boat on the ocean for seven days and nights, until he suddenly finds himself surrounded by four enemy ships. While Hammal is fully prepared to defend himself, it turns out that the others on the vessel are too cowardly to do so. Furthermore, all his trusty weapons, such as his sword and his ax, also slip out of his grasp and fall into the depths of the sea, an indication that Fate has turned its back on him. The suggestion is that the great warrior had grown too boastful, claiming that he would be able to defeat the Franks on his own while disregarding the power of the Almighty. This leads to his being captured and tied with tight ropes until blood gushes from his fingers. A somewhat enigmatic episode follows in which Hammal is taken to the country of the Franks, where he is offered a considerable position and a choice of Frankish women (who are all attracted to his charisma and valor). But the Baloch hero refuses them all, stating that he finds them unattractive on account of their immodesty, their lack of adherence to the true faith, and the fact that they are generally unfaithful; by contrast, the Baloch women not only had intoxicating eyes but were also exemplary in their modesty. Hammal is confined under difficult conditions where he will end his days, separated forever from his homeland, and must resort to sending pathetic messages home with the morning breeze, telling his family not to prepare feasts or weave fine clothes for him, and instructing his wife that if she marries again it should be to a worthy "killer of wild asses [*gorkush*]." The epic thus ends on a mournful note, with only the wild animals that were his usual prey rejoicing that Hammal would never return home to Kalmat. Imprecise about the actual historical context of the episode, as befits the oral epic tradition, the narrative nevertheless confirms the view that by the later decades of the sixteenth century the Baloch had in fair measure converted to Islam, unlike in the times when Tomé Pires wrote his account. This lends a further edge to the rivalry with the Portuguese beyond the mere question of the control of the waterways. When one adds to this the presence of a series of *lieux de mémoire* along the Makran coast, invested with more or less elaborate narratives concerning Portuguese maritime violence, one can see that texts like that of Couto do indeed have counterparts if we are willing to recognize them.

In the 1960s the French historian Jean Aubin launched a project and journal that he termed *Mare Luso-Indicum*, with a brief yet densely worded call to historians of the Indian Ocean world. At the time, Aubin was well aware that the dominant mode in which Indian Ocean history was written was that of "European expansion," usually done while deploying published European sources alone and with very little understanding of context, be it political, social, or cultural. At the same time, his own primary training—as a specialist of the Perso-Islamic world extending into Central Asia—also made him acutely conscious of the narrow horizons that many "orientalists" brought to the study of their subjects of predilection. In the preceding decades there had been some ambitious attempts by economic historians to go beyond these received frameworks, but it is noteworthy that Aubin showed some skepticism in the face of their universalizing claims. As he wrote,

> As the pioneers of a global view of universal history, economic historians invite us to seize the rhythms of the Indo-Islamic world from Aden, Ormuz, or Malacca. Their discipline allows them, up to a certain point, to already meet this wager. But it is above all from the perspective of Venice, Antwerp, or Lisbon, that one observes the cargoes. And cargoes are not everything. At times one has the feeling that a natural Eurocentrism, not always legitimate and frequently naïve, is behind not just the questions but also the answers.[27]

How, then, might one "restitute to Asian civilizations the role that they really played" in historical processes of the early modern period while at the same time acknowledging the potential of European texts, and above all understudied European archives such as those of the Portuguese, which he had begun already to explore in the 1950s? Aubin's answer, as might have been expected from a scholar who had spent considerable time producing critical editions of significant texts from the Islamic world, was philologically oriented. Textual, archival, and archaeological materials had to be unearthed or reexamined in as great a diversity as the questions demanded and subjected to relentless scrutiny with regard to classic questions such as authenticity, authorial motivation, and transmission. In this matter, Aubin saw himself in a (partly positivist) tradition that drew as much on the French school of Chartistes as on Russian scholars such as Vasily Bartold and Vladimir Minorsky. He also admitted a partiality for specific geographies: "local history is the natural framework for analytical research and only analysis at the level of regions, cantons, and cities will allow us to measure the cohesion and the interplay of social forces."[28]

With a primary focus on the sixteenth century and occasional forays into the seventeenth century, the outlines were thus clear enough. A crucial passage in his introduction then lays out the nuts and bolts of the project.

> The critical examination of [Portuguese] sources should be based on a systematic confrontation of the texts of chronicles, which all too often diverge, and the data in archival documents. It is only this collation that will allow us to interpret the contradictions in the narrative texts, their silences, and to distinguish

which versions are more reliable; this will, in passing, reveal the ways in which the chroniclers worked and will help in the preparation of critical editions, the absence of which have long been deplored. A no less systematic confrontation should be instituted between Portuguese and oriental sources. This can already be begun, even though the exploration of the Ottoman archives and Indian collections are less advanced than those of the Iberian collections. We have already stated that the two sets of sources do not overlap—one being maritime and the other continental, if one chooses an extreme simplification. But wherever they coincide, there are remarkable convergences, and they are extremely complementary. Portuguese documentation cannot be correctly understood if one treats it as a simple literary device, or as picturesque and exotic, because of the underlying social levels, the institutional practices, and the political conjunctures to which, in diverse and often implicit ways, they continue to refer.[29]

These are striking remarks that we would treat today with a certain degree of caution, notably on the subject of "convergences," which are more complex than they appear at first view. After a decade of experiments in this mode, found in the four remarkable volumes of *Mare Luso-Indicum*, the project was abandoned, at least in that form. But this was probably not so much an admission of defeat as recognition that in the same period academic fashions had instead dictated the dominance of works based on Weberian comparative simplifications, tired and reified stereotypes regarding both Asian and Iberian societies and the role therein of religion, caste, and the like.[30] In turn the 1980s brought forth a set of superficial syntheses claiming to do for the Indian Ocean what Braudel had done for the Mediterranean; reviewing the prominent work of K. N. Chaudhuri, Aubin noted that the book was "poorly organized" and nothing less than an *"essai manqué."* Since its author has been unable to "appreciate the difficulties of an important and complex subject," the consequence is that the book's superficial treatment of an enormous space over a very long time "leads inexorably, whatever qualities one has, to an accumulation of insipid summaries and poorly-linked comments, and the loss of a historical perspective."[31] Yet, in the later 1980s and 1990s, Chaudhuri's work became the slippery foundation for a series of other works, almost always monolingual in their orientation and bibliographical choices and driven above all by direct justifications in contemporary identity politics. The Indian Ocean thus was often not the space of a proper historiographical conversation but rather the canvas on which authors with competing projects, including those of revanchist nationalism, projected their views (not to say their fantasies), unfettered by the discipline of wide-ranging archival, textual, or material research.

It may be said, however, that the wheel has turned again in the twenty-first century, particularly in the context of the prominence of what is termed (for better and for worse) "global history." As a concept, this lacks precision and may cover a variety of both objects of study and methods; still, one may safely state that global history is largely intended to cover historical objects that do not fall within conventional regional or national boundaries. But it may still follow a panoply of methods ranging from classic comparative studies of two (or more) spaces to syntheses that draw for the most part on secondary literature and metahistorical reflections that do not have any clear spatial referent. In the context of the history of the Indian Ocean, we can find examples of all of these. This book has proposed to pursue a specific path, that of connected histories, in order to reconsider the history of the western Indian Ocean between the fifteenth and the seventeenth centuries. The purpose, it must be reiterated, has been to produce not an encyclopedic work but rather one that juxtaposes a set of analytical incisions to permit a closer look at a number of themes, places, and objects. Readers in search of an encyclopedic vision will certainly have other resources.[32] For my part, I have tried constantly to bring together a diversity of sources, known and unknown, and read them together, exploiting their tensions and—where possible—their convergences. The history that emerges is inevitably not merely connected but polyphonic, perhaps at times even discordant. But there is no proper history, whether of an ocean or a continent, where all the voices from the past will sing for us either in unison or in harmony.

Notes

INTRODUCTION

1. Seydi 'Ali Reis, *Kitabül-Muhit*, ed. Fuat Sezgin (Istanbul: Topkapı Sarayı Müzesi, 1997); Maximilian Bittner and Wilhelm Tomaschek, eds., *Die topographischen Capitel des indischen Seespiegels "Mohît"* (Vienna: K. K. Geographischen Gesellschaft, 1897).
2. Bittner and Tomaschek, *Die topographischen Capitel*, 53.
3. See Gerald R. Tibbetts, *Arab Navigation before the Coming of the Portuguese: Being a Translation of "Kitab al-Fawa'id fi usul al-bahr wa'l- qawa'id" of Ahmad b. Majid al-Najdi together with an Introduction on the History of Arab Navigation, Notes on the Navigational Techniques and on the Topography of the Indian Ocean, and a Glossary of Navigational Terms* (London: Royal Asiatic Society, 1972).
4. Bittner and Tomaschek, *Die topographischen Capitel*, 53.
5. Seydi 'Ali Re'is, *Le miroir des pays: Une anabase ottomane à travers l'Inde et l'Asie centrale*, trans. Jean-Louis Bacqué-Grammont (Paris: Actes Sud, 1999).
6. For two recent general volumes that broadly reconsider maritime history, see Jerry H. Bentley, Renate Bridenthal, and Kären Wigen, eds., *Seascapes: Maritime Histories, Littoral Cultures, and Transoceanic Exchanges* (Honolulu: University of Hawai'i Press, 2007); and David Armitage, Alison Bashford, and Sujit Sivasundaram, eds., *Oceanic Histories* (New York: Cambridge University Press, 2017).
7. See, for example, the reflections in Denys Lombard, "Une autre 'Méditerranée' dans le Sud-Est asiatique," *Hérodote* 88 (1998): 184–193, as well as in Heather Sutherland, "Southeast Asian History and the Mediterranean Analogy," *Journal of Southeast Asian Studies* 34, no. 1 (2003): 1–20.
8. See David Abulafia, *The Great Sea: A Human History of the Mediterranean* (London: Allen Lane, 2011), xxiii–xix.
9. See Fernand Braudel, *Autour de la Méditerranée*, ed. Paule Braudel and Roselyne de Ayala (Paris: Editions de Fallois, 1996).

10. Alison Games, "Atlantic History: Definitions, Challenges, and Opportunities," *American Historical Review* 111, no. 3 (2006): 741–757.
11. Jean Aubin, *Études sur l'Iran médiéval: Géographie historique et société*, ed. Denise Aigle (Paris: Association pour l'avancement des études iraniennes, 2018), 63–90.
12. Ibn Battuta, *The Travels of Ibn Battuta, AD 1325–1354*, tr. H.A.R. Gibb (Cambridge, UK: Hakluyt Society, 1962), 2:400–402.
13. Ralph Kauz and Roderich Ptak, "Hormuz in Yuan and Ming Sources," *Bulletin de l'École française d'Extrême-Orient* 88 (2001): 27–75.
14. Kauz and Ptak, "Hormuz in Yuan and Ming Sources," 56.
15. Ma Huan, *Yingyai Shenglan: "The Overall Survey of the Ocean's Shores" (1433)*, ed. and trans. Feng Chengjun and J. V. G. Mills (Cambridge, UK: Hakluyt Society, 1970).
16. See the discussion in Muzaffar Alam and Sanjay Subrahmanyam, *Indo-Persian Travels in the Age of Discoveries, 1400–1800* (Cambridge: Cambridge University Press, 2007), 59–60; and for the text, 'Abdur Razzaq ibn Ishaq Samarqandi, *Matla' us-Sa'dain wa Majma' ul-Bahrain*, ed. Muhammad Shafi', 2nd ed. (Lahore: Gilani, 1946–1949), 2:768–769.
17. Jean Aubin, "Le royaume d'Ormuz au début du XVIe siècle," in Aubin, *Le Latin et l'astrolabe*, 3 vols. (Paris: Centre Culturel Calouste Gulbenkian, 1996–2006), 2:287–376.
18. João de Barros, *Da Ásia, década segunda*, part 2 (Lisbon: Régia Officina Typográfica, 1777), 422: "humas grandes casas . . . que serviam de hospital, a que elles chamam madraçal, as quaes eram junto da fortaleza."
19. "Ha mais grande e formosa mesquita que ay em toda moramma": Gaspar Berze S.J. to the Society of Jesus, Hurmuz, 10th December 1549, in *Documenta Indica, Vol. 1 (1540–49)*, ed. Josef Wicki, (Rome: Monumenta Historica Societatis Iesu, 1948), 690.
20. Ahmad Iqtidari, ed., *Asar-i shahrha-yi bastani: Sawahil wa jazayir-i Khalij-i Fars wa Darya-yi 'Uman*, 2nd ed. (Tehran: Anjuman-i Asar wa Mufakhir-i Farhangi, 1375/1996), 682–739.
21. Aubin, "Cojeatar et Albuquerque," in Aubin, *Le Latin et l'astrolabe*, 2:149–196.
22. It is surprising to find it largely ignored in such survey essays as Michael Pearson, "Islamic trade, shipping, port-states and merchant communities in the Indian Ocean, seventh to sixteenth centuries," in David O. Morgan and Anthony Reid, eds., *The New Cambridge History of Islam*, vol. 3, *The Eastern Islamic World, Eleventh to Eighteenth Centuries* (Cambridge: Cambridge University Press, 2010), 315–365.
23. The chronicle was since published: 'Abdul Karim Nimdihi, *Kanz al-ma'ani: Munsha'at-i Nimdihi*, ed. Muhammad Riza Nasiri and Muhammad Baqir Wusuqi (Tehran: Farhangistan-i Zaban wa Adab-i Farsi, 1394 Sh./2015–2016). For a discussion of this source, see Meia Walravens, "Arabic as a Language of the South Asian Chancery: Bahmani Communications to the

Mamluk Sultanate," *Arabica* 67 (2020): 409–435. For Nimdihi's chronicle, see Cambridge University Library, Eton Pote 271 (on permanent loan from Eton College Library), *Tabaqat-i Mahmud Shahi*, fols. 381v–469r (ninth *tabaqa*).

24. Jean Aubin, "Indo-islamica I: La vie et l'oeuvre de Nimdihi," *Revue des Études Islamiques* 34 (1966): 61–81.
25. Jean Aubin, "Les documents arabes, persans et turcs de la Torre do Tombo," in Aubin, *Le Latin et l'astrolabe*, 2:424–425.
26. Aubin, "Les documents arabes, persans et turcs de la Torre do Tombo," 426–427.
27. For an earlier critique of such stereotypes, see Sanjay Subrahmanyam, "Of *Imârat* and *Tijârat*: Asian Merchants and State Power in the Western Indian Ocean, 1400–1750," *Comparative Studies in Society and History* 37, no. 4 (1995): 750–780.
28. Max Weber, *The City*, trans. and ed. Don Martindale and Gertrud Neuwirth (New York: Free Press, 1958). For a trenchant critique, which includes the views of orientalists such as Jean Sauvaget, see André Raymond, "Islamic City, Arab City: Orientalist Myths and Recent Views," *British Journal of Middle Eastern Studies* 21, no. 1 (1994): 3–18.
29. Simon Kuznets, *Modern Economic Growth: Rate, Structure, and Spread* (New Haven, CT: Yale University Press, 1966).
30. Alexander Gerschenkron, *Economic Backwardness in Historical Perspective: A Book of Essays* (Cambridge, MA: Belknap Press of Harvard University Press, 1962).
31. For an early overview of such attempts, see B. R. Tomlinson, "Writing History Sideways: Lessons for Indian Economic Historians from Meiji Japan," *Modern Asian Studies* 19, no. 3 (1985): 669–698. See the special issue entitled "India and Indonesia: General Perspectives," in *Itinerario* 13, no. 1 (1989). My own contributions to this comparative exercise may be found in Sanjay Subrahmanyam, "Aspects of State Formation in South India and Southeast Asia, 1500–1650," *Indian Economic and Social History Review* 23, no. 4 (1986): 357–377; and in Sanjay Subrahmanyam, "State Formation and Transformation in Early Modern India and Southeast Asia," *Itinerario* 12, no. 1 (1988): 91–109.
32. This remains a popular topic, as seen in volumes such as Adam Clulow and Tristan Mostert, eds., *The Dutch and English East India Companies: Diplomacy, Trade and Violence in Early Modern Asia* (Amsterdam: Amsterdam University Press, 2018).
33. Niels Steensgaard, *The Asian Trade Revolution of the Seventeenth Century: The East India Companies and the Decline of the Caravan Trade* (Chicago: University of Chicago Press, 1974), 7.
34. Steensgaard, *The Asian Trade Revolution of the Seventeenth Century*, 151.
35. Steensgaard, *The Asian Trade Revolution of the Seventeenth Century*, 10.
36. C. R. Boxer, *The Dutch Seaborne Empire, 1600–1800* (New York: Knopf,

1965); C. R. Boxer, *The Portuguese Seaborne Empire, 1415–1825* (London: Hutchinson, 1969).
37. Holden Furber, *Rival Empires of Trade in the Orient, 1600–1800* (Minneapolis: University of Minnesota Press, 1976).
38. Holden Furber, *John Company at Work: A Study of European Expansion in India in the Late Eighteenth Century* (Cambridge, MA: Harvard University Press, 1948).
39. Marc Bloch, "A Contribution Towards a Comparative History Of European Societies," in *Land and Work in Mediaeval Europe: Selected Papers*, trans. J. E. Anderson (Berkeley: University of California Press, 1967), 44–81.
40. This unhealthy obsession with list-making can be found in Jürgen Osterhammel, *The Transformation of the World: A Global History of the Nineteenth Century*, trans. Patrick Camiller (Princeton, NJ: Princeton University Press, 2015). For a penetrating critique of this work, see Giuseppe Marcocci, "La grande metamorfosi del lungo Ottocento: Una via weberiana alla storia del mondo?," *Archivio Storico Italiano* 175, no. 2 (2017): 383–394.
41. Ian Morris, *Why the West Rules—for Now: The Patterns of History, and What They Reveal about the Future* (London: Profile Books, 2010).
42. Sanjay Subrahmanyam, "Connected Histories: Notes towards a Reconfiguration of Early Modern Eurasia," *Modern Asian Studies* 31, no. 3 (1997): 735–762.
43. The end product appeared in the two massive volumes of Victor Lieberman, *Strange Parallels: Southeast Asia in Global Context, c. 800–1830*, 2 vols. (Cambridge: Cambridge University Press, 2003–2009).
44. Victor Lieberman, "What 'Strange Parallels' Sought to Accomplish," *Journal of Asian Studies* 70, no. 4 (2011): 931–938.
45. Carlo Ginzburg, *Cinco reflexiones sobre Marc Bloch*, trans. Carlos Antonio Aguirre Rojas (Bogotá: Desde Abajo, 2016), 75.
46. For a sorry attempt to defend such intellectual slothfulness, see Indrani Chatterjee, "Connected Histories and the Dream of Decolonial History," *South Asia: Journal of South Asian Studies* 41, no. 1 (2018): 69–86, which may be compared to the brilliant work of Thibaut d'Hubert, *In the Shade of the Golden Palace: Alaol and Middle Bengali Poetics in Arakan* (New York: Oxford University Press, 2018).
47. Thibaut d'Hubert and Alexandre Papas, eds., *Jāmī in Regional Contexts: The Reception of 'Abd al-Raḥmān Jāmī's works in the Islamicate world, ca. 9th/15th–14th/20th Century* (Boston: Brill, 2018); Sebouh D. Aslanian, *From the Indian Ocean to the Mediterranean: The Global Trade Networks of Armenian Merchants from New Julfa* (Berkeley: University of California Press, 2010).
48. Joseph Fletcher, "Ch'ing Inner Asia c. 1800," in *The Cambridge History of China*, ed. John K. Fairbank (Cambridge: Cambridge University Press, 1978), 10:35–106; Jean Aubin, *Emirs mongols et vizirs persans dans les remous de l'acculturation* (Paris: Association pour l'Avancement des Études Iraniennes, 1995).

49. See, for example, William H. McNeill, *The Pursuit of Power: Technology, Armed Force, and Society since A.D. 1000* (Chicago: University of Chicago Press, 1982).
50. Jean Aubin, "Un chroniqueur méconnu, Šabānkāra'ī," in Aubin, *Études sur l'Iran médiéval*, 143–154; and Aubin, "Indo-islamica I: La vie et l'oeuvre de Nimdihi." In somewhat the same spirit, see Christopher Markiewicz, *The Crisis of Kingship in Late Medieval Islam: Persian Emigres and the Making of Ottoman Sovereignty* (Cambridge: Cambridge University Press, 2019).
51. I refer here to the unfortunate caricature of "connected history" in Huricihan İslamoğlu, *Dünya Tarihi ve Siyaset* (Istanbul: İletişim Yayınları, 2021), 11–13.
52. Romain Bertrand, *L'histoire à parts égales: Récits d'une rencontre Orient-Occident (XVIe–XVIIe siècles)* (Paris: Seuil, 2011). Few published critiques have noted the hundreds of inaccuracies and errors in the references to Dutch, Portuguese, and Malay sources that litter the pages of this book.
53. See, for example, the important writings of Claude Guillot, "Libre entreprise contre économie dirigée: Guerres civiles à Banten, 1580–1609," *Archipel* 43 (1992): 57–72; Claude Guillot, Lukman Nurhakim, and Sonny Wibisono, *Banten avant l'Islam: Etude archéologique de Banten Girang (Java, Indonésie) 932(?)–1526* (Paris: EFEO, 2005); special number, "Banten: Histoire d'une region," *Archipel* 50 (1995).
54. Serge Gruzinski, "Les mondes mêlés de la monarchie catholique et autres 'connected histories'," *Annales HSS* 56, no. 1 (2001): 85–117.
55. Gruzinski, "Les mondes mêlés de la monarchie catholique," 87.
56. Serge Gruzinski, *Les quatre parties du monde: Histoire d'une mondialisation* (Paris: La Martinière, 2004). I broadly concur with the critique of "globalization" as a concept in Frederick Cooper, "What is the Concept of Globalization Good For? An African Historian's Perspective," *African Affairs* 100, no. 399 (2001): 189–213.
57. Philippa Levine, "Is Comparative History Possible?," *History and Theory* 53, no. 3 (2014): 331–347. For a far more balanced view of the same question, see Deborah Cohen and Maura O'Connor, eds., *Comparison and History: Europe in Cross-National Perspective* (New York: Routledge, 2004).
58. Levine, "Is Comparative History Possible?," 336.
59. Sanjay Subrahmanyam, "Turning the Stones Over: Sixteenth-Century Millenarianism from the Tagus to the Ganges," *Indian Economic and Social History Review* 40, no. 3 (2003): 131–163.
60. We may thus consider Alison Bashford and Philippa Levine, eds., *The Oxford Handbook of the History of Eugenics* (Oxford: Oxford University Press, 2010), which Levine holds up in her essay as a model of comparative history. It is divided into a first "universal" section, and a second long section where almost all chapters are divided by national boundaries, or conventional regional classifications.
61. Dipesh Chakrabarty, *Provincializing Europe: Postcolonial Thought and Histori-*

cal Difference (Princeton, NJ: Princeton University Press, 2000), 4 (emphasis in original).

62. A slightly different perspective may emerge from reading Partha Chatterjee, *The Black Hole of Empire: History of a Global Practice of Power* (Princeton, NJ: Princeton University Press, 2012), which addresses some issues deriving from connected history.
63. Zoltán Biedermann, "(Dis)connected History and the Multiple Narratives of Global Early Modernity," *Modern Philology* 119, no. 1 (2021): 13–32.
64. Zoltán Biedermann, *(Dis)connected Empires: Imperial Portugal, Sri Lankan Diplomacy, and the Making of a Habsburg Conquest in Asia* (Oxford: Oxford University Press, 2018).
65. See Anne Blackburn, "Buddhist Connections in the Indian Ocean: Changes in Monastic Mobility, 1000–1500," *Journal of the Economic and Social History of the Orient* 58, no. 3 (2015): 237–266.
66. Jorge Manuel Flores, *Os portugueses e o Mar de Ceilão: Trato, diplomacia e guerra (1498–1543)* (Lisbon: Edições Cosmos, 1998).
67. Geneviève Bouchon and Denys Lombard, "The Indian Ocean in the Fifteenth Century," in *India and the Indian Ocean, 1500–1800*, ed. Ashin Das Gupta and M. N. Pearson (Calcutta: Oxford University Press, 1987), 47.
68. Maria Augusta da Veiga e Sousa, ed., *O livro de Duarte Barbosa*, 2 vols. (Lisbon: Centro de Estudos de História e Cartografia Antiga, 1996–2000); and Armando Cortesão, ed. and trans., *The Suma Oriental of Tomé Pires: An account of the East, from the Red Sea to Japan, written in Malacca and India in 1512–1515; and the book of Francisco Rodrigues, rutter of a voyage in the Red Sea, nautical rules, almanack and maps, written and drawn in the East before 1515*, 2 vols. (London: Hakluyt Society, 1944). For an example of such dependence, see André Wink, Al-Hind, the Making of the Indo-Islamic World, vol. 3, *Indo-Islamic Society, 14th–15th Centuries* (Leiden: E. J. Brill, 2004), 170–243. See my detailed critique in the *International History Review* 27, no. 2 (2005): 352–354.
69. Jane Hathaway (with Karl Barbir), *The Arab Lands under Ottoman Rule, 1516–1800* (New York: Pearson-Longman, 2013), 135.
70. Richard T. Mortel, "The Mercantile Community of Mecca during the Late Mamlūk Period," *Journal of the Royal Asiatic Society* 4, no. 1 (1994): 15–35. See also Mortel, "Madrasas in Mecca during the Medieval Period: A Descriptive Study Based on Literary Sources," *Bulletin of the School of Oriental and African Studies* 60, no. 2 (1997): 236–252.
71. Taddesse Tamrat, *Church and State in Ethiopia, 1270–1527* (Oxford: Clarendon Press, 1972), 302. For a more recent account of the Solomonids in this period from a source-critical viewpoint, see Marie-Laure Derat, *Le domaine des rois éthiopiens: Espace, pouvoir et monachisme (1270–1527)* (Paris: Publications de la Sorbonne, 2003).
72. See H. Neville Chittick, *Kilwa: An Islamic Trading City on the East African Coast*, 2 vols. (Nairobi: British Institute in Eastern Africa, 1974).

73. See Thomas Spear, "Early Swahili History Reconsidered," *International Journal of African Historical Studies* 33, no. 2 (2000): 257–290 (quotation on 281). Also see the more recent reflections in Stephanie Wynne-Jones and Adria LaViolette, eds., *The Swahili World* (London: Routledge, 2018), esp. 135–146, 253–259.
74. For an overview of these processes, see Sunil Kumar, "The Delhi Sultanate as Empire," in *The Oxford World History of Empire*, ed. Peter Fibiger Bang, C. A. Bayly, and Walter Scheidel (Oxford: Oxford University Press, 2021), 2:571–596.
75. William Foster, ed., *Early Travels in India, 1583–1619* (London: Oxford University Press, 1921), 133–134. This may be compared to the slightly later description in R. C. Temple, ed., *The Travels of Peter Mundy in Europe and Asia, 1608–1667* (London: Hakluyt Society, 1914), 2:29–34.

CHAPTER 1: AN EPOCH OF TRANSITIONS, 1440–1520

1. Edward A. Alpers, *The Indian Ocean in World History* (New York: Oxford University Press, 2014), 8.
2. Muzaffar Alam and Sanjay Subrahmanyam, *Indo-Persian Travels in the Age of Discoveries, 1400–1800* (Cambridge: Cambridge University Press, 2007), 60.
3. For a critique see Sanjay Subrahmanyam, "'World-Economies' and South Asia, 1600–1750: A Skeptical Note," *Review (Fernand Braudel Center)* 12, no. 1 (1989): 141–148.
4. Irfan Habib, "Population," in *The Cambridge Economic History of India, vol. I (c. 1200 to c. 1750)*, ed. Irfan Habib and Tapan Raychaudhuri, 163–172 (Cambridge: Cambridge University Press, 1982). Habib estimates the population in 1600 CE as between 140 and 150 million.
5. Patrick Manning, "African Population, 1650–2000: Comparisons and Implications of New Estimates," in *Africa's Development in Historical Perspective*, ed. Emmanuel Akyeampong, Robert Bates, Nathan Nunn, and James Robinson, 131–152 (Cambridge: Cambridge University Press, 2014).
6. André Wink, "From the Mediterranean to the Indian Ocean: Medieval History in Geographic Perspective," *Comparative Studies in Society and History* 44, no. 3 (2002): 416–445.
7. Fernand Braudel, *The Mediterranean and the Mediterranean World in the Age of Philip II*, trans. Siân Reynolds, 2 vols. (New York: Harper & Row, 1972).
8. Wink, "From the Mediterranean to the Indian Ocean," 435.
9. Roxani Margariti, "An Ocean of Islands: Islands, Insularity, and Historiography of the Indian Ocean," in *The Sea: Thalassography and Historiography*, ed. Peter Miller, 198–229 (Ann Arbor: University of Michigan Press, 2013).
10. Edward A. Alpers, "Indian Ocean Africa: The Island Factor," *Emergences* 10 (2000): 373–386, reproduced in Alpers, *East Africa and the Indian Ocean* (Princeton, NJ: Markus Wiener, 2009).
11. Murray P. Cox, Michael G. Nelson, Meryanne K. Tumonggor, François-X.

Ricaut, and Herawati Sudoyo, "A Small Cohort of Island Southeast Asian Women Founded Madagascar," *Proceedings of the Royal Society: Biological Sciences* 279, no. 1739 (2012): 2761–2768.

12. Philippe Beaujard, *The Worlds of the Indian Ocean: A Global History*, vol. 2, *From the Seventh Century to the Fifteenth Century*, trans. Tamara Loring, Frances Meadows, and Andromeda Tait (Cambridge: Cambridge University Press, 2019), 429.

13. For a balanced account, see Tansen Sen, "The Impact of Zheng He's Expeditions on Indian Ocean Interactions," *Bulletin of the School of Oriental and African Studies* 79, no. 3 (2016): 609–636.

14. Geoff Wade, trans., *Southeast Asia in the Ming Shi-lu: An Open Access Resource* (Singapore: Asia Research Institute and the Singapore E-Press, National University of Singapore), http://epress.nus.edu.sg/msl/reign/xuan-de/year-5-month-6-day-9.

15. Evrim Binbaş and Will Kwiatkowski, "Iskandar b. ʿUmar Shaykh's Farman in the David Collection," *Journal of the David Collection* 5 (2021): 26–79 (quotation on 50).

16. Malika Dekkiche, "New Source, New Debate: Re-evaluation of the Mamluk-Timurid Struggle for Religious Supremacy in the Hijaz (Paris, BnF MS ar. 4440)," *Mamluk Studies Review* 18 (2014–2015): 247–271.

17. Joseph F. Fletcher, "China and Central Asia, 1368–1884," in *The Chinese World Order: Traditional China's Foreign Relations*, ed. John King Fairbank, 206–224 (Cambridge, MA: Harvard University Press, 1968).

18. Walther Hinz, "Quellenstudien zur Geschichte der Timuriden," *Zeitschrift der Deutschen Morgenländischen Gesellschaft* 90 (1936): 357–398 (quotation on 381–382).

19. Syed Ejaz Hussain, *Shiraz-i Hind: A History of the Jaunpur Sultanate* (New Delhi: Manohar, 2017).

20. Peter Jackson, *The Delhi Sultanate: A Political and Military History* (Cambridge: Cambridge University Press, 1999), 322.

21. Mehrdad Shokoohy, "Architecture of the Sultanate of Maʿbar in Madura, and Other Muslim Monuments in South India," *Journal of the Royal Asiatic Society*, 3d ser., 1, no. 1 (1991): 31–92.

22. Éric Vallet, *L'Arabie marchande: État et commerce sous les sultans rasūlides du Yémen (626–858/1229–1454)* (Paris: Presses Universitaires de la Sorbonne, 2010), 581.

23. Éric Vallet, "Les sultans rasūlides du Yémen, protecteurs des communautés musulmanes de l'Inde (VIIe-VIIIe/XIIIe–XIVe siècles)," *Annales Islamologiques* 41 (2007): 149–176.

24. M. G. S. Narayanan, *Cultural Symbiosis in Kerala* (Trivandrum: Kerala Historical Society, 1972), 38–42, 95–96.

25. V. V. Haridas, *Zamorins and the Political Culture of Medieval Kerala* (Hyderabad: Orient Blackswan, 2016), 206–213.

26. Haridas, *Zamorins and Political Culture*, 33.

27. Vallet, *L'Arabie marchande*, 655.
28. See R. B. Serjeant, "Fifteenth Century 'Interlopers' on the Coast of Rasūlid Yemen," *Res Orientales* 6 (1994) (Itinéraires d'Orient: Hommages à Claude Cahen): 83–91.
29. Vallet, *L'Arabie marchande*, 660.
30. For his account, see 'Abdur Razzaq ibn Ishaq Samarqandi, *Matla' us-Sa'dain wa Majma' ul-Bahrain*, part 2, ed. Maulavi Muhammad Shafi' (Lahore: Chapkhana-yi Gilani, 1946–1949), 764–771, 775–791, 796–830, 842–851. An abridged translation by Wheeler Thackston may be found in "Kamaluddin Abdul-Razzaq Samarqandi: Mission to Calicut and Vijayanagar," in *A Century of Princes: Sources on Timurid History and Art* (Cambridge, MA: Aga Khan Program for Islamic Architecture, 1989), 299–321. This text has been closely analyzed in Alam and Subrahmanyam, *Indo-Persian Travels in the Age of Discoveries*, 54–82.
31. Alam and Subrahmanyam, *Indo-Persian Travels in the Age of Discoveries*, 64.
32. Francisco Apellániz, *Breaching the Bronze Wall: Franks at Mamluk and Ottoman Courts and Markets* (Leiden: Brill, 2020), 54.
33. Alam and Subrahmanyam, *Indo-Persian Travels in the Age of Discoveries*, 69.
34. Burton Stein, *Vijayanagara (The New Cambridge History of India)* (Cambridge: Cambridge University Press, 1989), 29–30, 42, 55.
35. K. V. Ramesh, *A History of South Kanara: From the Earliest Times to the Fall of Vijayanagara* (Dharwar: Karnatak University, 1970), 264.
36. İlker Evrim Binbaş, *Intellectual Networks in Timurid Iran: Sharaf al-Din 'Ali Yazdi and the Islamicate Republic of Letters* (Cambridge: Cambridge University Press, 2016), 45.
37. Elizabeth Lambourn, "India from Aden: *Khutba* and Muslim Urban Networks in Late Thirteenth-Century India," in *Secondary Cities and Urban Networking in the Indian Ocean Realm, c. 1400–1800*, ed. Kenneth R. Hall (Lanham, MD: Lexington Books, 2008), 55–97.
38. Mehrdad Shokoohy, "Sasanian Royal Emblems and their Reemergence in the Fourteenth-Century Deccan," *Muqarnas* 11 (1994): 65–78.
39. Beatrice Forbes Manz, *Power, Politics and Religion in Timurid Iran* (Cambridge: Cambridge University Press, 2010).
40. Mohammad Suleman Siddiqi, "The Ethnic Change at Bidar and Its Influence (AD 1422–1538)," in *Medieval Deccan History: Commemoration Volume in Honour of Purushottam Mahadeo Joshi*, ed. A. R. Kulkarni, M. A. Nayeem, and T. R. De Souza (Bombay: Popular Prakashan, 1996), 33–51.
41. See Jean Aubin, "De Kûhbanân à Bidar: La famille Ni'matullâhi," *Studia Iranica* 20 (1991): 233–261.
42. Muhammad Qasim Firishta, *Tarikh-i Firishta*, ed. Mohammad Reza Nasiri, 4 vols. (Tehran: Anjuman-i Asar wa Mafakhir-i Farhangi, 2009–2016), 2:352; *History of the Rise of Mahomedan Power in India till the Year A.D. 1612*, trans. John Briggs (with Mir Khairat 'Ali Khan Akbarabadi "Mushtaq") (London: Longman, Rees, Orme, Brown and Green, 1829), 2:392.

43. Firishta, *Tarikh*, 2:364, 399; Firishta, *History of the Rise of Mahomedan Power*, 2:404, 439.
44. ʿAbdul Karim Nimdihi, *Kanz al-maʿani (Munshaʾat-i Nimdihi)*, ed. Muhammad Reza Nasiri and Muhammad Baqir Wusuqi (Tehran: Farhangistan-i zaban wa adab-i farsi, 1394 Sh./2015); Mahmud Gawan, *Riyaz al-inshaʾ*, ed. Shaikh Chand and Ghulam Yazdani (Hyderabad: Government Press, 1948). For an analysis of the latter from a literary perspective, see Stephan Popp, "Persische diplomatische Korrespondenz im Südindien des 15. Jahrhunderts," *Zeitschrift der Deutschen Morgenländischen Gesellschaft* 162, no. 1 (2012): 95–125.
45. For a discussion, see Alam and Subrahmanyam, *Indo-Persian Travels in the Age of Discoveries*, 82–91; see also Mary Jane Maxwell, "Afanasii Nikitin: An Orthodox Russian's Spiritual Voyage in the Dar al-Islam, 1468–1475," *Journal of World History* 17, no. 3 (2006): 243–266.
46. See Muzaffar Alam, "Scholar, Saint, and Poet: Jāmī in the Indo-Muslim World," in *Jāmī in Regional Contexts: The Reception of ʿAbd al-Raḥmān Jāmī's Works in the Islamicate World, ca. 9th/15th–14th/20th Century*, ed. Thibaut d'Hubert and Alexandre Papas (Leiden: Brill, 2018), 136–176, esp. 136–139.
47. Jean Aubin, "Le royaume d'Ormuz au début du XVIe siècle," in Aubin, *Le Latin et l'astrolabe*, 3 vols. (Paris: Centre Culturel Calouste Gulbenkian, 1996–2006), 2:373–374.
48. Jean Aubin, "Indo-islamica I: La vie et l'oeuvre de Nimdihi," *Revue des Études Islamiques* 34 (1966): 61–81 (quotation on 66); ʿAbdul Husain Tuni, *Tarikh-i Mahmud Shahi*, ed. S. C. Misra (Baroda: M.S. University, 1988), 185–186.
49. H. K. Sherwani, "The Bahmanis," in *History of Medieval Deccan (1295–1724)*, ed. H. K. Sherwani and P. M. Joshi, 1:189–190 (Hyderabad: Government of Andhra Pradesh, 1973).
50. Aubin, "Le royaume d'Ormuz," 374–375; Keelan Overton, ed., *Iran and the Deccan: Persianate Art, Culture, and Talent in Circulation, 1400–1700* (Bloomington: Indiana University Press, 2020), 105–116.
51. Vladimir Minorsky, "The Qara-qoyunlu and the Qutb-Shahs (Turkmenica, 10)," *Bulletin of the School of Oriental and African Studies* 17, no. 1 (1955): 50–73.
52. Armando Cortesão, ed., *The Suma Oriental of Tomé Pires and the Book of Francisco Rodrigues*, 2 vols. (London: Hakluyt Society, 1944), 1:50–51 (translation), and 2:371 (text).
53. M. N. Pearson, *Merchants and Rulers in Gujarat: The Response to the Portuguese in the Sixteenth Century* (Berkeley: University of California Press, 1976). For an early and trenchant critique, see Geneviève Bouchon, "Pour une histoire du Gujarat du XVe au XVIIe siècle," *Mare Luso-Indicum* 4 (1980): 145–158.
54. Samira Sheikh, *Forging a Region: Sultans, Traders, and Pilgrims in Gujarat, 1200–1500* (Delhi: Oxford University Press, 2009), 63.
55. Sheikh, *Forging a Region*, 5.

56. Z. A. Desai, "Inscriptions of the Sultans of Gujarat from Saurashtra," in *Epigraphia Indica, Arabic and Persian Supplement*, 1953–54, 49–77.
57. Jyoti Gulati Balachandran, *Narrative Pasts: The Making of a Muslim Community in Gujarat, c. 1400–1650* (Delhi: Oxford University Press, 2020).
58. See Ajaz Bano, "Political Condition of Gujarat during the Fifteenth Century," PhD thesis, Department of History, Aligarh Muslim University, 1988, 141–217 (for a listing of 280 nobles of the sultanate with short biographies).
59. Firishta, *Tarikh*, 4:52–53; Tuni, *Tarikh-i Mahmud Shahi*, 99–103.
60. Aparna Kapadia, *In Praise of Kings: Rajputs, Sultans and Poets in Fifteenth Century Gujarat* (Cambridge: Cambridge University Press, 2018), 104.
61. Z. A. Desai, "The 15th Century *Ma'athir-i-Mahmud Shahi* Written in Gujarat: Dynastic History, Monographic History or Universal History?," *Journal of the Pakistan Historical Society* 46, no. 3 (1998): 63–68.
62. Firishta, *Tarikh*, 4:70–71; Tuni, *Tarikh-i Mahmud Shahi*, 174–183.
63. João de Barros, *Da Ásia, décadas I–IV* (Lisbon: Régia Officina Typografica, 1777), Década segunda, part 1, book 2, 210–212.
64. Firishta, *Tarikh*, 4:77–78.
65. Cortesão, ed., *The Suma Oriental of Tomé Pires*, 2:369 (text). I have preferred here to set aside the somewhat approximate translation by Cortesão.
66. Cortesão, ed., *The Suma Oriental of Tomé Pires*, 2:366–367 (text).
67. Fernão Lopes de Castanheda, *História do descobrimento e conquista da Índia pelos portugueses*, ed. M. Lopes de Almeida, 2 vols. (Oporto: Lello and Irmão, 1979), vol. 1, book 2, chap. 59, p. 343: "[There were] a hundred foreign ships which were in the port [Hurmuz] being laden, amongst which there was one of the king of Cambay called *Meri* which was of 800 *toneis*, and it carried nearly a thousand armed men, and there was another large one of the son of the king of Cambay, and they were well equipped."
68. Letter from Silvestre de Bachom to Dom Manuel (n.d., 1516–1517), Arquivo Nacional da Torre do Tombo, Lisbon (henceforth ANTT), Gavetas, XV/1-36, in António da Silva Rego, ed., *As gavetas da Torre do Tombo*, 12 vols. (Lisbon: CEHU, 1960–1977), 4:44.
69. Geneviève Bouchon, "L'inventaire de la cargaison rapportée de l'Inde en 1505," *Mare Luso-Indicum* 3 (1976): 101–136. For a more general view of these return cargoes, see Luís Filipe F. R. Thomaz, "O sistema das viagens e a rede comercial portuguesa na Ásia Oriental," *Anais de História de Além-Mar* 19 (2018): 53–86.
70. Francisco Apellániz, "A Mamluk-Venetian Memorandum on Asian Trade, 1503," *Journal of the Royal Asiatic Society*, 3rd ser., 32, no. 3 (2022): 557–580.
71. Luís de Albuquerque, ed., *Crónica do descobrimento e primeiras conquistas da Índia pelos portugueses* (Lisbon: Imprensa Nacional, 1986), 328.
72. Archibald Lewis, "Maritime Skills in the Indian Ocean 1368–1500," *Journal of the Economic and Social History of the Orient* 16, nos. 2–3 (1973): 238–264 (quotation on 264).
73. Roxani Eleni Margariti, "Mercantile Networks, Port Cities, and 'Pirate'

States: Conflict and Competition in the Indian Ocean World of Trade before the Sixteenth Century," *Journal of the Economic and Social History of the Orient* 51, no. 4 (2008): 543–577.

74. Hermann Kulke, "Śrīvijaya Revisited: Reflections on State Formation of a Southeast Asian Thalassocracy," *Bulletin de l'Ecole française d'Extrême-Orient* 102 (2016): 45–95.

75. Geoff Wade, "The Zheng He Voyages: A Reassessment," *Journal of the Malaysian Branch of the Royal Asiatic Society* 78, no. 1 (2005): 37–58.

76. Hassan S. Khalilieh, *Islamic Law of the Sea: Freedom of Navigation and Passage Rights in Islamic Thought* (Cambridge: Cambridge University Press, 2019), 9, 35.

77. ANTT, Manuscritos da Livraria No. 805, fl. 168v. For a discussion of this text, see Manuel Lobato, "Notas e correcções para uma edição crítica do Ms. da Livraria n. 805 (IAN/TT), a propósito da publicação de um tratado do Pe. Manuel de Carvalho SJ," *Anais de História de Além-Mar* 3 (2002): 389–408.

78. Albuquerque to the King Dom Manuel, from the ship *Santo António*, dated 30 October 1512, in ANTT, Gavetas, XV/14-38, in *Cartas de Affonso de Albuquerque, seguidas de documentos que as elucidam*, ed. Raymundo António de Bulhão Pato and Henrique Lopes de Mendonça, 7 vols. (Lisbon: Academia Real das Ciências, 1884–1935), 1:97.

79. For examples of such "powerful men," see Georg Schurhammer, *Francis Xavier: His Life, His Times*, trans. M. Joseph Costelloe, 4 vols. (Rome: Jesuit Historical Institute, 1973–1982), 2:173–176.

80. Brás de Albuquerque, *Commentários do Grande Afonso Dalboquerque, capitam geral que foy das Indias Orientaes* (Lisbon: João de Barreira, 1576), 322, gives a figure of "over six thousand" and notes that some women and children were among those massacred.

81. "Inquirição de Vasco de Vilhana, ouvidor," 18 October 1514, ANTT, Corpo Cronológico (henceforth CC), II-52-116, in *Cartas de Affonso de Albuquerque*, 4:3–15.

82. Rafael Moreira, "Goa em 1535: Uma cidade manuelina," *Revista da Faculdade de Ciências Sociais e Humanas* 2, no. 8 (1995): 177–221.

83. See the discussion in Sanjay Subrahmanyam, *The Career and Legend of Vasco da Gama* (Cambridge: Cambridge University Press, 1997), 86–94, 112–121.

84. Malyn Newitt, *A History of Portuguese Overseas Expansion, 1400–1668* (London: Routledge, 2005), 111.

85. Edward A. Alpers, *Ivory and Slaves: Changing Pattern of International Trade in East Central Africa to the Later Nineteenth Century* (Berkeley: University of California Press, 1975), 43–44.

86. João de Barros, *Da Ásia, década primeira*, part 2, 211, 224–231, 388–390.

87. S. Arthur Strong, "The History of Kilwa," *Journal of the Royal Asiatic Society of Great Britain and Ireland* 54 (1895): 385–430. For a more modern edition,

see Sa'id bin 'Ali al-Mughiri, *Juhaynat al-akhbar fi tarikh Zanjibar*, ed. 'Abdul Mun'im 'Amir (Masqat: Wizarat al-Turas al-Qaumi, 1979), 37–58.
88. For discussions, see Gabriel Ferrand, "Les sultans de Kilwa," in *Mémorial Henri Basset: Nouvelles études nord-africaines et orientales*, 239–260 (Paris: Paul Geuthner, 1928); Elias Saad, "Kilwa Dynastic Historiography: A Critical Study," *History in Africa* 6 (1979): 177–207. See also G. S. P. Freeman-Grenville, *The East African Coast: Select Documents from the First to the Earlier Nineteenth Century* (London: Rex Collings, 1975).
89. Neville Chittick, "The 'Shirazi' Colonization of East Africa," *Journal of African History* 6, no. 3 (1965): 275–294 (discussion on 289–290); and Randall L. Pouwels, "A Reply to Spear on Early Swahili History," *International Journal of African Historical Studies* 34, no. 3 (2001): 639–646.
90. "Descrição da situação, costumes e produtos de alguns lugares de África [c. 1518]," in *Documentos sobre os Portugueses em Moçambique e na África Central, 1497–1840* (henceforth abbreviated as DPMAC), 9 vols. (Lisbon: Centro de Estudos Históricos Ultramarinos, 1962–1989), 5:367–369.
91. Alpers, *Ivory and Slaves*, 45.
92. "Descrição da situação, costumes e produtos," in DPMAC, 5:370–371.
93. ANTT, Núcleo Antigo 872, "Sumário de uma carta de Duarte Teixeira, feitor de Melinde (n.d.)," in DPMAC, 2:572–573.
94. These letters are located in ANTT, Núcleo Antigo 891, Maço 1, "Documentos em caracteres árabes provenientes do Oriente," Nos. 18, 19, 20 and 46. A full presentation and translation may be found in Muzaffar Alam and Sanjay Subrahmanyam, "A Handful of Swahili Coast Letters, 1500–1520," *International Journal of African Historical Studies* 52, no. 2 (2019): 255–281. Additionally, letters 7 and 54 have to do with Portuguese interference in the affairs of Angoche and Shaikh Wej Rukh.
95. ANTT, Núcleo Antigo 872, "Sumário de uma carta do Xeque de Moçambique para el-Rei, feito por António Carneiro, secretário do Estado [1510]," in DPMAC, 2:578.
96. ANTT, Núcleo Antigo 872, "Sumário de uma carta de Diogo Vaz, feitor de Moçambique," in DPMAC, 2:574–577.
97. For a broad contextual analysis, see Jeff Fleisher, "Behind the Sultan of Kilwa's 'Rebellious Conduct': Local Perspectives on an International East African Town," in *African Historical Archaeologies*, ed. Andrew M. Reid and Paul J. Lane, 91–123 (New York: Kluwer, 2004).
98. Subrahmanyam, *Career and Legend of Vasco da Gama*, 201–203, which includes a translation of Gama's letter written at Kilwa in July 1502.
99. Saad, "Kilwa Dynastic Historiography," 184.
100. It is claimed by the chronicler Castanheda that Ibrahim sent Muhammad Rukn as a hostage on board Gama's fleet in 1502 because he "wished him ill secretly, since he feared that he would take the kingdom from him"; Castanheda, *História*, 1:98–99.
101. Barros, *Da Ásia, década primeira*, part 2, 230–231.

102. For another account of Muhammad Rukn's elevation, see Castanheda, *História*, 1:215–216.
103. Barros, *Da Ásia, década primeira*, part 2, 432–447.
104. ANTT, Gavetas, XX/4-15, summary of a letter from Pedro Ferreira to the King, dated 31 August 1506, in DPMAC, 1:616–617.
105. On Tristão da Cunha and his voyage to India, see António Alberto Banha de Andrade, *História de um fidalgo quinhentista português: Tristão da Cunha* (Lisbon: Instituto Histórico Infante D. Henrique, 1974).
106. Gaspar was already present when D. Francisco de Almeida took Kilwa in 1505 and had extensive dealings with Muhammad Rukn on that occasion. See his letter in ANTT, Cartas dos Vice-Reis e Governadores da Índia, No. 76, undated [1505], published in *Cartas de Affonso de Albuquerque*, 3:200–204.
107. Barros, *Da Ásia, década primeira*, Part 2, 443.
108. ANTT, CC, II-12-98, inquiry dated 25 February 1507, in DPMAC, 2:170–177.
109. ANTT, CC, II-2-45 and III-4-13, 20 March 1510, documents regarding the "presas de uma nau de Cambaia que se tomou em Melinde," in DPMAC, 2:422–427. On Sidi Bu Bakr, or Abu Bakr, see ANTT, Gavetas, XV/19-22, document dated 25 January 1509, in DPMAC, 2:326–329; and ANTT, CC, I-8-40, letter from Diogo Vaz, *feitor* at Mozambique, dated 4 September 1509, in DPMAC, 2:374–375.
110. ANTT, CC, I-18-27, letter from the *feitor* of Sofala, Pero Vaz Soares, to the King, dated 30 June 1513, in DPMAC, 3:464–465. See also M. D. D. Newitt, "The Early History of the Sultanate of Angoche," *Journal of African History* 13, no. 3 (1972): 397–406.
111. Manuel Lobato, "Relações comerciais entre a Índia e a costa africana nos séculos XVI e XVII: O papel do Guzerate no comércio de Moçambique," *Mare Liberum* 9 (1995): 157–173 (quotation on 160).
112. ANTT, Cartas dos Vice-Reis e Governadores da Índia, No. 12, letter from Diogo Lopes de Sequeira at Cochin to the King, 23 December 1518, in DPMAC, 5:596–597.
113. ANTT, Cartas dos Vice-Reis e Governadores da Índia, no. 112, "Traslado da carta de Ali, Rei de Melinde, para D. Manuel," in DPMAC, 6:44–47.
114. See ANTT, Gavetas, XX/10-26, report by Jordão de Freitas, Goa, 17 September 1530, in DPMAC, 6:424–433, for a proposal to heavily constrain and restrict all aspects of Malindi's trade.
115. Alpers, *Ivory and Slaves*, 46.
116. See Kesavan Veluthat, *The Political Structure of Early Medieval South India* (New Delhi: Orient Longman, 1993), 114–117.
117. Shaykh Zainuddin Makhdum, *Tuhfat al-Mujahidin: A Historical Epic of the Sixteenth Century*, trans. S. Muhammad Husayn Nainar (Kuala Lumpur: Islamic Book Trust, 2006), 30–32.
118. Geneviève Bouchon, "Les musulmans du Kerala à l'époque de la décou-

verte portugaise," *Mare Luso-Indicum* 2 (1973): 3–59; Bouchon, *Mamale de Cananor: Un adversaire de l'Inde portugaise (1507–1528)* (Geneva: Librairie Droz, 1975). The latter book was translated into English as *"Regent of the Sea": Cannanore's Response to Portuguese Expansion, 1507–1528*, trans. Louise Shackley (Delhi: Oxford University Press, 1988). For reasons of convenience, I will cite the English translation. Bouchon's work may be contrasted with the loose reading of Portuguese material in Stephen Frederic Dale, *Islamic Society on the South Asian Frontier: The Mappilas of Malabar, 1498–1922* (Oxford: Clarendon Press, 1980).

119. For the later history of this dynasty, also see Binu John Mailaparambil, *Lords of the Sea: The Ali Rajas of Cannanore and the Political Economy of Malabar (1663–1723)* (Leiden: Brill, 2012).
120. Subrahmanyam, *Career and Legend of Vasco da Gama*, 210–213.
121. Jean Aubin, "L'apprentissage de l'Inde: Cochin, 1503–1504," in Aubin, *Le Latin et l'astrolabe*, 1:68.
122. Álvaro Vaz in Cochin to the King, 24 December 1504, ANTT), Gavetas, XV/2-36, in *Cartas de Affonso de Albuquerque*, 3:256–267 (quotation on 258).
123. Nuno de Castro to the King, Cochin, October 31, 1520, ANTT, CC, I-9-92, in *Cartas de Affonso de Albuquerque*, 7:172–186 (quotation on 175).
124. Bouchon, *Regent of the Sea*, 19–20.
125. *Les voyages de Ludovico di Varthema, ou le Viateur, en la plus grande partie de l'Orient*, trans. J. Balarin de Raconis, ed. C. Schefer (Paris: E. Leroux, 1888), 141–142.
126. Castanheda, *História do descobrimento e conquista da Índia*, book 2, 1:251–253.
127. Barros, *Da Ásia, década segunda*, Part 1, 54–55, 62–63.
128. Letter from the Kolattiri to Dom Manuel, 6 December 1507, ANTT, CC, I-6-68, in *Cartas de Affonso de Albuquerque*, 2:400–402.
129. Bouchon, *Regent of the Sea*, 132.
130. Albuquerque to Dom Manuel, Kochi, 1 April 1512, ANTT, CC, I-11–50, in *Cartas de Affonso de Albuquerque*, 1:38.
131. Albuquerque to Dom Manuel, Kannur, 30 November 1513, ANTT, CC, I-13-106, in *Cartas de Affonso de Albuquerque*, 1:131. Similar themes can be found in another letter by him on the same date, ANTT, CC, I-13-107, in *Cartas de Affonso de Albuquerque*, 1:152.
132. For Barbosa's role in these years, see Subrahmanyam, *Career and Legend of Vasco da Gama*, 262–265.
133. For an analysis, see Sanjay Subrahmanyam, "Making India Gama: The Project of Dom Aires da Gama (1519) and Its Meaning," *Mare Liberum* 16 (1998): 33–55.
134. *Tuhfat*, 75. For an account of the circumstances of the assassination, see the letter from the Kolattiri to the Portuguese governor (1545), reproduced in Bouchon, *Regent of the Sea*, 214–215.
135. Bouchon, *Regent of the Sea*, 174.

136. ANTT, Núcleo Antigo 891, Maço 1, "Documentos em caracteres árabes provenientes do Oriente."

137. Jean Aubin, "Les documents arabes, persans et turcs de la Torre do Tombo," in Aubin, *Le Latin et l'astrolabe*, 2:417–452. For an attempt at a comprehensive survey of "oriental" documents in Portuguese archives, see Georg Schurhammer, S.J., "Orientalische Briefe aus der Zeit des Hl. Franz Xaver (1500–1552)," *Euntes Docete* 21 (1968): 255–301. The versions presented in Frei João de Sousa, *Documentos arábicos para a história portugueza copiados dos originaes da Torre do Tombo com permissão de S. Magestade e vertidos em portuguez* . . . (Lisbon: 1790), are wholly unreliable.

138. Muzaffar Alam and Sanjay Subrahmanyam, "Letters from a Sinking Sultan," in Alam and Subrahmanyam, *Writing the Mughal World: Studies on Culture and Politics* (New York: Columbia University Press, 2012), 33–87; Dejanirah Couto, "Trois documents sur une demande de secours ormouzi à la Porte ottomane," *Anais de História de Além-Mar* 3 (2002): 469–493; Jorge M. dos Santos Alves and Nader Nasiri-Moghaddam, "Une lettre en persan de 1519 sur la situation à Malacca," *Archipel*, no. 75 (2008): 145–166. For an Arabic letter from Pasai (in Sumatra) dating 1516, also see A. C. S. Peacock, "Three Arabic letters from North Sumatra of the sixteenth and seventeenth centuries," *Indonesia and the Malay World* 44, no. 129 (2016): 188–210.

139. The popular Malayalam historical film *Urumi* (2011), directed by Santosh Sivan, attempted to develop a villainous character by the same name in the context of Vasco da Gama's expeditions to Kerala.

140. António Carneiro (1460–1545) was a powerful figure under Dom Manuel and his son Dom João III, although he had suffered some difficulties (and a period of exile) earlier in his career.

141. Aubin, "Les documents arabes, persans et turcs de la Torre do Tombo," 433.

142. For a full translation of these documents, see Muzaffar Alam and Sanjay Subrahmanyam, "Letters from Kannur, 1500–1550: A Little Explored Aspect of Kerala History," in *Clio and Her Descendants: Essays for Kesavan Veluthat*, ed. Manu Devadevan, 99–131 (Delhi: Primus Books, 2018). An additional document in the series is misclassified with Ottoman letters in ANTT, Gavetas, XV/14-20.

143. See Aubin, "L'apprentissage de l'Inde," 107.

144. ANTT, CC, I-83-56: "Carta do Guazil de Cananor, Guaripo, dando conta ao rei . . .," 20 December 1549.

145. For other letters from the same *alguazil* to Dom João de Castro, written from Kannur in 1546 and 1547, see Elaine Sanceau et al., eds., *Colecção de São Lourenço* (Lisbon: Instituto de Investigação Científica Tropical, 1983), 3:335–136, 349–351, 370–372, 381–383.

146. Christopher Markiewicz, *The Crisis of Kingship in Late Medieval Islam: Persian Emigres and the Making of Ottoman Sovereignty* (Cambridge: Cambridge University Press, 2019), 67–70.

147. Firishta, *Tarikh*, 4:87–88.
148. Letter from Dom Manuel to the bishop of Segovia, 12 July 1511, ANTT, CC, 1-10-60, in *Cartas de Affonso de Albuquerque*, 3:20–21.
149. Brás de Albuquerque, *Commentários*, 235.
150. Cihan Yüksel Muslu, *The Ottomans and the Mamluks: Imperial Diplomacy and Warfare in the Islamic World* (London: I. B. Tauris, 2014), 165–166.
151. Alam and Subrahmanyam, *Writing the Mughal World*, 43–50.
152. For an ambitious but controversial account of Ottoman ambitions in the Indian Ocean, see Giancarlo Casale, *The Ottoman Age of Exploration* (New York: Oxford University Press, 2010), as well as the more conventional reading in Salih Özbaran, *Ottoman Expansion towards the Indian Ocean in the 16th Century* (Istanbul: Istanbul Bilgi University Press, 2009).

CHAPTER 2: THE VIEW FROM THE HIJAZ, 1500–1550

Research for this chapter was done jointly with Muzaffar Alam in 2013–2014 at the Kluge Center of the Library of Congress, in Washington, DC.

1. For a critique of center-periphery theory, see David Washbrook, "South Asia, the World System, and World Capitalism," *Journal of Asian Studies* 49, no. 3 (1990): 479–508. More generally, on conceptualizations of Asia, see Sanjay Subrahmanyam, "One Asia, or Many? Reflections from Connected History," *Modern Asian Studies* 50, no. 1 (2016): 5–43.
2. For a recent reconsideration, see Alexis Wick, *The Red Sea: In Search of Lost Space* (Berkeley: University of California Press, 2017). Wick's work is largely unconcerned with the period I address here.
3. Shlomo D. Goitein and Mordechai A. Friedman, *India Traders of the Middle Ages: Documents from the Cairo Geniza ("India Book")* (Leiden: E. J. Brill, 2008). For a significant attempt to reinterpret the Geniza materials for the history of Indian Ocean trade, see Roxani E. Margariti, *Aden and the Indian Ocean Trade: 150 Years in the Life of a Medieval Arabian Port* (Chapel Hill: University of North Carolina Press, 2007).
4. Li Guo, *Commerce, Culture and Community in a Red Sea Port in the Thirteenth Century: The Arabic Documents from Quseir* (Leiden: E. J. Brill, 2004).
5. See Oscar Löfgren, ed., *Arabische Texte zur Kenntnis der Stadt Aden im Mittelalter*, 2 vols. (Uppsala: Almqvist & Wiksells, 1936–1950); and Lein Oebele Schuman, ed. and trans., *Political History of the Yemen at the Beginning of the 16th Century: Abu Makhrama's Account of the Years 906–927 H. (1500–1521)* (Groningen, Netherlands: V. R. B. Kleine, 1960).
6. Éric Vallet, *L'Arabie marchande: État et commerce sous les sultans rasūlides du Yémen (626–858/1229–1454)* (Paris: Presses Universitaires de la Sorbonne, 2010).
7. Vallet, *L'Arabie marchande*, 700.
8. John L. Meloy, *Imperial Power and Maritime Trade: Mecca and Cairo in the Later Middle Ages* (Chicago: Center for Middle Eastern Studies, 2010), 4; Richard T. Mortel, "The Mercantile Community of Mecca during the

Late Mamluk Period," *Journal of the Royal Asiatic Society of Great Britain and Ireland*, 3rd ser., 4, no. 1 (1994): 15–35.

9. Meloy, *Imperial Power and Maritime Trade*, appendix C: "Maritime Traffic between Jedda and Indian Ocean and Red Sea Ports, 876–944 / 1471–1537," 249–254. The data on arrivals appears far more complete than that on departures, but even here there are some gaps in relation to the sources for the period after 1517. Also, "Daybul" appears to be a misidentification for Dabhol on the Konkan coast.

10. For a modern edition, see ʿIzz-ud-Din ʿAbdul ʿAziz ibn al-Najm ibn Fahd al-Makki, *Bulugh al-qira fi zail ithaf al-wara bi-akhbar Umm al-Qura*, 4 vols., ed. Salah-ud-Din ibn Khalil Ibrahim, ʿAbdul Rahman ibn Husain Abuʾl Khair and ʿUlyan ibn ʿAbdul ʿAli al-Majlabdi (Cairo: Dar al-Qahira, 2005).

11. For a discussion, see Margariti, *Aden and the Indian Ocean Trade*, 11–22.

12. For two recent examples, see Samira Sheikh, *Forging a Region: Sultans, Traders and Pilgrims in Gujarat, 1200–1500* (Delhi: Oxford University Press, 2010); and Jyoti Gulati Balachandran, *Narrative Pasts: The Making of a Muslim Community in Gujarat, c. 1400–1650* (Delhi: Oxford University Press, 2020).

13. Jarullah ibn al-ʿIzz ibn al-Najm ibn Fahd al-Makki, *Kitab Nail al-muna bi-zail bulugh al-qira li-takmilat Ithaf al-wara: Tarikh Makka al-Mukarrama min sanat 922 H ila 946 H.*, ed. Muhammad al-Habib al-Hila (Riyadh: Muʾassasat al-furqan lil-turas al-Islamiya, 2000). For a survey of the chronicle literature, see the erudite work by al-Hila, *Tarikh wa al-muʾarrikhun bi-Makka min al-qarn al-salis al-Hijri ila al-qarn al-salis ʿashar: Jamʿ wa ʿard wa taʿrif* (Mecca: Muʾassasat al-furqan lil-turas al-Islamiya, 1994).

14. The fruits of his research only appeared posthumously in Jean Aubin, *Le Latin et l'astrolabe*, vol. 3, *Études inédites sur le règne de D. Manuel, 1495–1521*, ed. Maria da Conceição Flores, Luís Filipe F. R. Thomaz and Françoise Aubin (Paris: Centre Culturel Calouste Gulbenkian, 2006).

15. Nahrawali (1511–1582) was a brilliant and prolific author in Arabic, best known for two works, *Al-Iʿlam bi aʿlam Bayt Allah al-haram* and *Al-Barq al-Yamani fi al-fath al-ʿUthmani*. For a useful biographical note on him, see Richard Blackburn, "Introduction," in *Journey to the Sublime Porte: The Arabic Memoir of a Sharifian Agent's Diplomatic Mission to the Ottoman Imperial Court in the Era of Suleyman the Magnificent* (Beirut: Ergon Verlag, 2005), xi–xvi.

16. For discussions of this author, see William Millward, "Taqi al-Din al-Fasi's Sources for the History of Mecca from the Fourth to the Ninth Centuries A.H.," in *Sources for the History of Arabia*, ed. A. R. al-Ansary, vol. 1, part 2, 37–49 (Riyadh: University of Riyadh, 1979); and Richard T. Mortel, "Madrasas in Mecca during the Medieval Period: A Descriptive Study Based on Literary Sources," *Bulletin of the School of Oriental and African Studies* 60 (1997): 236–252.

17. Najm-ud-Din ʿUmar ibn Fahd, *Ithaf al-Wara bi-Akhbar Umm al-Qura*, vols.

1–3, ed. Fahim Muhammad Shaltut; vol. 4, ed. 'Abdul Karim 'Ali al-Baz; vol. 5 (Indexes) (Mecca: al-Mamlaka al-'Arabiya al-Sa'udiya, Jami'at Umm al-Qura, Ma'had al-Buhus al-'Ilmiya wa-Ihya' al-Turas al-Islamiya, Markaz Ilhya' al-Turas al-Islamiya, 1983–1990). See Li Guo's short but useful review of the edition in *Mamluk Studies Review* 5 (2001): 189.
18. See 'Izz-ud-Din ibn Fahd, *Bulugh al-qira fi zail ithaf al-wara*, ed. Salah-ud-Din ibn Khalil Ibrahim et al., 4 vols.
19. See Nasir bin Sa'd al-Rashid, "Banu Fahd mu'arrikhu Makka al-mukarrama wa al-ta'rif bi makhtut al-Najm ibn Fahd," *Masadir Tarikh al-Jazira al-'Arabiyya*, vol. 1, part 2 (1979): 69–90.
20. For details, see Shams-ud-Din Muhammad ibn Tulun, *Mufakahat al-khillan fi hawadith al-zaman: Tarikh Misr wa al-Sham*, ed. Muhammad Mustafa, 2 vols. (Cairo: Al-Mu'assassat al-Misriyya al-'amma li al-ta'lif wa al-tarjama wa al-tiba' wa al-nashr, 1964), 2:63.
21. See the editor's introduction in al-Hila, *Nail al-muna*, 10–13.
22. This work is analyzed in depth by Guy Burak, "Between Istanbul and Gujarat: Descriptions of Mecca in the Sixteenth-Century Indian Ocean," *Muqarnas* 34 (2017): 287–320.
23. On the question of coffee in the period, also see Ralph Hattox, *Coffee and Coffeehouses: The Origins of a Social Beverage in the Medieval Near East* (Seattle: University of Washington Press, 1985).
24. See Kristina L. Richardson, *Difference and Disability in the Islamic World: Blighted Bodies* (Edinburgh: Edinburgh University Press, 2012), 110–131; see also Mohammed Ghaly, *Islam and Disability: Perspectives in Theology and Jurisprudence* (New York: Routledge, 2010), and Ghaly, "Writings on Disability in Islam: The 16th-Century Polemic on Ibn Fahd's *al-Nukat al-Ziráf*," *Arab Studies Journal* 13, no. 2 / 14, no. 1 (2005–2006): 9–38.
25. Muhyi-ud-Din 'Abdul Qadir al-'Aydarusi, *Tarikh al-Nur al-Safir 'an akhbar al-qarn al-'ashir*, ed. Ahmad Halu, Mahmud al-Arna'ut, and Akram al-Bushi (Beirut: Dar Sadir, 2001).
26. See the editor's introduction in al-Hila, *Nail al-muna*, 26–29.
27. It is therefore tempting to compare him to at least two other sixteenth-century chroniclers with similar antinomian proclivities: the Portuguese Gaspar Correia and the Mughal intellectual 'Abdul Qadir Badayuni. On the former, see António Alberto Banha de Andrade, "Gaspar Correia inédito," *Revista da Universidade de Coimbra* 26 (1977): 5–49; and on the latter, Ali Anooshahr, "Mughal Historians and the Memory of the Islamic Conquest of India," *Indian Economic and Social History Review* 43, no. 3 (2006): 275–300.
28. Jean-Louis Bacqué-Grammont, "Les premiers fonctionnaires ottomanes dans le Hedjaz: Un rapport de Kāsim Širvānī de septembre 1517," *Annales Islamologiques* (Cairo) 21 (1985): 129–145; Jean-Louis Bacqué-Grammont and Mohammad Mokri, "Une lettre de Qāsim Širvānī à Muzaffar Šāh du Gujarat: Les premières relations des Ottomanes avec l'Inde?," in *Zafar*

Name: Memorial Volume of Felix Tauer, ed. Rudolf Veselý and Eduard Gombár, 35–47 (Prague: Enigma, 1996).
29. 'Abdul Qadir ibn Muhammad al-Jaziri, *Durar al-fara'id al munazzama fi akhbar al-hajj wa tariq Makka al-mu'azzama*, ed. Hamd al-Jasir, 3 parts (Riyadh: Dar al-Yamama, 1983), part 2, 849, 856 and 861.
30. This is based on the editor's analysis of Qutb-ud-Din Muhammad Nahrawali's *al-Barq al-Yamani*.
31. No comparable annals to those of the Banu Fahd were apparently composed for Jiddah. The brief text of 'Abdul Qadir ibn Ahmad ibn Faraj, *Kitab al-sila wa al-'udda fi tarikh bandar Jiddah: Bride of the Red Sea, a 10th/16th Century Account of Jeddah*, ed. and trans. Ahmad bin 'Umar al-Zayla'i and G. Rex Smith (Durham, UK: Centre for Middle Eastern and Islamic Studies, 1984), adheres largely to the conventions of hagiography (*faza'il*).
32. I have benefited from the useful discussion by Islam Dayeh, "Islamic Casuistry and Galenic Medicine: Hashish, Coffee and the Emergence of the Jurist-Physician," in *A Historical Approach to Casuistry: Norms and Exceptions in a Comparative Perspective*, ed. Carlo Ginzburg and Lucio Biasiori, 132–150 (London: Bloomsbury, 2019).
33. Salih Özbaran, *Ottoman Expansion towards the Indian Ocean in the 16th century* (Istanbul: Bilgi University Press, 2009); Suraiya Faroqhi, *Pilgrims and Sultans: The Hajj under the Ottomans, 1517–1683* (London: I. B. Tauris, 1994); Jean-Louis Bacqué-Grammont and Anne Kroell, *Mamlouks, ottomans et portugais en Mer Rouge: L'affaire de Djedda en 1517* (Cairo: Supplément aux Annales Islamologiques, 1988); and Giancarlo Casale, *The Ottoman Age of Exploration* (New York: Oxford University Press, 2010). Besides, much useful information may be found in Muhammad Yakub Mughul, *Kanuni Devri Osmanlıların Hint Okyanusu Politikası ve Osmanlı-Hint Müslümanları Münasebetleri, 1517–1538* (Istanbul: Fetih Yayınevi, 1974).
34. Naimur Rahman Farooqi, *Mughal-Ottoman Relations: A Study of Political and Diplomatic Relations between Mughal India and the Ottoman Empire, 1556–1748* (Delhi: Idarah-i Adabiyat-i Dilli, 1989).
35. E. Denison Ross, "The Portuguese in India and Arabia, 1517–38," *Journal of the Royal Asiatic Society of Great Britain and Ireland* 1 (1922): 1–18; Vitorino Magalhães Godinho, *Os descobrimentos e a economia mundial*, 2nd ed., 4 vols. (Lisbon: Editorial Presença, 1982–1983).
36. R. B. Serjeant, *The Portuguese off the South Arabian Coast: Hadrami Chronicles* (Oxford: Clarendon Press, 1963). This highly useful compendium is frustrating to use because of Serjeant's rather approximate manner of indicating his sources. For an explanation of the chief sources, see R. B. Serjeant, "Historians and Historiography of Hadramawt," *Bulletin of the School of Oriental and African Studies* 25, no. 2 (1962): 239–261. For a more recent edition of one of the key texts, see Muhammad ibn 'Umar al-Tayyib Ba Faqih, *Tarikh al-Shahar wa akhbar al-qarn al-'ashir*, ed. 'Abdullah Muhammad al-Habshi (Beirut: 'Alam al-Kutub, 1999).

37. Alam and Subrahmanyam, *Indo-Persian Travels in the Age of Discoveries*, 95–120, 303–312; Alam and Subrahmanyam, *Writing the Mughal World: Studies in Political Culture* (New York: Columbia University Press, 2011), 33–87.
38. Aubin had also gathered a body of materials for an extended essay he was planning, tentatively titled "Nuno da Cunha et Soltão Bador." These included a microfilm of the manuscript of Jarullah's chronicle. This was intended to extend the analysis he had begun in Aubin, "Albuquerque et les négociations de Cambaye," *Mare Luso-Indicum* 1 (1971): 3–63.
39. Jarullah, *Nail*, 1:53.
40. Jarullah, *Nail*, 1:72.
41. Jarullah, *Nail*, 1:130, 138, 140–141.
42. Jarullah, *Nail*, 1:165.
43. Jarullah, *Nail*, 1:158–159.
44. Jarullah, *Nail*, 1:255. Compare Serjeant, *Portuguese off the South Arabian Coast*, 51–52.
45. Jarullah, *Nail*, 1:311.
46. Jarullah, *Nail*, 1:323.
47. For the Portuguese naval campaigns of 1521 against Gujarat, see Arquivo Nacional da Torre do Tombo, Lisbon (henceforth AN/TT), Corpo Cronológico (henceforth CC), I-27-80, letter from Nuno Fernandes de Macedo to the King, 23 December 1521.
48. Jarullah, *Nail*, 1:325–326.
49. Fernão Lopes de Castanheda, *História do descobrimento e conquista da Índia pelos portugueses*, ed. Manuel Lopes de Almeida (Oporto: Lello e Irmão, 1979), book IV, ch. 12, 888. The meaning of this passage is misread in M. N. Pearson, *Pious Passengers: The Hajj in Earlier Times* (New Delhi: Sterling Publishers, 1994), 159–160.
50. Özbaran, *Ottoman Expansion*, 330–335.
51. Letter from Sier Piero Bragadin in Pera, dated 29 December 1525, paraphrased in Federico Stefani, Guglielmo Berchet, and Nicolò Barozzi, eds., *I Diarii di Marino Sanuto* (Venice: Privately printed, 1894), 40:824–825.
52. Jarullah, *Nail*, 1:369–370.
53. There is a distinct possibility that Jarullah has confounded the siege of Belgrade (in 1521) with the Ottoman victory at the Battle of Mohács on August 29, 1526 (21 Zi-Qaʻda 932 AH).
54. Jarullah, *Nail*, 1:392.
55. Jarullah, *Nail*, 1:421.
56. Jarullah, *Nail*, 1:503.
57. Jarullah, *Nail*, 1:513.
58. Jarullah, *Nail*, 1:541–542; also see Serjeant, *Portuguese off the South Arabian Coast*, 61–65; Ba Faqih, *Tarikh al-Shahar*, 203–204, 205–207.
59. Jarullah, *Nail*, 1:545.
60. Serjeant, *Portuguese off the South Arabian Coast*, 63, 65–67; Ba Faqih, *Tarikh al-Shahar*, 205, 214–215. On the activities of this particular captain, a cer-

tain Manuel de Vasconcelos, see Castanheda, *História do descobrimento*, vol. 2, book 8, chap. 50, 647–648.

61. There were a number of Portuguese attacks and raids on coastal Gujarat and the shipping there in these years, including on Rander in 1530 and the areas around Patan (Somnath), Mangrol, Pata, and Porbandar in 1532. The reference seems to be to the latter raids, led by Diogo da Silveira; see Diogo do Couto, *Década quarta da Ásia*, ed. Maria Augusta Lima Cruz (Lisbon: Imprensa Nacional-Casa da Moeda, 1999), 1:421–426.

62. Compare Suraiya Faroqhi, "Trade between the Ottomans and the Safavids: The Acem *Tüccarı* and Others," in *Iran and the World in the Safavid Age*, ed. Willem Floor and Edmund Herzig, 237–252 (London: I. B. Tauris, 2012).

63. Jarullah, *Nail*, 2:552–554.

64. The sending of these ships under the charge of Asaf Khan, laden with boxes (*sanduq*) of *ashrafis* and *sikka* (possibly a misreading for *tanka*) is noted in Sayyid Mahmud bin Munawwar al-Mulk Bukhari, *Tarikh-i Salatin-i Gujarat*, ed. S. A. I. Tirmizi (Bombay: Asia Publishing House, 1964), 31–32.

65. The fact of the unseasonal departure (*ghair mausim*) and many other details can be found in 'Abdullah Hajji al-Dabir Ulughkhani, *Zafar al-Walih bi-Muzaffar wa Alihi: An Arabic History of Gujarat*, ed. E. Denison Ross, 3 vols. (London: John Murray, 1910–1929), 1:257. He notes that the chief royal ship was called *Daryasara* and that a thousand men, largely Yemenis, Rumis, Habshis, Maharas, and Yafi'is, accompanied Asaf Khan. Ulughkhani obtained these details from the pilot (*mu'allim*), Hayut al-Mahri, whom he met many decades later in Hurmuz. For a discussion of Ulughkhani as a chronicler, see Jyoti Gulati Balachandran, "Counterpoint: Re-assessing Ulughkhani's History of Gujarat," *Asiatische Studien/Études Asiatiques* 74, no. 1 (2020): 137–161.

66. In 1536, the Ottoman court also received as an exile Burhan Lodi, ostensibly the son of Sikandar Lodi (though this has been doubted). This could not have had a favorable effect on their image of the Mughals either. See Bernard Lewis, "The Mughals and the Ottomans," in Lewis, *From Babel to the Dragomans: Interpreting the Middle East* (New York: Oxford University Press, 2004), 108–114 (citing the chronicler Ferdi).

67. The place name is misread as "Satayir" in the edited text, which the editor therefore could not identify.

68. On Asaf Khan's embassy, also see Casale, *Ottoman Age of Exploration*, 56–58. Casale bases himself on a mix of Ottoman and Portuguese sources (including the Ottoman translation of Nahrawali's work) and on the Arabic chronicle of Ulughkhani, *Zafar al-Walih*, in its English translation. As we will see, the *Nail al-muna* surpasses these in its level of detail and precision by some distance. For a different account, see Scott Kugle, *Hajj to the Heart: Sufi Journeys across the Indian Ocean* (Chapel Hill: University of North Carolina Press, 2021), 46–54.

69. This was the same person as Mustafa Bairam and had held the title of Rumi Khan in Gujarat before his defection to the Mughals; see Casale, *Ottoman Age of Exploration*, 54.
70. Jarullah, *Nail*, 2:602–609.
71. The reader may get a sense of these numbers by noting that the total revenues of Aleppo and Damascus in 1527–1528 amounted to 22.8 million akçe. For Ottoman revenues in that year, see Halil İnalcık, *An Economic and Social History of the Ottoman Empire*, vol. 1 *(1300–1600)* (Cambridge: Cambridge University Press, 1994), 80–83.
72. The Gujarat Sultanate's gold tanka in the sixteenth century weighed 11.97 grams, which made it the equivalent of 208 akçe. If the coins were indeed tankas, their total value would have been 509 million akçe, in comparison to the annual Ottoman revenues in 1527–1528 of 538 million akçe. In the lesser likelihood that these gold pieces were smaller, like the Ottoman sultani (which weighed 3.45 grams and was valued at 60 akçe), the total value still translates as 147 million akçe. See Şevket Pamuk, *A Monetary History of the Ottoman Empire* (Cambridge: Cambridge University Press, 2000), 63.
73. Topkapı Sarayı, Istanbul, E. 10895/1, reproduced in Fevzi Kurtoğlu, "Hadım Süleyman Paşa'nın mektupları ve Belgradın muhasara Pilânı," *Belleten* 4/13, no. 9 (1940): 53–87 (61–62, and plate V). I have benefited here from a draft translation into French of this letter in the unpublished notes of the late Jean Aubin.
74. Jarullah, *Nail*, 2:604. This 'Imad-ul-Mulk (or 'Umdat ul-Mulk) needs to be separated from several others who held the same title before and after in Gujarat, such as one who assassinated Sultan Sikandar Gujarati in the 1520s.
75. The month of the hajj itself would have been Zi al-Hijja 942 AH, that is, May–June 1536, whereas the Gujarati party probably arrived in Mecca around November or December 1535.
76. Jarullah, *Nail*, 2:606. The reference is to the Ottoman conquest of Tabriz and Baghdad in this period, a move that would culminate in the 1540s with the conquest of Basra. The taking of Baghdad in particular had a great symbolic importance; see Colin Imber, *The Ottoman Empire, 1300–1650: The Structure of Power*, 2nd ed. (Basingstoke, UK: Palgrave Macmillan, 2009), 44–45.
77. Jarullah, *Nail*, 2:609, 613, 623.
78. Jarullah, *Nail*, 2:625. A fuller list of amirs who eventually found themselves in Mecca may be found in Ulughkhani, *Zafar al-Walih*, 1:385. The names there include Shams Khan, Qaysar Khan (described as a troublemaker), 'Umdat al-Mulk, Malik 'Abdul Wahid Multani, Malik Ibrahim, Tahir Khan, and Hamid al-Mulk ibn Shams-ud-Din Muhammad.
79. Jarullah, *Nail*, 2:627.
80. Jarullah, *Nail*, 2:629.

81. Jarullah, *Nail*, 2:635. This letter from Asaf Khan, dated 17 Zi al-Hijja 942 AH (or June 7, 1536), has come down to us as Topkapı Sarayı, Istanbul, E. 1351; see Alam and Subrahmanyam, *Writing the Mughal World*, 68–69, for a summary and discussion.
82. Jarullah, *Nail*, 2:641.
83. Jarullah, *Nail*, 2:643.
84. Jarullah, *Nail*, 2:664.
85. Jarullah, *Nail*, 2:665.
86. The reference here (and henceforth) can no longer be to Mustafa Bairam but must instead be to Khwaja Safar al-Salmani.
87. Jarullah, *Nail*, 2:666.
88. Jarullah, *Nail*, 2:667–668.
89. Jarullah, *Nail*, 2:673–674.
90. Jarullah, *Nail*, 2:701.
91. Jarullah, *Nail*, 2:675, 684, 687.
92. The dispute is described in highly dramatic terms in Ulughkhani, *Zafar al-Walih*, 2:xxii–xxiv (in Denison Ross's translation). It is suggested that the women of the party even feared for a time being seized, and "preferring death to capture, washed, clothed, and perfumed themselves, and gave what they were able in charity; while the chief of the harem, Melik Firuz, sharpened their blades for them."
93. Jarullah, *Nail*, 2:700–701.
94. Jarullah, *Nail*, 2:704, 710.
95. Jarullah, *Nail*, 2:720. The realities of the 1537 campaign were actually far more modest; Kaya Şahin, *Empire and Power in the Reign of Süleyman: Narrating the Sixteenth-Century Ottoman World* (New York: Cambridge University Press, 2013), 105–106.
96. Jarullah, *Nail*, 2:737.
97. Jarullah, *Nail*, 2:743, 745, 752–753.
98. Jarullah, *Nail*, 2:746–747.
99. AN/TT, CC, I-59-12, published in Luiz Augusto Rebello da Silva, ed., *Corpo diplomático portuguez, contendo os actos e relações políticas e diplomáticas de Portugal com as diversas potências do mundo desde e século XVI até os nossos dias* (Lisbon: Academia Real das Sciências, 1868), 3:396–397.
100. For a competent summing up of most generally available materials on this expedition, see Dejanirah Couto, "No rasto de Hadim Suleimão Pacha: Alguns aspectos do comércio do Mar Vermelho nos anos de 1538–40," in *A Carreira da Índia e as Rotas dos Estreitos: Actas do VIII Seminário Internacional de História Indo-Portuguesa*, ed. Artur Teodoro de Matos and Luís Filipe F. R. Thomaz, 485–508 (Angra do Heroísmo, Portugal: Privately printed, 1998).
101. Janim al-Hamzawi was a prominent Egyptian notable (and nephew of Khayr Bey, Mamluk governor of Aleppo) who had been *amir al-hajj* from Cairo in 1524–1525, after helping suppress Ahmad Pasha's rebellion in 1524. He is described as "not a Mamluk, but [one who] belonged to the

awlad al-nas class." See Michael Winter, "Ottoman Egypt, 1525–1609," in *The Cambridge History of Egypt*, vol. 2, *Modern Egypt from 1517 to the End of the Twentieth Century*, ed. Martin W. Daly (Cambridge: Cambridge University Press, 1998), 13. For a brief biography, also see Peter M. Holt, "A Notable in the Age of Transition: Janim Bey al-Hamzawi (d. 944/1538)," in *Studies in Ottoman History in Honour of Professor V. L. Ménage*, ed. Colin Heywood and Colin Imber, 107–115 (Istanbul: Isis Press, 1994).

102. Jarullah, *Nail*, 2:748.
103. Jarullah, *Nail*, 2:749–750.
104. Compare this to the ill-tempered letter from Hadim Süleyman Pasha to Ulugh Khan, vizier of Gujarat, in AN/TT, CC, III-14-44, dated 18 Rajab 945 AH (December 10, 1538), reproduced (with some errors) in Luciano Ribeiro, "O primeiro cerco de Diu," *Studia*, no. 1 (1958): 211–214. The Ottoman original is still untraced, but the contemporary Portuguese translation appears quite faithful.
105. Jarullah, *Nail*, 2:758–759. For Süleyman Pasha in Yemen, also see the interesting perspective provided in Frédérique Soudan, *Le Yémen ottoman d'après la chronique d'al-Mawza'i, 'al-Ihsan fi dukhul mamlakat al-Yaman taht zill 'adalat al-'Usman'* (Cairo: Institut Français d'Archéologie Orientale, 1999), 55–56.
106. The *Tarikh al-Shihr* apparently has it that "entering Jeddah and Mecca he [Hadim Süleyman Pasha] seized a quantity of goods from the merchants of them, and ordered the merchants [*atdjar*] of Mecca, may God honour it, to take up residence in Jeddah. But those who bribed him with what he liked continued to have their residence in Mecca." Serjeant, *Portuguese off the South Arabian Coast*, 93. I have corrected the translation on the basis of the phrase in Ba Faqih, *Tarikh al-Shahar*, 264–265: "*faman bartala ma yarziyahu sakana makanahu fi Makka.*" This account seems to be pure anti-Ottoman malice, based perhaps on the pasha's initial delay in coming to Mecca.
107. Nevertheless, Süleyman Pasha was finally not castigated; quite on the contrary, he rose to the post of Grand Vizier from 1541 to 1544, and after being removed from that high station, only died in 1547. On the other hand, we read in Godinho, *Os descobrimentos e a economia mundial*, 3:121: "In the end, having returned to Djedda on 13 March 1539, he [Süleyman Pasha] committed suicide for fear of being punished by the Porte." This quite absurd claim, which may be based on what Casale has called "fanciful accounts . . . by some authors from Muslim India" (*Ottoman Age of Exploration*, 65), could have been rectified by consulting any standard biographical entry, e.g., Cengiz Orhonlu, "Khadim Süleyman Pasha," *Encyclopaedia of Islam*, 2nd ed., ed. P. Bearman et al., 4:901–902.
108. Jarullah, *Nail*, 2:778.
109. Jarullah, *Nail*, 2:785.
110. Jarullah, *Nail*, 2:782–783.
111. Jarullah, *Nail*, 2:800.

112. Ulughkhani, *Zafar al-Walih*, 2:xxi–xxii, xxv–xxvii. Asaf Khan, the son of a certain Hamid al-Mulk, was born in 1503. The family claimed descent from the Samma ruler of Sind, Jam Nanda Nizam-ud-Din (r. 1463–1509). Asaf Khan became prominent in the 1530s under Sultan Bahadur. Denison Ross reports that he was so well respected in the Hijaz that Ibn Hajar al-Haytami even dedicated a work to him.

113. Thus, compare John-Paul Ghobrial, *The Whispers of Cities: Informational Flows in Istanbul, London and Paris in the Age of William Trumbull* (Oxford: Oxford University Press, 2013), and Filippo de Vivo, *Information and Communication in Venice: Rethinking Early Modern Politics* (Oxford: Oxford University Press, 2007).

114. See Aubin, "Psychose des caravelles et turbulences bédouines," in *Le Latin et l'astrolabe*, 3:432. The reference is to Godinho, *Os descobrimentos e a economia mundial*, vol. 3. Also compare the discussion in Meloy, *Imperial Power and Maritime Trade*, 219–221.

115. Aubin, "Psychose des caravelles et turbulences bédouines," 3:437. The larger implications of this argument are drawn out in Sanjay Subrahmanyam, "The Birth-Pangs of Portuguese Asia: Revisiting the Fateful 'Long Decade' 1498–1509," *Journal of Global History* 2, no. 3 (2007): 261–280.

116. Compare the more conventional view in Anthony Grafton, *What Was History? The Art of History in Early Modern Europe* (Cambridge: Cambridge University Press, 2007), with Sanjay Subrahmanyam, "On World Historians in the Sixteenth Century," *Representations* 91 (2005): 26–57.

117. For a striking example of such neglect, see José Rabasa, Masayuki Sato, Edoardo Tortarolo, and Daniel Woolf, eds., *The Oxford History of Historical Writing, Volume 3: 1400–1800* (Oxford: Oxford University Press, 2012), where the entire Egyptian and Hijazi tradition we have discussed here, including the Banu Fahd and Nahrawali (but also Ibn Iyas and Ibn Tulun), is absent.

118. Blackburn, "Introduction," in *Journey to the Sublime Porte*, xv. Blackburn notes that the best study of the scholar to date remains the editor's introduction to Nahrawali, *Ghazawat al-jarakisa wa al-atrak fi junub al-Jazira, al-Mussama al-Barq al-Yamani fi al-fath al-'Usmani*, ed. Hamd al-Jasir (Riyadh: Dar al-Yamama, 1967), 11–59. For further comments, see Clive R. Smith, *Lightning over Yemen: A History of the Ottoman Campaign, 1569–71* (London: I. B. Tauris, 2002).

119. See Jane Hathaway (with Karl Barbir), *The Arab Lands under Ottoman Rule, 1516–1800* (New York: Routledge, 2013), 135.

120. For a sign of early Orientalist interest, see Ferdinand Wüstenfeld, ed., *Die Chroniken der Stadt Mekka*, vol. 3: *Geschichte der Stadt Mekka und ihres Tempels von Cutb ed-Dîn Muhammed ben Ahmed el-Nahrawâli* (Leipzig: F. A. Brockhaus, 1857).

121. Blackburn, "Introduction," xvi.

122. Richardson, *Difference and Disability*, 15–16.

123. Compare Dejanirah Couto, "Entre confrontations et alliances: Aceh, Malacca et les Ottomans (1520–1568)," *Turcica* 46 (2015): 13–61, who resorts repeatedly to the reductionist formula of the "réseaux marchands de la *Khutba*" as a form of behavioral explanation.
124. Michel Tuchscherer, "Trade and Port-Cities in the Red Sea-Gulf of Aden Region in the Sixteenth and Seventeenth Century," in *Modernity and Culture: From the Mediterranean to the Indian Ocean*, ed. Leila T. Fawaz and C. A. Bayly, 28–45 (New York: Columbia University Press, 2002).
125. Casale, *Ottoman Age of Exploration*, 182, 202.

CHAPTER 3: THE AFRO-INDIAN AXIS

1. Mark Horton, "Port Cities and Their Merchants on the East African Coast," in *Cities in the World, 1500–2000*, ed. Adrian Green and Roger Leech, 15–29 (London: Maney, 2006).
2. For comparative purposes, I refer the reader to S. M. Stern, ed., *Documents from Islamic Chanceries* (Oxford, UK: Bruno Cassirer, 1965); and for a broad literature survey in an African context, John Hunwick, "Arabic Sources for African History," in *Writing African History*, ed. John Edward Philips, 216–253 (Rochester, NY: University of Rochester Press, 2005).
3. Ronit Ricci, *Islam Translated: Literature, Conversion, and the Arabic Cosmopolis of South and Southeast Asia* (Chicago: University of Chicago Press, 2011).
4. Mauro Nobili, "Introduction: African History and Islamic Manuscript Cultures," in *The Arts and Crafts of Literacy: Islamic Manuscript Cultures in Sub-Saharan Africa*, ed. Andrea Brigaglia and Mauro Nobili, 1–24 (Berlin: De Gruyter, 2017).
5. For the text, see H. A. R. Gibb, C. F. Beckingham and A. D. H. Bivar, eds., *The Travels of Ibn Battuta, AD 1325–54*, 5 vols. (Cambridge, UK: Hakluyt Society, 1958–2000); the East African sections appear at 2:374–381. See also the discussion in H. Neville Chittick, "Ibn Baṭṭūta and East Africa," *Journal de la Société des Africanistes* 38, no. 2 (1968): 239–241.
6. See H. Neville Chittick, *Kilwa: An Islamic Trading City on the East African Coast*, 2 vols. (Nairobi: British Institute in Eastern Africa, 1974).
7. See Thomas Spear, "Early Swahili History Reconsidered," *International Journal of African Historical Studies* 33, no. 2 (2000): 257–290; the quotation is at 281. See also the more recent reflections in Stephanie Wynne-Jones and Adria LaViolette, eds., *The Swahili World* (London: Routledge, 2018), esp. 135–146, 253–259.
8. Stephanie Wynne-Jones, "The Social Composition of Swahili Society," in Wynne-Jones and LaViolette, *The Swahili World*, 302.
9. Mark C. Horton, *Shanga: The Archaeology of a Muslim Trading Community on the Coast of East Africa* (Nairobi: British Institute in Eastern Africa, 1996).
10. Mark Horton, "Islamic Architecture of the Swahili Coast," in Wynne-Jones and LaViolette, *The Swahili World*, 487–499.
11. Abdul Sheriff, "The Swahili in the African and Indian Ocean Worlds to c.

1500," in *Oxford Research Encyclopedia of African History*, africanhistory.oxfordre.com. See also the older survey by A. I. Salim, "East Africa: The Coast," in *UNESCO General History of Africa, V: Africa from the Sixteenth to the Eighteenth Century*, ed. B. A. Ogot, 750–775 (Berkeley: University of California Press, 1992).

12. Edward A. Alpers, "Gujarat and the Trade of East Africa, c. 1500–1800," *International Journal of African Historical Studies* 9, no. 1 (1976): 22–44 (quotation at 24).
13. Alpers, "Gujarat and the Trade of East Africa," 24.
14. See Wynne-Jones and LaViolette, *The Swahili World*. For the older literature, see Abdul Sheriff, "The Swahili in the African and Indian Ocean Worlds to c. 1500"; see also Mark Horton and John Middleton, *The Swahili: The Social Landscape of a Mercantile Society* (Oxford, UK: Blackwell, 2000), and Thomas Spear, "Early Swahili History Reconsidered."
15. Mark Horton, "Artisans, Communities, and Commodities: Medieval Exchanges between Northwestern India and East Africa," *Ars Orientalis* 34 (2004): 62–80.
16. João de Barros, *Da Ásia, década primeira* (Lisbon: Régia Officina Typografica, 1777), part 1, 290–318, for the full narrative. See also the discussion in Sanjay Subrahmanyam, *The Career and Legend of Vasco da Gama* (Cambridge: Cambridge University Press, 1997), 86–94, 112–121.
17. Malyn Newitt, *A History of Portuguese Overseas Expansion, 1400–1668* (London: Routledge, 2005), 111–112.
18. Barros, *Da Ásia, década primeira*, part 2, 211, 224–231, 388–390. For discussions, see Elias Saad, "Kilwa Dynastic Historiography: A Critical Study," *History in Africa* 6 (1979): 177–207; see also G. S. P. Freeman-Grenville, *The East African Coast: Select Documents from the First to the Earlier Nineteenth Century* (London: Rex Collings, 1975).
19. Neville Chittick, "The 'Shirazi' Colonization of East Africa," *Journal of African History* 6, no. 3 (1965): 275–294 (discussion on 289–290); and Randall L. Pouwels, "A Reply to Spear on Early Swahili History," *International Journal of African Historical Studies*, 34, no. 3 (2001): 639–646.
20. Edward A. Alpers, *Ivory and Slaves: Changing Pattern of International Trade in East Central Africa to the Later Nineteenth Century* (Berkeley: University of California Press, 1975), 86–87.
21. Manuel Lobato, "Relações comerciais entre a Índia e a costa africana nos séculos XVI e XVII: O papel do Guzerate no comércio de Moçambique," *Mare Liberum* 9 (1995): 157–173. Lobato's essay is largely based on a close reading of *Documentos sobre os Portugueses em Moçambique e na África Central, 1497–1840* (henceforth abbreviated as DPMAC), 9 vols. (Lisbon: Centro de Estudos Históricos Ultramarinos, 1962–1989). See also the summary account in Michael N. Pearson, *Port Cities and Intruders: The Swahili Coast, India, and Portugal in the Early Modern Era* (Baltimore, MD: Johns Hopkins University Press, 1998).

22. Letter from Diogo Lopes de Sequeira at Cochin to the King, 23 December 1518, in DPMAC, 5:596–597.
23. "Traslado da carta de Ali, Rei de Melinde, para D. Manuel," in DPMAC, 6:44–47.
24. Anonymous, "Livro das Cidades, e Fortalezas, que a Coroa de Portugal tem nas Partes da Índia, e das capitanias, e mais cargos que nellas há, e da importância delles," ed. F. Mendes da Luz, *Studia* 6 (1960), fols. 39v–40r.
25. Richard B. Allen, "Satisfying the 'Want for Labouring People': European Slave Trading in the Indian Ocean, 1500–1850," *Journal of World History* 21, no. 1 (2010): 45–73. See also the essay by Stephanie Hassell, "Inquisition Records from Goa as Sources for the Study of Slavery in the Eastern Domains of the Portuguese Empire," *History in Africa* 42 (2015): 397–418. Jeanette Pinto, *Slavery in Portuguese India (1510–1842)* (Bombay: Himalaya Publishing House, 1992), is largely impressionistic.
26. See Giuseppe Marcocci, "Tra cristianesimo e Islam: Le vite parallele degli schiavi abissini in India (secolo XVI)," *Società e storia* 138 (2012): 807–822.
27. Pedro Machado, *Ocean of Trade: South Asian Merchants, Africa, and the Indian Ocean, c. 1750-1850* (Cambridge: Cambridge University Press, 2014), 124–126.
28. Pedro Machado, "Awash in a Sea of Cloth: Gujarat, Africa and the Western Indian Ocean, 1300–1800," in *The Spinning World: A Global History of Cotton Textiles, 1200–1850*, ed. Giorgio Riello and Prasannan Parthasarathi, 161–179 (New York: Oxford University Press, 2009), 165–166.
29. Luís Frederico Dias Antunes, "A actividade da companhia do comércio dos baneanes de Diu em Moçambique: A dinâmica privada indiana no quadro da economia estatal portuguesa (1686–1777)," *Mare Liberum* 4 (1992): 143–164.
30. See the detailed discussion in Jean Aubin, *Le Latin et l'astrolabe*, vol. 1, *Recherches sur le Portugal de la Renaissance, son expansion en Asie et les relations internationales* (Paris: Centre Culturel Calouste Gulbenkian, 1996), 133–210.
31. See Amélie Chekroun, "Dakar, capitale du sultanat éthiopien du Barr Saʻd ad-dīn (1415–1520)," *Cahiers d'Études Africaines* 55 (2015): 569–585.
32. For a contemporary account, see Miguel de Castanhoso, *Dos feitos de D. Christovam da Gama em Ethiopia*, ed. Francisco Maria Esteves Pereira (Lisbon: Imprensa Nacional, 1898). For a recent summary narrative, with some context, see Andreu Martínez d'Alòs-Moner, "Conquistadores, Mercenaries, and Missionaries: The Failed Portuguese Dominion of the Red Sea," *Northeast African Studies* 12, no. 1 (2012): 1–28.
33. The use of African slaves (often as infantry, but sometimes as cavalry) was certainly known in the Abbasid and Fatimid caliphates. See Jere L. Bacharach, "African Military Slaves in the Medieval Middle East: The Cases of Iraq (869–955) and Egypt (868–1171)," *International Journal of Middle East Studies* 13, no. 4 (1981): 471–495.

34. Paul E. Lovejoy, *Transformations in Slavery: A History of Slavery in Africa*, 3rd ed. (Cambridge: Cambridge University Press, 2012), 46–47, 61–62.
35. Thomas Vernet, "Slave Trade and Slavery on the Swahili Coast (1500–1750)," in *Slavery, Islam and Diaspora*, ed. Behnaz A. Mirzai, Ismael M. Montana, and Paul Lovejoy, 37–76 (Trenton, NJ: Africa World Press, 2009), 59–60.
36. See Marie-Laure Derat, "Chrétiens et musulmans d'Éthiopie face à la traite et à l'esclavage aux XVe et XVIe siècles," in *Traites et esclavages en Afrique orientale et dans l'océan Indien*, ed. Henri Médard, Marie-Laure Derat, Thomas Vernet, and Marie-Pierre Ballarin, 119–148 (Paris: Karthala, 2013).
37. Sunil Kumar, "When Slaves Were Nobles: The Shamsî *Bandagân* in the Early Delhi Sultanate," *Studies in History* 10, no. 1 (1994): 23–52; Peter Jackson, "The *Mamluk* Institution in Early Muslim India," *Journal of the Royal Asiatic Society* 2 (1990): 340–358. More generally, see Indrani Chatterjee and Richard M. Eaton, eds., *Slavery and South Asian History* (Bloomington: Indiana University Press, 2006).
38. Tomé Pires, *The Suma Oriental of Tomé Pires and the Book of Francisco Rodrigues*, ed. Armando Cortesão, 2 vols. (London: Hakluyt Society, 1944), 1:88 (translation), 2:377 (text).
39. See J. S. King, *The History of the Bahmani Dynasty: Founded on the Burhan-i Ma'asir* (London: Luzac, 1900), 119.
40. Pires, *Suma Oriental*, 1:50–51.
41. The unique manuscript of this *masnawi* is to be found in Anna Centenary Library, Chennai, Government Oriental Manuscripts Collection, Persian Ms. D. 92, fols. 108–137; for an edition, see A. H. Yusha, "Fathnama-i Mahmud Shahi," *Annals of Oriental Research, University of Madras: Arabic, Persian and Urdu Section* 11 (1953–4): 1–29. For a preliminary analysis of 'Iyani's work, see A. C. S. Peacock, "'Iyani, a Shirazi Poet and Historian in the Bahmani Deccan," *Iran* 59, no. 2 (2021): 169–186.
42. Yusha, "Fathnama-i Mahmud Shahi," 6. The translation here differs substantively from that in Peacock, "'Iyani, a Shirazi Poet," 181–182. Peacock repeatedly stresses that the poem is written in "racially charged terms," translating terms like *ham-jins* unjustifiably as "of the same race." While the term "black" (*siyah*) is indeed used to describe Dastur Dinar and the other habashis, one cannot easily equate color (*rang*) as used by the poet with ideas of "race."
43. 'Abdullah Hajji-ud-Dabir Ulughkhani, *Zafar al-Walih bi-Muzaffar wa Alihi: An Arabic History of Gujarat*, ed. E. Denison Ross, 3 vols. (London: John Murray, 1910–1929), 2:xii–xviii, xxxiii–xxxiv. On this author, see most recently Jyoti Gulati Balachandran, "Counterpoint: Reassessing Ulughkhānī's Arabic history of Gujarat," *Asiatische Studien* 74, no. 1 (2020): 137–161.
44. On Ahmedabad, see M. Abdulla Chaghatai, *Muslim Monuments of Ahmedabad through Their Inscriptions* (Poona: Deccan College Research Institute, 1942).

45. Sidi Bilal Jhujhar Khan was killed during the 1546 siege of the Portuguese fortress of Diu; for several references to him (as "Jusarcão"), see António Baião, ed., *História quinhentista (inédita) do segundo cêrco de Dio* (Coimbra: Imprensa da Universidade, 1927), 27, 45–47, 92. His body was buried at the celebrated Sarkhej Rauza.
46. To these we can add the devoutly Hanafite figure of Sidi Saʿid Sultani (d. 1576), the builder of a major mosque in Ahmedabad; see Chaghatai, *Muslim Monuments of Ahmedabad*, 17–18.
47. For a survey of these sources, see Gina Maria Cordeiro Antunes, "Os Abexins no Decão e no Guzarate no século XVI: Escravos e senhores," MA thesis, Universidade Nova de Lisboa, 1997.
48. The absence of notarial archives of the type used by historians of the Spanish Atlantic empire thus hinders the construction of a more nuanced and gendered history of the African presence in early modern India. See, by way of comparison, Danielle Terrazas Williams, "'My Conscience Is Free and Clear': African-Descended Women, Status, and Slave Owning in Mid-Colonial Mexico," *The Americas* 75, no. 3 (2018): 525–554.
49. See the discussion in Maria Augusta Lima Cruz, "A 'Crónica da Índia' de Diogo do Couto," *Mare Liberum* 9 (1995): 383–391; also see António Coimbra Martins, *Em torno de Diogo do Couto* (Coimbra: Biblioteca Geral da Universidade de Coimbra, 1985).
50. Diogo do Couto, *Da Ásia, década sexta* (Lisbon: Régia Officina Typografica, 1781), part 2, 515–517, 529–536.
51. Diogo do Couto, *Da Ásia, década sétima* (Lisbon: Régia Officina Typografica, 1782), part 1, 83–88.
52. For details of the dealings in 1556–1557, see Arquivo Nacional da Torre do Tombo, Lisbon (henceforth ANTT), Corpo Cronológico, I-100-31, letter from Dom João da Costa in Daman to the King, 20 December 1556; CC, I-102-47, letter from Dom Diogo de Noronha at Goa to Pero de Alcáçova Carneiro, 17 December 1557.
53. See the letter from Dom Constantino de Bragança to the Queen, January 1561, in António dos Santos Pereira, "A Índia a preto e branco: Uma carta oportuna, escrita de Cochim, por D. Constantino de Bragança, à Rainha Dona Catarina," *Anais de História de Além-Mar* 4 (2003): 449–486 (discussion on 474–475).
54. Couto, *Da Ásia, década sétima*, part 2, 502–512.
55. For further details on Távora, see ANTT, Miscelâneas Manuscritas do Convento da Graça, Tomo 280, fols. 72–77, four letters from Garcia Rodrigues de Távora, respectively from Cochin, Chaul, and Daman (1558–1561).
56. Ulughkhani, *Zafar al-Walih*, 2:580–581; M. S. Commissariat, *A History of Gujarat: Including a Survey of Its Chief Architectural Monuments and Inscriptions* (Bombay: Longmans, Green, 1938), 1:471–472.
57. Couto, *Da Ásia, década sétima*, part 2, 43.

58. See Artur Teodoro de Matos et al., eds., *O tombo de Damão, 1592* (Lisbon: CNCDP, 2001). For a statistical analysis of this text, see Livia Baptista de Souza Ferrão, "Tenants, Rents and Revenues from Daman in the Late 16th Century," *Mare Liberum* 9 (1995): 136–149. For a slightly later description of Daman and its territories (from the 1630s), see António Bocarro, *O livro das plantas de todas as fortalezas, cidades e povoações do Estado da Índia Oriental*, ed. Isabel Cid, 3 vols. (Lisbon: Imprensa Nacional-Casa da Moeda, 1992), 2:84–101.
59. See Munis D. Faruqui, *The Princes of the Mughal Empire, 1504–1719* (New York: Cambridge University Press, 2012), 172.
60. See Radhey Shyam, *The Kingdom of Ahmadnagar* (Delhi: Motilal Banarsidass, 1966), 155–156.
61. Farhad Khan was obviously already prominent in Ahmadnagar by the late 1550s; see the inscription in the mosque, shrine and rest house built by him in that city in 967 AH/1559–1560 CE, in *Epigraphia Indo-Moslemica*, 1933–34: 6.
62. António Pinto Pereira, *História da Índia no tempo em que a governou o visorei Dom Luís de Ataíde*, ed. Manuel Marques Duarte (Lisbon: Imprensa Nacional-Casa da Moeda, 1987), 368–369.
63. Diogo do Couto, *Da Ásia, década XI* (Lisbon: Régia Officina Typográfica, 1788), 171–172; see also Antonella Vignato, ed., "Vida e Acções de Mathias de Albuquerque, Capitão e Viso-Rei do Estado da Índia" (Part 2), *Mare Liberum* 17 (1999): 267–360. It is of interest to read Farhad Khan's career together with the case of another Ethiopian (apparently of "falaxa" origin) named Gabriel or Sidi Rahim ("Side Reme"), who was tried by the Inquisition at Chaul and Goa in 1595 after spending part of his career in Ahmadnagar service; for a careful analysis of his Inquisition file, see Marcocci, "Tra cristianesimo e Islam," 807–822.
64. King to Viceroy Rui Lourenço de Távora, 29 October 1609, in *Documentos Remettidos da Índia, ou Livros das Monções*, ed. R. A. de Bulhão Pato (Lisbon: Academia Real das Ciências, 1880), 1:253. For Portuguese dealings with Malik 'Ambar more generally, see Jorge Flores, *Nas margens do Hindustão: O Estado da Índia e a expansão mogol, ca. 1570–1640* (Coimbra: Imprensa da Universidade de Coimbra, 2015), 235–242.
65. Thus, see the popular account by Omar H. Ali, *Malik Ambar: Power and Slavery across the Indian Ocean* (New York: Oxford University Press, 2016).
66. Richard M. Eaton, *A Social History of the Deccan, 1300–1761: Eight Indian Lives* (Cambridge: Cambridge University Press, 2005), 105–128.
67. The most useful account is in the text of Fuzuni Astarabadi from the mid-seventeenth century, *Futuhat-i 'Adil Shahi* (British Library, Persian Ms., Addn. 27, 251). For a translation of relevant passages, see Jadunath Sarkar, "Malik Ambar: A New Life," in Sarkar, *House of Shivaji: Studies and Documents on Maratha History*, 3rd ed. (Calcutta: M. C. Sarkar and Sons, 1955), 5–25. On Chingiz Khan and the end of his career, see Wolseley Haig, *The*

History of the Nizam Shahi Kings of Ahmadnagar (Bombay: British India Press, 1923), 131–132.

68. See Ghulam Yazdani, "Inscriptions at the Fort of Qandhar, Nanded District, H.E.H. the Nizam's Dominions," *Epigraphia Indo-Moslemica, 1919–20*, 20–26. For a discussion of Kandhar and other sites, see Klaus Rötzer, "The Architectural Legacy of Malik Ambar, Malik Sandal, and Yaqut Kabuli Habshi," in *African Elites in India: Habshi Amarat*, ed. Kenneth X. Robbins and John McLeod (Ahmedabad: Mapin, 2006), 70–84.

69. See Ghulam Yazdani, "Inscriptions of Nizam Shahi Kings from Antur Fort, Aurangabad District," *Epigraphia Indo-Moslemica, 1919–20*, 12–15. For the inscription from Shivneri, see Pramod B. Gadre, *Cultural Archaeology of Ahmadnagar during Nizam Shahi Period, 1494–1632* (Delhi: B. R. Publishing, 1986), 125–125.

70. Jamshid Nauruzi, ed., *Risala-i Tarikh-i Asad Beg Qazwini* (Tehran: Pizhushishgah-i 'Ulum-i Insani wa Mutala'at-i Farhangi, 2014), 29, 31–34.

71. Muhammad Qasim Firishta, *Tarikh-i Firishta*, ed. Mohammad Reza Nasiri, 4 vols. (Tehran: Anjuman-i Asar wa Mafakhir-i Farhangi, 2009–11), 3:508; *History of the Rise of Mahomedan Power in India till the Year A.D. 1612*, trans. John Briggs (with Mir Khairat 'Ali Khan Akbarabadi "Mushtaq"), 4 vols. (London: Longman, Rees, Orme, Brown and Green, 1829), 3:314–315 (revised).

72. See William Foster, ed., *The English Factories in India, 1618–69* (hereafter *EFI*), 13 vols. (Oxford: Clarendon Press, 1906–1927), *EFI, 1618–21*, 272–273.

73. See the letters from Jeffries dated October and November 1621, in *EFI, 1618–21*, 287–290, 296–297, and 315–318. There are further references to the episode and its aftermath in *EFI, 1622–23*, 12–13, 18, and 200–204. For a full discussion see Ashin Das Gupta, "Indian Merchants and the Western Indian Ocean: The Early Seventeenth Century," *Modern Asian Studies* 19, no. 3 (1985): 481–499.

74. "William Minor's Account of the Voyage of the *Scout*" (1625), in *EFI, 1624–29*, 71.

75. For an account of his career, see Muhammad Jamal Sharif, *Dakan mein Urdu sha'iri Wali se pehle*, ed. Muhammad 'Ali Asar (Hyderabad: Idara-i Adabiyat-i Urdu, 2004), 416–432; for an edition of his most important work, see Malik Khushnud, *Jannat Singar (1056 H./1645)*, ed. Sayyida Ja'far (New Delhi: Qaumi Council bara'i Urdu Zaban, 1997).

76. See Jadunath Sarkar, "The Leading Nobles of Bijapur, 1627–1686," in *House of Shivaji*, 90–101.

77. For details, see Jadunath Sarkar, *Shivaji and His Times*, 3rd ed. (Calcutta: M. C. Sarkar and Sons, 1929), 254–278. On Janjira, also see the recent essay by Faeeza Jasdanwalla, "The Invincible Fort of the Nawabs of Janjira," *Journal of African Diaspora Archaeology & Heritage* 4, no. 1 (2015): 72–91.

78. For an overview, see Sanjay Subrahmanyam, "Iranians Abroad: Intra-

Asian Elite Migration and Early Modern State Formation," *Journal of Asian Studies* 51, no. 2 (1992): 340–362.

79. For a discussion, see Derek J. Mancini-Lander, "Tales Bent Backward: Early Modern Local History in Persianate Transregional Contexts," *Journal of the Royal Asiatic Society*, 3rd ser., 28, no. 1 (2018): 23–54.
80. See Tobias P. Graf, *The Sultan's Renegades: Christian-European Converts to Islam and the Making of the Ottoman Elite, 1575–1610* (Oxford: Oxford University Press, 2017), 164–165, 178–183.
81. See the account in Amélie Chekroun, "Le *Futūḥ al-Ḥabaša*: Ecriture de l'histoire, guerre et société dans le Bar Saʿad al-Din (Éthiopie, XVIe siècle)" (PhD diss., Université Panthéon-Sorbonne, Paris-I, 2013), 81–84. For a modern English translation of the text, see Shihab-ud-Din Ahmad bin 'Abdul Qadir 'Arab Faqih, *The Conquest of Abyssinia: 16th Century*, trans. and ed. Paul Lester Stenhouse and Richard Pankhurst (Los Angeles: Tsehai, 2003).
82. See Megan Vaughan, *Creating the Creole Island: Slavery in Eighteenth-Century Mauritius* (Durham, NC: Duke University Press, 2005).
83. An interesting case that tests the limits is that studied in Júnia Ferreira Furtado, *Chica da Silva: A Brazilian Slave of the Eighteenth Century* (Cambridge: Cambridge University Press, 2009). See also Mariana P. Candido, *An African Slaving Port and the Atlantic World: Benguela and Its Hinterland* (New York: Cambridge University Press, 2013), for a comparison of mobility on the two sides of the Atlantic.
84. João José Reis, *Slave Rebellion in Brazil: The Muslim Uprising of 1835 in Bahia*, trans. Arthur Brakel (Baltimore, MD: Johns Hopkins University Press, 1995); Sylviane A. Diouf, *Servants of Allah: African Muslims Enslaved in the Americas* (New York: New York University Press, 1998).
85. See Jane Hathaway, *The Chief Eunuch of the Ottoman Harem: From African Slave to Power-Broker* (Cambridge: Cambridge University Press, 2018); and Emine Fetvacı, *Picturing History at the Ottoman Court* (Bloomington: Indiana University Press, 2013), 149–190. For Ottoman political ambitions in relation to Ethiopia, see the classic work of Cengiz Orhonlu, *Habeş eyaleti: Osmanlı imparatorluğu'nun güney siyaseti* (Istanbul: Edebiyat Fakültesi Matbaası, 1974).

CHAPTER 4: THE VIEW FROM SURAT

1. Nancy Um, *The Merchant Houses of Mocha: Trade and Architecture in an Indian Ocean Port* (Seattle: University of Washington Press, 2009), 15.
2. Um, *The Merchant Houses of Mocha*, 189–190.
3. Denis Diderot and Jean Le Rond D'Alembert, eds., *Encyclopédie ou dictionnaire raisonné des sciences, des arts et des métiers*, 28 vols. (Paris: Briasson, David, Le Breton and Durand, 1751–1752), 4:297.
4. For a fuller discussion of Postel, see Jean-François Maillard, "Postel le

cosmopolite: Quelques documents nouveaux," in Sylvain Matton, ed., *Documents oubliés sur l'alchimie, la kabbale et Guillaume Postel, offerts à l'occasion de son 90e anniversaire à François Secret par ses élèves et amis* (Geneva: Droz, 2001), 197–222.
5. See Paul Hazard, "Cosmopolite," in *Mélanges offerts à Fernand Baldensperger* (Paris: Champion, 1930), 1:354–364.
6. See Noel Malcolm, ed., *The Correspondence of Thomas Hobbes*, vol. 1 (1622–1659) (Oxford: Oxford University Press, 1994), 212–213; I have preferred not to use the English translation on 214–215.
7. On this figure, see Sanjay Subrahmanyam, "Once Bitten, Twice Shy: A French Traveller and Go-between in Mughal India, 1648–1667," *Indian Economic and Social History Review* 58, no. 2 (2021): 153–312. For older studies, see Gaston Moreau, *Le Gouz de la Boullaie, gentilhomme angevin, ambassadeur de Louis XIV: Sa vie, son oeuvre et sa famille* (Baugé: Emmanuel Cingla, 1956); Henri Castonnet des Fossés, "La Boullaye le Gouz: Sa vie et ses voyages," *Mémoires de la Société Nationale d'Agriculture, Sciences, et Arts d'Angers*, 4th ser., 1 (1887): 145–175.
8. Jean-Baptiste Tavernier, "Relation de ce qui s'est passé dans la Negociation des Deputez qui ont esté en Perse et aux Indes," in Tavernier, *Recueil de plusieurs relations et traitez singuliers et curieux de J. B. Tavernier, Chevalier, Baron d'Aubonne* (Paris: n.p, 1679), 54–125.
9. See Margaret C. Jacob, *Strangers Nowhere in the World: The Rise of Cosmopolitanism in Early Modern Europe* (Philadelphia: University of Pennsylvania Press, 2006), 1; and compare Anthony Pagden, *The Enlightenment and Why It Still Matters* (New York: Random House, 2013), 7–8.
10. See Thomas T. Allsen, "Ever Closer Encounters: The Appropriation of Culture and the Apportionment of Peoples in the Mongol Empire," *Journal of Early Modern History* 1, no. 1 (1997): 2–23 (quotation on 2).
11. For a nuanced discussion of Shahjahanabad-Delhi as a cosmopolitan center, see Rajeev Kinra, *Writing Self, Writing Empire: Chandar Bhan Brahman and the Cultural World of the Indo-Persian State Secretary* (Berkeley: University of California Press, 2015), 127–140.
12. For an interesting analysis, see Fonna Forman-Barzilai, *Adam Smith and the Circles of Sympathy: Cosmopolitanism and Moral Theory* (Cambridge: Cambridge University Press, 2010).
13. The standard works on this port in the early modern centuries are Ashin Das Gupta, *Indian Merchants and the Decline of Surat, c. 1700–1750* (Wiesbaden: Franz Steiner Verlag, 1979), and Balkrishna Govind Gokhale, *Surat in the Seventeenth Century: A Study in Urban History of Pre-Modern India* (London: Curzon Press, 1979). Far more cursory is O. P. Singh, *Surat and Its Trade in the Second Half of the 17th century* (Delhi: University of Delhi Press, 1977). A collection of essays largely based on English Company materials may be found in Ruby Maloni, *Surat: Port of the Mughal Empire* (Mumbai: Himalaya Publishing House, 2003). The colonial period is well

represented in Douglas E. Haynes, *Rhetoric and Ritual in Colonial India: The Shaping of a Public Culture in Surat City, 1852–1928* (Berkeley: University of California Press, 1991).

14. See Jacques Henri Bernardin de Saint Pierre, *La chaumière indienne, Le Café de Surate & c.*, ed. L. T. Ventouillac (London: Treuttel, Würtz, et al., 1824), 95–108.

15. See Armando Cortesão, *The Suma Oriental of Tomé Pires: An Account of the East, from the Red Sea to China, Written in Malacca and India in 1512–1515*, 2 vols. (London: Hakluyt Society, 1944), 1:34–35.

16. For a description, see Richard Carnac Temple, ed., *The Travels of Peter Mundy in Europe and Asia, 1608–1667, vol. 2 (Travels in Asia, 1628–1634)* (London: Hakluyt Society, 1914), 31–32.

17. See Fernão Lopes de Castanheda, *História do descobrimento e conquista da Índia pelos portugueses*, ed. M. Lopes de Almeida, 4 vols. (Oporto: Lello e Irmão, 1979), vol. 4, book 8, 572–574.

18. See Giancarlo Casale, *The Ottoman Age of Exploration* (New York: Oxford University Press, 2010), 54–55.

19. Khwaja Nizam-ud-Din Ahmad, *The Tabaqat-i-Akbari*, trans. Brajendranath De (Calcutta: Asiatic Society of Bengal, 1936), 2:381–382.

20. See ʿAbdul Qadir Badayuni, *Muntakhab al-Tawarikh*, ed. Ahmad ʿAli and W. Nassau Lees, 3 vols. (Calcutta: Asiatic Society of Bengal, 1864–1869), 2:143–147; and Badayuni, *Muntakhab al-Tawarikh*, trans. G. S. A. Ranking, W. H. Lowe, and T. W. Haig, 3 vols. (Calcutta: J.W. Thomas, 1884–1925), 2:147–150.

21. Nizam-ud-Din Ahmad, *The Tabaqat-i-Akbari*, 2:382.

22. I draw here on the materials in Sanjay Subrahmanyam "A Note on the Rise of Surat in the Sixteenth Century," *Journal of the Economic and Social History of the Orient* 43, no. 1 (2000): 23–33.

23. See the documents from 1545 in Luís Filipe F. R. Thomaz, *A questão da pimenta em meados do século XVI: Um debate político do governo de D. João de Castro* (Lisbon: Universidade Católica Portuguesa, 1998), 131, 160.

24. See the letter from Gaspar de Sequeira at Bassein to D. João de Castro, 13 July 1546, in Elaine Sanceau et al. *Colecção de São Lourenço* (Lisbon: CEHU, 1983), 3:149–152. The author of the letter seems to confuse the name of the fortress commander, Caracen, with the term ethnic designation "coraçone" (for *khorasani*). He notes that the garrison includes "jaos e negros de portugueses" but also states that Khwaja Safar had had excellent relations with the neighboring Rajputs, who had helped him protect the fort from the land side.

25. Diogo do Couto, *Da Ásia, décadas IV–XII* (repr., Lisbon: Livraria Sam Carlos, 1973–1774), *Década sexta*, part 1, book 5, 384–397.

26. Seydi Ali Re'is, *Mir'âtül-Memâlik*, ed. Mehmet Kiremit (Ankara: Türk Dil Kurumu, 1999), 89–94; Seydi ʿAli Re'is, *Le miroir des pays: Une anabase ottomane à travers l'Inde et l'Asie centrale*, trans. Jean-Louis Bacqué-Grammont

(Paris: Actes Sud, 1999), 62–67. Seydi ʿAli mentions various notables at Surat, such as the *kotwal* Agha Hamza, as well as Khudawand Khan and Jahangir Khan. The French translation at times distorts these names (e.g., by referring to Khuda-bande Khan).

27. Couto, *Da Ásia, década sétima*, part 2, book 9, 385–417.
28. Couto, *Da Ásia, década sétima*, part 2, book 9, 413.
29. Letters from Marcus Prancudo and Fernão Álvares at Daman, February 1561, in Josef Wicki, ed., *Documenta Indica, vol. V (1561–1563)* (Rome: Society of Jesus, 1958), 103–108.
30. For Chingiz Khan's own assassination some years later, see António Pinto Pereira, *História da Índia no tempo em que a governou o visorei Dom Luís de Ataíde (1617)*, ed. Manuel Marques Duarte (Lisbon: Imprensa Nacional, 1987), 18–19.
31. Couto, *Da Ásia, década sétima*, part 2, book 9, 416. Couto adds: "Thus did matters remain for then, with no further occasion offering itself for the viceroys to seize hold of Surrate, which was so crucial to the *Estado*."
32. See Maria Augusta Lima Cruz, *Diogo do Couto e a década oitava da Ásia*, 2 vols. (Lisbon: Imprensa Nacional, 1993–94), 1:365–368.
33. Letter from the viceroy Dom Francisco Coutinho to the King, Goa, 20 December 1561, reproduced in Josef Wicki, "Duas cartas oficiais de Vice-Reis da Índia, escritas em 1561 e 1564," *Studia* 3 (1959): 36–89.
34. See Shireen Moosvi, "The Gujarat Ports and Their Hinterland: The Economic Relationship," in *Ports and Their Hinterlands in India (1700–1950)*, ed. Indu Banga (New Delhi: Manohar, 1992), 121–130. Moosvi's reasoning is broadly followed by Farhat Hasan, *State and Locality in Mughal India: Power Relations in Western India, c. 1572–1730* (Cambridge: Cambridge University Press, 2006), 10–11.
35. See Antoni Montserrat, *Commentary of Father Monserrate*, trans. S. N. Banerjee and John S. Hoyland (Oxford: Oxford University Press, 1922), 10–11.
36. See Couto, *Da Ásia, década sétima*, part 2, book 10, ch. 8, 502–512, for the account of the attack on Daman in October 1561; also see chapter 4.
37. See Das Gupta, *Indian Merchants and the Decline of Surat*, 29.
38. Letters from Luís de Mendonça at Diu to Philip II, 26 November 1589 (summary), in *Boletim da Filmoteca Ultramarina Portuguesa*, no. 15 (1960): 595; letter from Philip III to Martim Afonso de Castro, dated 27 January 1607, in R. A. de Bulhão Pato, ed., *Documentos Remettidos da Índia ou Livros das Monções* (Lisbon: Academia Real das Sciencias, 1880), 1:130.
39. Bayazid Bayat, *Tazkira-i Humayun wa Akbar*, ed. M. Hidayat Hosain (Calcutta: Asiatic Society of Bengal, 1941), 353–363. For a full discussion, see Muzaffar Alam and Sanjay Subrahmanyam, *Indo-Persian Travels in the Age of Discoveries, 1400–1800* (Cambridge: Cambridge University Press, 2007), 304–312.
40. Couto, *Da Ásia, década décima*, part 1, 169–179; part 2, 305–313.

41. Shireen Moosvi, *People, Taxation and Trade in Mughal India* (Delhi: Oxford University Press, 2008), 243–256.
42. For details, see William Foster, ed., *The Voyage of Thomas Best to the East Indies, 1612–14* (London: Hakluyt Society, 1934).
43. The best account of the first phase of Dutch trade in Surat and Gujarat remains Hans W. van Santen, *De Verenigde Oost-Indische Compagnie in Gujarat en Hindustan, 1620–1660* (Leiden: Privately printed, 1982). The next phase is dealt with in V. B. Gupta, "The Dutch East India Company in Gujarat Trade, 1660–1700: A study of selected aspects," PhD diss., Delhi School of Economics, 1991.
44. See Sanjay Subrahmanyam, "Masulipatnam Revisited, 1550–1750: A Survey and Some Speculations," in *Gateways to Asia: Port Cities of Asia in the 13th-20th Centuries*, ed. Frank Broeze (London: Kegan Paul, 1997), 33–65.
45. See Billy K. L. So, *Prosperity, Region, and Institutions in Maritime China: The South Fukien Pattern, 946–1368* (Cambridge, MA: Harvard University Press, 2000); Roxani Eleni Margariti, *Aden and the Indian Ocean Trade: 150 Years in the Life of a Medieval Arabian Port* (Chapel Hill: University of North Carolina Press, 2007); and Luís Filipe F. R. Thomaz, "The Malay Sultanate of Melaka," in *Southeast Asia in the Early Modern Era: Trade, Power and Belief*, ed. Anthony Reid, 69–90 (Ithaca, NY: Cornell University Press, 1993).
46. A seventeenth-century Jain narrative poem in Sanskrit describes Surat as a Jain center; it awaits a fuller analysis. See Vinayavijaya, "Indudutam," in *Kavyamala*, ed. Pandit Durgaprasada and Kasinath Pandurang Parab (Bombay: Nirnaya Sagar Press, 1938), 14:45–67; also Vinayavijaya, *Indudutam khandakavyam*, ed. Dhurandharavijaya Gani (Shirapurastha: Shrijaina Sahitya Vardhaka Sabha, 1946). For brief remarks on this text, see Gokhale, *Surat in the Seventeenth Century*, 132. In addition, the Bibliothèque Nationale de France, Paris, in its manuscript section houses some important commercial documents in Gujarati from Surat in the late eighteenth century (Mss. indien 762–764, 803, 979, etc.), which are well beyond the temporal scope of this chapter. For a preliminary analysis, see Dilbagh Singh and Ashok B. Rajshirke, "The Merchant Communities in Surat: Trade, Trade Practices and Institutions in the Late 18th Century," in Banga, *Ports and Their Hinterlands in India*, 181–198.
47. A small collection of these documents, now housed in the Aligarh Muslim University, has been published in Mahendra Pal Singh, *Town, Market, Mint and Port in the Mughal Empire, 1556–1707* (New Delhi: Adam Publishers, 1985), 289–314. But see also the mixed collection of documents in the Biblioteca Apostolica Vaticana, Vat. Persiano 33, which seem to have been acquired from the estate of Adriaan Reland (who in turn acquired it from Dutch Company factors in the seventeenth century).
48. Bibliothèque Nationale de France, Paris, Persian Ms. Blochet 707 (Supplément 482), *Munsha'at-i marbut bi Gujarat wa Surat ta sal-i 1057 Hijri*, fols. 139–140, *parwana* dated 13 October 1636 (20 Jumada I 1045 AH),

translated in Hasan, *State and Locality in Mughal India*, 50–51. A. H. Anquetil-Duperron purchased this collection of documents at Surat in the eighteenth century. Other selections from this collection may be found translated in Moosvi, *People, Taxation and Trade in Mughal India*, 252–256, 266–274, 281–287, including some intriguing documents on domestic disputes.

49. "Remonstrantie over den stant van Suratte," in Heert Terpstra, *De Opkomst der Westerkwartieren van de Oost-Indische Compagnie (Suratte, Arabië, Perzië)* (The Hague: Martinus Nijhoff, 1918), 203–216.

50. V. Ball and W. Crooke, trans. and eds., *Travels in India by Jean-Baptiste Tavernier, Baron of Aubonne*, 2 vols. (New York: Oxford University Press, 1925), 1:5–7; Jean-Baptiste Tavernier, *Les six voyages de Jean-Baptiste Tavernier, Chevalier, Baron d'Aubonne, qu'il a fait en Turquie, en Perse, et aux Indes . . .*, part 2 (Paris: Gervais Clouzier, 1681), book 1, 3–4.

51. Archives Nationales d'Outre-Mer, Aix-en-Provence (henceforth ANOM), Colonies, C² 65, fols. 49r–66r, letter from François Martin at Pondichéry, dated 15 February 1700 (passage cited on fols. 49v-50r).

52. Compare Martin's account from 1681, in Alfred Martineau, ed., *Mémoires de François Martin, fondateur de Pondichéry (1665–1694)*, 3 vols. (Paris: Société de l'Histoire des Colonies Françaises, 1931–1934), 2:268–269.

53. Das Gupta, *Indian Merchants and the Decline of Surat*, 30.

54. Das Gupta, *Indian Merchants and the Decline of Surat*, 31. Schreuder concluded that the 175 wealthiest merchants at Surat in about 1750 had a total capital of about 8.74 million rupees; see Holden Furber, *Bombay Presidency in the Mid-Eighteenth Century* (New York: Asia Publishing House, 1965), 64–66. This may be compared with the far poorer state of the sixteenth-century *casado* bourgeoisie in Goa; see Rafael Moreira, "Goa em 1535: Uma cidade manuelina," *Revista da Faculdade de Ciências Sociais e Humanas* 2, no. 8 (1995): 177–221.

55. See H. W. van Santen, *VOC-dienaar in India: Geleynssen de Jongh in het land van de Groot-Mogol* (Franeker: Van Wijnen, 2001).

56. For somewhat comparable maps of Banaras in the period, see Madhuri Desai, *Banaras Reconstructed: Architecture and Sacred Space in a Hindu Holy City* (Seattle: University of Washington Press, 2017), 35–44.

57. See Hiromu Nagashima, "Juhachi seiki zenhan sakusei no Mugaru teikoku koshi Sūrato no chizu ni tsuite" (The Map of the Mughal Empire's Port-City of Surat Composed in the First Half of the Eighteenth Century), *Nagasaki kenritsu daigaku ronso* (Nagasaki Prefectural University Journal) 40, no. 2 (2006): 89–132; also see the briefer discussion in H. Nagashima, "The Factories and Facilities of the East India Companies in Surat: Locations, Building Characteristics and Ownership," in *Asian Port Cities 1600–1800: Local and Foreign Cultural Interactions*, ed. Masashi Haneda (Singapore: NUS Press, 2009), 192–227.

58. Gothenburg University Library, Christopher Henrik Braad, "Beskrifning

på skeppet Götha Leyons resa till Surat och åtskillige andre indianske orte" (manuscript). For a discussion, see Jeremy Franks, "The Observant Braad: A Swedish Enquirer in Gujerat in the 1750s," *Moyen Orient et Océan Indien, XVIe-XIXe siècles* 10 (1998): 155–184.

59. See Nagashima, "Juhachi seiki zenhan sakusei no Mugaru teikoku koshi Sūrato no chizu ni tsuite," 114–120.
60. See John Ovington, *A Voyage to Surat in the Year 1689*, ed. H. G. Rawlinson (London: Oxford University Press, 1929). For an attempt to place Ovington's text in a larger context, see Pramod K. Nayar, "Marvelous Excesses: English Travel Writing and India, 1608–1727," *Journal of British Studies* 44, no. 2 (2005): 213–238.
61. See Alexander Hamilton, *A New Account of the East Indies* (Edinburgh: John Mosman, 1727), 1:xiv.
62. For a summary of European printed accounts of Surat in this period, see Donald F. Lach and Edwin J. Van Kley, *Asia in the Making of Europe*, vol. 3, *A Century of Advance*, book 2 (Chicago: University of Chicago Press, 1993), 739–756.
63. Compare ANOM, Colonies, C² 65, fols, 230r–34r, "Estat des officiers du Mogol qui sont dans la ville de Suratte à commencer par le Gouverneur" (1700).
64. Ovington, *A Voyage to Surat in the Year 1689*, 138.
65. See Jorge Flores, "The Sea and the World of the *Mutasaddi*: A Profile of Port Officials from Mughal Gujarat (c. 1600–1650)," *Journal of the Royal Asiatic Society*, 3rd ser., 21, no. 1 (2011): 55–71.
66. See Hasan, *State and Locality in Mughal India*, 102.
67. See Muhyi-ud-Din 'Abdul Qadir al-'Aydarusi, *Tarikh al-Nur al-Safir 'an akhbar al-qarn al-'ashir*, ed. Ahmad Halu, Mahmud al-Arna'ut, and Akram al-Bushi (Beirut: Dar Sadir, 2001). For a discussion of this and other texts relating to the 'Aydarusis, see Engseng Ho, *The Graves of Tarim: Genealogy and Mobility across the Indian Ocean* (Berkeley: University of California Press, 2006).
68. See Engseng Ho, "Names beyond Nations: The Making of Local Cosmopolitans," *Études Rurales* 163–164 (2022): 215–231.
69. See Hasan, *State and Locality in Mughal India*, 101–105. Hasan's account here depends largely on a late nineteenth-century account by a certain Shaikh Bahadur, *Guldasta-i Sulaha-i Surat*.
70. See Peter van der Veer, "Playing or Praying: A Sufi Saint's Day in Surat," *Journal of Asian Studies* 51, no. 3 (1992): 545–564.
71. See Ronald W. Ferrier, "Charles I and the Antiquities of Persia: The Mission of Nicholas Wilford," *Iran* 8 (1970): 51–56. For Charles's request, see W. Noel Sainsbury, ed., *Calendar of State Papers, Colonial Series, East Indies and Persia, 1630–1634, preserved in the Public Record Office and the India Office* (London: Her Majesty's Stationery Office, 1892), 523.
72. British Library, London, OIOC, E/3/15/1543A, Methwold, Mountney,

Fremlen, etc at Swally to the Company, 29 December 1634, in *The English Factories in India*, ed. William Foster, 13 vols. (Oxford: Clarendon Press, 1906–27) (henceforth cited as *EFI*), *EFI, 1634–36*, 74–75 (the summary of the whole letter occupies 59–85).

73. For a discussion, see John Seyller, *Workshop and Patron in Mughal India: The Freer Ramayana and Other Illustrated Manuscripts of 'Abd al-Rahim* (Zurich: Museum Rietberg, 1999), 257–263. The manuscript may be found in the Bodleian Library, Oxford, Ms. Laud Or, 149.

74. See Will Sweetman, *A Discovery of the Banian Religion and the Religion of the Persees: A Critical Edition of Two Early English Works on Indian Religions* (Lampeter: Edwin Mellen Press, 1999).

75. See Ovington, *A Voyage to Surat in the Year 1689*, 133. For an evaluation of varying claims on the Armenians in Surat, see Sebouh David Aslanian, *From the Indian Ocean to the Mediterranean: The Global Trade Networks of Armenian Merchants from New Julfa* (Berkeley: University of California Press, 2011), 47–48.

76. Georges Roques, *La manière de négocier aux Indes (1676–1691): La Compagnie des Indes et l'art du commerce*, ed. Valérie Bérinstain (Paris: Maisonneuve et Larose, 1996), 147–148.

77. For example, see the petition in Persian (with Gujarati signatures) from Cauth Thakur, Tulsidas Parekh, and Benidas, to the Padshah and high authorities in England, dated January 1655, in British Library, London, Royal Ms 16.B.xxi, fol. 12.

78. Gokhale, *Surat in the Seventeenth Century*, 119–120; also Ghulam A. Nadri, *Eighteenth-Century Gujarat: The Dynamics of Its Political Economy, 1750–1800* (Leiden: Brill, 2009), 202–203, "The Family Tree of Three Merchants of Surat."

79. See Shalin Jain, "Jain Elites and the Mughal state under Shahjahan," *Indian Historical Review* 42, no. 2 (2015): 210–225 (esp. 221–223). Vora is identified as specifically belonging to the Lonka Gaccha group and possessing "proficiency in Jain learning."

80. See Makrand Mehta, "Virji Vora: The Profile of an Indian Businessman in the 17th Century," in Mehta, *Indian Merchants and Entrepreneurs in Historical Perspective (with Special Reference to the Shroffs of Gujarat, 17th to 19th Centuries)* (Delhi: Academic Foundation, 1991), 53–63. For Virji's dealings with the Dutch Company, see Van Santen, *De Verenigde Oost-Indische Compagnie in Gujarat en Hindustan*, 45–47, 124–127.

81. "The Agreement between the English and the Surat Authorities," in Foster, *EFI, 1624–29*, 27–30.

82. See Foster, *EFI, 1634–36*, 24.

83. William Methwold and Council at Surat to the Company, 28 April 1636, in Foster, *EFI, 1634–36*, 218.

84. Hasan, *State and Locality in Mughal India*, 42.

85. British Library, London, OIOC, IOR/E/3/24, O.C. No. 2448, letter from

Virji Vora to the Company dated 25 January 1655 (the letter is signed in Gujarati: "Virji Vora Kendrua"). For a transcription, with several unfortunate errors, see Mehta, "Virji Vora," 61.
86. See Foster, *EFI, 1655–60*, 368–369.
87. See Jivanji Jamshedji Modi, "Rustam Manock (1635–1721 A.C.), the Broker of the English East India Company (1699 A.C.) and the Persian Qisseh (History) of Rustam Manock: A Study," *Asiatic Papers* (Bombay) 4 (1929): 101–320 (the Persian text appears on 281–309). On the Parsis of Surat, see also Temple, *The Travels of Peter Mundy*, 2:305–306.
88. For this important event, see William Foster, "Sivaji's Raid upon Surat in 1664" (in two parts), *The Indian Antiquary* 50 (1921): 312–321; 51 (1922): 1–6.
89. See Panduranga S. S. Pissurlencar, *Portuguese Records on Rustamji Manockji, the Parsi Broker of Surat* (Bastorá-Nova Goa: Tipografia Rangel, 1933), 96–107 (for the affair of ʿOsman Çelebi).
90. See Modi, "Rustam Manock," 145.
91. For Breton's view of the situation in Surat at the time of Boullaye's arrival, see the letter from Breton and Council at Surat to the Company, dated 20 April 1648, in Foster, *EFI, 1646–50*, 209–211.
92. For a serviceable account of his career, see Alexander R. Ingram, *The Gateway to India: The Story of Methwold and Bombay* (London: Oxford University Press, 1938); and for his will, see The National Archives, Kew (UK), Records of the Prerogative Court of Canterbury, PROB 11/231/31 (dated 15 April 1653). For an example of charges against Methwold and his response to them, see Foster, *EFI, 1637–41*, 16–18.
93. The National Archives, Kew (UK), Records of the Prerogative Court of Canterbury, PROB 11/229/7 (dated 31 May 1634), and PROB 11/231/594 (dated 20 July 1649). These are two wills by Francis Breton, one on the eve of his departure for India, and one just before his death in Surat. On Breton's death and the acrimonious dealings around it, see Foster, *EFI, 1646–50*, 275–276.
94. Roman Siebertz, "How to Obtain a *Farmān* from Shah Jahan: The Experience of Joan Tack at Delhi, 1648," in *The Mughal Empire from Jahangir to Shah Jahan: Art, Architecture, Politics, Law and Literature*, ed. Ebba Koch and Ali Anooshahr (Mumbai: Marg Publications, 2019), 144–165.
95. François le Gouz de la Boullaye, *Les voyages et observations du Sieur de la Boullaye-Le-Gouz gentil-homme angevin* (Paris: Gervais Clousier, 1653), 129. A revised edition of the text appeared from the same publisher in 1657, 141.
96. Le Gouz de la Boullaye, *Les voyages et observations*, 132 (1653 ed.); 143–144 (1657 ed.).
97. Le Gouz de la Boullaye, *Les voyages et observations*, 163–164 (1653 ed.); 176–177 (1657 ed.).
98. This passage is misread and misrepresented as an expression of intoler-

ance by Mary M. Rowan, "Extraordinary French Voyages: Real and Imaginary," in *From Linguistics to Literature: Romance Studies Offered to Francis M. Rogers*, ed. Bernard H. Bichakjian (Amsterdam: John Benjamins, 1981), 269–280 (on 271–273).

99. Richard Burghart, "The Founding of the Ramanandi Sect," *Ethnohistory* 25, no. 2 (1978): 121–139.
100. Biblioteca dell'Accademia Nazionale dei Lincei e Corsiniana, Rome, Fondo Corsini, Ms, 34.K.17, f, 76r. I am grateful to Carlo Ginzburg for obtaining access to this collection at short notice. This manuscript was first fully discussed by Michele Bernardini, "The Illustrations of a Manuscript of the Travel Account of François de la Boullaye le Gouz in the Library of the Accademia Nazionale dei Lincei in Rome," *Muqarnas* 21 (2004): 55–72.
101. Le Gouz de la Boullaye, *Les voyages et observations*, 184–185 (1653 ed.); 197 (1657 ed.). The same passage is slightly harsher in tone in the Lincei manuscript.
102. Le Gouz de la Boullaye, *Les voyages et observations*, 134 (1653 ed.); 146 (1657 ed.).
103. See the discussion in Kate Teltscher, *India Inscribed: European and British Writing on India, 1600–1800* (Delhi: Oxford University Press, 1995), 39–42.
104. Marta Becherini, "Staging the Foreign: Niccolò Manucci (1638-ca, 1720) and Early Modern European Collections of Indian Paintings," PhD diss., Columbia University, 2017, 355–356 (from a longer discussion, 348–364). Becherini's is the most detailed and sophisticated analysis to date of the manuscript's illustrations, drawing on the earlier work of Bernardini and others.
105. See the historiographical discussion in Ines G. Županov and Corinne Lefèvre, "Introduction," in *Cosmopolitismes en Asie du Sud: Sources, itinéraires, langues (XVIe–XVIIIe siècles)*, Collection Purusartha 33, ed. C. Lefèvre, I. Županov, and Jorge Flores, 13–41 (Paris: Éditions de l'EHESS, 2015).
106. My approach is entirely at odds with that in the "impressionistic survey" by Michael N. Pearson, "Reflections on the Port City of Surat as a Case Study," in *Port Towns of Gujarat*, ed. Sara Keller and Michael Pearson (New Delhi: Primus Books, 2015), 43–55. I refrain here from engaging with the misconceptions in that essay.
107. See Kinra, *Writing Self, Writing Empire*, 17–19.
108. See Jos Gommans and Jitske Kuiper, "The Surat Castle Revolutions: Myths of an Anglo-Bania Order and Dutch Neutrality, c. 1740–1760," *Journal of Early Modern History* 10, no. 4 (2006): 361–389.
109. See Ashis Nandy, "Time Travel to a Possible Self: Searching for the Alternative Cosmopolitanism of Cochin," *Japanese Journal of Political Science* 1, no. 2 (2000): 295–327.
110. See the analysis in Sanjay Subrahmanyam, "Cochin in Decline, 1600–1650: Myth and Manipulation in the Estado da Índia," in *Portuguese Asia: Aspects*

in History and Economic History, ed. Roderich Ptak, 59–85 (Stuttgart: Franz Steiner Verlag, 1987), which was then considerably extended and developed in José Alberto Rodrigues da Silva Tavim, *Judeus e cristãos-novos de Cochim, história e memória (1500–1662)* (Braga: APPACDM Distrital de Braga, 2003).

111. See Jonathan Schorsch, "Mosseh Pereyra de Paiva: An Amsterdam Portuguese Jewish Merchant Abroad in the Seventeenth Century," in *The Dutch Intersection: The Jews and the Netherlands in Modern History*, ed. Yosef Kaplan, 63–86 (Leiden: Brill, 2008). Mosseh (or Pedro) Pereyra was a specialist in jewels and resided for an extended period in Surat.
112. See Irfan Habib, "Merchant Communities in Precolonial India," in *The Rise of Merchant Empires: Long Distance Trade in the Early Modern World, 1350–1750*, ed. James D. Tracy (New York: Cambridge University Press, 1990), 371–399 (on 387, 397). The references are to K. N. Chaudhuri, *The Trading World of Asia and the English East India Company, 1660–1760* (Cambridge: Cambridge University Press, 1978), 150–151. Habib's intuitions are broadly confirmed in Singh and Rajshirke, "The Merchant Communities in Surat."
113. This view is proposed by Lakshmi Subramanian, *Indigenous Capital and Imperial Expansion: Bombay, Surat and the West Coast* (Delhi: Oxford University Press, 1996). For a critique (which is part of a larger exchange between these two historians), see Michelguglielmo Torri, "Mughal Nobles, Indian Merchants and the Beginning of British Conquest in Western India: The Case of Surat, 1756–1759," *Modern Asian Studies* 32, no. 2 (1998): 257–315.
114. See Ricardo Quintana, "The Butler-Oxenden Correspondence," *Modern Language Notes* 48, no. 1 (1933): 1–11.
115. See Chris Scarre and Judith Roberts, "The English Cemetery at Surat: Pre-Colonial Cultural Encounters in Western India," *The Antiquaries Journal* 85 (2005): 251–291 (esp. 254–255).

CONCLUSION

1. Henry Cousens, *The Antiquities of Sind with Historical Outline* (1929; repr., Varanasi: Bhartiya Publishing House, 1975); Sunita Zaidi, "The Mughal State and Tribes in Seventeenth Century Sind," *Indian Economic and Social History Review* 26, no. 3 (1989): 343–362.
2. William Foster, ed., *Letters received by the East India Company from its servants in the East, Vol. 2 (1613–15)* (London: Sampson Low, Marston, 1897), 106.
3. Foster, ed., *Letters received by the East India Company*, 2:171–172.
4. Sir Thomas Roe at Ahmedabad to the Company, 14 February 1618, in *The English Factories in India*, ed. William Foster, 13 vols. (Oxford, UK: Clarendon Press, 1906–1927; henceforth EFI) *EFI, 1618–21*, 14.
5. Armando Cortesão, ed., *The Suma Oriental of Tomé Pires and the Book*

of Francisco Rodrigues, 2 vols. (London: Hakluyt Society, 1944), 1:37–38 (translation) and 2:364 (text).
6. Adelino de Almeida Calado, ed., "Livro que trata das Coisas da Índia e do Japão," *Boletim da Biblioteca da Universidade de Coimbra* 24 (1960): 129.
7. Jorge Flores, *Nas margens do Hindustão: O Estado da Índia e a expansão mogol, ca. 1570–1640* (Coimbra: Imprensa da Universidade de Coimbta, 2015), 88–89.
8. Charles R. Boxer, "Diogo do Couto (1543–1616), Controversial Chronicler of Portuguese Asia," in *Iberia: Literary and Historical Issues—Studies in Honour of Harold V. Livermore*, ed. R. O. W. Goertz, 49–66 (Calgary: University of Calgary Press, 1985).
9. Diogo do Couto, *Da Ásia, décadas IV-XII* (repr., Lisbon: Livraria Sam Carlos, 1975), *Da Ásia, década sétima*, part 1, 233.
10. For an account of his actions and policies, see Nuno Vila-Santa, "Counter-Reformation Policies versus Geostrategic Politics in the Estado da Índia: The Case of Governor Francisco Barreto (1555–1558)," *Journal of Asian History* 51, no. 2 (2017): 189–222.
11. Diogo do Couto, *Da Ásia, década sexta*, part 2, 208.
12. Couto, *Da Ásia, década sétima*, part 1, 275.
13. Muhammad Abdul Ghafur, "A Persian Inscription of Shah Hasan Arghun," *Journal of the Asiatic Society of Pakistan* 7, no. 2 (1962): 277–287.
14. Sayyid Mir Muhammad ibn Sayyid Jalal Tattawi, *Tarkhan Nama*, ed. Sayyid Husam-ud-Din Rashidi (Hyderabad: Sindi Adabi Board, 1965), 46; also see Mir Muhammad Ma'sum, *History of the Arghuns and Tarkhans of Sind, 1507–1593*, trans. Mahmudul Hasan Siddiqi (Hyderabad: University of Sind, 1972), 132–133; and Sayyid Tahir Muhammad Nasyani Tattawi, *Tarikh-i Balda-yi Thatta al-ma'ruf bi Tarikh-i Tahiri*, ed. Nabi Bakhsh Khan Baluch (Hyderabad: Sindi Adabi Board, 1964), 111–115. For a discussion of this particular chronicling tradition, see Ali Anooshahr, "Indo-Persian Historian and Sindho-Persian Intermediary: The Tarikh-i Ma'sumi of Mir Muhammad Ma'sum Bhakkari (d. 1606)," *Bulletin of the School of Oriental and African Studies* 82, no. 2 (2019): 245–269.
15. Seydi 'Ali Re'is, *Le miroir des pays: Une anabase ottomane à travers l'Inde et l'Asie centrale*, trans. Jean-Louis Bacqué-Grammont (Paris: Actes Sud, 1999), 72–79; Seydi 'Ali Re'is, *Mirâtü'l-Memâlik*, ed. Mehmet Kiremit (Ankara: Türk Dil Kurumu, 1999), 99–106.
16. See, for example, R. A. de Bulhão Pato, ed., *Documentos remetidos da Índia ou livros das monções* (Lisbon: Academia Real das Sciências, 1884), 2:103.
17. For a full discussion, see Flores, *Nas margens do Hindustão*, 184–186.
18. Niels Steensgaard, *Carracks, Caravans and Companies: The Structural Crisis in the European-Asian Trade in the Early Seventeenth Century* (Copenhagen: Scandinavian Institute of Asian Studies, 1973), 197.
19. See António Bocarro, *O livro das plantas de todas as fortalezas, cidades e povoações do Estado da Índia Oriental*, ed. Isabel Cid (Lisbon: Imprensa Nacional-Casa da Moeda, 1992), 2:65–67.

20. Willem Floor, "The Dutch East India Company's Trade with Sind in the 17th and 18th Centuries," *Moyen Orient et Océan Indien* 3 (1986): 111–144.
21. Brian Spooner, "Baluchistan, I: Geography, History, and Ethnography," in *Encyclopedia Iranica*, (London: Encyclopedia Iranica, 1988), vol. 3, fasc. 6, 598–632.
22. Cortesão, *The Suma Oriental of Tomé Pires*, 1:31–32 (translation) and 2:345–346 (text).
23. João de Barros, *Da Ásia, décadas I–IV* (repr., Lisbon: Livraria Sam Carlos, 1973-74); *Da Ásia, década terceira*, part 2, book 7, 124–125.
24. Couto, *Da Ásia, década sexta*, part 2, book 8, 208–209.
25. Couto, *Da Ásia, década décima*, part 1, 97–102.
26. Sabir Badalkhan, "Portuguese Encounters with Coastal Makran Baloch during the Sixteenth Century: Some References from a Balochi Heroic Epic," *Journal of the Royal Asiatic Society* 10, no. 2 (2000): 153–169. See also Josef Elfenbein, *A Baluchi Miscellanea of Erotica and Poetry: Codex Oriental Additional 24048 of the British Library* (Naples: Istituto Universitario Orientale, 1983), 79–83 (for an early manuscript from about the 1820s). Badalkhan's translation is a distinct improvement on that of Elfenbein but still poses numerous problems.
27. Although it is not mentioned specifically, it is clear that Aubin had in mind works such as Vitorino Magalhães Godinho, *L'économie de l'Empire Portugais aux XVe et XVIe siècles* (Paris: SEVPEN, 1969).
28. Jean Aubin, "Liminaire," *Le Monde Iranien et l'Islam* 1 (1971): vii–ix.
29. Jean Aubin, "Liminaire," *Mare Luso-Indicum* 1 (1971): vii–x.
30. The two central works in this respect were Steensgaard, *Carracks, Caravans and Companies*, and M. N. Pearson, *Merchants and Rulers in Gujarat: The Response to the Portuguese in the Sixteenth Century* (Berkeley: University of California Press, 1976). Both works were given detailed and highly critical reviews in *Mare Luso-Indicum*.
31. Jean Aubin, review of K. N. Chaudhuri, *Trade and Civilization in the Indian Ocean: An Economic History from the Rise of Islam to 1750* (Cambridge: Cambridge University Press, 1985), in *Bulletin Critique des Annales Islamologiques* 4 (1987): 143.
32. For instance, David O. Morgan and Anthony Reid, ed., *The New Cambridge History of Islam*, vol. 3, *The Eastern Islamic World, Eleventh to Eighteenth Centuries* (Cambridge: Cambridge University Press, 2010), 317–527; and Philippe Beaujard, *The Worlds of the Indian Ocean: A Global History*, vol. 2, *From the Seventh Century to the Fifteenth Century*, trans. Tamara Loring, Frances Meadows, and Andromeda Tait (Cambridge: Cambridge University Press, 2019).

INDEX

Locators in *italics* refer to illustrations, tables, and maps.

'Abdur Rahim Khan-i Khanan (1556–1627), 154, 174, 176, 187
'Abdur Rahman al-Sakhawi, 101–102
'Abdur Rahman Diba', 101
'Abdur Rahman Jami (1414–1492), 15, 53, 220n47
'Abdur Razzaq Samarqandi: *Matla' us-Sa'dain* (travel account from the 1440s), 4–5, 26, 44–48; stay in Vijayanagara, 45–48, 92
Aden, 5, 26, 34, 42–44, 60, 88, 96, 108, 112–113, 132, 134, 174, 213, 225n37; Albuquerque's attempt to conquer (1513), 88; location of, *27*; Portuguese attacks on ships from, 108; Rasulid trade in, 96; trade in, 34, 42–43, 60, 132, 174
'Adil Shahi territory and rulers. *See* Bijapur territory and rulers
Ahmadnagar: Farhad Khan, 152, 248n61, 248n63; habashis' consolidation of power in, 152–153; Malik 'Ambar's defense of, 154–155; Mughal control over, 153–154; Mughals expelled by Malik 'Ambar, 155
Ahmedabad, xi, 1, 57, *58*, 133, 145, 148

'Ajamis, 103, 113, 130
'Arif 'Ajami, 123
Albergaria, Lopo Soares de, 69, 83, 89, 109
Albuquerque, Afonso de, 9–10, 62, 66–67, 69, 76, 81, 88–93, 109, 141; attempt to seize Hurmuz, 8, 9, 62; failed attempt to conquer Aden (1513), 88; gifts for Dom Manuel, 92; Goa seized by, 88, 92–93; as governor of the Estado da Índia, 66–67, 76, 88–89; Khwaja 'Ata's letter to, 9–10; letter to Dom Manuel, 66–67; Portuguese installed on Soqotra, 141
Alexandria, 43, 110–111, 126
Allsen, Thomas, 164
Almeida, Dom Francisco de, viceroy, 9, 61–63, 69, 75–78, 83, 88, 230n106
Alpers, Edward, 25, 31, 69, 72, 79; on trade between Gujarat and East Africa, 136; on trade between India and the Swahili coast, 138–139
'Ambar, Malik: birth as Chapu (1548), 154; inscription of, *155;* as a maritime trader, 156; Nizam Shahi Sultanate of Ahmadnagar rescued

INDEX / 263

from annexation by the Mughals, 154–155; political role in Ahmadnagar continued by his son Fath Khan, 156

Angoche, 69, 70, 72–73, 78, 138, 229n94

Aqquyunlu: and Safavids, 92; letter from Mahmud Gawan to Uzun Hasan Aqquyunlu, 53; rivalry with the Qaraquyunlu, 55; Salghur Shah's struggles with, 7

Arabic historiography, neglect of, 130–131, 242n117. *See also* Banu Fahd family; Ibn Tulun; Nahrawali, Qutb-ud-Din Muhammad

Asaf Khan, 'Abdul 'Aziz: embassy in Mecca, 118, 119–124, 129; family background, 242n112; flight to Jiddah, 114–115, 238n64; *Sura al-An'am* chapter of the Qur'an read for Bahadur Shah, 118; travel to Istanbul, 123–134

Aubin, Jean, 5, 8; on editing the letters of Baba 'Abdullah, 90; influence on Indian Ocean studies, xiv, 19–20, 213; on issues with the Islamic spice route, 130; on Jarullah's *Nail al-muna*, 98, 237n38; on K. N. Chaudhuri's work, 214; on a letter from Khwaja 'Ata to Dom Francisco de Almedia, 9–10; *Mare Luso--Indicum* project, 212–214, 262n30; materials employed to understand the spice trade, 98, 106, 130; on Persian emigration to India, 52; on spatial units, 15–16

Ayaz, Malik (or Malik Iyas, d. 1522): as governor of the port of Diu, 63, 94, 107; in service to Sultan Mahmud, 59; and Sultan Muzaffar, 109;

'Aydarusi Sufis, 133, 181, 185, 235n25, 256n67

Ba Faqih, Muhammad ibn 'Umar al-Tayyib, *Tarikh al-Shihr* (or *al-Shahar*), 237n58, 237n60; on Süleyman Pasha's entering Jeddah and Mecca, 241n106

Baghdad, 2, 154, 239n76; location of, 27; Ottoman conquest of, 239n76

Bahadur Shah (Sultan Bahadur of Gujarat): Asaf Khan's service to, 242n112; death in 1537, 122–123, 166; gift for Sultan Süleyman, 120, 122; response to Portuguese attacks on Diu, 113–114; *Sura al-An'am* chapter of the Qur'an read for, 118

Bahmani Sultanate: capital at Gulbarga, 4, 46, 50, 144; collapse of, 143–144; Mahmud Gawan's career in, 51–52; Mahmud Shah (r. 1482–1518), 144; military strength, 52–53

Balochistan and Balochi populations: coastal raids by Balochi corsairs, 210; oral epics concerned with Mir Hammal, 211–212; Portuguese raids on Balochi sailors, 209; Portuguese raids on Balochi settlements, 210

Banu Fahd family, writings by three generations of, 21, 96–97

Barreto, Francisco, 205

Barros, João de (1496–1570): on a "chronicle of the Kings of Kilwa," 71, 138; on coastal raids by Balochi corsairs, 210; on Vasco da Gama's voyage along the Swahili coast, 137–138; on Haj Hasan, 78; on Malik Ayaz, 59; on Muhammad Rukn, 75; on the Portuguese monopolistic use of the sea, 65

Barr Sa'ad-ud-Din (or Adal Sultanate), conflict with the Ethiopian-Solomonid kingdom, 22, 141–142

Basra, 6, 27, 239n76

264 / INDEX

Basrur, 27, 41, 173
Bassein, 139, 149, *150*, 169, 193, 205
Becherini, Marta, 199
Bernardin de Saint-Pierre, Jacques Henri, 165
Berze, Gaspar, 5
Bharuch, 55, 96, 109, 149, 166, 169, 177, 180, 186, 201
Bhatkal, 4, 47, 60, 83, 173
Bijapur territory and rulers: Dabhol in, 94; Ibrahim 'Adil Shah, 152, 154; loss of Goa to the Portuguese, 66; murder of 'Ali 'Adil Shah (1579), 152
Binbaş, Evrim, 35–36
Blackburn, Richard, 131
Black Sea, 27
Bloch, Marc, essay on comparative history, 1, 13–14, 15
Bocarro, António, 207–208
Bouchon, Geneviève, xiv, 80, 82, 90
Boxer, Charles R., 12–13
Braad, Christopher Henrik, plan of Surat, *175*, 181
Braudel, Fernand, 2, 30, 214
Bukhari, Sayyid Mahmud bin Munawwar al-Mulk, 117, 118, 124, 238n64

Cairo, 4, 35, 39, 43, 46, 92–93, 95, 97, 101, 110, 118, 123
Calicut (Kozhikode): location of, 27; long-distance trade, 26, 34, 138; Muslim merchants, 41, 45; trade in Surat compared with, 173
Cambay (Khambayat), 4, 27, 46, 60, 61, 97, 107, 109, 114, 119, 123, 126, 129, 136, 138, 140, 152, 165, 175, 190, 211
Carneiro, António (1460–1545), 73, 90, 91, 232n140
Carvalho, Manuel de, 65
Casale, Giancarlo, 106, 132, 238n68, 241n107

Caspian Sea, location of, 27
Castanheda, Fernão Lopes de, 83, 109, 165–166, 229n100
Castro, Dom João de: attack on Surat, 168–169; drawing of the port of Suakin, *124;* letters to him from an *alguazil* in Kannur, 232n145
Chakrabarty, Dipesh, 19
Chaudhuri, K. N., 201, 214
Chaul, xix, 49, 51, 54, 63, 79, 97, 139, 140, 141, 152, 155, 156, 158, 173, 193; Ahmadnagar attack on the Portuguese in, 152; location of, 27, *150;* Malik 'Ambar's maritime trade in, 155–156; Muslim trading colonies in, 49; Portuguese fort and factory in, 139; trade in Surat compared with, 173; westward trade in the fifteenth century from, 51
Chingiz Khan (Ahmadnagar), 154
Chingiz Khan (Gujarat), 167, 169–171, 253n30; assassination of, 253n30
Chittick, Neville, 134
Christians and Christianity: Carmelite church in Thatta, 208; Farhad Khan's alleged conversion to, 152; Jesuit reading of canon law on navigation of the sea, 65; La Boullaye on animals in Christian scriptures, 195; La Boullaye on Christianity in the East Indies, 194; La Boullaye on Christians in Surat, 194; participation in the slave trade, 142; in the religious geography of the Indian Ocean, 30; slave converts, 87–88
Cochin (Kochi): 9, 10, 34, 62, 63, 173, 200, 230n112, 231nn122–123, 245n22, 259n109
Comoro Islands, 27, 31, 70
comparative history: Marc Bloch on, 1, 13–14, 15; connected history as an alternative to, 14–20,

215, 220n46, 222n62; Weberian influence on, 11–13, 214
core-periphery relations model, 26, 28–29
Correia, Gaspar, xi, *106*, 235n27
cosmopolitanism: *citoyen du monde* (citizen of the world) associated with, 162; defined in the *Encyclopédie*, 161–162; place associated with, 163–164; Guillaume Postel's revival of the term, 162; of Qara Qorum, 164; Ricci on the "Arabic cosmopolis," 134; of Surat, 161, 164–165, 200–202
Couto, Diogo do (1542–1616), *Décadas da Ásia*, 205, 253n31; on Ethiopian elite in Gujarat, 147–149; on Farhad Khan, 152; on Habash Khan, 145–147; inclusion of figures excluded from Perso–Arabic materials, 146; on Mirza 'Isa Tarkhan, 205; on the Portuguese fleet sent to Surat, 171; on Portuguese raids on Balochi settlements, 210; on Qara Hasan as the captain of Surat, 168; on the sacking of Panwan, 211; on the sinking of Qilij Khan's ship, 173; on tensions between Khudawand Khan and Chingiz Khan, 170–171
Cunha, Tristão da, 77

Dabhol, 51, 55, 63, 94, 173, 200, 234n9; trade in Surat compared with, 173; westward trade in the fifteenth century in, 51
Dahanu, 148, *150*
Dahlak archipelago: location near Massawa, *27;* Muslim maritime state in, 31; Nakhuda Ibrahim's attempt to establish trade in, 43
Daman, ix, 24, 147–151, 157, 165–166, 169–170, 172–173, 177, 191, 193,
198; location of, *27, 150;* Sidi Bu Fath's regime, 147, 149
Das Gupta, Ashin, on Surat in the seventeenth century, 179–180, 202
Dekkiche, Malika, 36
Delhi and Delhi Sultanate, 23, 38–39, 46, 49, 55–57, 109, 114, 142–143; fragmentation of, 23; Sikandar Khan Lodi (Sikandar Shah), 114
Diu, *27*, 59, 63, 65, 78–79, 94, 107, 109, 113–114, 119, 121–123, 125–129, 136, 146–147, 152, 165–169, 173; fortress of the Estado da Índia at, 146; Mahmud Shah's campaign against, 128; Portuguese attacks on, 166–168; and Safar al-Rumi, 128; trade in Surat compared with, 173
Du Prat, Abraham, letter to Hobbes introducing La Boullaye, 162, 163
Dutch Company (Verenigde Oostindische Compagnie, VOC), 11–13, 174–175, 177–178, 180, 188, 192–193, 198–202, 209

Eaton, Richard M., 154
Egypt-Mamluk dynasty: commercial networks in the Indian Ocean, 4, 34, 62–63, 130, 141; defeat of, 21, 93; Janim Bey al-Hamzawi (d. 1538), 120–121, 127, 240–241n101; letters from Mahmud Gawan to Mamluk rulers, *53;* management of Jiddah, 43–44, 111; mercantile community in Mecca during, 21; Shafi'i rulers of, 45; Sultan Barsbay (r. 1422–1438), 34, 36, 43; Sultan Jaqmaq, 36; Sultan Qait Bay (r. 1468–1496), *53;* Sultan Qansuh al-Ghauri (r. 1501–1516), 62, 93, 110
Estado da Índia: Dutch Company contrasted with, 12; failed attempt

to control Surat, 253n31; fortress at Diu, 146
Ethiopia-Solomonid kingdom: conflict with Barr Sa'ad-ud-Din (or Adal), 22, 141; founding in the 1270s, 21; rule of 'Amdä Seyon (r. 1314–1344), 22; rule of Zär'a-Ya'iqob (r. 1434–1468), 22; rule of Eskender (r. 1478–1494), 141; regency of Queen Eleni (1507–1516), 141; rule of Lebnä Dengel (Dawid II, r. 1507–1540), 141

Fali clan: political differences with Khwaja 'Ata, 10; Ra'is Nur-ud-Din, 8; residence on Hurmuz, 5
Finch, William, 23–24
Firishta (Muhammad Qasim Hindushah Astarabadi, d. ca. 1623), 49, 50; on Khalaf Hasan, 50, 51; on Malik 'Ambar, 155
Fletcher, Joseph, 15–16, 37
Fogaça, Pedro Ferreira, 69, 75–76
Furber, Holden, 13

Gama, Cristóvão da, 142
Gama, Gaspar da, 77, 230n106
Gama, Vasco da: first expedition via the Cape of Good Hope (1497–1498), 61, 67, 69, 137–138; negotiations with the Kolattiri, 81; second expedition (1502–1503), 61–62, 69, 73, 81, 229n100; as viceroy of the Estado da Índia (1524), 90, 91
Gerschenkron, Alexander, 11
Ginzburg, Carlo, 15
global history: in Anglo-American historiography, 15; lack of precision as a concept, 215; world-systems models, 28
Goa, xiii, xix, 23, 26, 54, 55, 60, 65, 66, 67, 68, 79, 88, 92, 109, 140, 148, 153, 158, 169, 170, 173, 193, 207, 208, 228n82; *casados* (settlers) of,
66–67, 68, 140, 255n54; conquest by the Portuguese Estado (1510), 65–66, 88, 92–93; location of, 27; slaves in, 140; trade in Surat compared with, 173
Godinho, Vitorino Magalhães, 106, 130, 241n107, 262n27
Gruzinski, Serge, 17–18
Gujarat Sultanate: cultural politics of, 57–58; founding, 56; gold tanka of, 239n72; merchants and economy, 56, 128–129; *Sikandar Nama*, 58

habashis: appellation for Horn of Africa origins, 133; consolidation of power in Ahmadnagar, 152–153; Dilawar Khan Habashi, 143–144, 146, 152; Habash Khan, 145–147; Ikhlas Khan Habashi, 152, 156, 157; Malik Dinar Dastur-i Mamalik, 144–145; Sidi Miftah Habashi Khan (commander of Udgir), 151; Sidi Sa'id Sultani al-Habashi (d. 1576), 133, 247; the term "black" (*siyah*) used for, 246n42
Habib, Irfan, 201; on the population of South Asia, 223n4
Haj Hasan ibn Muhammad Rukn, 76; letter to Dom Manuel, 77
Hamilton, Alexander, *A New Account of the East Indies* (1727), 183
Hanuman, divinity, 194–195
Hathaway, Jane, 131
Hazard, Paul, 162
Herat: consolidation of the Timurid state based in, 34–35, 44; death of Sultan Husain Baiqara, 92; Vijayanagara compared with, 46
Hindu worship, 7, 169, 194–199
Horton, Mark, 135, 136–137
Hurmuz, ix, 2–10, 31, 34, 38, 40, 44–47, 52–54, 60–62, 65, 86, 90–91, 94–95, 109–110, 204, 207, 210
Hurmuz kingdom: 'Abdur Raz-

zaq on, 4–5, 45; importance for Indian Ocean historiography, 8–9; Kahuru, 6, 7; location of, 27; morphology in the later fifteenth century of, 5–7

Hurmuz Kingdom, Jarun: Ibn Battuta's visit to, 3; location of, 6, 7; as a political center in the kingdom of Hurmuz, 2–3; Qutb-ud-Din Tahamtan bin Turan Shah as sultan of, 3

Hurmuz kingdom, rulers: Tahamatan bin Turan Shah, 3; Salghur Shah (1475–1505), 7–8; Turan Shah (r. 1436–1471), 7, 45; Turan Shah, Fakhr-ud-Din (r. 1347–1377), 5. See also Fali clan; Khwaja 'Ata Sultani (d. 1513)

Ibn Battuta (1304–1377), 3, 8, 24, 39; *Rihla* (travel account) of, 134
Ibn Hajar al-Haytami (d. 1567), 131, 133, 242n112
Ibn Tulun: impact of his works, 130, 242n117; *Mufakahat,* 102, 130, 235n20
Ibrahim al-Kalikuti, Nakhuda, trade established in Jiddah, 43
'Imad al-Mulk al-Banani, 116–117, 120
'Imad-ul-Mulk Aslan Rumi, 125, 146, 147
Indian Ocean historiography: in the context of imperial and intellectual competition, 130–131; core-periphery relations model unsuited for, 28–29; efflorescence beginning in the 1990s of, 203; importance of the Hurmuz kingdom, 8–9; islands and insularity as crucial subjects for, 31; Mediterranean analogies used for, 29–30; Ottoman historians, 105–106; variety and complexity of, 20–21, 24
Isfahan, 27, 35

Istanbul, 21, 59, 101–102, 115, 118, 120–124, 128, 164, 166
'Iyani, *Fath-Nama-yi Mahmud Shahi,* 144–145, 246nn41–42
'Izz-ud-Din ibn Fahd al-Makki (d. 1429): *Bulugh al-qira,* 97, 99–100, 103; continuation (*zail*) of Najm-ud-Din's annals, 99
Jackson, Peter, 39
Jacob, Margaret, 163–164
Janjira, 27; location of, 150; Maratha attacks on, 156
Jarullah ibn Fahd (d. 1547): background of, 98, 100–101; impact of his work, 102, 130; *Jawahir al-Hassan fi manqib al-Sultan Sulayman ibn 'Usman,* 101; as Shafi'I Muslim, 103; sixteenth-century chroniclers compared with, 235n27; texts by, 101–102
Jarullah ibn Fahd (d. 954 AH/1547 CE), *Kitab Nail al-muna* (*Nail*): Asaf Khan mentioned in, 117, 122, 123–124, 129; on the behavior of Gujaratis in Mecca, 117; on the death of Bahadur Shah, 122; Nahrawali's annotated manuscript of, 102–103; Nahrawali's summary of passages from, 104; on the Ottoman conquest of Tabriz and Baghdad, 239n76; Ottomans critiqued by, 102–103; publication in Arabic in 2000, 98; secretive quality of, 103–104; on the siege of Belgrade (in 1521), 111, 237n53; title of, 100
Jarun. See Hurmuz Kingdom, Jarun
Jews and Judaism: Boullaye on Jews in Surat, 194; Khoja Abraham, 170; Kochi Jews, 200
Jiddah, xi, 5, 34, 42–44, 63, 96–97, 103, 105–116, 118–123, 125–130, 168–169, 171, 173–174, 178, 236n31; location on the Red Sea,

27; port of Jiddah drawn by Gaspar Correia, *106;* Süleyman Rumi as the *na'ib* of, 122
Joyce, James, 203

Kannur (Cannanore): economic role of, 80–81; horse trade in, 83, 89–91; letters on Portuguese dealings in, 84–88, 90–91; local rulers of, 85–86; Portuguese fortress projected for, 62, 83–84, 88; and Portuguese maritime expedition, 81–83
Kapadia, Aparna, 58–59
Khalilieh, Hassan S., 65
Khudawand Khan. *See* Khwaja Safar al-Salmani (or Safar Aqa, d. 1546)
Khwaja 'Ata Sultani (d. 1513): as defacto controller of Hurmuz, 9; Hurmuz defended against Portuguese attacks (1507–1508), 8, 62; letter to Afonso de Albuquerque, 9–10; political differences with the Fali clan, 10
Khwaja Khalil Gilani, 119, 120
Khwaja Khizr, shrine at Kahuru dedicated to, 7
Khwaja Nizam-ud-Din Ahmad, 166–168, 188, 203
Khwaja Safar al-Salmani (or Safar Aqa, d. 1546), 240n86; death during the Portuguese attack on Diu, 167, 168, 170–171; Khudawand Khan as his title, 166–167, 169; Marjan Shami (mausoleum in Surat), 149, 172–173, 181, 186; Surat defended against Portuguese attacks by, 145
Kilwa, 22, 62, 67, 69, 71–79, 134–136, 138, 222n72, 228n87, 229n88; location on the Swahili coast, *27, 70,* 134; Pedro Ferreira at, 77–78; Portuguese capture of (1505), 77; Portuguese fortress projected for, 62
Kolattiri (ruler of Kannur): 81, 83–91;

negotiations with Vasco da Gama, 81; residence at Valarapattanam, 80
Kollam, 40, 81, 96
Krishna, divinity, 195–196
Kuznets, Simon, 11

La Boullaye, François le Gouz de (1623–1667): background of, 162–163; as a *citoyen du monde,* 162, 163
La Boullaye, François le Gouz de (1623–1667), *Voyages*: on cosmopolitan aspects of Surat, 161; on emperor Shahjahan, 193–194; images in, 197, *199;* informants, 197, *198;* on religion in Surat, 194–197, *196*
Lamu Archipelago, *27, 70,* 139–140
Lavachha: Ethiopian-origin *foreiros* (grantees) based in, 149, *151;* location of, *150*
Levine, Philippa, 18, 221n60
Lewis, Archibald, 64
Lieberman, Victor, 14
Lobato, Bastião Lopes, on trade between Sind and Hurmuz in the 1540s, 204
Lobato, Manuel, 78–79, 139, 140, 244n21
Lombard, Denys, xiv
Lovejoy, Paul, 142

Ma Huan, 4
Machado, Pedro, on trade between East Africa and India, 139–140
Madagascar: continuous human habitation of, 31–32; location in the southwestern Indian Ocean, *27, 70;* Mahilaka, 32, *70*
Maddison, Angus, regional population estimates, 29
Mahmud Arghun, Sultan, 205, 206–207
Mahmud Begada, Sultan (r. 1458–

INDEX / 269

1511), 58–59; campaign against the Chudasama rulers of Kathiawar, 59; letter from Mahmud Gawan, 53; and Malik Ayaz, 59, 63; themes from his reign, 58–59; trade carried out by his family, 61; tradition of history writing promoted in his domains, 59; Yadgar Beg Qizilbash at his court, 92

Mahmud Gawan Gilani, Khwaja, (d. 1481), 9; career in the Bahmani Sultanate, 51–52; *Riyaz al-Insha'*, 51, 226n44

Mahmud Gujarati, Sultan: assassination of (1554), 129, 146; fortress at Diu besieged by, 167

Malawi, 70

Maldives, relationship to Kerala, 31

Malindi, 26, 69, 72, 77–79, 135, 138–139; deterioration of Portuguese diplomatic relations, 139; Gama's visit during his first voyage (1498), 69, 138; Haj Hasan's imprisonment in, 77; location of, 27, 70; the Portuguese kings' alliance with, 72, 78–79

Mamluks. *See* Egypt-Mamluk dynasty

Mappila families: influence on the Kotte kingdom in western Sri Lanka, 20; Mammali Marakkar, 88–90; Muslim dynasty in Kannur in Kerala, 80, 88–89

Margariti, Roxani: on islands and insularity in Indian Ocean history, 31; on maritime predation, 64

Martin, François, 178–179

Marxist and Neo-Marxist historical analysis, 11, 16, 19, 26, 28

Massawa, 27

Masulipatnam, 174, 200

McNeill, William, 15

Mecca: Asaf Khan in, 118, 119–124, 129; 'Imad al-Mulk's journey to, 116–117; Jarullah on the behavior of Gujaratis in, 117; location of, 27; mercantile community during the late Mamluk period, 21; Ottoman conquest of, 103; Süleyman Pasha's hajj pilgrimage, 128

Meccan families: appearance in Jarullah's *Nail,* 100

Mogadishu, location of, 27, 70

Mokha (Mocha): location of, 27; slave market in, 154; trade with Surat, 178; Nancy Um's study of, 161, 202

Mombasa, 27, 67, 69, 70, 72, 79, 134–37, 139, 140, 158

Montserrat, António, visit to Surat, 172

Mortel, Richard T., 21

Mughal Empire: cadastral data from the *A'in-i Akbari*, 28; conquest of Gujarat (1572–1573), 150; diplomatic relations with the Ottomans, 106; exclusion of habashis from the *mansabdari* system of, 150–151; prosperity of Surat claimed by, 172; Qilij Khan Andijani, 173

Mughal Empire, rulers, Humayun (Muhammad Humayun): 119, 121, 207; Seydi 'Ali's contact with, 207

Mughal Empire, rulers, Shahjahan: Boullaye's positive view of, 193–194; daughter Jahanara Begam, 183, 199; Dutch attack on Surat during his reign, 192

Muhammad Mikat, 76–77

Muhammad Rukn al-Daybuli: assassination of, 76; elevation of, 74–76; as a hostage on board Gama's fleet, 229n100

Mundy, Peter, 199

Muslims and Islam: Boullaye on Muslims in Surat, 194; Islamic Law of the Sea, 65; in Kerala, 80; Muslim maritime state in the Dahlak archipelago, 31; Muslim merchants in the Calicut (Ernadu) kingdom, 41; Muslim trading colonies in Chaul, 49; participation in the slave trade, 142; presence in coastal Africa, 22; in the religious geography of the Indian Ocean, 30

Mustafa Bairam (Rumi Khan): defection to the Mughals, 114–115, 238n69; as governor of Zabid, 112; and Gujarat politics, 145–146; ship sent from Gujarat to the Red Sea, 121

Muzaffar Shah Gujarati (r. 1511–1525), 92–93, 107–109, 117

Nagashima, Hiromu, 181

Nahrawali, Qutb-ud-Din Muhammad (d. 990 AH/1582): account of Mecca (*I'lam bi a'lam*), 21, 131; annotated manuscript of the *Nail al-muna*, 102–103; chronicle of the Ottoman conquest of Yemen (*al-Barq al-Yamani*), 21, 104, 131; impact of his writing, 21, 130–131, 234n15; as Jarullah's notional successor as a chronicler, 98; travel account of his visit to Istanbul (1550s), 21, 120

Najm-ud-Din 'Umar ibn Fahd (d. 885 AH/1480): annals *Ithaf al-wara*, 99; family history, *Bazl al-jahd* (The Profitable Use of Effort), 100

Navsari, 23, *150*, 190

Newitt, Malyn, 69, 138

Nimdihi, 'Abdul Karim: *insha'* (belles-lettres), 8, 51, 59, 218n23; as Khwaja Mahmud Gawan Gilani's secretary, 51; *Tabaqat-i Mahmud Shahi*, 8

Ottoman court and empire, xv, xvii, 1, 21, 28, 53, 59, 93–94, 97–98, 101, 103–107, 110–116, 118–120, 123, 125, 128, 130–132, 142, 145, 158–159, 163, 166–167, 169, 171, 207, 214; exiled Burhan Khan Lodi received by, 238n66; Ottoman administration of the Holy Cities, 105

Ovington, John: biographical details, 183; *Essay upon the Nature and Qualities of Tea* (1699), 183

Ovington, John, his account of Surat, 183–185; on Armenians in Surat, 188; Alexander Hamilton's account compared with, 183; La Boullaye's account compared with, 199

Oxenden, Christopher and George, *198*, 201–202

Parnera, 147, 149, *150*

Pearson, Michael N., 56, 259n106

Persian Gulf Islands, *27*; Qishm, 3, 31; relationship to African history, 31; in the study of Indian Ocean history and historiography, 31. See also Hurmuz

Pestana, Francisco Pereira, 69, 76

Pires, Tomé: on Balochi populations, 209–210; on the Bengal Sultanate, 143; on Gentiles of Cambay, 60; on Sind, 204

Portuguese Estado da Índia. See Estado da Índia

Portuguese kings, Dom Manuel: Albuquerque diverts gifts to, 92; letter from Albuquerque, 66; letter from Haj Hasan ibn Muhammad Rukn, 77; letter from Ibrahim bin Sulaiman, 77; letters from Nuno de Castro, 82; letters from a Portuguese factor, 81; letter from Silvestre de Bachom, 227n68; letters from Sultan 'Ali bin 'Ali, 78–79; letter written by the Kolattiri to, 84–88; letter written by Sharif Muhammad al-'Alawi to, 72–73

Portuguese kings, Dom João III, 91

Postel, Guillaume, 162

Qaraquyunlu: founding of Golconda by Sultan Quli (r. 1496–1543), 55; tribal disorders in, 52

Rajapuri, 150, 155, 156
Rander: Couto on the Nawayats, 170; location of, 24, 150, 179; as a prosperous Gujarat port, 55, 165; raids on, 165–166, 238n61
Rasulid dynasty. *See* Yemen-Rasulid dynasty
Red Sea: location in the western Indian Ocean, 27; port of Zayla', 21. *See also* Dahlak archipelago
Ricci, Ronit, on the "Arabic cosmopolis," 134
Roe, Sir Thomas, 193, 204
Roques, Georges, on Armenians in Surat, 188
Ross, E. Denison, 106, 145–146, 242n112
Rumis: Ethiopian loyalty to, 146; at the fortress of Diu, 168; Jiddah governor as a, 115; ship belonging to the Rumi *sanjakar,* 113; support of Khwaja Khalil Gilani, 119. *See also* Mustafa Bairam (Rumi Khan)

Saad, Elias, 73
Safavids: Aqquyunlu relations, 92; Shah Isma'il, 92–93; Sultan Süleyman's victory over, 93, 118; trade relations, 11
Samudri Raja, 44–45, 81, 88–89
Sanjan: Ethiopian-origin *foreiros* (grantees) based in, 149, 151; location of, 150; Portuguese attack on, 148
Scarre-Roberts, on the English graveyard in Surat, 201–202
Schreuder, Jan, 180, 255n54
Serjeant, Robert B., 106, 236n36, 241n106
Seydi 'Ali Re'is, 1, 94, 167, 169, 207, 251–252n26

Shahjahanabad-Delhi, 164
Sheikh, Samira, 56
Sheriff, Abdul, 135–136
Shiraz: coastal families with Shirazi origins, 22, 71, 134; Ghazal of Hafiz Shirazi, 25; location of, 27; *mutasaddi* Sadra Shirazi (titled Hakim Masih al-Zaman), 175; poet and historian 'Iyani, *Fath-Nama-yi Mahmud Shahi,* 144–145, 246nn41–42
Shokoohy, Mehrdad, 49–50
Sidi Bashir Mosque at Ahmedabad, 145, 148
Sidi Bilal Jhujhar Khan, 133, 247n46
Sidi Bu Fath, 147, 149
Sidi Sa'id Sultani al-Habashi (d. 1576), 133, 247
Silveira, António da, attack on Surat and Rander, 165–166, 238n61
Sind: Mirza 'Isa Tarkhan, 205, 206–207; necropolis in Makli, 203; Persian chronicling tradition of, 206; Samma ruler Jam Nanda Nizam-ud-Din (r. 1463–1509), 242n112
Sind-Thatta: Boccarro's account of Portuguese trade in, 207–209; described by English factors (1614), 203–204; location of, 27; Portuguese *casados* in, 208
Siraf, location of, 27
slaves and slavery: in Atlantic societies, 28, 142–143, 159; converts to Christianity, 87–88; in Goa, 140; military slaves, 142, 158; participation of Christians in the slave trade, 142; participation of Muslims in the slave trade, 142; royal slaves (*ghulams*), 8, 52, 59, 143; rule of former slave Baha-ud-Din Ayaz in Jarun, 3; slave market in Mokha, 154. *See also* 'Ambar, Malik; habashis; Khwaja 'Ata Sultani (d. 1513)

Sofala, location of, *27, 70*
Solomonid dynasty. *See* Ethiopia-Solomonid kingdom
Spear, Thomas, 134
Steensgaard, Niels, on the Dutch Company, 12
Suakin, *27;* Nakhuda Ibrahim's attempt to establish trade in, 43; port of Suakin drawn by Dom João de Castro, *124*
Süleyman Pasha (d. 1547): described in *Tarikh al-Shihr* of Ba Faqih, 241n106; as Grand Vizier, 241n107; hajj pilgrimage, 128; letter to Ulugh Khan, 241n104; motivation to enter the Indian Ocean (1538), 94; and Safar al-Salmani (*na'ib* of Diu), 128
Surat: Begam Pura named after princess Jahanara Begam, 183; cosmopolitan aspects of, 161, 164–165, 200–202; described by English East India company employee William Finch, 23–24; described in a seventeenth-century Jaina narrative poem, 254n46; eighteenth-century Persian-Hindawi cloth map of, 180–181, *181;* location of, *27, 150;* in the seventeenth century, 179–180. *See also* Ovington, John, account of Surat
Surat-Persian texts: in the collection of William Laud (archbishop of Canterbury), 186–188, *See also* La Boullaye, François le Gouz de (1623–1667), *Voyages*
Surat-locations: C. H. Braad's plan of, *175*, 181; eighteenth-century locations in the inner city north of the fort, 182–183, *182;* graveyards of, 201–202; map of the city of, *176;* Marjan Shami (mausoleum of Khwaja Safar Khudawand Khan), 149, 172–173, 181, 186

Tabataba'i, Sayyid 'Ali bin 'Azizullah, 49, 143–144
Tabriz, 92, 239n76
Tamrat, Taddesse, 22
Taqi al-Fasi (d. 1429), 21, 97, 98–99, 100
Tarapur: Ethiopian-origin *foreiros* (grantees) based in, 149, *151;* location of, *150;* Portuguese attack on, 148
Tarkhans: Mirza 'Isa Tarkhan, 205, 206–207; Persian chronicling tradition of Sind, 206
Tavernier, Jean-Baptiste, 163, 177–178
Thatta. *See* Sind-Thatta
Timurid state, rulers, Iskandar, Mirza ibn 'Umar Shaikh (d. 1415), 35
Timurid state, rulers, Shahrukh, Mirza (d. 1447): 'Abdur Razzaq sent to Kerala by, 4–5; consolidation of the Timurid state based in Herat, 34–35; diplomatic dealings with the Yongle emperor, 36; Mamluk sultans corresponded with, 36–37, 44; relations with Khizr Khan, 38

Ulugh Khan (Yaqut Habashi, d. 1557), 146, 241n104
Ulughkhani, 'Abdullah Hajji al-Dabir, *Zafar al-Walih,* 238n65, 246n43, 247n56; on habashis in the Gujarate Sultanate's administration, 145–146
Um, Nancy, 161

Vallet, Éric, 40
Valsad, 24, 147–148, *150*
Vijayanagara kingdom: 'Abdur Razzaq's stay in, 44–48, 92; defeat of the Sultanate of Ma'bar (1378), 39; frontier conflict in, 48, 51, 52, 55; Herat compared with, 46; horse trade with Kannur, 83; Hurmuzi merchants in, 46–47

Wallerstein, Immanuel, 28
Weber, Max, and Weberians, 11, 12, 13, 214
western Indian Ocean as a region: coastal navigation impacted by the monsoon system, 25–26; Green Sea (*al-bahr al-akhzar*) as a term for, 2; maritime space of the western Indian Ocean, 26, 27; regional population estimates, 28–29; role of islands and insularity, 31
Wink, André, 29–30
Wynne-Jones, Stephanie, 135

Yemen: Süleyman Pasha in, 127–128, 241n105; trading links, 42

Yemen-Rasulid dynasty: al-Nasir Ahmad (r. 1400–1434), 42; competition in the Indian Ocean, 4; ends in 1454, 44; trade centered on Aden, 96

Zain-ud-Din Ma'bari, *Tuhfat al-mujahidin*, 80
Zénon, Père, 193
Zheng He: diplomatic exchanges with the Timurids not mentioned, 37; Ma Huan's observations on his trips to Hurmuz, 4; Ming courts instructions to, 33–34